Mallorca

Northern Mallorca
p121

Western Mallorca
p93

The Interior
p139

Eastern Mallorca
p152

Palma & the Badia de Palma
p50

Southern Mallorca
p166

Josephine Quintero, Damian Harper

PLAN YOUR TRIP

ON THE ROAD

MARKET IN VALLDEMOSSA
P103

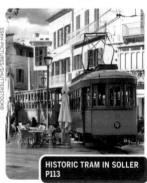

HISTORIC TRAM IN SOLLER
P113

REAL CARTUJA DE
VALLDEMOSSA P103

Contents

COVID-19

We have re-checked every business in this book before publication to ensure that it is still open after the COVID-19 outbreak. However, the economic and social impacts of COVID-19 will continue to be felt long after the outbreak has been contained, and many businesses, services and events referenced in this guide may experience ongoing restrictions. Some businesses may be temporarily closed, have changed their opening hours and services, or require bookings; some unfortunately could have closed permanently. We suggest you check with venues before visiting for the latest information.

Right: Port de
Sóller (p113)

BALATE DORIN/SHUTTERSTOCK ©

WELCOME TO
Mallorca

My parents chose Mallorca for their annual holiday for years, so when I later made Spain my home I made regular hops from the mainland to see what all the fuss was about. Although major sights (and famous bakeries) are still worth the elbow jostling – Palma cathedral and feather-light ensaïmades (sweet pastries) for starters – I have learned how to sidestep the well-trodden track of tourists. From meandering trails flanked with wild flowers to stuck-in-a-time-warp local restaurants, this grand dame of the Balearics has so many discoveries to offer.

By Josephine Quintero, Writer

For more about our writers, see p224

Mallorca

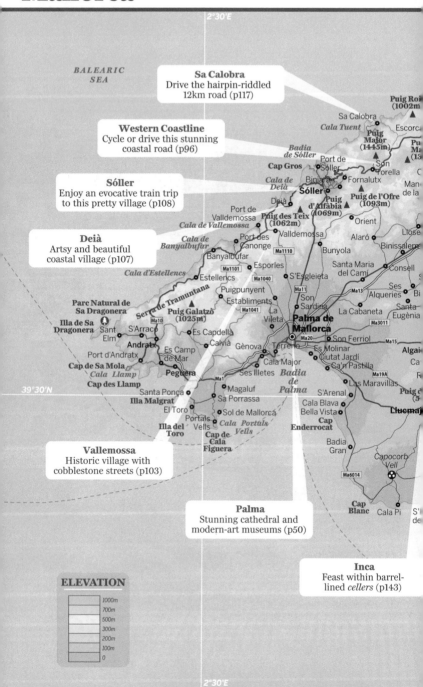

BALEARIC SEA

Sa Calobra
Drive the hairpin-riddled 12km road (p117)

Western Coastline
Cycle or drive this stunning coastal road (p96)

Sóller
Enjoy an evocative train trip to this pretty village (p108)

Deià
Artsy and beautiful coastal village (p107)

Vallemossa
Historic village with cobblestone streets (p103)

Palma
Stunning cathedral and modern-art museums (p50)

Inca
Feast within barrel-lined *cellers* (p143)

Puig Roi (1002m)
Escorca
Sa Calobra
Cala Tuent
Puig Major (1445m)
Pu Ma (15
Son Torella
C
Cap Gros
Badia de Sóller
Port de Sóller
Man de la
Biniaraix
Fornalutx
Cala de Deià
Sóller
Puig d'Alfàbia (1093m)
Deià
Puig des Teix (1062m)
Puig de l'Ofre (1069m)
Port de Valldemossa
Cala de Vallemossa
Port des Canonge
Orient
Valldemossa
Alaró
Llóse
Cala de Banyalbufar
Ma1110
Bunyola
Binissalem
Banyalbufar
Esporles
Santa Maria del Camí
Consell
Cala d'Estellencs
Ma1101
S'Esgleieta
Estellencs
Ma1040
Ma11
Ma13
Ses Alqueries
Bi
Puigpunyent
Son Sardina
Santa Eugènia
Parc Natural de Sa Dragonera
Serra de Tramuntana
Establiments
Ma1041
La Cabaneta
Ma3011
Illa de Sa Dragonera
Puig Galatzó (1025m)
Ma10
La Vileta
Palma de Mallorca
Sant Elm
S'Arracó
Es Capdellà
Ma20
Son Ferriol
Ma15
Andratx
Gènova
Terreno
Es Molinar
Algai
Es Camp de Mar
Calvià
Ciutat Jardí
Ca
Cap de Sa Mola
Cala Llamp
Peguera
Cala Major
Ca'n Pastilla
Ma19A
Cap des Llamp
Ma1
Ses Illetes
Badia de Palma
Las Maravillas
R
Santa Ponça
Magaluf
S'Arenal
Puig (5
Illa Malgrat
Sa Porrassa
Cala Blava
Llucma
El Toro
Sol de Mallorca
Bella Vista
Portals Vells
Cala Portals Vells
Cap Enderrocat
Illa del Toro
Cap de Cala Figuera
Badia Gran
Capocorb Vell
Ma6014
Cap Blanc
Cala Pi
S'
de

ELEVATION

	1000m
	700m
	500m
	300m
	200m
	100m
	0

2°30'E

39°30'N

Cap de Formentor
Breathtaking peninsula
high above the Med (p132)

Platja des Coll Baix
Isolated and near-perfect
wilderness beach (p136)

Pollença
Pilgrimage town with
medieval streets (p126)

Cala Ratjada
Unspoiled east-coast
beaches (p160)

Artà
Castle lookout and
great food (p156)

Parc Natural de S'Albufera
Best birdwatching in
the Mediterranean (p137)

Illa de Cabrera
Pristine archipelago with
stunning coves (p173)

MEDITERRANEAN
SEA

Mallorca's Top Experiences

1 SCENIC ESCAPADES

Mallorca's precipitous coastline and hair-pin riddled mountain roads demand slow and attentive touring – whether on gear-crunching drives or heart-and-thigh-pumping bike rides – with unexpected photo ops on every sweeping bend. Strategically located *miradores* (lookout points) allow you to appreciate the panoramic views as roads thread through lovely villages and diversions plunge to cooling dips in tiny coves. Cap de Formentor (p132)

Cycling in the Serra de Tramuntana

If you are ready to break a sweat on some serious pedal power, pump your way along the stunning scenic route between Andratx and the heady heights of the Monastir de Luc. p100

The Road to Sa Calobra

Loop down twisting hairpins on this heart-in-your-throat 12km drive to the scenic cove at Cala Tuent, cramming your car into clefts in the rock to let juddering coaches past, before winding back to the top. p117

Touring the Coast of Cap de Formentor

The narrow, precipitous peninsula of Cap de Formentor is one of the most dramatic mountain ranges in southern Europe, with thrusting peaks, sunlight-dappled forests of Aleppo pine and austere rocky outcrops that drop abruptly to beautiful and isolated coves. p132

2 COASTAL WALKABOUTS

The gorgeous turquoise Mediterranean is a constant backdrop to hikes that roam through forest, edge along cliffs, hop between coves and climb to high-up vantage points where you may only have goats – and spectacular views – for company. Expect drama, dreamlike views and a good cardio workout, as well as all the unexpected discoveries you make along the way. Below: Cap de ses Salines (p172)

Cap de ses Salines to Colònia de Sant Jordi

Step along this rocky 9km trail that takes you to bountiful swimming spots and opens onto beguiling sea views (but remember to don your sunhat and load up on water before you set out, there's precious little shade). p168

Ermita de la Victòria to Penya Rotja

Set out along this dramatic pine-cloaked peninsula, skirting bluffs, creeping under overhanging cliffs and treading along paths that hug sheer rock faces, with views plunging down to the cobalt waves below, to survey the entire north coast from a 360-degree vantage point. p124

Above left: Ermita de la Victòria (p136)

Parc Natural de la Península de Llevant

Quiet trails link pristine beaches, tranquil coves and pine valleys in this stunning nature park (pictured above right) in the island's east. p158

3 VILLAGE CHARMS

Mallorca is decorated with ancient towns and villages that ooze charm and insist on go-slow exploration. Many find themselves in the sublime valleys and hills of the Serra de Tramuntana, their charms amplified by the potent mountainous backdrop. To pull out all the scenic stops and lay claim to some superb memories, try to spend the night in at least one of them – you may never want to leave.

Valldemossa

One of the most charming villages in the Balearics, draped around the eastern foothills of the Serra de Tramuntana, Valldemossa (pictured top) is all flowerpots, cobblestone lanes and pretty church and stone architecture. p103

Deià

The mountains of Serra de Tramuntana rise like a natural amphitheatre above Deià (pictured above left), a bird's nest of a village perched high above the Mediterranean. p107

Medieval Artà

Artà's stone buildings line narrow medieval streets that gently climb up a hillside before ascending steeply to one of the island's most intriguing church-castle complexes.

Above: Santuari de Sant Salvador (p156)

4 HISTORIC HIGHLIGHTS

Slow Train from Palma to Sóller

Board the vintage train for a nostalgic, rattling journey through the evocative valleys and mountains of the Tramuntana and follow it up with a vintage tram ride from Sóller to the Port de Sóller. p85

Pol·lèntia

These riveting ruins (pictured top left) just beyond the walls of Alcúdia immerse you deep in Mallorca's Roman past. The highlight is the superb theatre amid the trees, but an abundance of interesting sights await. p132

Catedral de Mallorca

The island's architectural tour de force, Palma Catedral (pictured bottom left) dominates the skyline. You'll find yourself returning here either to get your bearings or simply to admire it from every angle – including the view from the roof terraces. p53

There's far more to Mallorca than beaches with powder-soft sand bordering the sapphire sea and gently lapping waves, though you may gravitate to the warm waters first. For a deeper involvement in the island, get versed in Mallorca's rich past: somnolent Bronze Age megaliths, inspiring Roman ruins, charming medieval hill towns, magnificent churches, stately palaces, grand patios and antique trains bring the island's eventful history vividly and colourfully to life.

5 GREAT ESCAPES

You don't have to travel far from the busier coastal resorts to discover an entirely different Mallorca: a treasure trove of isolated coves, hushed and pine-needle carpeted woods, tranquil farms and secluded pockets of total tranquillity, disturbed by nothing but the tinkling of goat bells or the soft lapping of water against the shore, overlooked by the almost impossibly clear and expansive night skies.

Barranc de Biniaraix

Head out of the small village of Biniaraix (pictured below) to immerse yourself in peace within this sublime gorge. p1

ALDORADO/SHUTTERSTOCK ©

Platja des Coll Baix

Few bays can rival Platja des Coll Baix (pictured above). Accessible only by sea or on foot through fragrant woods, this hidden beach on the pine-draped headland of Cap des Pinar is a stunning white crescent, backed by cliffs and pummelled by cobalt blue and turquoise waters. p136

Staying on a Farm

Mallorca's hinterland is sprinkled with *fincas* (estates), often quiet enough to hear an olive hit the ground. The rhythm is in an almost permanent siesta: lazy mornings by the pool and dinners under the stars to the tinkling of goat bells. p22

6 CULTURAL HIGHS

Pack away your towel, shake the sand from your shoes and break from the beach to discover Mallorca's cultural side, where artsy hill towns and a panoply of galleries celebrate the island's creative dimension. Pay homage to the works of Catalan artist Joan Miró or hunt down the former residence of composer Frédéric Chopin and George Sand.

Museu Fundación Juan March

Works by Picasso, Miró, Dalí, Juan Gris, sculptors Eduardo Chillida and Julio González as well as pieces from Mallorcan native Miquel Barceló, are all housed within the 17th-century mansion of Can Gallard del Canya in Palma. p64

Fundació Pilar i Joan Miró

Catalan artist Joan Miró's former home is filled with his works and spirit. With more than 2500 works by the artist, it's a rightful place of pilgrimage for Miró devotees. p90

Real Cartuja de Valldemossa

Make a beeline for this Carthusian monastery (pictured above) and former residence of royals and Chopin, or walk through the streets of Valldemossa, Chopin looping on your phone. p103

7 CELLERS, SOBRASSADA & ENSAÏMADES

Dining is a major source of pleasure in Mallorca, going to the very heart of the island's identity. Whether you aim for generous helpings of *conill amb ceba* (rabbit with onions), hunger-slaying *empanades* (pasties with savoury fillings) or tantalising delights at a *confiteria* (pastry shop), local dishes should top your to-do list. p32

ETORRES/SHUTTERSTOCK ©

AGEFOTOSTOCK/ALAMY STOCK PHOTO ©

Sobrassada

Synonymous with Balearic food, this tangy cured sausage made from ground pork, paprika, salt and spices is traditionally devoured on bread (pictured top left) or as a flavourful ingredient in Mallorcan dishes.

Eating at a Celler in Inca

A suckling pig turns slowly on a spit, the burble of animated conversation rises above the clamour of pans, while waiters bustle between tables in Inca's celler restaurants. Bottom left: Celler Ca'n Ripoll (p144)

Mallorcan Pastries

There is barely a more perfect start to the Mallorcan day than a delicious, light and fluffy *ensaïmada* pastry (pictured above right) and a *cafè amb llet* (espresso with milk).

8 GET ACTIVE

You can spend your entire visit to Mallorca horizontal on the beach or sedentary in one of the island's superb restaurants, but fleeing your parasol and getting active can put a spring in your step and take you to the island's wilder side, while giving you ample opportunity to explore less-visited regions. There's no shortage of choice and you can grade according to need, from low-calorific birdwatching to more high-octane thrills like cliff jumping and kite-surfing.

Water Sports

One glance at Mallorca's unfathomably blue seas has water-sports enthusiasts itching to slip into a wetsuit or hop on a board. Scuba divers swim around Formentor's caverns and islands, while coasteering, kite-surfing, kayaking and – deep breath now – cliff jumping also lure adrenaline-seekers. p41

Bird watching in Parc Natural de S'Albufera

Twitchers flock to Parc Natural de S'Albufera, one of the Mediterranean's premier sites for birdwatching. Bring your binoculars and look out for herons, ospreys and egrets. p137

Hiking

With some of the best hiking in Europe, Mallorca offers an astonishing choice of terrains and landscapes, whether you're a hardcore hiker or just seeking to mix a bit of trekking into your holiday experience. p38

Bottom left: Southern Mallorca hiking

Need to Know

For more information, see Survival Guide (p201)

Currency
Euro (€)

Language
Spanish, Mallorquin (a dialect of Catalan)

Visas
Generally not required for stays up to 90 days; not required for members of EU or Schengen countries. Some nationalities will need a Schengen visa.

Money
ATMs are widely available in towns and resorts. Credit cards are accepted in most hotels, restaurants and shops.

Mobile Phones
Local SIM cards are widely available and can be used in European and Australian mobile phones. Other phones may need to be set to roaming.

Time
Central European Time Zone (GMT/UTC plus one hour)

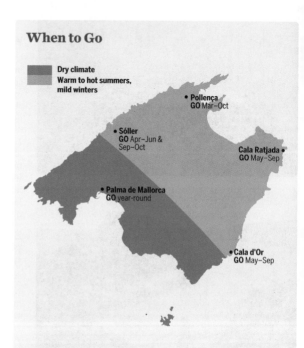

When to Go

Dry climate
Warm to hot summers, mild winters

• Pollença
GO Mar–Oct

• Sóller
GO Apr–Jun &
Sep–Oct

Cala Ratjada •
GO May–Sep

• Palma de Mallorca
GO year-round

• Cala d'Or
GO May–Sep

High Season
(Jul–Aug)
➡ Clear skies, sunny days and warm seas.

➡ Temperatures soar as do room rates. Book well ahead or try for a last-minute deal online.

➡ Fiesta time! The island's towns host high-spirited parties, parades and music festivals.

Shoulder
(Easter–Jun, Sep & Oct)
➡ Most hotels and restaurants open at Easter and stay open until October.

➡ Days are often still mild and crowds are few.

➡ Ideal season for hiking, climbing, mountain biking and canyoning.

Low Season
(Nov–Easter)
➡ Many hotels and restaurants close. Palma is the exception.

➡ Pack layers for cooler-than-expected evening temperatures.

➡ You'll have the island's trails, beaches and sights to yourself.

Useful Websites

Consell de Mallorca (www.info mallorca.net) Excellent website from the island's regional tourist authorities.

Lonely Planet (www.lonely planet.com/mallorca) Destination information, hotel reviews, traveller forum and more.

Rustic Booking (www.rustic booking.com) Directory and booking service for Mallorca's rural properties.

Balearsnatura.com (www.balearsnatura.com) Excellent resource for the natural parks of the Balearic Islands.

ABC Mallorca (www.abc-mallorca.com) Lifestyle portal for both residents and travellers.

TIB (www.tib.org) Public transport fares, times and routes across the island.

Important Numbers

International access code	☎00
Spain country code	☎34
International directory inquiries	☎11825
Emergency	☎112
Policía Nacional	☎91

Exchange Rates

Australia	A$1	€0.65
Canada	C$1	€0.70
Japan	¥100	€0.75
New Zealand	NZ$1	€0.60
UK	UK£1	€1.15
USA	US$1	€0.88

For current exchange rates, see www.xe.com.

Daily Costs

Budget: Less than €150

➡ Basic digs in a hostel, guesthouse or last-minute deal on resort hotel: €45–60

➡ Breakfast in hotel, three-course *menú del día* lunch: €15–20

➡ Bus ticket to nearby towns and beaches: €2–5

Midrange: €150–300

➡ Double room in midrange hotel: €75–150

➡ Cafe lunch, dinner at local restaurant: €30–40

➡ Car rental: from €30 per day

Top end: More than €300

➡ Double room in top-end hotel: €150 and up

➡ Sit-down lunch and dinner at first-rate restaurant: €80–100

➡ Boat tour or guided activity: around €50

Opening Hours

High-season hours are provided; hours generally decrease in the shoulder and low seasons. Many resort restaurants and hotels close from November to March.

Banks 8.30am–2pm Monday to Friday; some also open 4–7pm Thursday and 9am–1pm Saturday

Bars 7pm–3am

Clubs midnight–6am

Post offices 8.30am–9.30pm Monday to Friday, 8.30am–2pm Saturday

Restaurants 1–3.30pm and 7.30–11pm

Shops 10am–2pm and 4.30–7.30pm or 5–8pm Monday to Saturday; large supermarkets and department stores generally 10am–9pm Monday to Saturday

Arriving in Mallorca

Palma de Mallorca Airport (PMI; p208) Bus 1 runs every nine minutes from the airport (ground floor of Arrivals) to Plaça d'Espanya in central Palma (€5, 20 minutes); buy tickets from the driver. If you want to hire a car, most rental agencies are on-site. The drive takes 20-25 minutes to central Palma via Hwy MA-19. Metered taxis cost around €19 and €22 to Palma. Some hotels can arrange transfers.

Ferry Terminal, Palma (www.portsdebalears.com) Bus 1 (the airport bus) runs every 15 minutes from the ferry port (Estació Marítima) to Plaça d'Espanya (€3, 15 minutes). Metered taxis cost around €10–12 to the city centre.

Tap Water

Tap water is safe to drink across Mallorca and is better for the environment than buying water in plastic bottles. Don't be shy to request it when eating out (*agua del grifo, por favor*).

For much more on **getting around**, see p210

First Time Mallorca

For more information, see Survival Guide (p201)

Checklist

➡ Ensure that your passport is valid for at least six months after your arrival

➡ Check airline baggage restrictions

➡ Make advance bookings for accommodation, restaurants, travel and tours

➡ Arrange comprehensive travel insurance

➡ Verify what you need to hire a car (p211), including excess insurance

What to Pack

➡ Travel adapter plug

➡ High factor, waterproof sunscreen

➡ Mosquito/insect repellent

➡ Hiking boots for Tramuntana trails

➡ Chargers for mobile (cell) phones and other devices

➡ Earphones for your smartphone

➡ Sunhat and sunglasses

➡ Beach towel & swimwear

➡ Waterproof coin holder/ dry bag

➡ Phrasebook

➡ A sociable nature – the Mallorcans love a chat

Top Tips for Your Trip

➡ Detour off the well-trodden trail for a spell and you will find peaceful countryside, restful *fincas* (farms) and uncrowded beaches.

➡ Get high: the best views and photo ops are from the monasteries, forts and castles that crown Mallorca's hillsides. Time it right and you'll catch a fiery sunset.

➡ Allow ample time to get from A to Z. Looking at a map of Mallorca is deceptive. Yes, it is an island and fairly compact, but those twisting mountain roads bump up journey times.

➡ Walk. Whether it's pilgrim-style to a monastery, through the back alleys of a cobbled old town or to a hidden bay, many of Mallorca's most alluring sights can only be seen on foot.

➡ Mallorca is made for cycling: many professional teams do their winter training here. However, remember that the steep roads of the Serra de Tramuntana are a killer!

What to Wear

Mallorca is a laid-back island and most people find they over-pack, especially for beach and poolside holidays that require little more than bathing suits and a couple of changes of shorts and T-shirts. Going out is a casual affair and ties and jackets are rarely required.

Summers are hot, but layers are advisable for the rest of the year when the weather is patchier and evenings are cool. Forget wearing high heels on the cobbled streets of Mallorca's hill towns – flats it is.

Sleeping

Reserving a room is always wise – book well in advance (at least two months) if you are travelling in the peak months of July and August, when beds are like gold dust.

From November to Easter, the vast majority of hotels close in coastal resorts. Palma is a year-round option, though, and you'll also find a sprinkling of places open in towns like Pollença and Sóller.

Taxes & Refunds

Spain's IVA (VAT) goods-and-services tax of up to 21% is included in stated prices. Refunds are available on goods of any purchase amount, if taken out of the EU within three months. Collect a refund form when purchasing and present it (together with the purchases) to the customs IVA refunds booth when leaving the EU. For more information, see www.globalblue.com.

Bargaining

The only place haggling skills may be called for, or appropriate, is at markets. Otherwise it's not done. If you want something, be prepared to pay the asking rate.

Tipping

Hotels Discretionary: porters around €1 per bag and cleaners €2 per day.

Cafes and bars Not expected, but you can reward good service by rounding the bill to the nearest euro or two.

Restaurants Service charge is included, unless 'servicio no incluido' is specified, but many still leave an extra 5% or so.

Taxis Not necessary, but feel free to round up or leave a modest tip, especially for longer journeys.

Ornate steps in a Mallorcan manor garden

MARTINEZ STUDIO / SHUTTERSTOCK ©

Etiquette

Mallorcans are generally easygoing, and used to the different mores of foreigners, but will respond well to those who make an effort.

Greetings Shake hands on first meeting and say 'bon dia' (good day) or 'bona tarda' (good evening). In more casual situations, greet with two kisses – offer your right cheek first.

Socialising Mallorcans, like all Spanish, are a chatty, sociable lot. Don't be shy – try to join in their rapid-fire conversations, and be prepared for people to stand quite close to you when speaking.

Eating & Drinking If you are invited to a Mallorcan home, take a small gift of wine, flowers or chocolate. Wait for your host to say bon profit! (enjoy your meal) before getting stuck in. Dunking bread in soup is a no-no, but otherwise meals are fairly relaxed affairs. Join in a toast by raising your glass and saying salut!

Language

Travelling in Mallorca without speaking a single word of Spanish or Mallorquin is entirely possible, but picking up a smattering of these languages will go a long way to winning the affection of the locals. English is widely spoken in the beach resorts and in major towns, but in the rural hinterland and small villages you'll find it handy to have a grasp of a few basic phrases. Plus it's part of the fun! For more on the Spanish language, see p212.

Accommodation

Find more accommodation reviews throughout the On the Road chapters (from p49)

Accommodation Types

Apartments Airbnb is the go-to source for finding a rental with a range of options, including fully equipped villas.

Fincas Mallorca's rural properties range from serene *fincas* (rural estates), to country mansions and B&Bs.

Hostales A *hostal* (or *pensión*) is a small-scale budget hotel, usually family-run.

Hotels Range from no-frills digs through to design-focused boutique hotels and luxury hotels.

Monasteries Technically hermitages that offer basic digs in converted cells in a countryside setting.

Refugis Simple hikers' huts mainly located around the Serra de Tramuntana.

Best Places to Stay

Best on a Budget

Mallorca has a fairly good selection of budget options but those in the main resorts, as well as Palma's historic centre, book up fast. For the best deals consider basing yourself away from the most popular tourist spots, or near the Estació Intermodal de Palma (p210), from where it is easy to travel via bus or train.

Hotel Brick Palma, Palma (www.staybrick.es; r €45)

Hostal Pons, Palma (www.hostalpons.com; r €65)

L'Hostal, Pollença (www.pollensahotels.com; d €73)

Best for Families

For the largest choice of family-friendly hotels head for the beach resorts southwest of Palma, or opt for in and around Port de Pollença in the north. Although the collapse of Thomas Cook in 2019 caused several hotels in this bracket to close, most have reopened under new management.

HPC Hostal Porto Colom, Porto Colom (www.hostalportocolom.com; s/d €75/120)

Pension Bellavista Port de Pollença (www.pension bellavista.com; s €35-45, d €55-65, tr €65-75, q €70-80)

Best Rural Hotels & Retreats

Despite some 16 million tourists descending on Mallorca annually, it is still possible to venture beyond the crowds and discover sleepy villages and unspoiled countryside. Rural hotels and monasteries (or hermitages) are a great way to really appreciate this other lesser-known side of the island.

➡ **Cases de Son Barbassa** (www.sonbarbassa.com; s/d/ste €185/250/315)

➡ **Ca N'Ai** (www.canai.com; ste from €170)

➡ **Santuari de la Mare de Déu des Puig** (hermitage; 971 18 41 32; s/d/tr €14/22/30)

➡ **Petit Hotel Hostatgería Sant Salvador** (hermitage; www.santsalvadorhotel.com; d/ste €64/110)

Best for Solo Travellers

Palma is hands-down the best destination for solo travellers in Mallorca. Like in mainland Spain, both single men and single women can feel comfortable walking into a bar and there is plenty to keep solo folk occupied here, ranging from cultural to culinary.

House and gardens of Son Marroig (p106)

Hotel Sant Francesc (www.hotelsantfrancesc.com; s €195)

Protur Naisa Palma (www.protur-hotels.com; r €114)

Hotel Hostal Cuba (www.hotelhostalcuba.com; r €120)

Planning & Booking Services

Advance booking is always a good idea, especially in high season (May to September). Increasingly, Palma is becoming a weekend short-break destination, so even in low season, book ahead. Prices can skyrocket in high season.

Lonely Planet (lonelyplanet.com/hotels) Find independent reviews, as well as recommendations on the best places to stay.

Rustic Booking (www.rusticbooking.com) Covers a wide variety of rural properties.

See Mallorca (www.seemallorca.com) A separate accommodation section covers hotels, rural properties and *fincas*.

Fincas & Villas (www.fincavillamallorca.com) Accommodation ranges from sea-view villas to village townhouses.

Airbnb (www.airbnb.com) Book accommodation, including villas.

Apartment Rentals

Palma is the first European city to impose a ban on private homeowners from renting out their apartment to visitors. The regulation is a reaction to a surge of unlicenced apartments in the city, which has both contributed to overtourism and raised local rents approximately 40%.

Getting Around

For more information, see Transport (p208)

Travelling by Car

Car Hire

Hiring a car is an excellent way to explore Mallorca. All the main agencies have offices at the airport and costs vary from around €40 to €70 per day. You must have a valid driving licence, be aged 21 or older and have a credit card. Third-party motor insurance is a minimum requirement in Spain.

Driving Conditions

In general, Mallorca has a good network of well sign-posted roads, which makes navigating the island relatively straightforward. Be prepared for narrow roads and one-way systems, however, especially driving through villages. Reversing a 4x4 around tight narrow corners is never fun. Rental cars are inexpensive and, overall, having your own wheels is both a practical and enjoyable way of exploring the island.

Driving Licence

All EU member states' driving licences are recognised throughout Europe. Those with a non-EU licence are supposed to obtain an International Driver's Permit (one or three years duration) to accompany their national licence, although you will find that national licences from countries like Australia, Canada, New Zealand and the USA are often accepted.

Fuel & Spare Parts

Petrol (*gasolina*) prices vary between service stations (*gasolineras*). Lead-free (*sin plomo*; 95 octane) costs an average €1.32 per litre. Diesel (*gasóleo*) comes in at €1.20 per litre.

RESOURCES

Via Michelin (www.viamichelin.com) Upload a map of your destination and use the route planner to help you plan your journey.

Real Automóvil Club de España (www.race.es) Emergency breakdown service.

Epic Road Rides (www.epicroadrides.com) Scroll to Mallorca for some great tips on routes and bike hire.

Parking

Parking in Palma can be a taxing business due to a combination of congestion, narrow streets and a baffling one-way system. Parking in the historic centre is strictly limited to local residents. One solution is to park on the outskirts and catch a taxi or bus into the centre. There is also a mobile parking app, **MobiAPPark**, that you can download onto your mobile device. The app is free and once installed it allows you to pay for and extend your parking time in Palma's blue zone. You can also use the app to settle parking penalties from a mobile phone. You will need a password and to provide credit card details, your email address and the car registration number.

Parking in other towns is not as problematic, aside from July and August, and most beaches have metered parking. Parking costs around from €1 to €1.50 an hour throughout Mallorca.

Safety

Overall, rural roads are not lit at night so watch out for bicycles, motorbikes, donkeys and, of course, pedestrians. Be aware also that motorists here use their hazard warning lights when forced to slow rapidly, for example for an accident or road works, so it is wise to do likewise.

No Car?

Bus

Mallorca has a good network of buses that cover virtually all of the island. The buses are air conditioned and comfortable. In Palma all buses leave from the centrally located **Estació Intermodal** (p210) on Plaça d'Espanya. There are several bus companies; you can get a comprehensive list of timetables, routes and prices from www.tib.org. Frequency decreases considerably during the winter months and at weekends.

Train

There are just four train lines in Mallorca; all commence from **Estació Intermodal** (p210) on Plaça d'Espanya in Palma. The most popular (and recommended) line runs to **Sóller** (p85) via a historic wooden train and passes glorious scenery en route. The remaining three lines journey inland from Palma to Inca and beyond to Sa Pobla and Manacor. s

Bicycle

Whether you fancy the challenging climbs of the Serra de Tramuntana or the scenic flat roads of the east and south coasts, Mallorca is a great destination for **cyclists** (p39) with an ever increasing number of bicycle lanes to keep you safe. If you can't fit your bike into your hand luggage, never fear, there are countless bicycle hire outfits located throughout the island. .

DRIVING FAST FACTS

➡ Drive on the right.

➡ All vehicle occupants must wear a seatbelt.

➡ Minimum age for a full licence is 18 years.

➡ Carry your licence at all times.

➡ Maximum speed is 100km/h on major roads, 50km/h in built-up areas.

➡ Blood alcohol limit is 50mg per 100ml (0.05%).

ROAD DISTANCES (KM)

	Palma	Andratx	Deià	Pollença	Inca	Artà
Andratx	28					
Deià	33	47				
Pollença	55	80	60			
Inca	32	57	55	23		
Artà	73	102	98	41	46	
Santanyí	52	82	78	76	53	51

Month by Month

January

Winter wraps the island in a blanket of calm; some days are mild, some chilly. Beach resorts are in hibernation, with many hotels and restaurants closed; Palma is a notable exception.

Three Kings

The three kings *(tres reis)* rock up on 5 January, the eve of Epiphany, bearing gifts of gold, frankincense and myrrh. They are the stars of a flamboyant parade in Palma.

Festes de Sant Antoni Abat

The Festes de Sant Antoni Abat (16 and 17 January) are celebrated with concerts, prancing demons, huge pyres and fireworks; parading farm animals get a blessing. It's celebrated with gusto in Sa Pobla (p146) and Artà (p156).

Sant Sebastià

Palma pulls out the party stops on the eve of the feast day of its patron saint (20 January), with live music, fireworks and revelry in city squares. (p69)

February

Almond trees in bloom cast flurries of white blossom across the countryside. High-spirited carnivals shake the island out of its winter slumber for pre-Lenten feasting and parading. Many places are still closed.

Carnival

The pre-Lenten season kicks off with parades across the island. In Palma a children's procession, Sa Rueta, is followed by the grown-ups' version, Sa Rua, with pumping music, fancy dress and colourful floats. (p69)

March

A glorious month, with solemn Easter celebrations, wildflowers flourishing and fantastic birdwatching in the Parc Natural de S'Albufera.

Semana Santa

Follow the Semana Santa (Holy Week) processions around the island. Begin in Palma (p72) on Holy Thursday evening, then head to Pollença (p126) for its moving Good Friday Davallament ('Lowering'). On Easter Sunday, head to Montuïri's S'Encuentro (p148).

April

Mallorcan hotels and restaurants dust off the cobwebs, and resorts start to fill up. Milder days make this a perfect month for hiking and mountain biking.

Fira del Vi

Pollença pops a cork on regional wines at its Fira del Vi (Wine Fair) in the Convent de Sant Domingo in late April.

May

Coastal Mallorca has a real spring in its step as resorts come to life.

Sa Fira

Since 1318, Sineu has been the setting for Sa Fira, the island's largest and most authentic livestock and produce market, held on May's first Sunday. (p146)

⛊ Es Firó

On the second weekend of May, Sóller stages Es Firó, where the town's heroic defenders, led by the so-called Valiant Women, fight off Muslim pirates, as they did in 1561, to much merriment and festivities. (p110)

⛊ Corpus Christi

Corpus Christi, on the Thursday of the ninth week after Easter, is a major celebration in Palma. The weeks leading up to it are marked by concerts in the city's baroque courtyards. (p72)

June

Mallorca moves into top gear. Patron saints' festivals, where religious tradition mixes with good old-fashioned pagan partying, are the excuse for knees-up aplenty.

⛊ Nit de Sant Joan

The feast day of St John (24 June) is preceded the night before by fiery festivities on the Nit de Sant Joan. In Palma, it's *correfoc* (fire running), concerts and beach partying till dawn.

July

There's little to interrupt lazy days on the beach and long liquid nights.

⛊ Festa de la Verge del Carme

On 16 July, many coastal towns stage processions for the Festa de la Verge del

Carme, the patron saint of fisherfolk and sailors.

⛊ Festa de Sant Jaume

On 25 July, the inland town of Algaida sees *cossiers* perform traditional dances in the streets for the Festa de Sant Jaume. Six men and one woman dance alongside a demon, who ultimately comes unstuck. (p147)

August

The heat cranks up, festivals are in full swing and the hotels (and beaches) are full to bursting point.

⛊ Festes de la Patrona

One of Pollença's most colourful festivals culminates in a staged battle between townsfolk and a motley band of invading Moorish pirates during the week-long Festes de la Patrona. (p128)

☆ Festival Chopin

Valldemossa pays tribute to one-time resident, composer Frédéric Chopin, at the stately Real Cartuja de Valldemossa, with top-notch classical concerts, devoted mostly to Chopin, throughout August. (p105)

☆ Sa Pobla International Jazz Festival

Sa Pobla is an unlikely setting for one of the Mediterranean's most celebrated jazz festivals, but no matter – it swings with some of the genre's big names every August. (p147)

September

September is like the joyous last drink before the hangover. Autumn is good for migrating birds in the Parc Natural de S'Albufera, coastal hikes, bike rides and water-based activities.

🍷 Festes de la Verema

Mallorca's vine-cloaked interior celebrates the grape harvest with the Festes de la Verema in late September. Binissalem gets stuck into a big juicy mess of a grape fight. (p143)

October

Last drinks! People bid tearful farewells to new-found friends at resorts across the island.

⛊ Fira d'Alcúdia

Concerts, produce markets, music and parades come to Alcúdia on the first weekend in October. (p134)

November

As the weather turns chilly, most places close for the winter. Autumnal markets spring up selling wine, just-harvested olives and mushrooms.

December

Many resorts around the island are closed for the winter and most of the ports are hushed. Snow is likely to fall on the Puig de Massanella, Puig Major and other high points of the Serra de Tramuntana, and may dust some of the mountain villages.

Itineraries

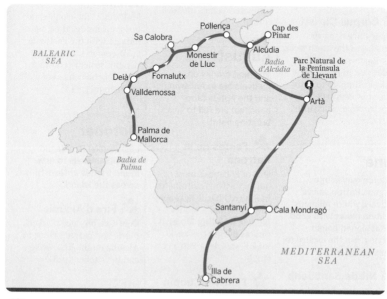

 The Grand Tour

This all-inclusive tour breaks the back of the island, whisking you from Palma's historic attractions along the mountainous coastline of the Serra de Tramuntana via charming mountain villages, seaside inlets, ancient towns and seaboard hikes, before concluding at the gorgeous coves of the Illa de Cabrera.

Spend a few days exploring fascinating **Palma**, then head north to the mountains and the stunning town of **Valldemossa**. Continue east along the coast road to restful, artsy **Deià** and the tranquil village of **Fornalutx**. Take the epic downhill corkscrew to **Sa Calobra**, then follow the pilgrims seeking spiritual restoration at the **Monestir de Lluc**. From here, aim for ravishing **Pollença** and the ancient sights of walled **Alcúdia**, cultured precursors to a breezy and bracing hike along the sublime **Cap des Pinar**. The ancient settlement of **Artà** lies to the south, a good base from which to explore the outstanding landscapes of the **Parc Natural de la Península de Llevant**. Continue to the charming town of **Santanyí** and nearby **Cala Mondragó**. Conclude your journey with a trip to the beautiful archipelago of **Illa de Cabrera**.

Palma to Pollença

1 WEEK

Kicking off in the island's capital, this must-do journey charts a dramatic course through many of Mallorca's signature sights.

Warm up with a day or two in sea-splashed **Palma** before drifting southwest to beach belle **Ses Illetes**, harbourside **Port d'Andratx** and low-key **Sant Elm**, before hopping to **Illa de Sa Dragonera**. Dramatic cliff-edge and mountain views unfurl northeast from **Andratx** through alley-woven **Estellencs** and **Banyalbufar** and hill-town stunner **Valldemossa**. Just north, photogenic **Deià** twirls delightfully up a hillside, with the minute village of Lluc Alcari just to the east. Swing north to valley-cupped **Sóller** for backstreet strolls, Modernista treasures, Picasso and Miró. Time permitting, detour to charming hill-toppers **Orient**, **Biniaraix** or **Fornalutx**, or board a rickety vintage tram down to **Port de Sóller**. As the Ma10 weaves inland, take the hair-raising road down to **Sa Calobra** en route to pilgrims' respite **Monestir de Lluc**. See the wild peaks of the Tramuntana unfurl in all their brooding splendour as you descend to the quintessentially Mallorcan town of **Pollença**.

Artà to Illa de Cabrera

10 DAYS

Mixing gorgeous beach panoramas and sheltered coves with an archipelago of hilly islands, this tour has a bit of everything.

Linger in fortress-topped **Artà** for a day, then tour the remote coastal loveliness of **Parc Natural de la Península de Llevant**. From Artà, squeeze in a visit to **Capdepera**, a town defined by its castle. Hopscotch along the east coast to beguiling half-moon bays, such as **Cala Mesquida** near Cala Ratjada, and inch south for the Coves d'Artà and medieval Torre de Canyamel around **Platja de Canyamel**. Head further south, pondering the glittering depths of Coves del Drac in **Porto Cristo**, then point your compass inland to vine-streaked **Petra** and **Sineu**, stopping off at wineries along the way. As you wend your way back to the coast, visit handsome Mallorcan estate **Els Calderers** and then head for the boho charms of **Santanyí** and the good-looking port of **Cala Figuera** before aiming for artsy **Ses Salines**, detouring via pretty beaches for a quick swim. Wrap up your trip in **Colònia de Sant Jordi**, springboard to the island-speckled **Parc Nacional Marítim-Terrestre de l'Arxipèlag de Cabrera**.

Off the Beaten Track: Mallorca

BANYALBUFAR

So you've swooned over Deià and visited Valldemossa, but what about Banyalbufar? Centuries-old farming terraces form steps down to the wave-lashed coast – this speck of a village is postcard stuff. (p101)

SA FORADADA

This finger of rock juts out into the water at the base of Son Marroig. Wander through sheep-dotted olive groves down to the sea and linger for a watercolour sunset. (p106)

ILLA DE SA DRAGONERA

This rippled island reposes like a slumbering dragon off the island's westernmost tip. Trails thread through this nature reserve to quiet capes, far from the beach resort swarms. (p99)

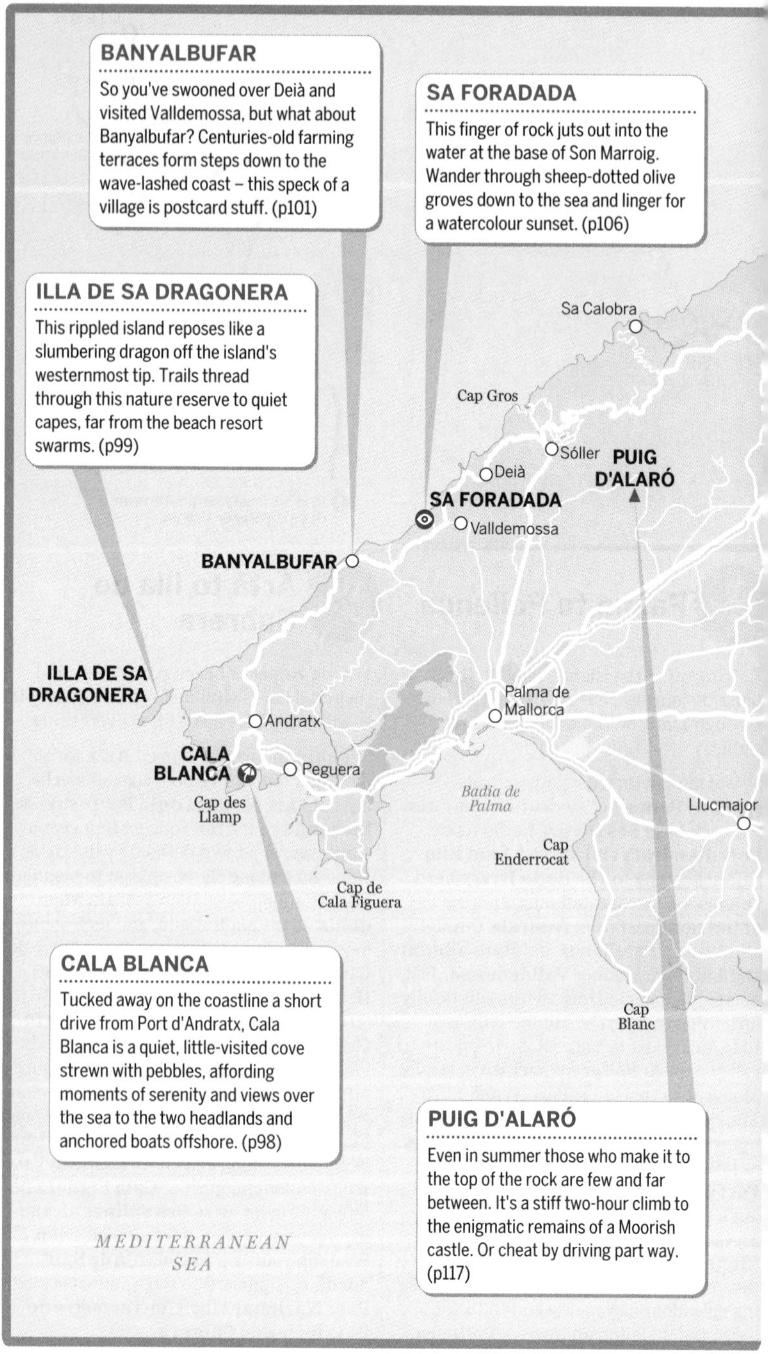

Sa Calobra

Cap Gros

Sóller **PUIG D'ALARÓ**

Deià

SA FORADADA

Valldemossa

BANYALBUFAR

ILLA DE SA DRAGONERA

Andratx

Palma de Mallorca

CALA BLANCA

Peguera

Cap des Llamp

Badia de Palma

Llucmajor

Cap Enderrocat

Cap de Cala Figuera

CALA BLANCA

Tucked away on the coastline a short drive from Port d'Andratx, Cala Blanca is a quiet, little-visited cove strewn with pebbles, affording moments of serenity and views over the sea to the two headlands and anchored boats offshore. (p98)

Cap Blanc

PUIG D'ALARÓ

Even in summer those who make it to the top of the rock are few and far between. It's a stiff two-hour climb to the enigmatic remains of a Moorish castle. Or cheat by driving part way. (p117)

MEDITERRANEAN SEA

N 0 — 20 km
0 — 10 miles

BALEARIC
SEA

Cap de
Formentor

Cap des
Pinar

Pollença

▲ TALAIA
D'ALCÚDIA

SANTUARI DE
LA MARE DE
DÉU DES PUIG

Badia de
Pollença

Parc
Natural de
S'Albufera

Badia
d'Alcúdia

Finca
Pública de
Son Real

Parc Natural de
la Península
de Llevant

Santa
Margalida

Artà

Cala Ratjada

Manacor

Felanitx

CALES DE
MALLORCA

Portocolom

PLATJA
DES TRENC

Parc
Natural de
Mondragó

Cala d'Or

Cap de Ses
Salines

MEDITERRANEAN
SEA

Illa des
Conills

Illa de
Cabrera

TALAIA D'ALCÚDIA

Hike up from the Ermita de la Victoria on a half-hour trek to this astonishing lookout point with 360-degree views over the peninsula and the sea. You may only have wild mountain goats for company. (p136)

SANTUARI DE LA MARE DE DÉU DES PUIG

Silence blankets the courtyards and chapel of this former nunnery, high above Pollença. It's hard to drag yourself away from the views that embrace the full sweep of the north coast. (p126)

CALES DE MALLORCA

Walking is the only way to reach the tiny coves that dot the coastline north of Cales de Mallorca, but chances are you'll have their iridescent waters all to yourself. (p154)

PLATJA DES TRENC

This 3km ribbon of frost-white, dune-backed sand hems Mallorca's southern coast and is lapped by aquamarine water. Even in August, there's space to breathe and go nude if you dare. (p171)

Caragols

Plan Your Trip

Eat & Drink Like a Local

Stopping to sit down and slowly savour a meal is one of the best things about Mallorca, where eating is not just a functional pastime but one of life's great pleasures. Eating on the hoof is thankfully not part of the culture and there is a refreshing lack of fast-food restaurants; the few here are mainly frequented by un-adventurous tourists.

The Year in Food

Spring

Sprigs of wild rosemary and thyme add flavour to *anyell de llet* (suckling lamb). *Espàrrecs* (asparagus) and *caragols* (snails) pop up on many menus.

Summer

You can pick *fonoll marí* (samphire), a coastal plant that's marinated and used in salads. Markets and menus fill with a bounty of fresh fruit, veg and fish.

Autumn

Join locals to comb the hills for *esclata-sang*, a mushroom of the milk-fungus family. The island's grape harvest and festivals in late September are great fun, especially the grape-throwing **festival in Binissalem** (☺Sep; 🎪).

Winter

Menus go meaty with *sobrassada* (paprika-flavoured cured pork sausage), *llom amb col* (pork wrapped in cabbage with pine nuts and raisins) and *lechona asada* (roast suckling pig).

Food Experiences
Meals of a Lifetime

➡ **Marc Fosh** (☎971 72 01 14; www.marcfosh.com; Carrer de la Missió 7A, Convent de la Missió Hotel; menús lunch €30-40, dinner €72-92; ☺1-3pm & 7.30-9.30pm; 🎫) Michelin-starred Marc Fosh's flagship restaurant in a stylish converted convent refectory (p74).

➡ **Es Verger** (☎971 18 21 26; Camí des Castell; mains €8-16; ☺9am-9pm Tue-Sun) Superbly tender slow-cooked lamb on the long, winding road up to Castell d'Alaró (p117).

➡ **Es Racó d'es Teix** (☎971 639 501; www.esracodesteix.es; Carrer de Sa Vinya Vella 6; mains €35-40, 3-course lunch menú €38, with wine €52, 4-/6-course tasting menú €78/115; ☺1-3pm & 7.30-10.30pm Wed-Sun Feb-Oct; 🎫) Michelin-starred fusion menu and a gorgeous mountain backdrop from the terrace (p108).

➡ **Trespais** (☎971 67 28 14; www.trespais-mallorca.com; Carrer Antonio Callafat 24; mains €22-35; ☺6-11pm Tue-Sun; 🎫) First-rate modern Med cuisine paired with an ultra-romantic setting (p99).

➡ **Celler Ca'n Amer** (☎971 50 12 61; www.celler-canamer.es; Carrer de la Pau 139; mains €16-18, lunch menú €24; ☺1-4pm & 7.30-11pm Mon-Sat, 1-4pm Sun; 🅿) Rustic charm, cracking Mallorcan menu (p144).

➡ **Cases de Son Barbassa** (☎971 56 57 76; www.sonbarbassa.com; Camí de Son Barbassa; mains from €24, 3-course menu €34.50; ☺12.30-3pm & 7-10pm) Tranquil and romantic *finca* (farm) setting for turbot in champagne with clams and oysters (p160).

Cheap Treats

➡ **Forn or confiteria (pastry shop)** You will generally have change from a €5 note, when you pop into one of these pastry shops.

➡ **Ensaïmades** Crispy, croissant-like pastry dusted with icing sugar, with a variety of fillings.

➡ **Empanades** Pasties with savoury fillings.

➡ **Cocarrois** Larger version of the *empanades*.

➡ **Tapas and pintxos (mini tapas)** Great way to stave off hunger and absorb local life; hit Palma's Ruta Martiana (p80) on a Tuesday or Wednesday evening when a drink and a tapa cost as little as €2.

Dare to Try

➡ **Caragols** Dig into snails cooked in a garlicky, herby broth or served in a rich stew.

➡ **Arròs brut** The name 'dirty rice' is off-putting, but trust us, this soupy wonder – with pork, rabbit and vegetables – is delicious.

➡ **Botifarró** Cured blood sausage (not unlike British black pudding) – surprisingly tasty.

➡ **Percebes** Goose barnacles – claw-like, filter-feeding crustaceans that cling to rocks – look ghastly but taste divine. Perfect finger food.

➡ **Frit Mallorquí** A flavoursome lamb offal and veg fry-up, born out of a desperate need for protein during periods of poverty.

PLAN YOUR TRIP EAT & DRINK LIKE A LOCAL

Cooking Courses

Mallorca's fledgling cooking-course scene is just starting to spread its wings, with restaurants and *fincas* occasionally offering the odd class where you can roll up your sleeves and learn the basics. East of Palma, at **Soqueta** (☏660 628430; www.soqueta.com; Carrer Gabriel Comas 20; €79; ⓧ10am-3pm; p89), you will learn how to prepare a three-course meal using local produce, while in Palma itself, there are two standout cooking schools: **Lonja 18** (☏672 233555; www.lonja18.com; Carrer de Sa Llotja 18; 3hr course €70; p69) where courses include a trip to the local market and **My Muy Bueno Cookery School** (☏971 72 00 17; www.mymuybuenocookeryschool.com; Carrer Tous Maroto 5B; half/full day €120/195; p69), which offers a range of courses ranging from vegan to solidly traditional Mallorcan fare.

TAKE IT HOME

For a lingering taste of Mallorca, save room to take home hand-harvested salt from des Trenc, fig bread, *sobrassada*, olives and almonds, wine, Hierbas liqueur and tangy orange preserves from Sóller – a burst of island sunshine when summer is long gone. Here's where you'll find them:

➡ **Típika** (☏971 68 58 10; Carrer d'en Morei 7; ⓧ10am-8pm Mon-Fri, to 6pm Sat, to 3pm Sun; p82)

➡ **Colmado Santo Domingo** (☏971 71 48 87; www.colmadosantodomingo.com; Carrer de Sant Domingo 1; ⓧ10am-8pm Mon-Sat; p82)

➡ **Malvasia de Banyalbufar** (☏971 14 85 05; www.malvasiadebanyalbufar.com; Carrer de Comte Sallent 5; ⓧ11am-2pm & 5-8pm Tue-Sat, to 2pm Sun Jun-Aug, shorter hours Sep-May; p102)

➡ **Mercat de l'Olivar** (www.mercatolivar.com; Plaça de l'Olivar 4; ⓧ7am-2.30pm Mon-Thu, to 8pm Fri, to 3pm Sat; p75)

➡ **Mercat de Santa Catalina** (www.mercatdesantacatalina.com; Plaça de la Navegació; ⓧ7am-5pm Mon-Sat; p75)

➡ **Sunday Market** (Plaça Major; ⓧ8.30am-1pm Sun)

Local Specialities

You might think of Mallorca's coastline and expect to find nothing but fish on menus, yet traditional dishes are surprisingly gutsy and meat-focused, especially in the rural interior. Pork is a very popular ingredient, working its way into countless wholesome sausages, stews, soups and even some vegetable dishes and desserts.

It's true that much of the fish eaten on Mallorca is flown in from elsewhere, but many species still fill the waters near the island. *Besugo* (sea bream) and *rape* (monkfish) are some of the most common fish caught here. Especially appreciated is *cap roig*, an ugly red fish found around the Illa de Cabrera.

Although you'll find fish and seafood cooked in a variety of sauces, this is largely a nod to foreign tastes. Mallorcans long ago learned that fresh seafood is best served grilled with just a bit of salt and lemon. Another delicious way to eat it is *a la sal*, or baked in a salt crust.

Paella may have its origins just across the water in Valencia, but this and other rice dishes have been taken to heart by Mallorcans to the extent that some of Spain's best paellas are found on the island.

Mallorcan Wine

Mallorca has been making wine since Roman times and the industry was flourishing by the mid-19th century, but in the late 1880s the Mallorcan vines were ravaged by the imported vine pest phylloxera. It's only in the past few decades that Mallorcan wine has made it back onto the world wine map. Just over 30 cellars, with 2500 hectares between them, comprise the island's moderate production, most of which is enjoyed in Mallorca's restaurants and hotels. The wineries are huddled in the island's two DOs (Denominaciones de Orígen), Binissalem and an area in the interior of the island that includes towns such as Manacor, Felanitx and Llucmajor, where growing conditions are ideal. International varieties such as cabernet sauvignon are planted alongside native varieties, like manto negro, fogoneu and callet. Local white varieties include prensal blanc and girò blanc, which are blended with Catalan grapes like parellada or with international varieties like chardonnay.

Cocarrois and empanades (pasties with savoury fillings)

Wine production also takes place on the seaward slopes of the Serra de Tramuntana, particularly around Banyalbufar, where the malvasia grape is enjoying a revival.

Tourist offices across the wine country generally have a list of local wineries and their opening hours.

How to Eat & Drink

English menus are a given in coastal resorts, but not necessarily elsewhere. That said, there is nearly always a waiter who can translate. It's handy to learn a few words of Mallorquin, though, so you can decipher some menu items for yourself. Tap water *(agua del grifo)* is perfectly safe to drink, although restaurateurs may push the more costly bottled mineral water *(agua mineral)*.

If you're extended the honour of being invited to dine in someone's home, bring a small gift of wine or chocolates and prepare yourself for a feast. A Mallorcan host will go all-out to entertain guests. Family lunches are often big, boisterous affairs – you'll barely get a word in edgeways but have fun trying! Say *bon profit* (enjoy your meal) before eating and *isalut!* (cheers) when drinking a toast.

The one who invites usually foots the bill. Service charge is included, but you might want to reward good service with an additional tip of around 5%.

When to Eat

Mallorcans eat late, no matter what the meal, although the large foreign population on the island means that restaurants tend to open an hour or more earlier than they do on the mainland.

Most Mallorcans kick-start the day with a shot of *cafè* (black coffee), but they might head out to *esmorzar* (breakfast) around midmorning. This is the ideal time to try a light, sugary *and* fluffy *ensaïmada* (Mallorcan pastry) and wash it down with a *cafè amb llet* (espresso with milk) or a delicious *suc de taronja natural* (freshly squeezed orange juice).

Lunch is the biggest meal of the day. On Sundays, the midday family meal may last until late afternoon. Even when not ordering a *menú*, Mallorcans generally order two courses and a dessert when they go out for lunch.

VEGETARIANS & VEGANS

There has been a marked increase in restaurants and cafes dishing up vegetarian and vegan fare in recent years, making the most of the island's abundant range of produce.

If you want something light, try *trempó*, a refreshing Mallorcan salad of chopped tomatoes, peppers and onions, drizzled in olive oil. *Pa amb oli* is another good option, as is *tumbet* (Mallorcan ratatouille). Spanish gazpacho (cold, garlicky tomato soup) and *tortillas de patatas* (thick omelettes made with potatoes) are popular too.

Bear in mind that many traditional veggie dishes are prepared with salted pork, meat broth or lard. For meat-free meals be sure to stress that you are vegetarian. *Soy vegetariano/a* (I'm a vegetarian m/f) or *no como carne* (I don't eat meat) should do the trick.

Mallorcans' stomachs start growling by 7pm or so. This is a great time to stop for tapas. An import from the mainland, many bars and cafes will have a small selection of snacky things to choose from. Olives or a dish of *ametlla* (almonds) are the ideal accompaniment to a *caña* (beer).

For most Mallorcans, the appropriate dinner time is around 9pm. A meal usually begins with *pa moreno* (brown bread) and perhaps a *pica pica,* when many small appetisers are put out for everyone to share. Next comes the *primer plato,* which may be a salad, pasta, grilled-vegetable plate or something more creative. Desserts are most often a simple *gelat* (ice cream), flan or fruit.

Where to Eat

➡ **Celler** A country-wine-cellar-turned-restaurant, with a solid menu of traditional home cooking, a local crowd and relaxed feel.

➡ **Cafe** Takes you through from morning coffee to evening tapas and alcoholic drinks. Great for light bites such as salads and *pa amb oli* (bread with oil).

➡ **Chiringuito** Beach shack serving drinks, snacks and sometimes tapas and seafood.

➡ **Confiteria** A pastry shop, alternatively called a *forn* or a *pastelería*. Find the best *ensaïmades* (round buns) here.

➡ **Gelateria** Ice-cream parlour, often with Italian-style *gelato* (made with milk and fresh fruit).

➡ **Marisquería** Specialises in seafood. Sometimes called a *restaurant de marisc*.

➡ **Restaurant** From simple to gourmet. Anything with *ca'n* or *ca's* in its name serves traditional fare in a family-style atmosphere.

➡ **Tabernas** Rustic taverns serving tapas or meals. *Tascas* work to a similar concept.

Menu Decoder

arròs bogavante – moist, juicy lobster rice

arròs brut – literally 'dirty rice', a soupy dish made with pork, rabbit and vegetables

arròs negre – rice dish, cooked in and coloured by squid ink, and sometimes served with shellfish

botifarra – flavourful pork sausage; some of the best island sausages

botiffarón – a larger version of *botifarra*

cocas de patata – bread-like pastry dusted with sugar and particularly famous in Valldemossa

conill amb ceba – rabbit with onions

ensaïmada – Mallorcan pastry par excellence; a round bun made with a spiral of sweet dough, topped with powdered sugar and sometimes filled with cream, chocolate or *cabell d'àngel* (pumpkin paste)

gató Mallorquí – dense almond cake

lechona – suckling pig, often roasted on an open spit

llom amb col – pork loin wrapped in cabbage, flavoured with garlic, tomatoes, *sobrassada,* parsley, sultanas and pine nuts

marisquada – heaped tray of steamed shellfish; plan to share

pa amb oli – literally bread with oil; traditional *pa moreno* (rye bread) usually topped with chopped tomatoes, as well as a variety of other toppings

sobrassada – tangy cured pork sausage flavoured with paprika and sea salt

suquet – stew cooked in rich fish stock and filled with fish and/or seafood

trempó – refreshing salad of chopped tomatoes, peppers and onions

tumbet – a kind of vegetable ratatouille made with aubergines, courgettes, potatoes, garlic and tomatoes.

Kitesurfers at Ca'n Pastilla (p88)

Plan Your Trip

Activities

Whether you're hiking along the north coast's ragged clifftops, negotiating the Tramuntana's limestone wilderness by mountain bike or kayaking to secluded coves too tiny to appear on maps, Mallorca's outdoors exhilarates and enthrals. Mountains, canyons and 550km of gorgeous coast are all squeezed into this island. Go forth and explore!

Best of the Outdoors

Best Hiking

The twin peninsulas of Cap de Formentor and Cap des Pinar offer coastal hiking at its finest, with pine-cloaked cliffs dropping suddenly to a sea of bluest blue.

Best Cycling

Mountain bikers and road cyclists are in their element in the high peaks of the Serra de Tramuntana, with thigh-crunching climbs, sweeping descents and hairpin bend after looping hairpin bend.

Best Scuba Diving

South Mallorca is a diver's dream. Go to Illa de Sa Dragonera and Illa de Cabrera (for divers with requisite permission) for wrecks, cave drops and pristine water swirling with rays, octopuses and barracuda.

Best Canyoning

The Serra de Tramuntana is rippled through with gorges and canyons. For drama, delve into Gorg Blau Sa Fosca or Torrent d'es Pareis.

Best Windsurfing & Kitesurfing

The thermal winds that whip off the sea rolling into Sa Marina in the Badia de Pollença create the ideal conditions for windsurfing and kitesurfing.

Planning Your Trip

When to Go

Mallorca's activities are, in theory, possible year-round thanks to the island's relatively mild winters and oft-touted 300 days of sunshine. That said, many organised activities will only be doable from roughly Easter to October, particularly water-based sports.

The ideal conditions for most activities, particularly hiking and cycling, are in spring and autumn. Daytime temperatures in summer can be uncomfortably hot and the traffic on the roads can make cycling a stop-start affair.

What to Take

Most activities operators in Mallorca can provide you with all of the necessary equipment, while high-quality bicycles can be rented all over the island. Although professional-standard equipment is available for purchase on Mallorca, anyone planning on hiking should bring their own boots.

On the Land

Hiking

From the bald and dramatic limestone mountains in the west to the rocky coastal trails of the north and east where the lure of the sea is never-ending, Mallorca offers some of the finest hiking anywhere in Europe. The Consell de Mallorca (www.conselldemallorca.net) has become serious about signposting and maintaining the island's trekking routes (many of which have been used for centuries by pack animals and wayfaring pilgrims), so following the route is often (but not always) fairly easy.

The Tramuntana cannot rival the Alps in height, but its serrated peaks, crags and ravines are every bit as wild and not to be underestimated, and the hiking season here is longer. A network of *refugis* (mountain refuges) gives weary hikers a place to bed down for the night, as do the hilltop monasteries and hermitages that have been converted into simple accommodation.

While short distances between trails mean you can cover more ground, it's worth bearing in mind that you may need your own wheels to reach many of the trailheads. But once you get there, you'll have them more or less to yourself.

There are hikes for almost every age and fitness level, so don't assume hiking is just for the hardcore.

Best Day Hikes

Just about every tourist office in Mallorca can advise on local day hikes in the area and help you find a route to match your fitness level. Five favourites:

Cap de Ses Salines to Colònia de Sant Jordi (p172) This half-day hike along the south coast takes in captivating seascapes. Plenty of opportunities for swimming.

Four Coves Hike (p154) Slip away from east-coast crowds with this glorious, easygoing cove-to-cove walk.

Sóller to Mirador de Ses Barques (p115) Stride through olive groves to a magical viewpoint, then return via pretty hill town Fornalutx.

Three Coastal Peaks (p124) Walk through forests of pine and gaze out across the north coast from this cliff-hugger of a hike.

Cala en Gossalba to Fumat (p125) Formentor's most dramatic coastal hike – begins gently and ends spectacularly with 360-degree views from the 334m crag of Fumat.

Multiday Hikes

There are two main long-distance hiking trails in Mallorca. As in the rest of Spain, the two GR (long-distance) trails are signposted in red and white.

Ruta de Pedra en Sec Keen hikers can tackle the Route of Dry Stone (GR221; www.gr221.info), a four- to seven-day walk going from Port d'Andratx to Pollença, crossing the Serra de Tramuntana. At a few points along the GR221 there are *refugis de muntanya* (rustic mountain huts) where trekkers can stay the night.

Ruta Artà-Lluc Signposting marks the GR 222, which has been under development for several years and was virtually completed at the time of research.

Hiking Maps & Guides

The best hiking maps are the 1:25,000 *Tramuntana Central, Tramuntana Norte* and *Tramuntana Sur* maps by Editorial Alpina (www.editorialalpina.com). These can be picked up at many bookshops around the island. Cicerone's *Walking in Mallorca* details and maps 80 routes.

If you need more than a map, there are some reputable guides on the island:

Tramuntana Tours (p209) Respected activities operator based in Sóller and Port de Sóller; its focus is on the Serra de Tramuntana.

Món d'Aventura (p128) This Pollença adventure specialist offers myriad hikes, graded from easy to advanced, including the Ruta de Pedra en Sec.

Rich Strutt (p130) An English-speaking guide with over 20 years of experience based in Port de Pollença offering a huge number of day hikes (or longer treks) to choose from for groups of four or more.

Cap de Ses Salines lighthouse (p172)

Hiking Resources

The Consell de Mallorca (www.conselldemallorca.net) publishes two excellent brochures, both of which should be available from the Consell de Mallorca tourist office (p206) in Palma. The brochures' maps are orientative in scope and you'll need to supplement them with detailed hiking maps:

Rutes per Mallorca (Mallorca Itineraries) Six treks ranging from 33.2km to 113.5km.

Caminar per Mallorca (Walking in Mallorca) Twelve day hikes from 4.5km to 14km.

Cycling

Mallorca's popularity as a destination for road cycling and mountain biking (p210) continues to soar. Nearly half of Mallorca's 1250km of roads have been harnessed for cycling, with everything from signposts to separate bike lanes. The lycra peak season in mountainous regions is from March to May and late September to November, when the weather is refreshingly cool.

Mountain bikers will find abundant trails, too, ranging from flat dirt tracks to

PLAN YOUR TRIP ACTIVITIES

VISIONSI/ SHUTTERSTOCK ©

Cyclist on the Sa Calobra route

rough-and-tumble single tracks. Be sure to get a good highway or trekking map before you set out on any cycling expedition.

Bike-rental agencies are ubiquitous across the island, and local tourist offices can usually point you in the right direction. Prices can vary between €10 per day for a basic touring bike and €30 for a high-end mountain or racing bike.

Best Cycling Routes

There are many great areas for biking; trails cover the island like a web and, depending on your skills and interests, anywhere can be the start of a fabulous ride. That said, here are some favourites:

Palma to Capocorb Vell (p70)

Andratx to Monestir de Lluc (p96)

Parc Natural de la Península de Llevant (p158)

Cap de Formentor (p132)

Port d'Alcúdia & Cap des Pinar (p135)

Santa Maria to Binibona, via Santa Eugenia, Binissalem, Lloseta and Caimari

Cycling Guides

If you don't fancy going it alone, you can hook onto some terrific excursions with guides that know Mallorca like the backs of their hands:

Tramuntana Tours (p209) As the name suggests, these guys take you into the heart of the Tramuntana.

Cycling Resources

The Federació de Ciclisme de les Illes Balears (www.webfcib.es) can provide contact information for local cycling clubs. A growing number of hotels cater specifically to cyclists, with garages and energy-packed menus.

Canyoning

The ultimate Mallorcan adrenaline rush, canyoning is an exhausting but exhilarating mix of jumping into ravines and trudging down gorges and gullies.

Going with a professional guide is essential. Among the best are Món d'Aventura (p128), Tramuntana Tours (p209) and Ex-

Golf

Palma is a popular golfing destination, which is not surprising given the mix of warm Mediterranean climate and fine natural setting. At last count there were around 22 golf courses scattered around the island; some of the best cluster around Capdepera and Artà in the east. Green fees for 18 holes start from €30 and can go as high as €130, although the average is €40 to €75.

Horse Riding

With its extensive network of rugged trails over hilly countryside and alongside the Mediterranean, Mallorca is a fine place to saddle up. Many towns and resorts have stables where you can join a class (€10 to €20) or a group excursion (about €15 for the first hour, with two five-hour rides generally costing around €25/60 per person). Longer trips are also possible. Some stables also offer pony rides for small children.

Golf course in Mallorca

perience Mallorca (p138), all of which cater to all levels, with tours graded from easy to difficult.

Rock Climbing

The mere thought of Mallorca's sublime limestone walls has climbers' hearts pounding. The island is among Europe's foremost destinations for sport climbers, with abundant overhangs, slabs and crags. Climbing here concentrates on three main areas: the southwest for multi-pitch climbing, the northwest for magnificent crags and the east for superb deep water soloing (DWS).

Caving

Mallorca's pocked limestone terrain means caving conditions are fantastic. Kitted out with headlamps, spelunkers can penetrate the cool twilight of the numerous cave complexes that burrow into the cliffs of the southern, northern and eastern coasts. A guide is highly recommended.

Experience Mallorca (p138) leads half-day caving excursions year-round.

Water Sports
Diving & Snorkelling

Mallorca is one of southern Europe's premier diving and snorkelling destinations. The combination of super-clear waters and professional dive centres make this an excellent place for a leisure dive or to undertake the open-water PADI diving-accreditation course. Diving is best from May to October.

Mallorca Diving (www.mallorcadiving.com) lists eight reputable dive centres with their prices.

Sailboarding & Kitesurfing

While the relatively calm wind and waves of Mallorca don't make the island a natural hot spot for fans of windsurfing or kitesurfing (aka kiteboarding), exceptions to the rule are the Badia de Pollença and Port d'Alcúdia, where stiff breezes ensure plenty of action.

Sail & Surf Pollença (p130) Sailing and windsurfing courses and rental in Port de Pollença.

Wind & Friends (p135) In Port d'Alcúdia, with a range of courses for adults and children.

MARINA KRYUCHINA / SHUTTERSTOCK ©

Top: Kayakers off Port de Sóller (p113)

Bottom: Stand-up paddleboarding in a sea

Sailing

Among the 35 marinas that ring Mallorca's coast, many offer yacht charters, sailboat rentals and sailing courses. There are large sailing schools in Palma, Port de Pollença and other resorts; expect a two-day course to cost €400 to €500; the Palma Sea School (p69) is the most professional outfit.

One place that rents yachts is Llaüts (p96) in Port d'Andratx; prices start at €120 per half day. Mezzo Magic (p113) in Port de Sóller is also recommended for all-inclusive yacht hire.

Sea Kayaking

Mallorca's craggy coastline is indented with lovely bays and coves – many of which can only be reached by boat. A sea kayak allows you to tune into the soothing rhythm of the sea and explore rock formations, caves and quiet beaches at your own pace. Marine falcons, cormorants and wild goats are frequently sighted, and you might even spot the odd dolphin or flying fish. The coves of the Parc Natural de la Península de Llevant (p156), inaccessible from the land, are a paradise of pristine waters, pitted rocks and thriving wildlife. The coasts around Sóller (p108) in the west, Porto Cristo (p164) in the east and Port de Pollença (p128) in the north are perfect for paddling.

Boat Trips

From Easter to October, glass-bottomed boats drift up and down the eastern coast and can be a fun way to enjoy the water without the responsibility of sailing your own boat. Most are half-day trips only and rarely last four hours. All operators sell return tickets, but on some east-coast routes you can travel one way. Here are four routes to get your started:

Transportes Marítimos Brisa (p135) Port d'Alcúdia to Cala Sant Vicenç and back, via Cap de Formentor.

Barcos Azules (p113) Port de Sóller to Sa Calobra.

Excursions a Cabrera (p171) Round-trip tours by speedboat or slower boats from Colònia de Sant Jordi to the Parc Nacional Marítim-Terrestre de l'Arxipèlag de Cabrera.

Starfish (p165) From Portocolom to Cala Figuera.

Plan Your Trip
Family Travel

Mallorca could be the poster child for stimulating and stress-free family travel. Undoubtedly an adults' playground, it's just as packed with diversions and distractions for the littl'uns: castles to scale, warm seas and wild water parks to splash in, caves to explore, beaches to burn energy at and warm welcomes all round.

Keeping Costs Down

Accommodation

Mallorca has plenty of family-friendly accommodation options. Many hotels in coastal resorts offer apartments or one-bedroom suites big enough for families. Most places will squeeze in a baby's cot for free or a child's bed for a small extra charge.

Transport

Children under five years travel free on public transport with discounts for those aged between five and 12 years. You can hire car seats from most car-rental firms, but be sure to reserve beforehand.

Eating

Eating out with children is a breeze in Mallorca, where large family lunches are the norm. Many resort restaurants offer inexpensive children's menus or are happy to whip up smaller portions. High chairs are generally available and, increasingly, restaurants have nappy-changing facilities within the disabled-toilet space.

Activities

There's no shortage of activities for children here, including water parks, museums and outdoor pursuits, such as hiking, swimming and surfing. Mallorca is a popular cycling destination; most bike-rental outfits have children's bikes available.

Children Will Love...

Natural Wonders

Coves del Drac, Porto Cristo Wend through watery caverns encrusted with stalactites, millennia in the making and a wondrous site for kids. (p164)

Serra de Tramuntana, Western Mallorca Fire up the kids' imaginations by marvelling at faces and the surreal weird formations in the bizarrely weathered peaks of this mountain range. (p100)

Sa Cova Blava, Illa de Cabrera Look in wonder at the surreal blue waters at the 'Blue Cave' on a boat trip to the Illa de Cabrera, part of Mallorca's only natural park. (p174)

Coves d'Arta, Canyamel Gawp at this magical cave with its veritable forest of formations, including the 'Queen of Columns' and the (kids' favourite) aptly named 'Chamber of Hell'! (p163)

Parc Natural de S'Albufera, Northern Mallorca Bring binoculars to spot wading birds, turtles and, if you're lucky, even water buffalo in this reed-fringed nature park (p137).

Beaches & Swimming

Cala Mondragó, Parc Natural de Mondragó Great for swimming and snorkelling, this southern Blue Flag bay is gorgeous with brilliantly clear waters and powder-soft sand. (p176)

Platja de Muro, Ca'an Picafort Fabulous sweep of silky sand and shallow turquoise sea which is ideal for both sandcastle creations and paddling tots. (p137)

GOOD TO KNOW

Look out for the 👪 icon for family-friendly suggestions throughout this guide.

Accommodation Most hotels can supply cots and the all-inclusive resorts generally have kids' clubs and loads of organised activities.

Breastfeeding Although most locals have a relaxed attitude about breastfeeding in public, the same might not be true for the tourists.

Baby-change facilities Most museums, theme parks and major sights have a bathroom with a baby-change table; increasingly, restaurants will have an accessible toilet with a changing table installed.

Child-safety seats Major car-hire companies can supply child-safety seats for a fee; install them yourself. Call taxi companies in advance to organise seats.

Eating out Restaurants that cater towards tourists generally include a separate children's menu (although the quality can be questionable), while local restaurants will normally be happy to prepare a smaller quantity of, probably, a healthier dish. Alternatively, tapas are a good option for kids.

Playgrounds Plentiful throughout Mallorca; ask at a tourist office for locations.

Timings Adjust your children to Spanish time (ie late nights) as quickly as you can, otherwise they'll miss half the fun. Also, bear in mind that many kid-geared sights and activities are only open from April to October, so always check before you set out to avoid disappointment (and tears).

Platja de Formentor, Cap de Formentor Getting to this north-coast beach by boat or the hair-raising coastal road is part of the family fun. Tiptoe away from the crowds on the pine-flanked slither of sand. (p131)

Cala Mesquida, Cala Ratjada An east-coast favourite, this gently shelving bay has dazzling clear water, which is terrific for snorkelling for older kids. (p162)

Going Back in Time

Castell de Bellver, Palma The Badia de Palma shrinks to postcard format from this mighty circular castle. (p76)

Ferrocarril de Sóller This rattling vintage train from Palma to Sóller is a real blast from the past – a hit with kids and parents. (p85)

Santuari de Sant Salvador, Artà Ramble along the ramparts of this hilltop castle above Artà. (p156)

Medieval Walls, Alcúdia Travel back in time with a walk atop the old city walls of Alcúdia. (p132)

Torre des Verger, Banyalbufar Play pirates at this watchtower precariously perched above the sea near Estellencs. (p98)

Energy Burners

Aqualand, S'Arenal Kids will gleefully exhaust themselves on the slides, rides and tides at the island's three waterparks. (p89)

Península de Llevant, Eastern Mallorca Treat natural parks, like this, as vast open-air playgrounds, full of secret coves, ancient stone towers and flocks of beady-eyed goats. (p158)

Parc Natural de S'Albufera, South of Alcúdia Gentle pedals along the coast and in the bird-rich wetlands of this natural park; mountain biking in the Tramuntana for active teens. (p137)

Port de Sóller, Western Mallorca Pair up with a nipper in a tandem sea kayak to explore the caves and coves around one of the island's prettiest ports. (p113)

Region by Region
Palma & Badia de Palma

The island's capital is like a history lesson come to life, whether playing spot-the-gargoyle at the cathedral (p53) or clambering up to Castell de Bellver (p76). Nearby, find giant water parks (p89) and a superb aquarium (p88) with brilliantly creepy shark sleepovers. See Palma for Kids (p68) for more family fun ideas in the city.

Western Mallorca

Older kids who like striding out will love this area for its wide range of hiking trails, particularly around the Serra de Tramuntana (p100) and the raw and unspoiled Illa de Sa Dragonera (p99). Watery pursuits, including paddle surfing and kayaking, are other options on the west coast, as well as entertaining boat rides (p113) from bustling Port de Sóller.

Northern Mallorca

Alcúdia and Port de Pollença are natural family pleasers, with giant gentle bays ideal for long sandy days. Hit Hidropark (p135) for whizzy slides and Parc Natural de S'Albufera (p137) for gentle bike rides and birdwatching expeditions. Plus, there are loads of activities for teens – from kayaking to spooky caving.

The Interior

Famed for its picturesque villages and countryside, this region is not the most riveting for youngsters, although the glassmaking demonstrations at the Museu de Gordiola (p147) may capture their imaginations, along with the eerie thicket of stalactites and stalagmites at the Coves de Campanet (p145).

Eastern Mallorca

Tell tales of troglodytes as you duck through the glittering chambers of vast caves – none more impressive than the Coves del Drac (p164). There are castles for fantasy play, pony rides, boat trips, safari encounters and a cluster of lovely, gently shelving bays in the island's east too.

Southern Mallorca

This region is all about the beaches and sea sports with plenty of seafaring options, including boat rides (p176) and scuba diving. There is also a genuine prehistoric village (p168).

Useful Resources

Lonely Planet Kids (www.lonelyplanetkids.com) Loads of activities and family travel blog content.

Book: First Words Spanish (shop.lonelyplanet. com) A beautifully illustrated introduction to the Spanish language for ages five to eight.

Travel with your Kids (www.travelwithyourkids. com) Tips for travelling with your children, including packing, resources and accommodation.

Kids' Corner

Say What?

Hello.	Hola
Goodbye.	Adiós
Thank you.	Gracias
My name is ...	Me llamo ...

Did You Know? ℹ

- Mallorca is home to a real prehistoric village
- The national anthem was adopted from an ancient nursery rhyme about a spider!

Have You Tried?

Ensaïmada Yummy flaky pastry with a choice of filling.

Regions at a Glance

Palma & the Badia de Palma

Architecture
Galleries
Food

Medieval Architecture

Palma is like a 3D textbook on Mediterranean architectural history. The Gothic cathedral is the show-stealer, but the old town's tightly packed lanes hide Modernista masterpieces, medieval mansions and baroque *patis* (patios).

Miró, Barceló, Picasso & Dalí

Many of Spain's premier 20th-century artists had a soft spot for Palma. Miró left his playful mark all over the city, Miquel Barceló came from nearby Felanitx, and Picasso and Dalí originals cram the city's stellar galleries.

The Mallorcan Kitchen

Mallorca's culinary star shines brightest in Palma, from the island's best seafood restaurants to the celebrated cuisine of master chef Marc Fosh, to intimate tapas bars around Plaça Major, innovative vegetarian and (increasingly) vegan options and those irresistible pastry shops.

p50

Western Mallorca

Villages
Landscapes
Hiking

Hilltop Villages

The honey-coloured stone architecture of Western Mallorca's hilltop villages form idyllic stops through a stunning mountain panorama. Slow tour the Tramuntana's foothills and charms of Valldemossa, Deià, Fornalutx, Binaraix and Orient.

Spectacular Uplands

In Mallorca's repertoire of lovely landscapes, the Serra de Tramuntana deserves a standing ovation, with its wild limestone peaks, plunging cliffs and backdrop of azure waters.

Mountain Hikes

The multiday Ruta de Pedra en Sec traversing the Tramuntana is the real biggie, but you can also scramble up Puig de Massanella, trek through Sóller's citrus groves or do the pilgrimage to Monestir de Lluc.

p93

Northern Mallorca

Landscapes
Towns
Beaches

Cap de Formentor

The Serra de Tramuntana reaches a crescendo along this peninsula of dizzying mountain peaks and cliffs that plunge to sheltered coves.

Pollença & Alcúdia

The northern coastal hinterland harbours two of Mallorca's most engaging towns: glorious Pollença, with its cobblestone streets and 365 steps to Calvari, and ancient Alcúdia, with Roman ruins and walls.

Superlative Sands

The masses gravitate to the broad beaches and crystal-clear waters of the north's twin bays: Badia de Pollença and Badia d'Alcúdia. Quieter coves punctuate Cala Sant Vicenç, Cap de Formentor and Cap des Pinar.

p121

The Interior

Wine
Food
Architecture

Wineries & Bodegas

Mallorca's wine-producing areas range across the island's vine-cloaked interior; some of the wineries – such as Bodegas Castell Miquel – offer tours.

Mallorcan Country Cooking

From the *celler* restaurants of Inca and Sineu to the rural *fincas* (farms) transformed into hotels and restaurants, eating dishes such as *lechona* (roast suckling pig) or *tumbet* (a kind of vegetable ratatouille) in the interior is all about authenticity.

Monasteries & Medieval Towns

Almost every hilltop in inland Mallorca was long ago colonised by a monastery from where the views ripple for miles, while towns like Sineu and Petra are places of quiet, underrated charm.

p139

Eastern Mallorca

Beaches
Caves
Landscapes

Secluded Beaches & Coves

Explore the wild beaches northeast of Cala Ratjada, home to some of Mallorca's most desirable real estate. The serene *cales* (coves) south of Porto Cristo are similarly lovely.

Subterranean Cathedrals

The epic formations and stalactite forests of eastern Mallorca's caves rank among the island's most eye-catching phenomena – try Coves del Drac, Coves d'Artà and Coves dels Hams.

The Península de Llevant

North of Artà, the Parc Natural de la Península de Llevant lures birdwatchers and hikers. Cap Ferrutx bookends the peninsula, while Ermita de Betlem affords quiet contemplation.

p152

Southern Mallorca

Beaches
Scenery
Archaeology

Unspoiled Sands

The south has a prized collection of beaches and limpid waters for diving. Loll on the seemingly never-ending sands of Platja des Trenc, or cove-hop to coastal lovelies like Cala Pi, Cala Llombards and the Parc Natural de Mondragó.

Coastal Ramparts

The high cliffs of the coast have spared much of the south from developers' bulldozers, especially from Cap Blanc to Cap de Ses Salines. Illa de Cabrera is a treasure.

Talayotic Sites

The island's prehistory is shrouded in uncertainty; Talayotic sites such as Capocorb Vell and those close to Ses Salines offer insights into pre-Roman Mallorca.

p166

On the Road

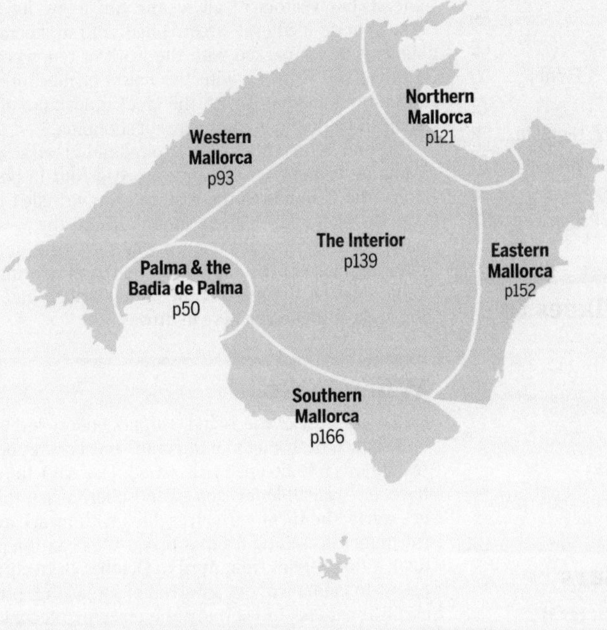

Northern Mallorca p121

Western Mallorca p93

The Interior p139

Eastern Mallorca p152

Palma & the Badia de Palma p50

Southern Mallorca p166

Palma & the Badia de Palma

Best Places to Eat

➡ Marc Fosh (p74)

➡ El Camino (p73)

➡ Beatnik (p76)

➡ Mola (p78)

➡ Simply Delicious (p76)

Best Bars

➡ Bar Flexas (p79)

➡ Clandestino Cocktail Club (p79)

➡ Lórien (p78)

➡ Idem Café (p80)

➡ Atlantico Café (p79)

Why Go?

Visually magnificent, culturally spoiled, historically fascinating and geographically blessed, Palma should be better known as one of Europe's great destinations. Yes, it's a playground of the elite (and, increasingly, a port of call for cruise liners), but visitors of all means can enjoy its wonders: atmospheric medieval streets lined with aristocratic mansions; galleries packed with the work of renowned artists; a broad bay bristling with the masts of maritime wealth; restaurants mixing it with the great innovators of modern Spanish food; and endless acres of shopping.

Beyond Palma, Mallorca's capital and greatest asset, the Badia de Palma (Bay of Palma) spreads out in both directions: the flatlands to the east and the wrinkled hills that presage Mallorca's highest mountains to the west. These parts are also culturally uneven: one *cala* (cove) may be the mooring place of the superwealthy; the next brilliant with neon, lighting the way for the young British and German fun seekers that come here in droves.

When to Go

Unlike the rest of the island, Palma's energy levels remain fairly constant throughout the year – most sights, hotels and restaurants remain open year-round. That said, the city does have an irresistible feel-good atmosphere when the weather's warm, the yacht harbour is filled with masts and one of the numerous sailing regattas brings the beautiful people to town – this applies from April to October. Scarcely a month passes in Palma without a festival of some kind: pre-Lenten carnival parades in February, the crazy pyrotechnics of Nit de Foc in June and December's Christmas market are top diary dates. The beach resorts of the Badia de Palma effectively shut down in winter.

What's New

➔ Catedral Roof Terraces (p53) You can now visit the cathedral's roof terraces on a guided one-hour tour. The steep climb of some 280 steps rewards you with views of the splendid bells, four of which date from the 14th century, and you can get up close to the vast Gothic rose window (largest in Europe), the dramatic flying buttresses and, of course, enjoy superlative views of the city and sea.

➔ Can Balaguer (p65) The permanent exhibition here covers 4000 years of history, expressed in the decor and furnishings of the various rooms, which are impressively faithful to their era.

PALMA'S PATIOS

Few experiences in Palma beat simply milling around the backstreets of the city's Old Town, which spreads east of the cathedral. Iron gates conceal the city's *patis* (patios), the grand courtyards where nobles once received guests and horse-drawn coaches clattered to a halt. *Patis* were the intersection of public and private life, and as such they were showpieces – polished until they gleamed and filled with flowers and plants.

There are still around 150 patrician houses with *patis* in Palma today, though most can only be observed through locked wrought-iron gates. They vary in style from Gothic to renaissance, baroque to Modernista, but most have the same defining features: graceful arches and Ionic columns, sweeping staircases with wrought-iron balustrades and a well or cistern.

Top Five Galleries

➔ Museu Fundación Juan March (p64) Contemporary art stars, including Mallorca's own Miquel Barceló.

➔ Es Baluard (p66) Picasso, Miró and fine city views at this gallery atop the Renaissance sea wall.

➔ Fundació Pilar i Joan Miró (p90) Total Miró immersion, with 2500 works on show.

➔ Centre Cultural Contemporani Pelaires (p63) Fetching 17th-century building with Palma's first dedicated contemporary-art gallery, still going strong.

➔ Palau March (p56) Etchings by Dalí and sculpture by Moore, Rodin and Chillida in an exquisite palace.

CATHEDRAL PHOTO OPS

For that must-have cathedral snapshot, head to Parc de la Mar during the blue hour (twilight) to frame it perfectly and see it spectacularly illuminated.

Need to Know

➔ Many of Palma's headline attractions close on Mondays, including the Fundació Pilar i Joan Miró and Es Baluard.

➔ Sunday closures include the Catedral and Palau March.

➔ Don't attempt to drive or park in the Old Town unless approved by your hotel in advance. Parking is strictly restricted to residents and there are steep fines.

To/From the Airport

➔ Mallorca's international airport is in Ca'n Pastilla, just 8km from central Palma. From here, a taxi to the centre of town should cost around €20, slightly less if you're headed to the eastern Badia de Palma, and €40 or more if you're bound for Magaluf.

➔ Bus 1 loops around Palma from the airport to Porto Pi in the west; bus 21 heads east to S'Arenal. Both cost a flat €5.

Resources

Ajuntament de Palma (www.palmademallorca.es) Civil administration website.

Consell de Mallorca tourist office (www.infomallorca. net) Easily navigated and up to date.

Visit Palma (www.visit palma.com) Comprehensive info.

Visit Calvia (www.visit-calvia.com) Low-down on resorts to the west.

EMT Palma public transport (www.emtpalma.es) Search routes and fares.

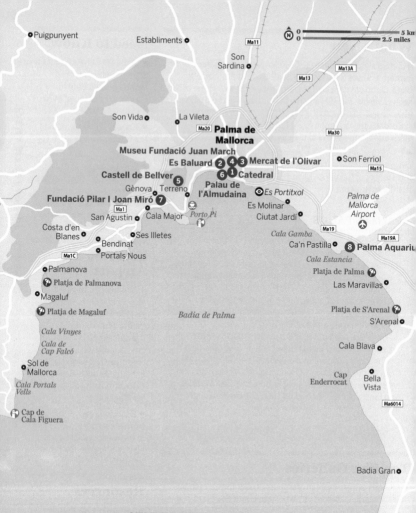

Palma & the Badia de Palma Highlights

1 Catedral (p53) Admiring the work of Barceló, Gaudí and other visionaries.

2 Es Baluard (p66) Wandering the ramparts and galleries of this historic fortress-turned-museum.

3 Mercat de l'Olivar (p75) Tasting the plenty of Palma's largest market.

4 Museu Fundación Juan March (p64) Getting up close to Picasso, Miró and Dalí, minus the crowds.

5 Castell de Bellver (p76) Commanding the heights above the Badia de Palma.

6 Palau de l'Almudaina (p54) Walking in the footsteps of Moorish governors and Spanish royalty.

7 Fundació Pilar i Joan Miró (p90) Feeling inspired from the hilltop studio of the great Catalan artist.

8 Palma Aquarium (p88) Coming face to face with the denizens of the Mediterranean deep.

PALMA DE MALLORCA

POP 409,661

Palma is a real stunner. Rising in honey-coloured stone from the broad waters of the Badia de Palma, this enduring city dates back to the 13th-century Christian reconquest of the island, and to the Moors, Romans and Talayotic people before that. A richly studded diadem of historical sites, Palma also shelters a seemingly endless array of galleries, restaurants, craft studios and bars – it's without doubt Mallorca's greatest treasure. Wander in any direction from the stunning Gothic Catedral at its geographic and historical heart and you'll find twisted medieval streets lined with aristocratic townhouses, looming baroque churches, teeming public squares, vibrant bohemian neighbourhoods and markets overflowing with all the bounty of the island. Palma is a supremely liveable city with an intrinsic Spanish feel; you could spend several weeks here and still uncover fresh joys every day.

History

Founded by the Romans in 123 BCE, Palma (or Palmeria) was built on a prominence naturally commanding the broad Badia de Palma, on the site of an earlier, Talayotic settlement. Later falling into dereliction, it was given fresh impetus by the arrival of the island's new Muslim masters in the 10th century. By the 12th century Medina Mayurka (City of Mallorca) was one of the most prosperous Muslim capitals in Europe. The upheaval of Christian reconquest in 1229 didn't interrupt this growth for long – by the 14th century Ciutat de Mallorca had become one of the western Mediterranean's richest trading ports.

By the 16th century, along with the rest of the island, the city was sinking into a protracted period of torpor, suffering from the plunder of pirates. The great seaward walls (today's Dalt Murada) were largely built in the 16th and 17th centuries, when the city's seasonal torrent, the Riera, was diverted from its natural course along Passeig d'es Born to its present location west of the city walls. The Old Town centre then went into decline, and the bulk of the sea walls were demolished at the beginning of the 20th century to allow rapid expansion of the city. But the heart of the city has been spruced up beyond recognition, since tourist cash began to flow into the island in the 1960s. The 2000s marked a new period of prosperity and property around the Dalt Murada became among the most expensive in all Spain. The introduction, in 2016, of restricted traffic zones in the historic centre has helped maintain the Old Town's integrity and charm.

⊙ Sights

⊙ Old Palma

★**Catedral de Mallorca** CATHEDRAL
(La Seu; Map p60; www.catedraldemallorca.org; Plaça del Almoina; €8, incl roof terraces €12; ⊙10am-6.15pm Mon-Fri Jun-Sep, to 5.15pm Apr,

PALMA & THE BADIA DE PALMA PALMA DE MALLORCA

PALMA IN TWO DAYS

Palma makes a fabulous city break and with a will you can cram a lot into a weekend. Start with the obvious: the colossal Gothic Catedral and Palau de l'Almudaina (p54). You'll spend hours meandering the Old Town's mazy lanes, and may wish to find some contemplative space at the Jardí del Bisbe (p59) and Banys Àrabs (p59). Grab a stool at the full-length bar at super stylish and sociable El Camino (p73) to dine on traditional tapas treated to the gourmet touch. Continue touring the nearby Basílica de Sant Francesc (p58) and Es Baluard (p66), where you can stop to snack alongside the battlements. For a night out, make for nearby Santa Catalina, with dinner at Koh (p77), drinks at Idem Café (p80) and clubbing along Passeig Marítim. The following day, head east out of town up to Castell de Bellver (p76) and the Fundació Pilar i Joan Miró (p90), book lunch at Ca'n Eduardo (p77) and spend the afternoon exploring the Museu Fundación Juan March (p64), then end with a drink and a view at the Guinness House (p79). Later, have an *ensaïmada* (a delicate, croissant-like pastry dusted with icing sugar, and sometimes filled with cream) at Ca'n Joan de S'Aigo (p74), a splash-out dinner at Marc Fosh (p74), or traditional fare at Restaurant Celler Sa Premsa (p74), then hit the bars of Sa Gerreria, beginning at L'Ambigú (p73).

May & Oct, to 3.15pm Nov-Mar, 10am-2.15pm Sat year-round, terraces 10am, 11am, noon, 4pm, 5pm & 6pm) Palma's vast cathedral ('La Seu' in Catalan) is the city's major architectural landmark. Aside from its sheer scale, treasures and undoubted beauty, its stunning interior features, designed by Antoni Gaudí and renowned contemporary artist Miquel Barceló, make this unlike any cathedral elsewhere in the world. The awesome structure is predominantly Gothic, apart from the main facade, which is startling, quite beautiful and completely mongrel. The stunning rose window is the largest in Europe; see it up close by visiting the roof terraces.

The Catedral occupies the site of what was the central mosque of Medina Mayurka, capital of Muslim Mallorca for three centuries. Although Jaume I and his marauding men forced their way into the city in 1229, work on the Catedral – one of Europe's largest – did not begin until 1300. Rather, the mosque was used in the interim as a church and dedicated to the Virgin Mary. Work wasn't completed until 1601.

The original was a Renaissance cherry on the Gothic cake, but an earthquake in 1851 (which caused considerable panic but no loss of life) severely damaged it. Rather than mend the original, it was decided to add some neo-Gothic flavour. With its interlaced flying buttresses on each flank and soaring pinnacles, it's a masterful example of the style. The result is a hybrid of the Renaissance original (in particular the main doorway) and an inevitably artificial-feeling, 19th-century pseudo-Gothic monumentalism.

For an additional €4, visitors can enjoy the cathedral's roof terraces, which includes the bell tower, buttresses and corridor between the two main towers, all affording magnificent views of the city and sea. Note that there are around 280 steps and no available lift. The one-hour visits are guided at set times and must be booked in advance as numbers are limited.

Mass times vary, but one always takes place at 9am Monday to Saturday.

★ **Palau de l'Almudaina**   PALACE
(Map p60; https://entradas.patrimonionacional.es; Carrer del Mirador; adult/child €7/4, audio guide €3, tour €4, Wed afternoon free; ⊙ 10am-8pm Tue-Sun Apr-Sep, to 6pm Oct-Mar) Originally an Islamic fort, this mighty construction opposite the cathedral was converted into a residence for the Mallorcan monarchs at the end of the 13th century. The King of Spain resides here still, at least symbolically. The royal family is rarely in residence, except for the occasional ceremony, as they prefer to spend summer in the Palau Marivent (in Cala Major). At other times you can wander through a series of cavernous stone-walled rooms that have been lavishly decorated.

The Romans are said to have built a *castrum* (fort) here, possibly on the site of a prehistoric settlement. The Wālis (Governors) of Muslim Mallorca altered and expanded the Roman original to build their own *alcázar* (fort), before Jaume I and his successors modified it to such an extent that little of the *alcázar* remains.

The first narrow room you enter has a black-and-white Mudéjar ceiling, symbolising the extremes of night and day, darkness and light (and only discovered during restoration in 1967). You then enter a series of three grand rooms. Notice the bricked-in Gothic arches cut off in the middle. Originally these three rooms were double their present height and formed one single great hall added to the original Arab fort and known as the **Saló del Tinell** (from an Italian word, *tinello*, meaning 'place where one eats'): this was once a giant banqueting and ceremonial hall. The rooms are graced by period furniture, tapestries and other curios. The following six bare rooms and terrace belonged to the original Arab citadel.

In the main courtyard, **Patio de Armas**, troops would line up for an inspection and

TOP TREASURES OF PALMA CATHEDRAL

Enter the Catedral (p53) from the north flank. You get tickets in the first room and then pass into the **sacristy**, which hosts the main part of the small **Museu Capitular** (Chapter Museum). At the centre of this is a huge gold-plated monstrance, dating to 1585, which comes out for the annual Corpus Christi procession. Interesting items include a portable altar, thought to have belonged to Jaume I. Its little compartments contain saints' relics; other reliquaries include one purporting to hold three thorns from Christ's crown of thorns.

Next come two chapter houses. In the **Gothic chapter house** by Guillem Sagrera, note the tomb of Bishop Gil Sánchez Muñoz (Antipope Clement VIII), the *Tabla de l'Almoina* (Alms Panel) and two paintings by the master Monti-Sion – *El Calvario* (the Calvary) and *Nuestra Señora de la Misericordia* (Our Lady of Mercy) – which allude to a terrible flood in Palma in 1403 that left 5000 dead. The **baroque chapter house** is exquisite, with its delicately carved stonework and 16th-century *relicario de la Vera Cruz* (reliquary of the True Cross) encrusted with gemstones.

On passing through one of the side **chapels** into the cathedral itself, your gaze soars high to the cross vaults, supported by slender, octagonal pillars. The broad **nave** and aisles are flanked by chapels. The walls are illuminated by kaleidoscopic curtains of stained glass, including 87 windows and eight magnificent rose windows. The grandest (the **oculus maior** or 'great eye', featuring a Star of David) comprises 1115 panes of glass shimmering ruby, gold and sapphire, and is the largest Gothic rose window in the world (yes, even bigger than Notre-Dame!). Visit in the morning to see the stunning effect of its coloured light and shapes, reflected on the west wall. To see the rose window up close, opt for a tour of the roof terraces.

The cathedral's three strikingly different **apses** show the Eucharist in three stages from left to right: institution, celebration and adoration. The left apse displays the golden wonder of the Corpus Christi altarpiece, an elaborate baroque confection by Jaume Blanquer (1626–41) devoted to the institution of the Eucharist at the Last Supper.

Antoni Gaudí carried out renovations from 1904 to 1914. His most important contribution was the strange **baldachin** that hovers over the main altar. Topped by a fanciful sculpture of Christ crucified and flanked by the Virgin Mary and St John, it looks like the gaping jaw of some oversized prehistoric shark dangling from the ceiling of an old science museum. Some 35 lamps hang from it, and what looks like a flying carpet is spread above. The genius of Barcelona Modernisme seems to have left behind an indecipherable pastiche, but then this was supposed to be a temporary version. The definitive one was never made (typical Gaudí).

Not content with this strangeness, the parish commissioned contemporary Mallorcan artist Miquel Barceló (an agnostic) to remake the **Capella del Santíssim i Sant Pere**, in the right apse. Done in 15 tonnes of ceramics, this dreamscape representing the miracle of the loaves and fishes was unveiled in 2007. On the left, fish and other marine creatures burst from the wall; the opposite side has a jungle look, with representations of bread and fruit. In between the fish and palm fronds, and standing above stacks of skulls, appears a luminous body that is supposed to be Christ, but is modelled on the short and stocky artist himself.

Other notable elements of the interior include the **giant organ**, built in 1798 (free recitals are held at noon on the first Tuesday of each month), and the two **pulpits**, the smaller of which was partly redone by Gaudí.

parade before heading out into the city. The 11th century lion fountain here is one of the palace's rare Arab remnants. Up the grand Royal Staircase are the **royal apartments**, a succession of lavishly appointed rooms (look up to the beautiful coffered timber *artesonado* ceilings). Next door to the apartments is the royal **Capella de Sant'Anna**, a Gothic chapel whose entrance is a very rare Mallorcan example of late Romanesque in rose and white marble.

After the death of Jaume III in 1349, no king lived here permanently again.

Palma

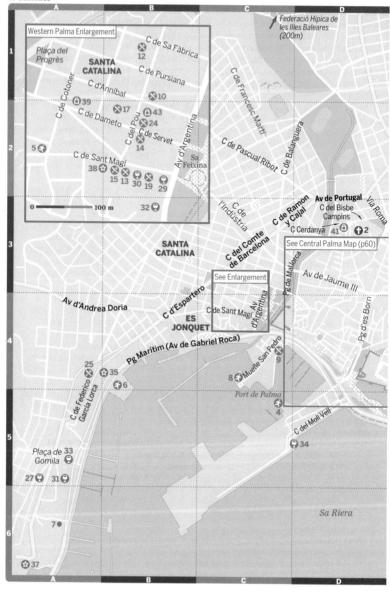

In the shadow of the Almudaina's walls, along Avinguda d'Antoni Maura, is S'Hort del Rei (the King's Garden).

★ Palau March   MUSEUM
(Map p60; ☎ 971 71 11 22; www.march.es; Carrer del Palau Reial 18; adult/child €4.50/free; ⊙ 10am-6.30pm Mon-Fri Apr-Oct, to 5pm Nov-Mar, to 2pm Sat year-round) This house, palatial by any definition, was one of several residences of the phenomenally wealthy March family. Sculptures by 20th-century greats, including Henry Moore, Auguste Rodin, Barbara Hepworth and Eduardo Chillida, grace the

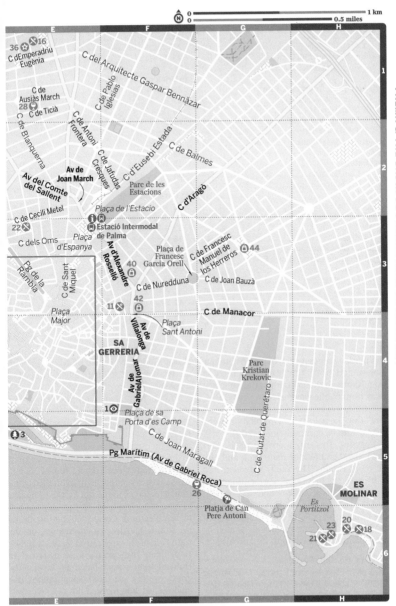

outdoor terrace. Within lie many more artistic treasures. Not to be missed are the meticulously crafted figures of an 18th-century Neapolitan *belén* (nativity scene).

Entry is through an outdoor terrace display of modern sculptural works, of which centre stage is taken by Corberó's enormous *Orgue del Mar* (1973).

Inside, more than 20 lithographs by Dalí around the themes 'Alchemy and Eternity' catch the eye, as do the 1000-plus detailed figures of the *belén*, ranging from angels to kings, including shepherds, farm animals

Palma

and market scenes, which make up a unique representation of Christ's birth. Brought from Naples in the 1970s and originally kept away from public view, aside from at Christmas time, you can watch a short video documenting the painstaking installation of the display into its current home in 2007.

Upstairs, the artist Josep Maria Sert (1874–1945) painted the main vault and music room ceiling. The vault is divided into four parts, the first three representing three virtues (audacity, reason and inspiration) and the last the embodiment of those qualities in the form of Sert's patron, Juan March (1917–98). The dining room is decorated by large paintings of local bird life, also by Sert.

Basílica de Sant Francesc   CHURCH
(Map p60; Plaça de Sant Francesc 7; adult/child €16/5; ⊙10am-1.30pm & 2.15-5pm Mon-Sat Nov-Mar to 6pm Apr-Oct) One of Palma's oldest churches, the Franciscan Basílica de Sant Francesc was begun in 1281 in Gothic style, while the baroque facade, with its carved postal and rose window, was completed in 1700. In the splendid Gothic cloister – a two-tiered, trapezoid affair – the elegant columns indicate it was also some time in the making. Inside, the high vaulted roof is classic Gothic, while the glittering high altar is a baroque lollipop, albeit in need of a polish.

In the first chapel on the left is the church's pride and joy, the tomb of the 13th-century scholar and mystic Ramon Llull. Also a fervid evangelist and the inventor of literary Catalan, Llull lays fair claim to the title of Mallorca's favourite son (apart perhaps from tennis champ Rafael Nadal). His alabaster tomb is high up on the right – drop a few coins in the slot for the campaign to have him canonised (he has only made it to beatification). Check out the Capilla de los Santos Mártires Gorkomienses, on the right side of the apse. In 1572, 19 Catholics, 11 of them Franciscans, were martyred in Holland. In this much-faded portrayal of the event, you can see them being hanged, disembowelled, and more.

Església de Santa Eulàlia   CHURCH
(Map p60; ☑971 71 46 25; Plaça de Santa Eulàlia 2; church free, belfry visit €5; ⊙10am-6pm Mon-Sat) The oldest parish church in Palma, raised after the 1229 conquest, the Església de Santa Eulàlia is a soaring Gothic structure with a neo-Gothic facade. Note that you can visit the church for free; the admission price is

to visit the 50m-high belfry, from where you have a magnificent view of the Basílica de Sant Francesc and Palma's historic quarter with sights easily identifiable with the help of a diagrammed guide.

Museu Diocesà
MUSEUM

(Map p60; Carrer del Mirador 5; adult/child €3/free; ⊗10am-6.15pm Mon-Fri Jun-Sep, to 5.15pm Apr, May & Oct, to 3.15pm Nov-Mar, 10am-2.15pm Sat year-round) Located in the Palau Episcopal (Bishop's Residence; a mainly Gothic ensemble dating to the 13th century), the Museu Diocesà, behind the cathedral to the east, is a fascinating excursion for those interested in Mallorca's Christian artistic history. It contains works by Antoni Gaudí, Francesc Comes and Pere Niçard, and a mind-boggling *retaule* (altarpiece) depicting the Passion of Christ (c 1290–1305) and taken from the Convent de Santa Clara.

The episodes of the Passion are shown in precise detail: Palm Sunday, the Last Supper, St Peter's kiss of betrayal, Christ flailed. Off to the right, a key work is Comes' *St Jaume de Compostela* (St James; known to the Spaniards as the Moor slayer). Niçard's *Sant Jordi* (St George), from around 1468–70, is remarkable for its busy detail. The City of Mallorca (Palma) is shown in the background as St George dispatches the dragon. Below this painting is a scene by Niçard and his boss Rafel Mòger depicting the 1229 taking of Palma. The final room in this wing is the Gothic **Oratori de Sant Pau**, a small chapel. The stained-glass window was a trial run done by Gaudí in preparation for his windows in the cathedral.

Otherwise, a succession of rooms showcases Mallorcan artists such as Pere Terrencs and Mateu López (father and son), while upstairs is a slim collection of baroque art and ceramics, plus some lovely views out over the bay.

Jardí del Bisbe
GARDENS

(Map p60; Carrer de Sant Pere Nolasc 6; ⊗7am-1.30pm Mon-Sun) **FREE** Adjoining the Palau Episcopal is the Jardí del Bisbe, a small, tranquil botanic garden that offers cool respite from a day's hot sightseeing. Stroll among the palms, pomegranates, water lilies, thyme, artichokes and olive, orange and lemon trees, or just sit on a bench and contemplate.

Banys Àrabs
HISTORIC BUILDING

(Map p60; Carrer de Serra 7; adult/child €3/free; ⊗10am-7pm Apr-Nov, to 6pm Dec-Mar) These baths, dating from the 10th to 12th centuries, are the single most important remaining monument to the Muslim domination of the island, although all that survives are two small underground chambers, one with a domed ceiling supported by a dozen columns, some of whose capitals were recycled from demolished Roman buildings. The site may be small, but the two rooms – the **caldarium** (hot bath) and the **tepidarium** (warm bath) – evoke a poignant sense of abandonment. Normally there would also have been a third, cold bath, the frigidarium. As the Roman terms suggest, the Arabs basically took over a Roman idea, here in Mallorca and throughout the Arab world. These ones probably were not public but attached to a private mansion. The baths are set in one of Old Palma's prettiest gardens, where you can sit and relax.

Museu de Mallorca
MUSEUM

(Map p60; ☎971 17 78 38; http://museudemallorca.caib.es; Carrer de la Portella 5; adult/child €2.50/free, Sun free; ⊗10am-6pm Tue-Fri, 11am-2pm Sat & Sun) This excellent city museum is housed in a rambling ensemble of 17th-century mansions on Carrer de la Portella. It showcases a collection of archaeological artefacts, religious art, antiques and Arabic ceramics – from Talayotic bronzes to intricate Almohad gold jewellery. The museum also hosts high-quality temporary exhibitions.

Dalt Murada
HISTORIC SITE

(Map p60) Most of Palma's defensive walls were destroyed in the late 19th century to allow the overcrowded city to expand. Only a section of the Renaissance sea wall, the Dalt Murada (begun in 1562, finished in 1801), remains impressively intact. The adjoining Parc de la Mar (p62) is an appealing place for a breezy drink at a terrace cafe in summer and is one of the best vantage points for photographing the cathedral in all its glory.

Sa Portella
GATE

(Map p60; Dalt Murada) An original seaward gate in the medieval walls can still be seen here.

Arab City Wall
HISTORIC SITE

(Map p56; Carrer de Mateu Enric Lladó) On the eastern rim of the Old Town you strike a portion of the 12th-century Arab city wall (with some heavy blocks from the Roman wall at the base), beyond which is a park named after the city gate that once stood here: Porta d'es Camp (Gate of the Countryside).

Central Palma

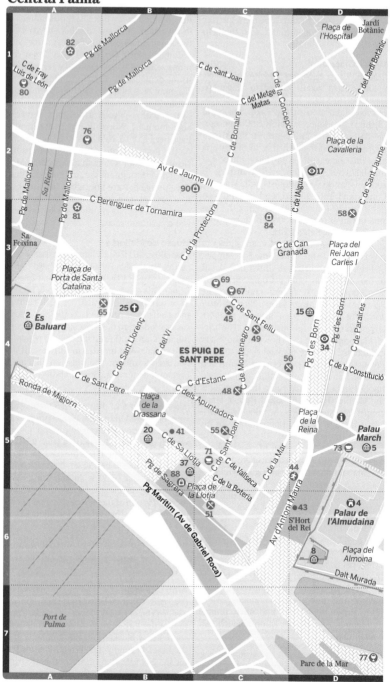

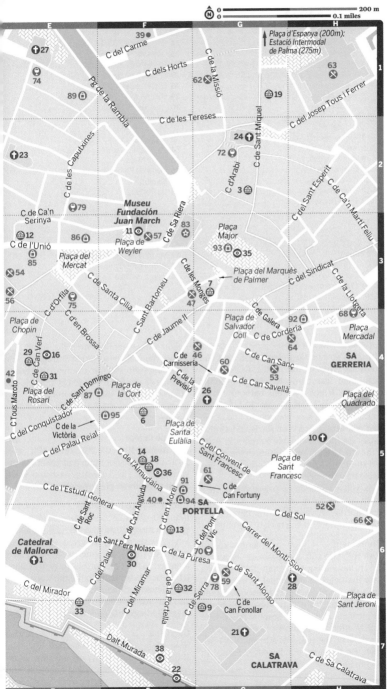

200 m
0.1 miles

Plaça d'Espanya (200m);
Estació Intermodal
de Palma (275m)

27
74
89
23

39
C del Carme
C dels Horts
C de les Tereses

62
C de la Missió
19
24
72
3
63

Pg de la Rambla

C de les Caputxines

79
C de Ca'n
Serinya
12
C de l'Unió
85
86

Museu
Fundació
Juan March
11 57
Plaça de
Weyler
83

Plaça
Major
93 35

C de Sant Miquel
C d'Arabi
C del Josep Tous i Ferrer
C del Sant Espert
C de Ca'n Martí Feliu

54
56
Plaça de
Chopin
29 16
42
31
C de Can Verí
Plaça del
Rosari
87
C de Sant Domingo

Plaça del
Mercat
75
C d'Orfila
C d'en Brossa
C de Santa Cilia
C Sant Bartomeu

C de les Monges
7
47

Plaça del Marquès
de Palmer
C del Sindicat
C de la Llotgeta
68

Plaça
Mercadal

Plaça de
Salvador
Coll
C de Galera
C de Corderia
64
92

SA
GERRERIA

C de
Carnisseria
46
C de la
Previsió
60
26
C de Can Sanç
53
C de Can Savellà

Plaça del
Quadrado

Plaça de
la Cort
95
6

Plaça de
Santa
Eulàlia
C del Convent de
Sant Francesc

10

Plaça de
Sant
Francesc

C del Palau Reial
C de la
Victòria
C del Conquistador
C Tous Maroto

14 18
36
91
61
C de
Can Fortuny

C de l'Almudaina
C de l'Estudi General
C de Ca'n Angulda
40 94
SA
PORTELLA
C d'en Morei

52
66

C del Sol

Catedral
de Mallorca
1
C del Mirador
33

C de Sant Roc
C de Sant Pere Nolasc
C del Palau
30
C del Miramar
C de la Portella
32
13
70
C del Pont
i Vic
C de la Puresa
C de Serra
9
78 59
21
C de
Can Fonollar
C de Sant Alonso
Carrer del Monti-Sion
28

Plaça de
Sant Jeroni

Dalt Murada
38
22
SA
CALATRAVA
C de Sa Calatrava

Central Palma

◎ Top Sights

1 Catedral de Mallorca E6
2 Es Baluard A4
3 Museu Fundación Juan
   March.. G2
4 Palau de l'Almudaina......................... D6
5 Palau March D5

◎ Sights

6 Ajuntament F5
7 Almacenes El Águila G3
8 Arc de sa Drassana D6
9 Banys Àrabs....................................... G7
10 Basílica de Sant Francesc H5
11 CaixaForum.. F3
12 Can Balaguer..................................... E3
13 Can Oleza F6
14 Can Oms F5
15 Casal Solleric.................................... D4
16 Centre Cultural
    Contemporani Pelaires E4
17 Centre de Cultura Sa
    Nostra.. D2
18 Centre Maimó ben Faraig.................. F5
19 Claustre de Sant Antoniet................. G1
20 Consolat de Mar................................. B5
21 Convent de Santa Clara G7
22 Dalt Murada.. F7

23 Església de Sant Jaume E2
24 Església de Sant Miquel G2
25 Església de Santa Creu B4
26 Església de Santa Eulàlia G4
27 Església de Santa Magdalena........... E1
28 Església del Monti-Sion.................... H6
29 Galeria K.. E4
30 Jardí del Bisbe F6
31 La Caja Blanca E4
32 Museu de Mallorca F6
33 Museu Diocesà E7
34 Passeig d'es Born D4
35 Plaça Major G3
36 Porta de l'Almudaina F5
37 Sa Llotja.. B5
38 Sa Portella... F7

◎ Activities, Courses & Tours

39 Akzent F1
40 Die Akademie..................................... F5
41 Lonja 18 .... B5
42 My Muy Bueno Cookery School E4
43 Palma City Sightseeing D6
44 Palma on Bike D5

◎ Eating

45 13%.. C4
46 Bagel.. G4

Església del Monti-Sion CHURCH
(Map p60; Carrer del Monti-Sion; ⊗ 5.15-7pm) The gaudy baroque facade of the Església del Monti-Sion was converted from a Gothic synagogue. It got a serious baroque makeover, inside and out, in the 16th to 17th centuries, and is now considered one of the high points of the style on the island. Gothic giveaways include the ogive arches in front of the chapels, the key vaulting in the ceiling and the long, low Catalan Gothic arch just inside the entrance.

As you wander in, a priest sitting in a booth by the entry may flip a switch and light up the curves-and-swirls baroque *retablo* (altarpiece) at the back of the church.

Ajuntament HISTORIC BUILDING
(Town Hall; Map p60; www.palma.ca; Plaça de la Cort 1) Dominating the square that has long been the heart of municipal power in Palma is the *ajuntament*. The baroque facade hides a longer history: the town hall building grew out of a Gothic hospital raised here shortly after the island's conquest. On the top floor of the main facade sits the town clock, **En Figuera**, purchased in France in 1863.

You can generally enter the foyer only where you will see a Gothic entrance, a fine sweeping staircase and around half a dozen *gegants* (huge figures of kings, queens and other characters that are paraded around town on people's shoulders during fiesta) in storage.

Parc de la Mar PARK
(Map p56) In 1984 the Parc de la Mar (with its artificial lake, fountain and green spaces) was opened. Head slightly east and you'll reach a children's playground.

Centre Maimó ben Faraig MUSEUM
(Map p60; ☑ 971 22 55 99; Carrer de l'Almudaina 9A; ⊗ 9.30am-1.30pm Mon-Fri) FREE Palma's long Jewish history is given some recognition in this small interpretation centre, attached to the Can Bordils. As well as illustrated panels bringing to life the story of the city's Jews (and their various persecutions), you can see sections of masonry from Roman buildings that once occupied the site.

Can Oms HISTORIC BUILDING
(Map p60; Carrer de l'Amudaina 7) The 18th-century baroque *pati* of this grand house is one of Palma's most beautiful, and it's visible from the street.

Porta de l'Almudaina
GATE

(Map p60; Carrer de l'Almudaina) The arch over Carrer de l'Almudaina east of Can Bordils is intriguing for history buffs, part of a rare stretch of defensive wall and tower. It is said to have been in use from antiquity until about the 13th century and is almost certainly part of the original Roman wall.

Centre Cultural Contemporani Pelaires
CULTURAL CENTRE

(Map p60; ☑ 971 72 03 75; www.pelaires.com; Carrer de Can Verí 3; ☺ 4.30-8pm Mon, 10.30am-8pm Tue-Fri, to 1.30pm Sat) FREE This private cultural centre – Palma's first dedicated contemporary-art space – is as interesting for its architecture as for its ever-changing exhibitions. The building, Can Verí, is a beautiful 17th-century townhouse that was also used for a while as a convent.

Convent de Santa Clara
CONVENT

(Map p60; Carrer de Can Fonollar 2; ☺ 9am-12.30pm & 4.15-5.30pm Mon-Sat, 9-11am & 4.15-6.45pm Sun) The 'Poor Clares' were one of the first orders to establish a presence in Palma, following the Reconquesta of 1229. The land on which the convent stands was granted them in 1260, although much of the baroque and Gothic structure dates to the 16th and 17th centuries. The current church (the third on the site) has been extensively restored, and the handful of nuns still cloistered here maintain a centuries-old tradition of baking sweets for sale.

You will see a *torno,* a kind of timber turnstile set in a window. Ring for a nun, order what you want and put money into the turnstile. This swivels around and out come your *bocaditos de almendra* (almond nibbles) or *rollitos de anís* (aniseed rolls), at €4.50 for 200g. They also sell homemade ice cream (€2.50).

Arc de sa Drassana
HISTORIC BUILDING

(Map p60; off S'Hort del Rei) A grand arch dominated by the Palau de l'Almudaina, the Arc de sa Drassana is one of the city's few extant reminders of its Arab past. When the Riera, the city's river, coursed along what is now Passeig d'es Born and the sea lapped the city walls, this was the seaward entrance into the Arab palace and early shipyards.

⊙ Plaça Major & Around

Plaça Major
SQUARE

(Map p60) Plaça Major is a typically Spanish grandiose central square, lined with arcades, shops, cafes and restaurants (the burger

GET YOUR BEARINGS

Use the Catedral (p53) as your compass. The heart of the Old Town (the districts of **Sa Portella** and **Sa Calatrava**) has always been centred on its main place of worship, and the one-time seat of secular power opposite it, the Palau de l'Almudaina (p54). Many of Palma's sights are jammed into this warren of tight, twisting lanes and sunny squares, where massive churches jostle noble houses. The bright Mediterranean light and glittering sea are never far away.

To the north lies Plaça Major (p63), a typically Spanish public square lined with arcades, shops and cafes. To the east, Carrer del Sindicat spokes out towards the avenues that mark the limits of historic Palma, following the zigzag pattern of its now-demolished walls. It crosses a district known as **Sa Gerreria** – for decades a rundown part of town, but which is now enjoying a revival boasting some of Palma's more edgy nightlife. Off Plaça Major, the shopping boulevard, **Carrer de Sant Miquel**, leads north towards the vast **Plaça d'Espanya**, the city's major transport hub. Plaça Major and Carrer de Sant Miquel are on high ground that falls away to the west, down to tree-lined **Passeig de la Rambla** boulevard.

West of the cathedral is **Passeig d'es Born**, a classic boulevard for strollers and window shoppers, and one of Palma's major arteries. It borders the historic quarter of **Es Puig de Sant Pere**, buttressed by the fortress-turned-gallery Es Baluard (p66) to the west, and the shop-lined **Avinguda de Jaume III** to the north. Crossing the **Sa Riera** river brings you to the former sailors' district **Santa Catalina**, with its long, grid-pattern streets and traditional low-slung one- and two-storey houses. As early as the 17th century, windmills were raised in the area still known as **Es Jonquet**, just south of **Carrer de Sant Magí**, the oldest street in the *barri* (district). In recent years gentrification has transformed Santa Catalina into an artsy, bohemian quarter, filled with one-of-a-kind boutiques, galleries, bars and restaurants. Follow the seafront **Passeig Marítim** further west still and you reach the ferry port and Western Palma's major sight: Castell de Bellver (p76).

To the east, a 1km walk from the city-centre end of the **Platja de Can Pere Antoni** brings you to **Es Portixol**. The 'little port', once a fishing town beyond Palma and now a delightful dining destination, has a quiet abundance of pleasure craft and is closed off inland by the motorway (at a discreet distance). From central Palma it's an easy walk, cycle or rollerblade here along the Passeig Marítim. From Portixol, walking around the next point brings you to **Es Molinar**, a simple, waterfront 'suburban' district of fishing folks' houses. Over the bridge is **Ciutat Jardí**, another low-key residential area with a broad, sandy beach.

chain jars somewhat). Lively by day, it falls eerily silent at night.

To the east, Carrer del Sindicat spokes out towards the avenues that mark the limits of historic Palma. It crosses a district known as Sa Gerreria. For decades rundown and slightly dodgy, Sa Gerreria is enjoying a revival and becoming a trendy hub of the city's nightlife. Off Plaça Major, the shopping boulevard, Carrer de Sant Miquel, leads north towards the vast Plaça d'Espanya. Plaça Major and Carrer de Sant Miquel are on high ground that falls away to the west down to shady Passeig de la Rambla.

⭐ **Museu Fundación Juan March**   GALLERY
(Map p60; 📞 97 171 35 15; www.march.es; Carrer de Sant Miquel 11; ⏱ 10am-6.30pm Mon-Fri, 10.30am-2pm Sat) **FREE** Can Gallard del Canya, a

17th-century mansion overlaid with minor Modernist touches, now houses a small but significant collection of painting and sculpture. The permanent exhibits – some 80 pieces held by the Fundación Juan March – constitute a veritable who's who of contemporary Spanish art, including Miró, Picasso, fellow cubist Juan Gris, Dalí, and the sculptors Eduardo Chillida and Julio González.

After starting with the big names, the collection skips through various movements in Spanish art, such as that inspired in Barcelona by the Dau al Set review (1948–53) and led by Antoni Tàpies. Meanwhile, in Valencia, Eusebio Sempere and Andreu Alfaro were leading the way down abstract paths. Sempere's *Las Cuatro Estaciones* (1980) reflects the four seasons in subtle changes of colour in a series of four panels with interlocking shapes made of fine lines. Other names to watch for are Manuel Millares, Fernando Zóbel and Miquel Barceló, who is represented by works including his large-format *La Flaque* (The Pond; 1989).

Can Balaguer
MUSEUM

(Map p60; ☑971 22 59 00; Carrer de l'Unió 3; ⊙9.30am-8.30pm Tue-Sat) FREE One of Palma's most emblematic buildings, the permanent exhibition, entitled *La Casa Posible*, re-creates rooms of this former noble house from 1600–1951. Rooms are evocative of their period, including the 17th-century music room with its magnificent organ, the opulent 18th-century bedchamber sporting sumptuous damask fabrics and a canopied bed, and the extraordinary Louis XV room, a style that was in vogue in the late 19th century. The house's last owner was Josep Balaguer (1869–1951), a musician, entrepreneur and patron of the arts.

Don't miss Balaguer's fine collection of Modernista paintings near the entrance which highlight Mallorcan painter Antoni Gelabert (1877–1932). There is also a 20-minute audiovisual presentation (subtitled in English) about the history of Can Balaguer, plus a downstairs cafe and small bookshop.

Església de Sant Miquel
CHURCH

(Church of St Michael; Map p60; Carrer de Sant Miquel 21; ⊙9.30am-1.30pm & 5-7.30pm) A striking mix of styles, St Michael's is one of Palma's first four churches, built on the site of a mosque where the island's first Mass was celebrated on 31 December 1229. The facade and entrance, with its long, low arch, are a perfect example of 14th-century Catalan Gothic, as is the squat, seven-storey bell tower. Otherwise the church, with its barrel-vaulted ceiling, is largely the result of a baroque makeover.

Note the statue of Pope John Paul II on the right as you enter.

Claustre de Sant Antoniet
GALLERY

(Map p60; Carrer de Sant Miquel 30; ⊙10am-2pm & 3.30-8pm Mon-Fri, 10am-1.30pm Sat) FREE The Claustre de Sant Antoniet is a baroque gem that belongs to the BBVA bank. The two-tiered, oval-shaped enclosure was built in 1768 and is now used for temporary art exhibitions. It was originally attached to the Església de Sant Antoni de Viana, next door, but was transferred to the stewardship of the church of St Miquel when the Order of Sant Antoni was abolished by Charles III in 1788.

Almacenes El Águila
HISTORIC BUILDING

(Map p60; Plaça del Marqués de Palmer 1) Gaspar Bennázar (1869–1933) – one of the most influential architects in modern Palma, his native city – played with various styles during his long career, including Modernisme. An outstanding example of this is the Almacenes El Águila, originally built as a department store in 1908, but recently converted into a boutique hotel: L'Aguila Suites. Note the generous use of wrought iron in the main facade, typical of the Modernisme style of the time.

CaixaForum
CULTURAL CENTRE

(Map p60; ☑971 17 85 00; https://obrasociallacaixa.org/en/cultura/caixaforum-palma; Plaça de Weyler 3; adult/child €6/free; ⊙10am-8pm Mon-Sat, 11am-2pm Sun) Housed in the wonderful Modernisme building (the island's first) that was once the Grand Hotel, this cultural centre and gallery is run by one of Spain's biggest building societies, the Barcelona-based La Caixa (members get free entry). The permanent collection of paintings by Hermenegildo Anglada Camarasa is complemented by temporary exhibitions (on themes such as Roman female statuary from the Louvre):

GALLERY ALLEY

Contemporary-art enthusiasts will get a buzz out of the plethora of galleries that populate the narrow streets just east of the Passeig d'es Born.

La Caja Blanca (Map p60; www.lacajablanca.com; Carrer de Can Verí 9; ⊙11am-2pm & 5-8pm Mon-Fri, 11.30am-2pm Sat) FREE Edgy Mallorcan and international artists are showcased in this stark, minimalist space. It stages three to four exhibitions annually.

Galeria K (Map p60; www.galeria-k.com; Carrer de Can Verí 10; ⊙10.30am-8pm Mon-Fri, 11am-3pm Sat) FREE This innovative little gallery presents Spanish and international painters and sculptors.

Centre Cultural Contemporani Pelaires (p63) This contemporary-art space, Palma's first such dedicated gallery, occupies a lovely 17th-century building.

pick up a program at reception and flick through it at the ground-level cafe, or browse the excellent bookshop.

Centre de Cultura
Sa Nostra CULTURAL CENTRE
(Map p60; www.fundaciosanostra.es; Carrer de la Concepció 12; ☺10.30am-1.30pm & 5-8pm Mon-Fri) FREE The big Balearic building society, Sa Nostra, runs this cultural foundation in Can Castelló, where it stages exhibitions, performances and talks. Keep an eye out for temporary shows, which are often worth a look. The original house dates to the 17th century, with Modernista touches from renovation work in 1909, and it's worth popping in just to check out the fine 18th-century courtyard, which now hosts a stylish cafe.

Just in front of the centre is **Font del Sepulcre**, a Gothic baptismal font left over from a long-disappeared church. Inside it is a 12th-century Muslim-era well. Carrer de la Concepció used to be known as Carrer de la Monederia, as the Kingdom of Mallorca's mint was on this street.

Església de Sant Jaume CHURCH
(Map p60; Carrer de Sant Jaume 10; ☺11.30am-1.30pm & 5.30-8.30pm) Despite its baroque facade, this is one of Palma's older surviving Gothic churches. This grey soaring eminence is one of the first four parish churches to be built 'under the protection of the Royal House of Mallorca' from 1327. It is said that the Bonapart family (later Bonaparte) lived around here until they moved to Corsica in 1406. Napoleon could have been a Mallorcan!

Església de Santa Magdalena CHURCH
(Map p60; Plaça de Santa Magdalena; ☺7.30am-1.15pm & 5.30-7.30pm) The main claim to fame of the baroque Església de Santa Magdalena is as the resting place of Santa Catalina Thomàs of Valldemossa. Her clothed remains are visible through a glass coffin held in a chapel to the left of the altar and are an object of pilgrimage.

It is said that the future saint sat weeping by a great clump of stone one day as none of the convents would accept her because she was too poor. When someone told her that the convent once attached to the Església de Santa Magdalena would take her in, she was overjoyed. The stone in question is now embedded in the rear wall of the 14th-century **Església de Sant Nicolau** on Plaça

del Mercat. The nuns here make pastas de Santa Magdalena (sponge buns) and other sweet treats for sale to the public from a hatch located on a side street to the right of the entrance.

Església de Sant Crist de la Sang CHURCH
(Map p56; Plaça de l'Hospital; ☺7.30am-1pm & 4-8pm) Within the Hospital General (founded in the 16th century), you can behold the Gothic facade of this church. It is an object of pilgrimage and devotion, since the *paso* (a sculpted image used in processions) of 'Holy Christ of the Blood' is considered to be miraculous. Just on your left as you enter the church is a 15th-century nativity scene, probably imported from Naples. Mass is held at 11.30am weekdays, 8.30am on Saturday and at 9am and 6.30pm on Sunday.

⊙ Es Puig de Sant Pere

★ Es Baluard GALLERY
(Museu d'Art Modern i Contemporani; Map p60; ✆971 90 82 00; www.esbaluard.org; Plaça de Porta de Santa Catalina 10; adult/child €6/free; ☺10am-8pm Tue-Sat, to 3pm Sun) Built with flair and innovation into the shell of the Renaissance-era seaward walls, this contemporary art gallery is one of the finest on the island. Its temporary exhibitions are worth viewing, but the permanent collection – works by Miró, Barceló and Picasso – gives the gallery its cachet. Anyone turning up on a bike is charged just €2.

The 21st-century concrete complex is cleverly built among the fortifications, including the partly restored remains of an 11th-century Muslim-era tower (on your right as you arrive from Carrer de Sant Pere). Inside, the ground floor houses the core of the permanent exhibition, starting with a section on Mallorcan landscapes by local artists and others from abroad; the big names here include Valencia's Joaquín Sorolla, Mallorca's own Miquel Barceló and the Catalan Modernista artist Santiago Rusiñol.

Also on the ground floor and part of the permanent collection is a room devoted to the works of Joan Miró, while on the top floor is an intriguing collection of ceramics by Pablo Picasso; after viewing the latter, step out onto the ramparts for fine views. In sum, it's an impressive rather than extraordinary collection that's well worth a couple of hours of your time.

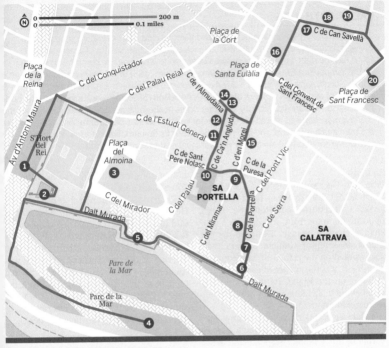

Town Walk
Historic Palma & Hidden Patios

START S'HORT DEL REI
END BASÍLICA DE SANT FRANCESC
LENGTH 2.5KM; TWO TO THREE HOURS

Begin in ❶ **S'Hort del Rei** (King's Garden), where ❷ **Arc de sa Drassana** (p63) arches above a pond. Amble north to Miró's bronze sculpture ('the egg'). Climb the steps past Palau March to the immense Gothic ❸ **Catedral** (p53). Head down to ❹ **Parc de la Mar** (p59), with its fountain-draped lake.

Soak up views along the Renaissance sea-wall ❺ **Dalt Murada** (p59). Turn left at medieval gateway ❻ **Sa Portella** (p59), noting its keystone and coat of arms. Carrer de la Portella hides many historic courtyards: 17th-century ❼ **Cal Marquès de la Torre** at No 14, and 19th-century ❽ **Can Espanya-Serra** at No 8, with a neo-Gothic staircase. Swing left onto Carrer de la Puresa, pausing at No 2, ❾ **Can Salas**, one of Palma's oldest *patis*, with carved pillars, a beautiful loggia and 13th-century coat of arms.

Pause in tiny ❿ **Jardí del Bisbe** (p59) or continue north up Carrer de Ca'n Angluda to ⓫ **Cal Poeta Colom** at No 4, named for its one-time resident poet. Its baroque patio features fine wrought-iron and tapered columns. Further along at No 2A is grand medieval manor ⓬ **Can Marquès**.

On Carrer de l'Almudaina, the medieval gateway ⓭ **Porta de l'Almudaina** (p63) was originally part of the Roman walls. Close by is ⓮ **Can Oms** (p62), with its impressive Gothic portal. Nearby, ⓯ **Can Oleza** (Map p60; Carrer d'en Morei 9) is a baroque patio with loggia, Ionic columns, low arches and wrought-iron balustrade. Pass spired ⓰ **Església de Santa Eulàlia** (p58) – climb to the rooftop if time permits – to Carrer de Can Savellà, home to Corinthian column-lined ⓱ **Can Vivot** at No 4 and ⓲ **Can Catlar del Llorer** at No 15, one of Palma's oldest Gothic *patis*. Detour a street north for hot chocolate at old-school ⓳ **Ca'n Joan de S'Aigo** (p74) before heading back to venerable ⓴ **Basílica de Sant Francesc** (p58).

PALMA WITH KIDS

With its beaches, parks, water activities and plentiful cafes and ice-cream shops, Palma is a wonderful city to visit with children. What kid doesn't love castles? Castell de Bellver (p76) has the right, imposing story-book dimensions, while you can combine art with fun on the ramparts at Es Baluard (p66). Palma Aquarium (p88) to the east is outstanding, and you could easily spend half a day there (kids can even spend a, possibly sleepless, Friday night at a monthly 'Shark Sleepover'). Aqualand (p89), the island's largest water park, is another sure-fire hit, with its slides, rides, pools and speedball flumes.

Playgrounds are scattered about town, for instance in Parc de les Estacions, behind the train and bus station, and Sa Feixina park near Es Baluard. There's a brilliant adventure playground further along near the walls just east of Parc de la Mar (p62).

Sa Llotja   HISTORIC BUILDING
(Map p60; Plaça de la Llotja 5; ⊙11am-2pm & 5-9pm Tue-Sat, 11am-2pm Sun) FREE The gorgeous 15th-century sandstone Sa Llotja, opposite the waterfront, was built as a merchants' stock exchange. Designed by the Mallorcan sculptor Guillem Sagrera (who also worked on the cathedral) and completed in 1448, it is the apogee of civilian Gothic building on the island. Its mercantile past well behind it, Sa Llotja is now used for temporary exhibitions.

Inside, six slender, twisting columns lead to the ribs of a lofty groined vault. In each corner of the building rises a fanciful octagonal tower. The flanks are marked with huge arches, fine tracery and monstrous-looking gargoyles leaning out overhead.

Consolat de Mar   HISTORIC BUILDING
(Map p60; Passeig de Sagrera 7) The 'Consulate of the Sea' was founded in 1326 as a maritime tribunal, adjudicating disputes among merchants, sailors and captains. The present building – one of Mallorca's few examples of Renaissance design, albeit an impure one – was completed in 1669. It was tacked onto, and faces, a late-Gothic chapel completed around 1600 for the members of Sa Llotja.

The Consolat de Mar houses the presidency of the Balearic Islands regional government.

Passeig d'es Born   AREA
(Map p60) One of Palma's most appealing boulevards, Passeig d'es Born is capped by Plaça del Rei Joan Carles I (named after the former king and formerly after Pope Pius XII), a traffic roundabout locally known as Plaça de les Tortugues, because of the obelisk placed on four bronze turtles. On the east side of the avenue, on the corner of Carrer de Jovellanos, the distorted black face of a Moor, complete with white stone turban, is affixed high on a building.

Known as the Cap del Moro (Moor's Head), it represents a Muslim slave who is said to have killed his master, a chaplain, in October 1731. The slave was executed and his hand lopped off and reportedly attached to the wall of the house where the crime was committed. Chronicles claim the withered remains of the hand were still in place, behind a grille, in 1840. The Passeig was renamed in honour of Franco, but reverted to its original title after the dictator's death.

Casal Solleric   HISTORIC BUILDING
(Map p60; ☑971 72 96 04; https://casalsolleric. palma.cat; Passeig d'es Born 27; ⊙11am-2pm & 3.30-8.30pm Tue-Sat, 11am-2.30pm Sun) FREE This grand 18th-century baroque mansion with the typical Palma courtyard of graceful broad arches and uneven stone paving is at once a cultural centre with temporary exhibitions, bookshop and tourist information office. Displays are usually free and found over a couple of floors. The part facing Passeig d'es Born was actually the rear of the original house, built in 1763. Archduke Ludwig Salvador thought its courtyard 'one of the most beautiful in Palma'.

Església de Santa Creu   CHURCH
(Map p60; Carrer de Sant Llorenç 4) Work on the original Gothic Church of the Holy Cross, one of Palma's original parish churches, began in 1335. The main entrance (Carrer de Santa Creu 7) is a baroque (18th-century) addition. What makes it particularly interesting is the Cripta de Sant Llorenç (Crypt of St Lawrence), an early Gothic place of worship possibly dating to the late 13th century. Some paintings by Rafel Mòger and Francesc Comes are scattered about the interior.

Activities

Magic Catamarans BOATING
(Map p56; ☑971 45 61 82; http://magic-catamarans.com/es; 1st fl, Passeig Marítim 8; adult/child €52/26; ⏲10am-3pm & 3.30-8.30pm Apr-Oct; 🖐)
Magic puts on twice-daily, five-hour catamaran tours to either Cala Portals Vells or Cala Vella, just east of the Badia de Palma. The price includes food on board and snorkeling gear, and hotel pickups can be arranged (adult/child €10/5). Note that the 2½-hour tour to Ses Illetes is cheaper, at just €18/10 (without food and drink).

Cruceros Marco Polo BOATING
(Map p56; ☑647 843667; www.crucerosmarcopolo.com; off Passeig Marítim; 1hr cruise €12; ⏲hourly 11am-4pm Mon-Sat, 2-4pm Sun Mar-Oct)
Marco Polo, one of the first tour operators in the Badia de Palma, offers a one-hour whiz around the bay, up to six times daily aboard the *Mar y Sol II*. There's a bar on board, and limitless opportunities to snap Palma's scenic attractions from the water.

Real Club Náutico BOATING
(Map p56; www.rcnp.es; Plaza de San Pedro 1) The most prestigious of Palma's yacht clubs has been around since 1948, and now organises more than 20 events during the year. The club also organises sailing courses for adults and children.

Courses

Akzent LANGUAGE
(Map p60; ☑971 71 99 94; www.akzent-palma.com; Carrer del Carme 14; 2-week course €395; ⏲9.30am-1.30pm Mon-Fri) This bookshop offers well-regarded, two-week intensive Spanish courses. Each day's tuition lasts four hours, and classes are capped at 10 students. They also run one-to-one tuition and evening classes.

My Muy Bueno Cookery School COOKING
(Map p60; ☑971 72 00 17; www.mymuybueno cookeryschool.com; Carrer Tous Maroto 5B; half/full day €120/195) A highly professional cookery school which offers accredited long courses as well as half- and one-day courses with a diverse choice of culinary experiences, ranging from classic Spanish cuisine to raw desserts and street food. They also run a deli-cum-cafe next door which concentrates on vegan baked goodies, fresh juices and similar.

Lonja 18 COOKING
(Map p60; ☑672 233555; www.lonja18.com; Carrer de Sa Llotja 18; 3hr course €70) The most popular cooking class here is the Spanish Cooking Class, a hands-on course where you will learn to make classic Spanish dishes. Other options include tapas and *pintxos* and vegan cooking. The courses include a visit to the Santa Catalina market (p75) as well as a full meal and drinks.

Die Akademie LANGUAGE
(Map p56; ☑971 71 82 90; www.dieakademie.com; Carrer d'en Morei 8; 1-week course €198; ⏲9am-1.30pm & 5-7.30pm Mon-Fri) Housed in a 16th-century, late-Gothic mansion, Die Akademie runs a variety of Spanish-language courses based on the impressive sounding 'Superlearning' method. Standard classes run for four hours each morning, from 9.30am to 1.30pm.

Palma Sea School BOATING
(Map p56; ☑971 10 05 18; www.palmaseaschool.com; Passeig Marítim 38; 2-day yachting course from €299; ⏲9am-5pm) Whether you're cutting your teeth or honing your skills, this Royal Yachting Association–affiliated school offers a wide range of courses in yachting, sailing, powerboating and jet-skiing.

Tours

Palma City Sightseeing BUS
(Map p60; ☑902 10 10 81; www.city-ss.es/en/destination/palma; Avinguda d'Antoni Maura; adult/child bus €18/9, boat €12/6, bus & boat €28/14; ⏲9.30am-10pm, reduced hours outside summer; 🖐) Run by the *ajuntament* (town hall) this hop-on-hop-off bus departs from Avinguda d'Antoni Maura every 20 minutes, with commentary in various languages. It follows a circuit of the city centre, waterfront and the Castell de Bellver, and can be combined with a boat tour of the bay.

Festivals & Events

Fiesta Sant Sebastiá MUSIC
(⏲18-20 Jan) On the eve of the feast day of Palma's patron saint, concerts (from funk to folk) are staged in the city squares, along with flaming pyres and the *aiguafoc*, a fireworks display over the bay. It's a big (if chilly) night.

Sa Rueta & Sa Rua CARNIVAL
(⏲Feb/Mar; 🖐) Palma's version of Carnaval (celebrated in the last days before Lent

CYCLING & SAILING AROUND PALMA

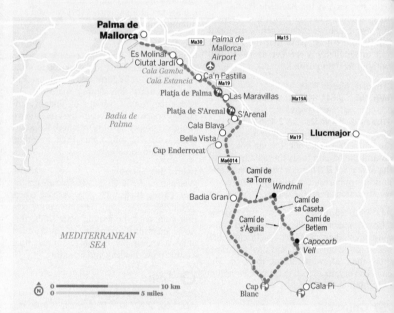

Palma de Mallorca
Ma30
Palma de Mallorca Airport
Ma15
Es Molinar
Ciutat Jardí
Cala Gamba
Cala Estancia
Ca'n Pastilla
Ma19
Platja de Palma
Las Maravillas
Ma19A
Platja de S'Arenal
S'Arenal
Badia de Palma
Cala Blava
Bella Vista
Llucmajor
Ma19
Cap Enderrocat
Ma6014
Camí de sa Torre
Windmill
Badia Gran
Camí de sa Caseta
Camí de s'Àguila
Camí de Betlem
Capocorb Vell
MEDITERRANEAN SEA
Cap Blanc
Cala Pi

0 — 10 km
0 — 5 miles

PALMA TO CAPOCORB VELL

START/END PALMA DE MALLORCA
DISTANCE 67KM
DIFFICULTY EASY TO MODERATE

Bicycle is a great way to explore Palma and Badia de Palma: there's a coastal bike path between Palma's port and S'Arenal, and bike lanes in the city itself, where cyclists are an accepted fact of life. There are also plenty of operators who rent out city and mountain bikes.

Covering a huge swath of the Badia de Palma, this circular ride follows an easygoing seafront cycle path, then heads slightly inland towards Cap Blanc on the island's south coast. The return journey winds through peaceful country lanes, before a deserved downhill reverses the route back to town. Take a road or touring bike for this ride.

Pick up the waterfront bike path in **Central Palma** and head southeast. Hugging the coast for most of the way, the path is a breezy sweep to Ca'n Pastilla (p88). From here fol-

low the seafront road to the end of the long sandy strip of **Platja de Palma** and its extension S'Arenal (p89), although you'll have to mind the crowds that will wander onto the bike-only zone the whole way. Then follow the wooden signs for **Cap Blanc**. Although along a major road (the Ma6014), this 23km section cuts through pleasant countryside, and motorists are used to lycra-clad cyclists plying the route. The road rises to 150m, but the ascent is not too gruelling.

Follow the signs up a slight hill to reach the lighthouse at the cape, where you can take a breather to appreciate the sensational coastal views. Once back on the main road, continue northeast to a junction, with signs right to Cala Pi (p170); bear left and watch out for signs to **Capocorb Vell** (p170), whose entrance is on the left. There's a simple coffee bar at the ruins.

Exit the bar to the right and take the Camí de Betlem, a quiet country lane (also signed Carreró de Betlem). Follow this road to the junction, and continue on to the Camí Est-

Palma, with its tight tangle of galleries, palaces, ancient streets and good road infrastructure, is a great place for cycling, while the harbour and broad Badia de Palma is made for sailing.

• •

abits de s'Àguila, surrounded by farmland. Turning sharp right, it becomes the Camí de s'Àguila. After 200m, a left turn will bring you onto the Camí de sa Caseta, shaded by overhanging trees and lined by dry-stone walls. The end of the lane is marked by a **windmill** and, to the left, a church. Turn left here, where a wooden sign points along tranquil Camí de sa Torre and onwards to S'Arenal. Take a right when you hit the Ma6014 and follow the wooden signs to Platja de Palma. From here, retrace your tracks back to the capital.

BIKE RENTAL

Palma on Bike (Map p60; ☑ 971 71 80 62; www.palmaonbike.com; Avinguda d'Antoni Maura 10; city/mountain/e-bike per day €12/36/28; ⊙ 9.30am-1pm & 3-7pm) has city bikes to get around Palma, as well as road bikes, rollerblades and kayaks. Rates include insurance and a helmet. It also runs Palma city tours (€25 per person; minimum two people), including tapas (€35) and a winery tour (€55).

You'll find plenty of rental outlets along S'Arenal's beachfront but if you're after a decent road bike, try **Ciclos Quintana** (☑ 971 44 29 25; www.ciclosquintana.com; Carrer de San Cristóbal 32; aluminium/carbon bikes per day €20/30; ⊙ 9.30am-1pm & 4-8pm Mon-Fri), just up from the main drag.

Palma Lock & Go (p88) is on the underground level of the train station; it's a handy place to leave your luggage if you are considering renting a bike for a day.

SAILING IN PALMA

Sailing is a big deal in Palma and numerous regattas are held in the course of the year. In addition to those listed, the **Real Club Náutico** (p69), the most prestigious of Palma's yacht clubs, organises more than 20 events (some in collaboration with other clubs) throughout the year.

Copa del Rey (p72) The King's Cup in July/August is one of the summer highlights of Palma's regatta calendar.

PalmaVela (www.palmavela.com; ⊙ late Apr/early May) The PalmaVela has hundreds of yachts of all classes from around the world.

Trofeo SAR Princesa Sofía (www.trofeoprincesasofia.org; ⊙ Mar/Apr) This is one of six regattas composing the World Cup Series, attracting Olympic crews from all over the world.

Superyacht Cup (www.thesuperyachtcup.com; ⊙ Jun) Held over three days in June, this is one of the major races for super yachts of anything from 25m to 90m in size.

Trofeo Ciutat de Palma (p72) A huge event for smaller boats, held over four days in December.

CRUISES & COURSES

For boat tours and cruises, try **Magic Catamarans** (p69), **Cruceros Marco Polo** (p69) or **Real Club Náutico** (p69) around Palma. **Attraction** (p89) is another option in nearby Ca'an Pastilla while, in Magaluf, **Cruceros Costa de Calvià** (p92) offers a range of different boat trips, including day-long cruises.

Palma Sea School (p69) offers a wide range of courses in yachting, sailing, powerboating and jet-skiing.

Deep Blue Sea (Map p56; ☑ 971 90 21 00; www.deepbluesea.training; Calle de Sant Magi 46, Santa Catalina; 2-day yachting courses from €30; ⊙ 8-45am-6pm Mon-Fri) Located in Santa Catalina and offering a comprehensive choice of yachting classes and courses.

starts) involves a procession for children (Sa Rueta) followed by a larger parade (Sa Rua) with extravagant floats.

Semana Santa
RELIGIOUS

(Holy Week; ⊙ Mar-Apr) Processions dot the Easter week calendar, but the most impressive are those on Holy Thursday evening. In the Processó del Sant Crist de la Sang (Christ of the Blood), robed and hooded members of *confraries* (lay brotherhoods) parade with a *paso* (heavy sculpted image of Christ). The procession starts at 7pm, in the Església del Crist de la Sang.

Corpus Christi
RELIGIOUS

(⊙ May/Jun) The feast of the Body of Christ (the Eucharist) falls on the Thursday of the ninth week after Easter, although the main procession from the cathedral takes place on the following Sunday, when carpets of flowers are laid out in front of the cathedral. Concert cycles (many held in the city's *patis*) add a celebratory note.

Nit de Foc
FIESTA

(⊙ 23 Jun) In Palma, the night before the midsummer feast of St John is celebrated with fiery abandon. The *correfoc* (fire running) begins in the Parc de la Mar, as costumed demons leap and dance in an infernal procession. To finish, the city's beaches host musical groups, bonfires and a crowd that parties until dawn.

Cinema a la Fresca
FILM

(⊙ 9.30pm Tue, Wed, Sat & Sun Jul-Sep) Running each summer since 1986, Cinema a la Fresca has become something of a Palma institution, bringing free open-air cinema to the Parc de la Mar, beneath the Catedral.

Copa del Rey
SAILING

(www.regatacopadelrey.com; ⊙ Jul/Aug) The 'King's Cup', held over eight days in July and August, is a high point in the sailing calendar. Felipe VI and his father, former king Juan Carlos I, frequently raced on competing boats.

Nit de l'Art
CULTURAL

(www.nitdelartartpalma.com; ⊙ mid-Sep) One Saturday night in the middle of September Palma's historic heart is given over to the arts, as the city's many galleries throw open their doors, and the streets are illuminated by installations, exhibitions and live performances.

TaPalma
FOOD & DRINK

(www.tapalma.es; ⊙ late Nov) Nibble your way around Palma at this event celebrating the city's best tapas. Some 40 restaurants and bars take part and there are dedicated tapas trails to follow – see the website for a map.

Christmas Market
CHRISTMAS MARKET

(Plaça Major; ⊙ 10am-9pm mid-Dec–early Jan; 🐾) The Christmas market takes over Plaça Major, Plaça d'Espanya and Las Ramblas. Expect handicraft stalls, music and multiple Santas.

Trofeo Ciutat de Palma
SAILING

(www.trofeociutatdepalma.com; ⊙ Dec) Run by the Royal Nautical Club of Palma, the Ciutat de Palma-Regata is a huge event for smaller boats, held over four days in early December.

🍴 Eating

Palma's dining scene, starting from the already-strong base you'd expect in a major Spanish city, just keeps improving. As well as bold experiments with traditional Mallorcan dishes by innovative young chefs, you'll find excellent tapas and typical Spanish food as well as very good renditions of a wide range of world cuisines (and we are not talking about all-day English breakfasts!).

🍴 Old Palma

Temple Natura
VEGETARIAN €

(Map p60; ☎ 971 71 86 88; Carrer del Temple 4; mains €8.50-10; ⊙ 12.30-5.30pm Mon-Sat; 🛜 🌿) This appropriately named restaurant offers a tranquil respite from pavement pounding. Head for the 'secret garden' out back with its sprawling wisteria, citrus and banana trees. The menu concentrates on light healthy bites like smoked tofu salad and guacamole with white corn *arepas* while rumbling tummies can opt for a veggie burger with all the trimmings. There are regular art exhibitions.

Forn del Santo Cristo
BAKERY €

(Map p60; ☎ 971 71 26 49; www.hornosanto cristo.com; Carrer de Paraires 2; ensaïmades from €1.50; ⊙ 8am-8.30pm Mon-Sat, 8.30am-1pm Sun) The 'Oven of Holy Christ' has been baking up *ensaïmades* (a light, spiral pastry emblematic of the island) since 1910, and offers a choice of 12 fillings ranging from velvety marzipan to white chocolate with nuts. It also offers a range of other traditional goodies, including *cocas patatas* (sweet potato buns).

★ El Camino MODERN SPANISH €€
(Map p60; www.elcaminopalma.es; Carrer de San
Brondo 4; tapas €7-10; ☺1-4pm & 6-10.45pm Mon-
Sat; 🐾) Worthy of all the hype, this concept
tapas bar is superstylish, with coffered ceilings, oak panelling, mosaic tiles and a long
marble bar from where you can watch your
tasty bites being prepared. The dishes are
classic, the execution superb: slices of moist
tortilla, garlicky fried squid, blistered Pa-
drón peppers, crispy melt-in-your-mouth
croquettes. No reservations.

L'Ambigú MODERN EUROPEAN €€
(Map p60; ☑971 57 21 51; www.elambigubar.com;
Carrer de Carnissería 1; mains €12-18; ☺noon-mid-
night Mon-Sat; 🐾) Tucked in behind the Església de Santa Eulàlia with an inviting terrace,
this irresistible little bar-restaurant specialises in fresh seasonal ingredients in dishes
like avocado and strawberries tartar and
smoked sardines. It does retain something
of the vibe of the tapas bar it once was and
can get crowded with a convivial crowd on
Fridays and Saturdays.

Las Olas VIETNAMESE, FRENCH €€
(Map p60; ☑971 21 49 05; www.lasolasbistro.
com; Carrer de Can Fortuny 5; mains €14-17, tapas €2-9; ☺12.30-3.30pm & 8.15-11pm Wed-Sat,
12.30-3.30pm Mon & Tue) Las Olas divides
the day into two: lunch is all about rein-
terpreted French Mediterranean flavours
(perhaps cod with apples and soft garlic),
while dinner is a Vietnamese-Cambodian
affair, with fresh, herby dishes such as *chao
tom* (prawn patties on a bed of citronella
shoots). The accomplished chef-cum-own-
er is French of southeast Asian descent, so
that explains a lot.

La Taberna del Caracol TAPAS €€
(Map p60; ☑971 71 49 08; www.tabernacaracol.
com; Carrer de Sant Alonso 2; tapas €4.50-19, tapas
tasting plate €16; ☺noon-3pm & 7.30-11pm Tue-
Sat, noon-3pm Mon) Descend three steps into
this high-ceilinged Gothic basement to find
traditional tapas, such as grilled artichokes,
snails, *jamón* (cured ham) and mushrooms
with garlic. Through a broad sandstone
arch at the back you can see what's cooking,
which may tempt you to try the tapas plate
(minimum two people); a meal in itself. Reservations recommended.

Can Cera Gastro-Bar MEDITERRANEAN €€€
(Map p60; ☑971 71 50 12; www.cancerahotel.com;
Carrer del Convent de Sant Francesc 8; tapas €10-

THE PERFECT ENSAÏMADA

Most Mallorcans and just about every
Spanish visitor to the island has one
culinary favourite above all others – the
humble *ensaïmada*, a delicate, feather-
light, croissant-like pastry dusted with
icing sugar, and sometimes filled with
cream. Getting them to agree on where
to buy the best is surprisingly simple.
These choices are considered by the
locals to be the best you'll find in Palma,
and possibly the entire island:

➡ Horno San Antonio (p74)
➡ Ca'n Joan de S'Aigo (p74)
➡ Fornet de la Soca (p73)
➡ Forn del Santo Cristo (p72)

24, mains €18-27; ☺12.30-10.30pm; 🐾) This
restaurant spills onto a lovely inner patio at
the Can Cera hotel, housed in a *palau* that
originally dates from the 13th century. Dine
by lantern light on tapas-sized dishes, such
as Andalucian squid with orange alioli, or
opt for an unfussy main, like roast shank of
lamb or grilled octopus.

✖ Plaça Major & Around

★ Fornet de la Soca BAKERY €
(Forn des Teatre; Map p60; ☑673 499446; www.forn
etdelasoca.com; Plaça de Weyler 9; pastries from
€1.50; ☺9am-8pm Mon-Sat) Tomeu Arbona is
the master baker here. He is also the author
of the cookery book *Traditional Cooking
in Mallorca* and something of a culinary
legend in town. Arbona describes himself
as a gastronomic archaeologist, seeking out
age-old recipes and reinventing them. The
mouthwatering selection of cakes, pastries
and savoury pies here, including vegetarian,
is testimony to his dedication.

Bagel BAGELS €
(Map p60; ☑871 57 10 10; www.bagelpalma.
es; Carrer dels Set Cantons 4; bagels from €3;
☺10am-5pm Mon-Fri; ✓) The bagels are made
here daily and have that authentic, slightly
chewy, texture that can be so hard to find
outside New York. The fillings are vegetarian and vegan with combos like avocado,
hummus and beetroot and mozzarella, pesto
and tomato or, for traditionalists, the more
conventional lightly toasted with butter and
strawberry jam.

Restaurant Celler Sa Premsa MALLORCAN €
(Map p56; ☑971 72 35 29; www.cellersapremsa.
com; Plaça del Bisbe Berenguer de Palou 8; mains
€9-14, menús €14; ☺noon-4pm & 7.30-11.30pm
Mon-Sat) A visit to this local institution, going strong since 1958, is almost obligatory.
It's a cavernous tavern filled with huge old
wine barrels and faded bullfighting posters – you find plenty of these places in the
Mallorcan interior but they're a dying breed
here in Palma. Mallorcan specialities dominate the menu.

Come for the well-prepared roast lamb,
tumbet (Mallorcan-style vegetable ratatouille), *frito mallorquín* (sautéed lamb
offal with fried potatoes, onions and herbs),
pork with cabbage, and rabbit with onion.
Service is quietly excellent, but it's the atmosphere you'll remember.

Ca'n Joan de S'Aigo BAKERY €
(Map p60; ☑971 71 07 59; www.canjoande
saigo.com; Carrer de Can Sanç 10; pastries €1.30-
3; ☺8am-9pm) Tempting with its sweet creations since 1700, this glorious cafe is *the*
place for thick hot chocolate (€2.20) and
pastries in atmospheric, stuck-in-a-time-
warp surroundings complete with chandeliers, dark wood fittings and decorative
tiles. The house speciality is *quarto,* a feath-
er-soft sponge cake that children love, with
almond-flavoured ice cream.

Horno San Antonio BAKERY €
(Map p56; ☑971 71 59 32; www.hornosanantonio.
com; Plaça Sant Antoni 6; ensaïmades from €1.35;
☺8am-8pm Tue-Fri, to 2pm Sat & Sun) Considered by most Mallorcans to be the best of
the best when it comes to *ensaïmades,* this
traditional old pastry shop does a roaring
trade in all sizes and types, from plain to
chocolate, with cream or apricot filling. You
can get them nicely packed if you plan on
taking one home.

Bar España SPANISH €€
(Map p60; ☑971 72 42 34; Carrer de Ca'n Escur-
rac 12; tapas menus €12-22; ☺6.30pm-midnight
Mon-Fri, 12.30-4.30pm & 6.30pm-1am Sat) Happening upon this place in the evening when
everything else in the vicinity is closed is like
discovering a hidden secret. Hugely popular
and deservedly so, it has stone walls and an
agreeable hum of conversation accompanies
the fine *pintxos* (Basque tapas), which are
lined up along the bar or chalked up on a
board.

Quina Creu TAPAS €€
(Map p60; ☑971 71 17 72; www.quinacreu.com;
Carrer de Corderia 24; mains €17-23, cocktails from
€6.50; ☺noon-1am Mon-Sat; ☎) With its mish-
mash of vintage furniture, flickering chandeliers and poster-plastered walls, Quina
Creu nails bric-a-brac chic. Deep sofas, a ta-
pas-lined bar and blackboards touting such
delights as grilled tuni *tataki,* or lamb shank
with couscous, add to the appeal. There is
also an exotic cocktail menu, ranging from
a mint julep to a Moscow mule (vodka, lime
and ginger beer).

★**Marc Fosh** MODERN EUROPEAN €€€
(Map p60; ☑971 72 01 14; www.marcfosh.com;
Carrer de la Missió 7A, Convent de la Missió Hotel;
menús lunch €30-40, dinner €72-92; ☺1-3pm &
7.30-9.30pm; ☎) Located within a former
17th-century convent, now the luxury Convent de la Missió Hotel, this stylish gastronomic destination introduces novel twists
to time-honoured Mediterranean dishes
and ingredients. The weekly lunch *menú* is
a very reasonable way to enjoy dishes such
as sweetbread and truffle ravioli or braised
beef cheek with a nasturtium-and-plum jus.
Vegetarian options available.

Flavours are clean, bright and seasonal,
with much of the produce and herbs grown
at a dedicated culinary garden, the Fosh
Farm. Reservations essential.

La Bodeguilla SPANISH €€€
(Map p60; ☑971 71 82 74; www.la-bodeguilla.com;
Carrer de Sant Jaume 3; mains €22-28; ☺1-11pm;
☎) This proper foodie's restaurant reinter-
prets dishes from across Spain in a modern
dining room lined with wine and hams. Try
the *porc negre* (rare-breed pork) from Mallorca or the *lechazo* (young lamb, baked
Córdoba-style in rosemary). Also on offer is
an enticing range of tapas – the grilled octopus with potato foam is a perfectly cooked
mouthful of the sea.

✕ **Es Puig de Sant Pere**

13% TAPAS €
(Map p60; ☑971 42 51 87; www.13porciento.com;
Carrer de Sant Feliu 13A; tapas €5-9, lunch menú
€12; ☺12.30-11.30pm Mon-Sat, from 6pm Sun; ☑)
✑ This L-shaped barn of a place is a wine
and tapas bar, bistro and delicatessen combined. Most items are organic and there's
plenty of choice for vegetarians. Alongside
classics such as Galician octopus, you'll find

DON'T MISS

TO MARKET

Nosing around the colourful stalls of Palma's produce markets is a great way to take in the flavour of the city. There's all you need to assemble your own picnic, from cheeses and cold meats to fruit and veg. The largest and best is the central Mercat de l'Olivar, where you'll find everything from plump olives to never-heard-of legumes, melons as big as footballs, strings of *sobrassada* (paprika-flavoured cured pork sausage), hunks of Serrano ham and enough fish to fill a small ocean. Make a morning of it and linger for lunch at the deli stalls for tapas or oyster shucking. Equally busy but with fewer tourists are the Mercat de Santa Catalina and **Mercat de Pere Garau** (Map p56; ☑971 24 46 74; https://mercatperegarau.es; Plaça de Pere Garau; ⊘7am-3pm Mon-Sat). Gourmets should head to the Mercado Gastronómico San Juan, a hub of fine food housed in a redeveloped abattoir in the northern part of the city.

Mercado Gastronómico San Juan (St John Gastronomic Market; Map p56; ☑971 78 10 04; www.mercadosanjuanpalma.es; Carrer d'Emperadriu Eugènia 6; ⊘noon-midnight) This gastronomic market occupies a coral-pink Modernista building in the S'Escorxador cultural centre, which was once a slaughterhouse. With a bar, cafe, terrace and some 20 stalls selling *fideuá* (like paella, but made with fine noodles), silky *croquetas*, top-grade acorn-fed *jamón, sobrassada* (paprika-flavoured cured pork sausages) and a galaxy of other Mallorcan and Spanish treats, it's a gourmand's dream.

Mercat de l'Olivar (Map p60; www.mercatolivar.com; Plaça de l'Olivar 4; ⊘7am-2.30pm Mon-Thu, to 8pm Fri, to 3pm Sat) Palma's main retail produce market is a wonderland of Mallorcan (and Spanish) comestibles. Cheese, meat, fish, vegetables and prepared dishes are just some of the delights gathered under one roof. It's a place to linger, with cafes and tapas bars mixed among the stalls.

Mercat de Santa Catalina (Map p56; www.mercatdesantacatalina.com; Plaça de la Navegació; ⊘7am-5pm Mon-Sat) Local produce markets like this are the lifeblood of Palma's neighbourhoods, and are always the best bet for fresh fruit and vegetables (including organic), seafood, charcuterie, bread and other staples. Inside, four tapas bars are placed at intervals convenient for refuelling.

more daring concoctions like *bacallà* (salt cod) with sage butter and honey. There are also salads, carpaccios and pastas.

The lunch *menú* is a choice selection of three tapas.

Bon Lloc VEGETARIAN €€
(Map p60; ☑971 71 86 17; www.bonllocrestaurant .com; Carrer de Sant Feliu 7; mains €9-18, lunch menú €15; ⊘1-4pm & 7.30-10.30pm Tue-Sat, 1-4pm Mon; 🕾🖉) 🖉 Longstanding favourite of the hip and health-conscious, this vegetarian (and increasingly vegan) place does great work with organic produce. Palma's first veggie restaurant, it's light, open and airy with a casual but classy atmosphere. At lunchtime there's a four-course *menú* (juice or salad, entrée, main and dessert), while dinner is à la carte. It's always popular, so ring to reserve.

Forn de Sant Joan SPANISH €€
(Map p60; ☑971 72 84 22; www.forndesant joan.com; Caller de Sant Joan 4; menú €20-24;

⊘1-4pm & 7-11.30pm; 🕾🖉) Yet another example of Palma's forward-thinking food scene, this former bakery is all stripped-brick, perfectly mixed cocktails and Mallorcan/Mediterranean food taken to the next level. As far as possible, all the ingredients and produce are local, showcased in such dishes as tuna tartar with guacamole. The three-course regular or vegetarian lunch *menú* provides an excellent introduction to the cuisine.

Saranna INTERNATIONAL €€
(Map p60; ☑971 53 64 32; www.sarannacafe.com; Forn de l'Olivera 4; mains €12-16; ⊘8.30am-6pm Sun-Wed, to 8pm Thu-Sat; 🕾) This restaurant has a Scandi feel with its stripped-back cream-and-turquoise decor and laid-back feel. There is nothing minimalist about the dishes though: from the fusion flavours of the Thai-style curries to the Cajun chicken burger with guacamole, jalapeño peppers and red onion, the flavours here sing loud and clear. The staff are a delight – and so are the desserts.

WORTH A TRIP

CASTELL DE BELLVER

Straddling a wooded hillside, the **Castell de Bellver** is a 14th-century circular castle (with a unique round tower), the only one of its kind in Spain. Jaume II ordered it built atop a hill known as Puig de Sa Mesquida in 1300 and it was largely completed within 10 years. Perhaps the highlight of any visit is the spectacular view over the woods to Palma, the Badia de Palma and out to sea.

The castle was conceived above all as a royal residence but seems to have been a white elephant, as only King Sanç (in 1314) and Aragón's Joan I (in 1395) moved in for any amount of time. In 1717 it became a military prison, and was subsequently used in both the Napoleonic and Spanish Civil Wars. Climb to the roof and check out the prisoners' graffiti, etched into the stonework.

The ground-floor **Museu d'Història de la Ciutat** (City History Museum) traces the development of the city from the prehistoric Talayotic civilisation to the present day. As well as Roman and Arabian ceramics there are explanatory panels, the classical statues of the Despuig Collection and other artefacts. Upstairs you can visit a series of largely empty chambers, including the one-time kitchen.

About the nearest you can get to the castle by bus (3, 46 or 50) is Plaça de Gomila, from where you'll have to walk for about 15 minutes (1km) up a steep hill. Instead, combine it with the Palma City Sightseeing open-top bus, which climbs to the castle as part of its circuit of the city. Alternatively, if you have a car, there is parking available.

There is a small cafe available for refreshments.

Bruselas   STEAK €€
(Map p60; ☑971 71 09 54; www.restaurante bruselas.net; Carrer d'Estanc 4; mains €15-20; ⊙1-3.30pm & 8-11.30pm Mon-Sat; ☎) Bruselas basically provides red meat to aesthetes, with Argentine steaks – such as *solomillo con foie* (sirloin with foie gras) – gourmet hamburgers and kobe beef served in a stone-vaulted basement. There are some innovative tapas (though few non-meaty options), and all goes down well with a throaty Mallorcan red, such as Son Bordils Negre.

★ Beatnik   AMERICAN FUSION €€€
(Map p60; ☑971 28 28 72; www.beatnikpalma. com; Puro Oasis Urbano, Carrer de Montenegro 12; mains €20-32, lunch menú €25; ⊙12.30-5pm & 7-11.30pm Mon-Fri, to 1am Sat & Sun; ☎) This place has a gee-whizz American '60s vibe with its retro bucket chairs and Jack Kerouac pics and quotes on display. Dishes are faithful to the era with a menu that includes chicken lollipop with buffalo sauce, lobster tacos, a Tex Mex salad with black beans and New York cheesecake. The attached bar stays open later than the restaurant.

Caballito de Mar   SEAFOOD €€€
(Map p60; ☑971 72 10 74; www.caballito demar.info; Passeig de Sagrera 5; mains €19-34; ⊙1pm-midnight; ☎) One of Palma's dining beacons, the 'Little Seahorse' is a dependable, if touristy, seafood destination overlooking the harbour. There are monkfish medallions, *sobrassada* (spicy Mallorcan sausage) and *butifarrón* (blood sausage) wrapped in cabbage leaves in a nut sauce. Or you could go for something more traditional, such as turbot with confit vegetables or red shrimp from Sóller.

On sunny days, grab a seat on the terrace.

✖ Santa Catalina & Around

El Perrito   SWEDISH €
(Map p56; ☑971 45 59 16; Carrer d'Anníbal 20; mains €8-11; ⊙8am-5pm Mon-Sat; ☎) The 'Little Dog' takes its canine moniker from the black-and-white photos of customers' pooches that hang on its walls. Run by Swedes, this cute-as-a-button cafe is a pleasantly bohemian haunt for bagels, homemade cakes, fresh juices and hearty specials, such as goulash, meatballs with lingonberries or 'Jansson's Temptation' (potatoes baked with anchovies and cream).

★ Simply Delicious   ISRAELI €€
(Map p56; ☑871 23 37 05; http://simplydelicious. es; Plaça Navegació 5; mains €10-15; ⊙11am-5pm Mon-Sat; ☎) Seek out this corner cafe which has a comforting boho feel and a menu that concentrates on heart-warming dishes like *shakshuka* (poached eggs in a rich tomato,

pepper and garlic sauce) with five subtle variations, including *picante* and with crumbly feta cheese. The hummus has similar varied options, and the falafel are simply superb.

Japo Sushi Bar
SUSHI €€

(Map p56; ☑971 73 83 21; Carrer de Sant Magí 25; menus €19-29; ⊙1.30-4pm & 7-11.30pm; 🛜) Locals in the know reckon this is the best Japanese restaurant around. All the standards are here, including fresh sushi, maki, sashimi and nigiri, plus a choice of fabulously light and crisp tempura, including vegetable tempura with the added perk of a topping of avocado. The decor is all cool greys and tasteful oriental artwork, and the service is exemplary.

Koh
SOUTHEAST ASIAN €€

(Map p56; ☑971 28 70 39; Carrer de Servet 15; mains €13-15; ⊙7-11pm Mon-Sat) This stylish, friendly Southeast Asian restaurant in Santa Catalina prepares (chiefly Thai) curries, soups and stir-fries with real panache. The flavours are punchy, whether you go for bouncy prawn and chive dumplings, or a perfectly balanced yellow seafood curry. Produce comes from neighbouring Santa Catalina market and there's a pretty patio to enjoy a ginger mojito in warm weather.

Nola
CAJUN €€

(Map p56; ☑971 66 70 06; www.disfrutadenola. com; Carrer de Sant Magí 13; mains €15-18; ⊙7.30-11pm Mon-Sat; 🛜) Funky Santa Catalina is the logical neighbourhood for this dedicated Cajun-Creole restaurant, the first outpost of New Orleans cool in Palma. Bayou classics like jambalaya, gumbo and ribs are given some refinement (a slick of Calvados jus here, a touch of truffle oil there) but basically the food and soundtrack stick close to the Louisiana originals.

La Baranda
ITALIAN €€

(Map p56; ☑971 45 45 25; www.labaranda.net; Carrer de Sant Magí 29; pizza €8.50-12, mains €14.50-20, tapas from €6.50; ⊙1-3.30pm & 6.30pm-midnight Wed-Sun) An easygoing Italian with Tuscan affinities, La Baranda is a good choice for wood-fired pizzas, pasta dishes and homemade cakes. It's a pleasant place to linger over a meal, with exposed stone, warm-yellow-hued walls, simple timber furniture and art scattered about. If you can't decide on Italian or Spanish, there's also a tapas menu.

Hórreo Veinti3
SPANISH €€€

(Map p56; ☑649 033806; http://horreoveinti3. jimdo.com; Carrer de Sa Fàbrica 23; mains €19-27; ⊙1pm-12.30am Thu-Mon, 7pm-12.30am Tue & Wed; 🛜) Transparent chairs, gleaming tiles and wicker lampshades set the scene at this modern, upbeat pick, with tables spilling out onto a pavement terrace. Dishes range from mussels in Albariño to grilled tuna and, a speciality, chateaubriand cooked on a hot stone at your table.

✗ Passeig Marítim & Western Palma

★ Toque
INTERNATIONAL €€

(Map p56; ☑971 28 70 68; www.restaurante-toque.com; Carrer Federico García Lorca 6; mains €17-19, 3-course lunch menú €16.50; ⊙1-4pm & 7-11pm Tue-Sat; 🍴) A father-and-son team run this individual little place with real pride and warmth. The food is Belgian-meets-Mallorcan (perhaps steak tartar with fries and salad, or suckling pig on a sweet potato puree) and has generated a loyal following among *palmeros*. Wines are well chosen and modestly priced, and the three-course €16.50 lunch *menú* is a dead-set bargain.

El Náutico
SEAFOOD €€

(Map p56; ☑971 72 66 00; https://tast.com/en/restaurant/el-nautico; Real Club Náutico, Plaza de San Pedro 1; mains €18-22; ⊙1pm-midnight; 🛜🍴) One of Palma's standout seafood options in the Royal Sailing Club (p69), 'The Nautical' does hake in a variety of ways (including 'Roman-style' – with vinegar and raisins), simply grilled shellfish and other spanking-fresh marine delights. The space, with wraparound windows overlooking the marina and a decked terrace, is beautifully designed in a nautical theme.

Ca'n Eduardo
SEAFOOD €€€

(Map p56; ☑971 72 11 82; www.caneduardo.com; Es Mollet, 3rd fl, Travesía Contramuelle; mains €23-29; ⊙1-11pm; 🛜) What better place to sample fish than right above the fish market? Ca'n Eduardo, in business since the 1940s, is hardly cutting-edge, but makes the most of stunning harbour views and super-fresh ingredients. Black-vested waiters serve seafood and some fantastic rice dishes (minimum of two) – the *arroz bogavante* (lobster rice; €26 per person) is a favourite.

✖ Es Portixol & Es Molinar

★ Mola
MODERN MEDITERRANEAN €€

(Map p56; ☑ 634 339344; www.grupomola.com; Carrer del Vicari Joaquim Fuster 83; mains €13-19; ☺ 1-10.30pm; 🐾) A hip and intimate small space decorated with striking abstract paintings, Mola has just a handful of tables (inside and out) where you can expect to find deliciously fresh and flavoursome food served in innovative ways. Unusual pairings like a pea hummus with snow peas and mint or turbot with a truffle vinaigrette are the order of the day. Reservations recommended.

Portixol
MEDITERRANEAN €€

(Map p56; ☑ 971 27 18 00; www.portixol.com; Carrer de la Sirena 27; mains €19-27, 3-course lunch menú €19; ☺ 7.30am-11pm; 🐾☑) The harbourside restaurant at Hotel Portixol is bright and breezy with sea views and a blue-white colour scheme. The menu is ingredient-driven, treating Med produce to the occasional international twist: perhaps a seafood laksa with rice rather than noodles, or grilled red tuna with edemame beans and wasabi mayonnaise. Vegetarian options include a miso burger with sweet potato fries.

Sa Roqueta
SEAFOOD €€

(Map p56; ☑ 971 24 94 10; www.restaurante saroqueta.com; Carrer Sirena 11, Portixol; mains €20-24; ☺ 1-3.30pm & 7.30-10.30pm Mon-Sat) One of former-fishing-village Portixol's excellent seafood restaurants, Sa Roqueta has been doing as little as possible to the daily catch since 1987. Grilled fish, clams with artichokes, lobster rice and seafood *fideuà* (pasta) are all prepared simply and expertly. Grab a table on the small terrace overlooking the bobbing boats.

Ola del Mar
SEAFOOD €€€

(Map p56; ☑ 971 27 42 75; www.oladelmar.es; Carrer del Vicari Joaquim Fuster 1; mains €22-26; ☺ 1-4pm & 7.30-11.30pm; 🐾) Ola del Mar specialises in top-quality fresh fish and seafood and rice dishes. There are no surprises on the menu, but everything's executed with flair, and the sprawling seafront terrace and switched-on service invite you to linger.

🍷 Drinking & Nightlife

Palma's clubbing epicentre is around the Passeig Marítim and the Club de Mar.

Most clubs open around midnight, but don't get going until 2am. Things go strong until 5am, when the early-morning clubs (some around Plaça de Gomila) begin.

Admission costs €10 to €20, usually including your first drink, although if you're not dressed to impress you may be turned away no matter how much cash you're willing to spend.

🍷 Old Palma

★ Lórien
CRAFT BEER

(Map p60; ☑ 971 72 32 02; www.sauep.com; Carrer de les Caputxines 5; ☺ 5pm-1am Tue-Fri; 🐾) The helpful owner can guide you through the vast choice of craft ales on offer here, be they local, Spanish or international. It's a friendly, cosy and informal pub where recent taps have included a highly touted brown ale from Mallorca's Sa Cerviseria brewery.

La Vinya de Santa Clara
WINE BAR

(Map p60; ☑ 666 664330; Carrer de Santa Clara 8A; ☺ 1pm-midnight Mon-Sat, from 5pm Sun) With over 60 varieties by the glass (from €4), this convivial little cubby hole gives you every opportunity to get to grips with the wines of Mallorca (and beyond, if you choose). Basic tapas – cheese, *sobrassada*, empanadas and the like – keep you on your feet and socialising.

Bodega Santa Clara
BAR

(Map p60; ☑ 655 770193; Carrer de Santa Clara 4; ☺ 6pm- 9pm Tue-Sat) This cavernous and quirkily cluttered small bar is easy to mistake for a shop. Step inside, perch on an old soda case and allow yourself to be guided by the enthusiastic owner. The speciality here is vermouth and soda, a classic Mallorcan tipple, but local wines are also on offer.

Gibson
BAR

(Map p60; ☑ 971 71 64 04; www.gibsonbar.es; Plaça del Mercat 18; ☺ 8am-2am Sun-Thu, to 3am Fri & Sat) This chirpy cocktail bar with outside seating is still busy with (mostly local) punters on a weekday night when everything else around has pulled the shutters down.

Cappuccino
CAFE

(Map p60; www.grupocappuccino.com; Carrer del Conquistador 13; ☺ 8.30am-1am Sun-Wed, to midnight Thu-Sat; 🐾) Part of a cafe chain (albeit a stylish one), it's Cappuccino's location in the lee of the Palau March that's the attraction here. Light meals, cakes and good (if overpriced) coffee are all perfectly fine, but

LGBTIQ+ PALMA

....

The bulk of LGBTIQ+ life on the island happens in and around Palma. The biggest concentration of gay bars is on Avinguda de Joan Miró, south of Plaça de Gomila. To get your night going, you could start with Bar Michel, Siente and Dark Cruising Bar. Ben Amics (p84) has an LGBTIQ+ advice service. Useful websites for plugging into Palma's queer community include www.mallorcagaymap.com and www.gaymallorca.es.

Bar Michel (Map p56; ☑971 90 02 84; Avinguda de Joan Miró 58; ⊗8am-2.30am Mon-Sat, 4pm-midnight Sun; 🛜) This friendly terraced bar in the heart of Palma's gay 'district' is a great place to kick-start your night. Very reasonable cocktails and tapas and chatty bar staff are part of the charm. Check out the Facebook page.

Siente (Map p60; ☑971 77 39 33; www.sientespa.com; Carrer de Fray Luis de León 5; ⊗3-11pm Mon-Wed & Sun, to 4pm Fri, to 8am Sat) With a pool, Jacuzzi, wet and dry saunas and private rooms, Siente is the best-equipped gay sauna in central Palma.

Dark Cruising Bar (Map p56; www.darkcruisingmallorca.com; Carrer de Ticià 22; ⊗7pm-3am) For all your (male-only) dark-room encounters, including naked and fetish parties, this is the place. Look for the small illuminated sign and the deep blue glow.

it's the people-watching from the raised outdoor terrace you'll appreciate the most.

Guinness House   BAR
(Map p60; Parc de la Mar; ⊗8am-1am) This otherwise unremarkable bar is blessed with a stunning location, between the cathedral and the Parc de la Mar. It's at its best for an early-morning coffee before the crowds arrive, or after dark. The terrace tables are also well placed to enjoy the outside cinema screenings (p72) that take place just west of here in summer, on Tuesday, Wednesday, Saturday and Sunday at 9.30pm.

🍽 Plaça Major & Around

⭐**Clandestino Cocktail Club**   COCKTAIL BAR
(Map p60; ☑618 189237; Carrer de Sant Jaume 12; ⊗7pm-2am Tue & Thu-Sat, 9pm-2am Wed; 🛜) Well worth seeking out if you are up for a sophisticated, big-city feel; Clandestino offers smoochy jazz on the soundtrack, candlelit tables, excellent cocktails and a great choice of spirits, including a wide range of gins (in proper balloon glasses). Check out the Facebook page.

Café L'Antiquari   BAR
(Map p60; ☑871 57 23 13; Carrer d'Arabi 5; ⊗11.30-1am Mon-Sat) This old antique shop has been transformed into one of the most original places in Palma to nurse a drink and nibble on tapas. Curios, prints and knick-knacks adorn every corner and inch of wall space, and even the tables and chairs belong to another age. Occasionally there's music or

photo exhibitions, and the coffee is always excellent. Check out the Facebook page.

⭐**Bar Flexas**   BAR
(Map p60; www.barflexas.com; Carrer de la Llotgeta 12; ⊗6.30pm-midnight Tue-Thu, from noon Fri & Sat) A lively locals' bar with a hint of grunge, Bar Flexas took up residence long before the streets southeast of the Plaça Major became trendy and remains a great spot for a tipple far from the tourist haunts.

🍽 Es Puig de Sant Pere

⭐**Atlantico Café**   BAR
(Map p60; ☑971 72 62 85; www.cafeatlantico.es; Carrer de Sant Feliu 12; ⊗7pm-2.30am Mon-Thu, to 3am Fri-Sun) Spangled with an upended cornucopia of bric-a-brac, blessed with welcoming, laid-back staff and capable of cranking the merriment up to 11, this is one of Palma's most charismatic bars. Ever-expanding swaths of graffiti testify to the numberless nights of bonhomie and cocktails downed since the place opened in 1997.

Bodega Can Rigo   BAR
(Map p60; ☑971 41 60 07; www.bodegacanrigo.es; Carrer de Sant Feliu 16; ⊗10.30am-midnight Mon, Tue, Thu & Fri, from noon Sat, from 7pm Sun) The tapas and *pintxos* at this charismatic little place, which has been going strong since 1949, are rated as some of the best in Palma. As if the intimate vibe, profusion of cosy nooks and great wine list weren't enough incitement to linger!

Café La Lonja
CAFE

(Map p60; ☑971 72 27 99; Carrer de Sa Llotja 2; ⊙10am-2am Mon-Sat, 11am-1am Sun) With its curved marble bar, tiled-chessboard floor, smattering of tables, padded benches and eclectic decor of old luggage and portraits, this place is as appealing for breakfast as it is for tapas and a *pomada* (Menorcan gin and lemon soft drink). Sit outside when the weather's warm, in the shadow of Sa Llotja.

Ginbo
BAR

(Map p60; ☑971 72 21 75; Passeig de Mallorca 14A; ⊙4pm-3am Mon-Fri, from 6pm Sat & Sun; ☜) Not in the hippest neighbourhood, Ginbo nonetheless does the best G&T in Palma. Besides over 120 different kinds of gin, it mixes some superb cocktails, including the lip-smacking Tangerine (basically a gin sour made with rosemary syrup), which you can sip in the buzzy, stylishly urban, backlit bar or on the terrace. Check out the Facebook page.

Santa Catalina & Around

★Idem Café
BAR

(Map p56; ☑619 356295; Carrer de Sant Magí 15A; ⊙7pm-2am, to 3am summer; ☜) Slink into this bordello-chic cocoon of deep, dark-red velvet, chandeliers, baroque mirrors and risqué art. With a fabulously burlesque look and pre-clubbing vibe, Idem is a unique spot to sip a mojito or gin.

Hotel Hostal Cuba
BAR

(Map p56; ☑971 45 22 37; www.hotelhostalcuba.com; Carrer de Sant Magí 1; ⊙8am-2am Sun-Thu, to 4am Fri & Sat; ☜) Inhabiting an early-20th-century Santa Catalina landmark for sailors passing through Palma, this place has been reborn as a watering hole of a more sophisticated kind. With a kitchen open from 9am to midnight, DJs on busy nights, and a rooftop Skybar with superb 27-degree views of central Palma and the Badia de Palma, it covers most bases.

Soho Bar
BAR

(Map p56; ☑971 45 47 19; www.sohobarpalma.com; Avinguda d'Argentina 5; ⊙6pm-3am; ☜) This self-proclaimed 'urban vintage bar' has a green-lit beer fridge, vintage 1960s decor and a dedication to indie music. The laid-back crowd seems oblivious to the traffic pounding past the footpath tables, and there are old-school game consoles for the easily distracted. Cocktails go for €7 – the bar prides itself on its mojito.

Passeig Marítim & Western Palma

Pacha
CLUB

(Map p56; www.pachamallorca.es; Passeig Marítim 42; ⊙10pm-6am daily Jul & Aug, Thu-Sat Sep-Jun; ☜) This glamour puss of a club brings a splash of Ibiza to Palma's late-night scene. Set away from the town centre, down by the port, it's a three-floor temple to hedonism, with regular fiestas, DJs pumping out dance music of all flavours and multiple chill-out terraces. Entry costs around €15.

Tito's
CLUB

(Map p56; www.titosmallorca.com; Passeig Marítim 33; €15-20; ⊙11pm-6am daily Jun-Sep, Fri & Sat Oct-May; ☜) Ray Charles, Marlene Dietrich and Frank Sinatra once used to let their hair down at this clubbing classic, which has been going strong since the 1950s. Today DJs spin Euro-house and popular dance to a crowd that comes for the upbeat vibe, sweeping city views and the occasional sexy floor show. There's also an outdoor stage in warm weather.

Varadero
BAR

(Map p56; ☑971 72 64 28; www.varaderomallorca.com; Camí de l'Escullera; ⊙8am-1am Sun-Thu, to 3am Fri & Sat; ☜) This minimalist, glass-fronted

---

DON'T MISS

LA RUTA MARTIANA

••

The Sa Gerreria neighbourhood of Palma, southeast of the Plaça Major, has undergone an extraordinary makeover, from the no-go area of central Palma to one of its hottest nightlife districts. Part of the momentum is attributable to the inexplicably named La Ruta Martiana (The Martians' Route), where 25 bars clustered tightly around a few streets offer a small morsel to eat (a tapa, or a *pintxo*) and a drink for €2 from 7.30pm to midnight on Tuesday and from 7.30pm to 2am on Wednesday. Apart from being great value and allowing you to go on a tapas and bar crawl without breaking the bank, it has breathed life into this long-neglected corner of town. Among the bars taking part is excellent L'Ambigú (p73) which is also well-located at the centre of the action. Check out the Facebook page.

bar's splendid situation, jutting out into the Badia de Palma, makes it feel as though you've weighed anchor. The squawking of seagulls mixes with lounge sounds as you sip your favourite tipple and contemplate the majesty of the cathedral from the teak-timbered terrace.

Es Portixol & Es Molinar

Anima Beach
BAR

(Map p56; ☑971 59 55 91; www.animabeachpalma.com; Platja de Can Pere Antoni; ☉10.30am-1.30am May-Oct, 11am-8pm Nov-Mar; ☜) Beachfront chill-out lounge and much-loved spot for a sundowner and tapas. DJs bring the beats Thursday to Sunday. You can reserve a sunbed for €25, and add a cocktail, water and towel for €35. You can also order food here, which is geared towards its international clientele, with salads, pasta and similar.

☆ Entertainment

From rock concerts to opera, movies to folk dancing, international regattas to football matches, there's always an entertaining diversion happening in Palma. Most events can be booked online through www.ticketmaster.es, or through the department store El Corte Inglés (www.elcorteingles.es).

Go to http://ocio.diariodemallorca.es for up-to-date event listings. Alternatively, pick up the free bi-monthly *YouThing Guia de Mallorca* available at tourist offices as well as many bars and entertainment venues.

Cinema

Palma has at least seven cinema complexes, each with several screens, but only one shows films not dubbed into Spanish.

Cine Ciutat
CINEMA

(Map p56; ☑971 20 54 53; www.cineciutat.org; Carrer de Emperadriu Eugènia 6) About 2km north of central Palma, this cinema programs arthouse films, many in their original language with Spanish subtitles. On Mondays the ordinary ticket price of €7.75 drops to €5.50.

Theatre

Teatre Principal
THEATRE

(Map p60; ☑box office 971 21 96 96; www.teatreprincipal.com/en; Carrer de la Riera 2; ☉box office 5-9pm Wed & Thu, 11am-2pm & 5-9pm Fri & Sat) Built in 1854 on the site of a 17th-century predecessor, destroyed by fire in 1858, rebuilt in 1860 and again restored in 2007, this is the city's prestige theatre for drama, clas-

sical music, opera and ballet. The renovation recreated the theatre's neoclassical heyday and combined it with the latest technology, resulting in great acoustics.

Teatre Municipal
DANCE

(Map p60; ☑971 73 91 48; www.palmacultura.cat; Passeig de Mallorca 9; ☉box office 1hr before show) Here you might see anything from contemporary dance to drama. The telephone line is open 9am to 2pm.

Live Music

Most of Palma's live acts perform on the stages of intimate bars around Sa Llotja. Concerts begin between 10pm and midnight and wrap up no later than 2am.

Novo Café Lisboa
LIVE MUSIC

(Map p56; ☑661 785667; Carrer de Sant Magí 33; ☉9pm-3am Wed-Sun) One of Palma's best live music/DJ venues, the New Lisbon Cafe's curved wooden bar is thronged three-deep on the more popular nights. Expect jazz-funk, disco, electro, synthpop and much else besides. Most nights are free. Check out the Facebook page.

Auditòrium
LIVE MUSIC

(Map p56; ☑971 73 47 35; www.auditoriumpalma.es; Passeig Marítim 18; ☉box office 10am-2pm & 4-9pm) This spacious, modern theatre is Palma's main stage for major performances, ranging from opera to light rock, ballet, musicals, tribute bands and gospel choirs. The Sala Mozart hosts part of the city's opera program (with the Teatre Principal), while the Orquestra Simfónica de Balears (Balearic Symphony Orchestra) is a regular from October to May.

Garito Cafe
LIVE MUSIC

(Map p56; ☑971 73 69 12; www.garitocafe.com; Dàrsena de Can Barberà; ☉8pm-4am, closed Sun-Wed Oct-May; ☜) DJs and live performers – slinging anything from jazz to disco classics and electro – get the Garito going from around 10pm Thursday to Saturday nights. The food's quite funky, too: expect riffs on traditional classics, such as quinoa risotto or fried black ravioli. Admission is generally free, but you're expected to buy a drink.

Blue Jazz Club
LIVE MUSIC

(Map p60; ☑971 72 72 40; www.bluejazz.es; 7th fl, Passeig de Mallorca 6; ☉10pm-late Thu-Sat, 8.30pm-late Mon; ☜) Located on the 7th floor of the Hotel Saratoga, this sophisticated club with high-altitude views over Palma offers after-dinner jazz, soul and blues concerts from 11pm to 1am Thursday to Saturday, and a Monday-evening jam session from 9pm to 11pm. Admission is free, but you're expected to buy a drink.

Football

RCD Mallorca FOOTBALL
(☑ booking 971 22 15 35; www.rcdmallorca.es; Iberostar Estadi, Camí dels Reis, Polígon Industrial) Palma's RCD Mallorca, which plays at the Iberostar Estadi, about 3km north of central Palma, is one of the better sides battling it out in La Liga. Never champions, they usually wind up achieving mid-table respectability. You can get tickets at the stadium or call the ticket booking number.

Iberostar Estadi STADIUM
(☑ booking 971 22 15 35; www.rcdmallorca.es; Camí dels Reis, Polígon Industrial) The Iberostar Estadi is about 3km north of central Palma, and hosts football games, including those featuring Palma's top division RCD Mallorca. Tickets are available at the stadium or by phoning the booking number. Take bus No 6 or 8.

🏠 Shopping

Start browsing the chic boutiques around Passeig d'es Born. The Passeig itself is equal parts high street and highbrow, with chain stores like Massimo Dutti and Zara alongside elitist boutiques. In the maze of pedestrian streets west of the Passeig, you'll find some of Palma's most tempting (and expensive) stores. Another good shopping street is pedestrianised Carrer de Sant Miquel.

🏠 Old Palma

Colmado Santo Domingo FOOD
(Map p60; ☑ 971 71 48 87; www.colmadosantodomingo.com; Carrer de Sant Domingo 1; ⊙ 10am-8pm Mon-Sat) It's almost impossible to manoeuvre in this narrow little shop, so crowded are its shelves with local Mallorcan food products – cheeses, honey, olives, olive oil, pâté, fig bread, balsamic vinegar and Sóller marmalade to name just a few – while *sobrassada* hangs from the ceiling.

Vidrierias Gordiola GLASS
(Map p60; ☑ 971 66 50 46; www.gordiola.com; Carrer de la Victòria 2; ⊙ 10.15am-1.45pm & 4.30-8pm Mon-Fri, 10.15am-1.45pm Sat) The Gordiola family can call on nearly 300 years of glass-

making skill, everywhere evident in the fantastically shaped and coloured vases, lamps, stemware and other vitreous works of art on display in this shop.

Típika ARTS & CRAFTS
(Map p60; ☑ 971 68 58 10; Carrer d'en Morei 7; ⊙ 10am-8pm Mon-Fri, to 6pm Sat, to 3pm Sun) This small shop is dedicated to promoting the craftsmanship and gastronomy of Mallorca. Here you'll find wines, olive oils, salts and liquors, as well as ceramics and other handicrafts from small family artisan businesses across the island.

Chocolate Factory CHOCOLATE
(Map p60; ☑ 971 22 94 93; www.chocolatfactory.com; Plaça des Mercat 9; ⊙ 10.30am-8.30pm Mon-Sat, 11am-3pm Sun) The Chocolate Factory does precisely what it says on the tin. Besides irresistible pralines, macaroons and slabs of amazingly intense 100% cocoa chocolate, it also does a fine line in chocolate-filled *ensaïmades*, chocolate fondues, cakes and ice cream.

Carmina SHOES
(Map p60; www.carminashoemaker.com; Carrer de l'Unió 4; ⊙ 11am-8.30pm Mon-Sat) A classic of traditional Mallorcan shoemaking, Carmina makes a virtue of dark tones, brogues and loafers that will set you back €340 to €500. If you want Cordoban leather, expect to pay €600 and more.

Fine Books BOOKS
(Map p60; ☑ 971 72 37 97; Carrer d'en Morei 7; ⊙ 10am-8pm Mon-Sat) This extraordinary collection of secondhand books, including some really valuable treasures, rambles over three floors. It's *the* place for secondhand, English-language books in Palma: if you can't find what you're looking for, Rodney will try to track it down for you. In this increasingly digital age, Fine Books is a rare gem indeed.

🏠 Plaça Major & Around

El Paladar FOOD & DRINKS
(Map p56; ☑ 971 71 74 04; www.elpaladar.es; Carrer de Bonaire 21; ⊙ 9am-9pm Mon-Sat) 'The Palate' is a wonderland for *jamón* lovers. The flavour of air-cured pig scents the air, mingling with the cheese, *sobrassada* and other delights on display. There's plenty of other Mallorcan produce, including wines and canned

fish, and you can perch on a stool to enjoy a glass and tasting plate.

El Corte Inglés
DEPARTMENT STORE

(Map p56; ☑971 77 01 77; www.elcorteingles.es; Avinguda d'Alexandre Rosselló 12-16; ☺9.30am-10pm Mon-Sat) This flagship branch of Palma's biggest department store sells clothes, cosmetics, homewares and accessories, and tickets to local shows and events. There's also a smaller store in Palma.

Mimbreria Vidal
ARTS & CRAFTS

(Map p60; ☑971 71 12 43; Carrer de Cordería 13; ☺9.30am-1.30pm & 4.30-8pm Mon-Sat) This sprawling shop showcases wickerwork, much of it made in Mallorca as well as in mainland Spain. There are mats, baskets, hats and smaller decorative items that may just fit in your hand luggage.

Dialog
BOOKS

(Map p60; ☑971 66 63 31; www.dialog-palma.com; Carrer de Santa Magdalena 3; ☺11am-2pm & 4.30-8pm Mon-Fri, 10am-2pm Sat) The selection of German- and English-language books here is small but very carefully chosen, with especially good sections on languages and books about Mallorca.

🏠 Es Puig de Sant Pere

Camper
SHOES

(Map p60; ☑971 71 46 35; www.camper.com; Avinguda de Jaume III 5; ☺10am-8.30pm Mon-Sat, to 8pm Sun) Best known of Mallorca's famed shoe brands, funky, eco-chic Camper is now incredibly popular worldwide.

El Corte Inglés
DEPARTMENT STORE

(Map p60; ☑971 77 01 77; www.elcorteingles.es; Avenida de Jaime III 15; ☺9.30am-9.30pm Mon-Sat, 11am-8.30pm Sun) This branch of the huge Spanish department store franchise is good for getting many things under one roof.

🏠 Santa Catalina & Around

★Magatzem de Santa Catalina
SHOES

(Map p56; ☑606 40 29 40; Plaça Navegació 2; ☺10am-3pm Mon-Sat) Master shoemaker Domingo Moya makes the most wonderful espadrilles, that Mallorcan summer sandal classic, with several styles to choose from. Prices start at around €26.

B Connected Concept Store
HOMEWARES

(Map p56; ☑971 28 21 95; www.bconnected-conceptstore.com; Carrer de Dameto 6; ☺10am-2.30pm & 5-9pm Mon-Fri, 10am-3pm Sat) Part of a

---

FLEA MARKETS

Flea markets, speciality markets and artisan markets abound in Palma. For handicrafts, head to the **Plaça Major Artisan Market** (Map p60; Plaça Major; ☺10am-2pm daily Jul-Sep, Mon, Tue, Fri & Sat Feb-Jun & Oct-Dec, Fri & Sat Jan & Feb) or the street-long summer **craft market** (Map p60; Passeig de Sagrera, La Llonja; ☺10.30am-1.30pm & 5.30-11pm Tue-Sun May-Sep) near La Llonja. A sprawling **flea market** (Map p56; Avinguda de Gabriel Alomar & Avinguda de Villalonga; ☺8am-2pm Sat) takes over the *avingudes* east of the city centre each Saturday. The Christmas Market (p72) takes over the Plaça Major from 16 December to 5 January.

---

local cluster of B Connected stores focusing on various facets of stylish living, this designer 'concept' store is very much at home in Santa Catalina. Dedicated to homewares and interior design, it sells all sorts of knick-knacks that you never knew you needed. The look is generally contemporary with the occasional retro touch.

ℹ Information

SAFE TRAVEL

➡ In general, Palma is a safe city. The main concern is petty theft – pickpockets and bag snatchers.

➡ Some streets are best avoided at night, when the occasional dodgy character comes out to play; if you're alone after dark, perhaps avoid Plaça de Sant Antoni and nearby avenues, such as Avinguda de Villalonga and Avinguda d'Alexandre Rosselló. But really, the risks are very slight.

EMERGENCY

Ambulance	☑061
Country code	☑+34
General EU Emergency Number	☑112
Policía Local	☑092 (emergency), ☑971 22 55 00
Policía Nacional	☑091 (emergency), ☑71 22 55 00

MEDIA
Foreign-language newspapers include the following:

→ *Daily Bulletin* (www.majorcadailybulletin.es) English-language paper established in 1962.

→ *The Olive Press* (www.theolivepress.es) English-language paper covering local and national Spanish news.

→ *Mallorca Magazin* (www.mallorcamagazin.net) A substantial German-language weekly.

→ *Mallorca Zeitung* (www.mallorcazeitung.es) A German-language weekly.

For an idea of what's on, look for free printed listings in tourist offices and bars:

→ *Youthing* (www.youthing.es) Published fortnightly.

→ *Dígame* (www.digamemallorca.com) A monthly island-wide round-up of events, activities and up-to-date listings.

→ See Mallorca (www.seemallorca.com) A useful online-only source of events and listings.

Palma has a growing field of glossy mags and lifestyle websites, in English and German:

→ *abcmallorca* (www.abc-mallorca.com) Free, with articles on the city and island.

→ Anglo Info (www.angloinfo.com) This website has a forum, events listings and a directory of English-speaking businesses.

→ *Mallorca Geht Aus!* (www.mallorca-geht-aus. de) Published annually (€10) and also available in Germany, Austria, Switzerland and online, this glossy has more than 200 pages of stories and reviews of anything from *fincas* (rural estates) to clubs.

MEDICAL SERVICES

In the main newspapers (such as the *Diario de Mallorca*) you will find a list of pharmacies open late.

Farmácia Castañer-Buades (☑ 971 07 06 35; Plaça del Rei Joan Carles I 3; ⊙ 8.30am-10.30pm)

Farmácia Salvà Saz (☑ 971 45 87 88; Carrer de Balanguera 15; ⊙ 24hr)

Hospital Universitari Son Espases (☑ 871 20 50 00; www.hospitalsonespases.es; Carretera de Valldemossa 79) Situated 4km north of town, this hospital is best reached with bus lines 20, 29, 33 and 34.

TOURIST INFORMATION

Airport Tourist Office (☑ 971 78 95 56; www. visitpalma.com; Aeroport de Palma; ⊙ 8am-8pm Mon-Sat, to 2pm Sun) Has a lot of useful information about the city, as well as a good map.

Ben Amics (☑ 871 96 54 66; www.benamics. com; Carrer del General Riera 3; ⊙ 9am-3pm) Ben Amics is the island's umbrella association for gays, lesbians and transsexuals. There's also a bookable advice service at the office.

Consell de Mallorca Tourist Office (Map p60; ☑ 971 17 39 90; www.infomallorca.net; Plaça

de la Reina 2, Palma de Mallorca; ⊙ 8.30am-8pm Mon-Fri, to 3pm Sat; ☎) The provincial tourist office can help with information about the island, as well as provide maps.

Oficinas del Parque Nacional Marítimo y Terrestre de Cabrera (☑ 971 17 76 45; http://en.balearsnatura.com; Carrer Gremí de Corredors 10, Palma de Mallorca; ⊙ 11am-3pm Mon-Fri) Can help with information and permits for visiting the Parc Nacional Marítim-Terrestre de l'Arxipèlag de Cabrera (p173).

Parc de ses Estacions Tourist Office (Map p56; ☑ 902 102365; www.infomallorca.net; Plaça d'Espanya; ⊙ 9am-8pm) A small tourist office conveniently located near the train and bus stations.

USEFUL WEBSITES

City of Palma Tourist Site (www.visitpalma. com) The city's main tourist portal.

Empresa Municipal de Transports Urbans de Palma de Mallorca (www.emtpalma.es) Palma's public transport corporation.

Federación Empresarial Hotelera de Mallorca (www.fehm.info) Has hotel and general information for Palma de Mallorca.

Getting There & Away

AIR

Palma de Mallorca Airport (PMI; ☑ 902 404704; www.aena-aeropuertos.es) lies 8km east of the city and receives an impressive level of traffic. Sometimes referred to as Son Sant Joan Airport, it's Spain's third largest, with direct services to 105 European and North African cities.

BOAT

Palma is the island's main port. There are numerous boat services (p209) to/from Mallorca's Estació Marítima from mainland Spain and the other islands of the Balearics. Palma is also becoming increasingly (and somewhat controversially) popular as a cruise-liner destination (p54).

BUS

All island buses to/from Palma depart from (or near) the Estació Intermodal de Palma (p210). Services head in all directions, including Valldemossa (€2, 30 minutes, up to 17 daily), Sóller (€2.45 to €3.90, 45 minutes, regular daily), Pollença (€5.50, 45 to 60 minutes, up to 14 daily) and Alcúdia (€5.45, one hour, up to 18 daily). All other significant coastal and inland centres are connected to Palma by usually frequent services (although some are served instead by one of the island's three train lines).

THE SLOW TRAIN TO SÓLLER

Welcome to one of the most rewarding excursions in Mallorca. Since 1912 a narrow-gauge train has trundled along the winding 27.3km route north to Sóller (p108). The train, which originally replaced a stagecoach service, departs from Plaça de l'Estació seven times a day (five times from November to February) and takes about 1¼ hours, with between four and five return trains daily. The route passes through ever-changing countryside that becomes dramatic in the north as it crosses the 496m-high Serra de Alfàbia, via 13 tunnels (some over 2km long) and a series of bridges and viaducts.

The train initially rolls through the streets of Palma, but within 20 minutes you're in the countryside. At this stage the view is better to the left, towards the Serra de Tramuntana. The terrain starts to rise gently and to the left the eye sweeps over olive gardens, the occasional sandy-coloured house and the mountains beyond. Half an hour out of Palma you call in at Bunyola (an alternative boarding place that costs just €9/15 single/return from Palma or Sóller).

Shortly after Bunyola, as the mountains close in (at one point you can see Palma and the sea behind you), you reach the first of a series of tunnels. Some trains stop briefly at a marvellous lookout point, the **Mirador Pujol de'n Banya**, shortly after the **Túnel Major** (Main Tunnel; which is almost 3km long and took three years to carve out of the rock in 1907–10). The view stretches out over the entire Sóller valley. From there, the train rattles across a viaduct before entering another tunnel that makes a slow 180-degree turn on its descent into Sóller, whose station building is housed in an early-17th-century mansion. Return tickets are valid for two weeks.

TRAIN

The **Ferrocarril de Sóller** (Sóller Railway; 971 75 20 51; www.trendesoller.com; Carrer Eusebio Estada 1; single/return €25/50; 10.10am-7.40pm Apr-Oct, 10.30am-6pm Nov-Mar;) is a popular heritage railway running from the old station on Carrer Eusebio Estada, next to Palma's Estació Intermodal (p210), to the northwestern town of Sóller, stopping en route at Bunyola. The Estació Intermodal itself is the terminus for Mallorca's three regular lines: the T1 (to Inca; €3.15, 25 to 40 minutes), the T2 (Sa Pobla; €3.75, one hour) and the T3 (Manacor; €3.44, 55 minutes). Services start at 5.45am and finish at 10.20pm on weekdays.

Make sure your service isn't an express bypassing the station you want; look for the bike symbol that indicates a peak service on which you can't bring your bike; and be aware that some trains require you to transfer at Enllaç. The T1 to Inca doesn't run on weekends, as the T2 and T3 both stop there anyway, and there are no express services.

Getting Around

TO/FROM THE AIRPORT

Bus 1 runs around every nine minutes from the airport to Plaça d'Espanya/Estació Intermodal de Palma in central Palma (€5, 20 minutes) and on to the entrance of the ferry terminal. It makes several stops along the way, entering the heart of the city along Avinguda de Gabriel Alomar i Villalonga, skirting around the city centre and then running back to the coast along Passeig de Mallorca and Avinguda d'Argentina. It heads along Avinguda de Gabriel Roca (aka Passeig Marítim) to reach the Estació Marítima (Ferry Port) before turning around. Buy tickets from the driver.

Taxis are generally clean, honest and abundant (when not striking), and the ride from the airport to central Palma will cost around €19 to €22.

TO/FROM THE FERRY PORT

Bus 1 (the airport bus) runs every 15 minutes from the **Estació Marítima** (Ferry Port) across town (via Plaça d'Espanya/Estació Intermodal de Palma) and on to the airport. A taxi from/to the city centre will cost around €10 to €12.

BUS

There are 29 local bus services around Palma and its bay suburbs run by **EMT** (971 21 44 44; www.emtpalma.es). These include line 1 between the airport and port (€5), and line 23 serving Palma–S'Arenal–Cala Blava via Aqualand. Single-trip tickets on lines other than those to the airport and port cost €2, or you can buy a 10-trip card for €15.

BICYCLE

For details on bike rental in Palma, see the special section (p70).

CAR & MOTORCYCLE

Parking in the city centre can be complicated. Most streets in the Old Town are limited to residents or are pedestrian only and most of the

LAZY DAYS

It has to be the quintessential combo – sunshine, sea and sand. And Mallorca offers this beachlife in buckets and spades, especially around the capital, Palma, where the choices vary from secluded coves to family geared strips of sand with seaports, sunbeds and ice-cold cerveza (beer).

QUIET COVES & BEACHES

Despite the sheer numbers of tourists that come to the coast, there remain beaches where you can snooze under your Panama lulled only by the sound of seagulls and surf. Head to the less developed south for beaches like **Platja des Trenc** (p171), which is mixed nudist and clothed, and **Cala Pi** (p170). Rocky footpaths connect the pretty cove of **Cala Mondragó** (p176) to a string of quiet coves in the **Parc Natural de Mondragó** (p176) while, at the other end of the island, **Platja des Coll Baix** (p136) is hidden beneath sheer wooded cliffs and only accessible by boat or foot, which means this gleaming crescent of pearl-white sand is seldom busy.

FAMILY BEACHES WITH GOOD FACILITIES

A family day on the beach generally goes a lot smoother if food, drink, ice cream (and toilets) are all close by. East of Palma, **Cala Estancia** (p88) and **Cala Major** (p90) are both family-friendly options while, in the north, low-key **Port de Pollença** (p130) boasts a wide sandy strip with shallow waters ideal for paddling tots plus plenty of facilities nearby. In the Port de Sóller, **Platja d'en Repic** (p113) is just far enough away from the hordes of passers by, yet still close to cafes and the possibility of boat rides.

1. Cala Pi (p170)
2. Cave at Platja des Coll Baix (p136)
3. Platja de Palma, Ca'n Pastilla (p88)

WORTH A TRIP

CALA BLAVA
....

Despite being within whistling distance of the beer gardens of the Platja de Palma, Cala Blava (population 339) is altogether different: it's residential rather than nakedly touristic, and offers a few quiet coves (several rocky; one sandy) to test the waters. It's really absurdly close to the hubbub of S'Arenal – only a few kilometres south on the Ma6014, then a short side road to Cala Blava. Just beyond is Bella Vista: part of the coast here is protected, and off-limits, but you can still slip down to the **Calò des Cap d'Alt** for a swim in crystal-clear waters. Bus 23 from Plaça d'Espanya to S'Arenal continues on to Cala Blava, but only every two hours (€2).

---

remainder, including the ring roads (the *avingudes*, or *avenidas*) around the centre, are either no-parking zones or metered parking. Metered areas are marked in blue and generally you can park for up to two hours (€2.50), although time limits and prices can vary. The meters generally operate from 9am to 2pm and 4.30pm to 8pm Monday to Friday, and 9am to 2pm on Saturday.

Rent one of Mallorca Vintage's Vespas or Ducatis to zip around town or across the island from **Mallorca Vintage Motors** (☑620 476285; www.mallorcavintage.com; Plaça Espanya; ☺9am-7pm). A day's high-season rental is €38 for a scooter, and €98 for a Ducati, including two helmets and insurance. It's located on the underground level of the train station; luggage can be left at the affiliated **Palma Lock & Go** (☑971 71 64 17; www.palmalockandgo.com; Estación Intermodal de Palma, Plaça d'Espanya; large bag per day €5.90; ☺9am-8pm Apr-Oct, 9.30am-7pm Nov-Mar), and there's another **branch** (Plaza de Porta de Santa Catalina 5; ☺9am-7pm) near Es Baluard museum.

METRO
Of limited use to most travellers, a metro line operates from Plaça d'Espanya to the Universidad de las Islas Baleares (UIB; the city's university). Single trips cost from €1.60.

TAXI
For a taxi, call 971 40 14 14. For special taxis for people with disability, call 971 70 35 29.

Taxis are metered, but for trips beyond the city fix the price in advance. A green light indicates a taxi is free to hail or you can head for one of the taxi stands in the city centre, such as those on

Passeig d'es Born. Flagfall is €2.45, thereafter you pay €1.05 per kilometre (more on weekends and holidays). There's a minimum fare from the airport of €19, and a supplement to visit Castell de Bellver.

BADIA DE PALMA

The broad Badia de Palma (Bay of Palma) stretches east and west away from the city centre. Some of the island's densest holiday development is to be found on both sides, but the beaches, especially to the west, are quite striking, in spite of the dense cement backdrop. The beaches are mostly very clean, but get very crowded (with very different crowds) in peak periods. Further south the coast quietens considerably before rounding Cap de Cala Figuera.

East of Palma

On the east side of the bay, vast neon *bier kellers* and German-language menus alert you to which Western European nation's young choose to let their hair down here. A couple of nearby escape hatches allow respite from the madding crowds.

Ca'n Pastilla
POP 5125

In the shadow of the airport, heavily built-up Ca'n Pastilla is where Palma's eastern package-holiday coast begins. The Platja de Ca'n Pastilla marks the western and windier end of the 4.5km stretch of beach known as **Platja de Palma** (the windsurfing here can be good). Just west of Ca'n Pastilla is the pleasant **Cala Estancia**, a placid inlet whose beach is perfect for families. The waterfront, with a broad pedestrian walkway traversed by bikes, tourist trains and the odd Segway, is backed by thick midrise developments of hotels, eateries, cafes and bars.

◉ Sights & Activities

Palma Aquarium   AQUARIUM
(☑902 70 29 02; www.palmaaquarium.com; Carrer de Manuela de los Herreros i Sorà 21; adult/child €22.50/14; ☺9.30am-5pm May-Sep, shorter hours Oct-Apr; ⊕) Marine research, conservation and preservation programs offset any animal-welfare qualms you may have visiting the excellent Palma Aquarium. Five million litres of salt water fill the 55 tanks, home to sea critters from the Mediterranean (rays, sea horses, coral and more) and

faraway oceans. The central tank, which you walk through via a transparent tunnel, is patrolled by 20 sleek sharks, with which you can dive for €175. You could spend half a day here.

In total some 8000 specimens are found here ranging across a number of marine environments, with some stirring exhibits covering the threat to world tuna stocks. If the kids fancy spending the night, the monthly Friday shark sleepover will certainly crank up the fear factor for little nippers.

Attraction　　　　　　　　　　BOATING
(☑971 74 61 01; www.attractioncatamarans.com; Carrer de Nanses; adult/child €55/49; ⊘mid-Apr–Sep) Attraction arranges five-hour trips on a 24m catamaran around the Badia de Palma, taking in caves and bathing spots and including a paella lunch. The boarding point in Ca'n Pastilla is Carrer Nanses, and either daytime or sunset cruises are on offer.

Segway Palma　　　　　　　　　　TOURS
(☑971 49 19 15; www.segwaypalma.com; Carretera del Arenal 9; 1-/2-/3-hr tours €40/75/110; ⊘9.30am-6pm) See the city by Segway (zippy battery-powered two-wheel scooters), with one-hour beach tours, two-hour tours to Es Portixol and three-hour excursions that go to the cathedral and back to Platja de Palma.

🍃 Courses

Soqueta　　　　　　　　　　COOKING
(☑660 628430; www.soqueta.com; Carrer Gabriel Comas 20; €79; ⊘10am-3pm) Paula is the enthusiastic teacher here who will teach you to prepare traditional recipes covering a three-course meal, using local produce bought at the market. Participants will sample their fare and taste local wines.

🍷 Drinking & Nightlife

A predominantly German crowd pours into Ca'n Pastilla for endless drinking and deafening music, a phenomenon known as Ballermann. The action centres on enormous beer gardens around Carrer del Pare Bartomeu Salvà (aka Schinkenstrasse) and about three-quarters of the way along the beach east towards S'Arenal.

Puro Beach　　　　　　　　　　LOUNGE
(☑971 74 47 44; www.purobeach.com; ⊘10am-10pm May-Aug, to sunset Mar, Apr & Sep-Nov; 🛜)

The pure-white beach bar carries more than a hint of Ibiza with a tapering outdoor promontory over the water that's perfect for sunset cocktails, DJ sessions and open-air spa treatments. Most of the toned, bronzed bods here wear white to blend in with the slinky decor – it's that kind of place.

Our tip: go for a drink or two and skip the sky-high-priced fusion food. It's a two-minute walk east of Cala Estancia.

❶ Getting There & Away

Bus 23 runs from Plaça d'Espanya to Ca'n Pastilla and parallel to Platja de Palma through S'Arenal and on to Aqualand. Buses run every half-hour or so and once every two hours they continue on to Cala Blava. Bus 15 runs from Plaça de la Reina and passes through Plaça d'Espanya on its way to S'Arenal every 10 minutes. For the Aquarium, get off at 366 (Ses Fontanelles).

S'Arenal

POP 6599

S'Arenal has so long been a favourite destination of young sunseekers, especially German ones, that its portion of the lengthy, broad Platja de Palma has been entirely developed. The hotels, bars, souvenir shops and kebab joints now spread several blocks back from the shore, for kilometres in each direction. Of course, that means there's lots of fun to be had by the young and feckless, and only the most curmudgeonly would deny that this is one of Mallorca's liveliest spots.

Aqualand　　　　　　　　　　AMUSEMENT PARK
(☑971 44 00 00; www.aqualand.es; Ma6014; adult/child €30/21; ⊘10am-6pm Jul & Aug, to 5pm mid-May–Jun, Sep & Oct; 🅿🚼; 🚍23) With 12 rides and pools, Mallorca's largest water park has plenty of splashy fun, including dedicated pools for tots, rapids, flumes and thrill-a-minute slides with names like anaconda, harakiri and kamikaze that leave little to the imagination. Parking is €4 and 'minis' (kids between three and 10) cost only €12.

❶ Getting There & Away

Buses 15 and 25 (express) run along Platja de Palma from Palma's Plaça de la Reina to S'Arenal; bus 21 runs between S'Arenal and the airport; and bus 23 links Cala Blava and S'Arenal with Plaça d'Espanya. A single trip is €2, unless it's to the airport, in which case it's €5.

West of Palma

Cala Major

POP 5633

Cala Major, a once-fashionable resort about 4km southwest of the city centre, boasts a pretty, rock-sheltered beach, and is the first of the coves that spread south from Palma, down the western shore of the Badia. It's quiet and residential in comparison to what lies further down the Ma1, but there are still plenty of midrise hotels, cafes, restaurants and clubs packed in between the hills and the beach.

Aside from the beach, the main attraction here is the wonderful Fundació Pilar i Joan Miró, inland and uphill from the waterfront.

Avinguda de Joan Miró, the main coastal road, has the most eating options.

★**Fundació Pilar i Joan Miró**　　MUSEUM
(☑971 70 14 20; http://miro.palma.cat; Carrer de Saridakis 29; adult/child €7.50/free; ☉10am-7pm Tue-Sat, to 3pm Sun mid-May–mid-Sep, to 6pm mid-Sep–mid-May; ℗) The Catalan artist Joan Miró lived and worked at this beautiful hilltop compound, now a major museum celebrating his life and work. Miró's friend, the architect Josep Lluís Sert, designed the studio space (much of which is preserved as it was during his working life) while the major exhibition space was designed by top Spanish architect Rafael Moneo, in 1992. With more than 2500 works by Miró (including sculpture, sketches and 118 paintings), it's a major collection.

No doubt influenced by his Mallorcan wife and mother, Miró moved to Palma in 1956 and remained here until his death in 1983.

A selection of his works hangs in the Sala Estrella, an angular, jagged part of Moneo's creation that is the architect's take on the artist's work. The rest of the building's exhibition space is used for temporary shows. Miró sculptures are scattered about outside. Beyond the studio is **Son Boter**, an 18th-century farmhouse Miró bought to increase his privacy. Inside, giant scribblings on the whitewashed walls served as plans for some of his bronze sculptures.

Guided 45-minute tours in English take place every Tuesday and Friday at 12.30pm costing an additional €1. Reserve via the website.

Il Paradiso　　EUROPEAN €€€
(☑971 10 33 79; www.ilparadiso.es; Avinguda de Joan Miró 243; mains €25-36; ☉12.30-4pm & 6pm-midnight; ℗🐾) Priceless views across the Badia de Palma are not the only forte of this slick beachside restaurant. The long list of pastas, including penne with scampi in saffron sauce and *spaghetti al pescatore*, suggests an Italian hand in the kitchen, but it's the simple seafood, perhaps grilled red tuna, or hake with broccoli and new potatoes, that really shines.

❶ Getting There & Away

From Palma take bus 3 or 46 (from Plaça d'Espanya) or bus 20 (from Plaça del Mercat) to get here (all fares €2).

Gènova

POP 3962

Most visitors to Palma come up to Gènova, around 1km north of Cala Major, to visit the closest caves to the capital, the Coves de Gènova. Aside from views, and some good Mallorcan restaurants, there probably isn't much else to tempt travellers. If you have wheels, follow the signs to **Na Burguesa** off the main road from the centre of Gènova (a short way north of the Coves turn-off). About 1.5km of winding, poor road takes you past the walled-in pleasure domes of the rich to reach a rather ugly monument to the Virgin Mary, from where you have sweeping views over the city (this is about the only way to look down on the Castell de Bellver) and bay.

Coves de Gènova　　CAVE
(☑971 40 23 87; www.covesdegenova.com; Carrer d'es Barranc 45; adult/child €10/5; ☉10am-5.45pm; ℗) Discovered in 1906, these caves are worth visiting, their chambers dripping with curlicued stalactites and studded with pinnacled stalagmites. You descend 36m, and see all sorts of fanciful, backlit shapes. The temperature is always around 20°C in the caves, where water has been dripping for many millennia to create these natural 'sculptures'. Take bus 46 from Palma (€2, 40 minutes, every 30 minutes), with a stop at Cala Major.

Mesón Ca'n Pedro　　MALLORCAN €€
(☑971 70 21 62; www.canpedro.es; Carrer del Rector Vives 14; mains €16-20; ☉12.30pm-12.30am) One of Gènova's best, hearty, traditional Mallorcan restaurants is Mesón Ca'n Pedro,

famous for its *frit mallorquí* (a lamb, liver and vegetable hash) snails and *pa amb oli* (bread rubbed with oil, garlic and super-fresh tomato). Running since 1976, it's a local favourite, with a terrace that's packed with *palmeros* when it's warm.

Casa Jacinto
MALLORCAN €€

(☑971 40 18 58; www.casajacinto.es; Camí de la Tramvía 37; mains €14-20, menús €15-22; ☺1-5pm & 7pm-12.30am; P) A classic family-run restaurant since the 1980s, this huge and no-nonsense eatery attracts Mallorcans from far and wide for copious servings of mainland Spanish and local food, especially grilled meats, including game cuts such as venison and wild boar. Vegetarians may go hungry. It has the added perk of private parking.

ⓘ Getting There & Away

Bus 46 runs from Carrer del Sindicat, on the eastern edge of Old Palma, to Gènova (€2, every 20 to 40 minutes).

Ses Illetes & Portals Nous

Ses Illetes (population 3209) and Portals Nous (population 2356) lie between narrow, picturesque coves and steep pine-stubbled hills. Together they comprise an upmarket holiday-residential zone and perhaps the most appealing stretch of the Badia de Palma. The coast is high and drops quite abruptly to the turquoise coves, principally Platja de Ses Illetes and, a little less crowded, Platja de Sa Comtesa. Parking is a minor hassle.

Virtually part of Ses Illetes is **Bendinat** (which takes its name from a nearby, neo-Gothic reworking of a 13th-century castle original that can only be seen from the Ma1 motorway). Next up is Portals Nous, with its super marina for the super yachts of the super rich at restaurant-lined **Puerto Portals**. The beach that stretches north of the marina is longer and broader than that in Ses Illetes.

Restaurante Illetas Playa
MALLORCAN €€

(☑971 70 18 96; www.illetasplaya.es; Passeig d'Illetes 75, Ses Illetas; mains €16-18; ☺1-3.30pm & 7-11.30pm Thu-Mon, 7-11.30pm Wed) With a plumb spot, overlooking the beach, this slightly old-fashioned Mallorcan restaurant is a welcome alternative to the glitz that dominates this part of the bay. It's not humble, but it isn't exorbitantly fancy either:

ideal if you feel like just-so grilled squid, or lamb shoulder roasted to tender perfection. The paella also receives a thumbs up from readers.

Roxy Beach Bar
BAR

(☑696 062831; Portals Nous; ☺10am-10pm Apr-Sep) You will build up a thirst just getting here (unless via private yacht). This bar is on a rocky headland at the far east end of the main beach; you have to clamber over rocks or climb down steep steps from Portals Nous town. With a terrace located right at edge of the sea, the views are blissful, especially at sunset.

They also serve reasonable food (as in price and quality). Note that this bar is not recommended for young children due to the sheer drop to the sea from the terrace.

ⓘ Getting There & Away

Local Palma bus 3 reaches Ses Illetes from central Palma (€2, 30 minutes, more than 15 daily); you can pick it up on Passeig de la Rambla or Avinguda de Jaume III). Buses 103, 104, 106 and 111 from Palma's bus station call in at Portals Nous (€2, 30 to 50 minutes, frequent).

Palmanova & Magaluf

About 2km southwest from Portals Nous' elite yacht harbour is a whole other world. Palmanova (population 6577) and Magaluf (population 4288) have merged to form what is the epitome of the sea, sand, sunburn, sangria and shagging resort that has unfairly coloured perceptions of Mallorca in general. But the real Wild West days are substantially over: civic investment and public order laws have managed to rein in the worst of the bacchanalian behaviour.

If you crave peace, head south of Magaluf to explore a couple of pretty *calas* (coves). **Cala Vinyes** has placid water, and the sand stretches inland among residential buildings. The next cove, Cala de Cap Falcó, is an emerald lick of an inlet surrounded by tree-covered rocky coast. Unfortunately, developers are getting closer and closer. Follow signs south for Sol de Mallorca and then the signs for each of these locations. Bus 107 from Palma reaches Cala Vinyes via Magaluf (€3.90, one hour, nine daily).

◉ Sights & Activities

There is a reason for Palmanova's and Magaluf's popularity: the four main beaches between Palmanova and Magaluf are broad,

PALMA & THE BADIA DE PALMA WEST OF PALMA

beautiful and immaculately maintained. The lavish sweeps of fine white sand, in parts shaded by strategically planted pines and palms, are undeniably tempting. And, to be fair, the development behind them could be considerably worse.

Western Water Park AMUSEMENT PARK
(☑ 971 13 12 03; www.westernpark.com; Carretera de Cala Figuera a Sa Porrasa, Magaluf; adult/child €30/21; ⊙ 10am-6pm Jul & Aug, to 5pm May, Jun & Sep; ℗ ⛲) This is the bucking bronco of Magaluf water parks, with wave pools and slides such as the Tijuana Twins, the Boomerang and the Beast, with a near-vertical 30m drop. There are quieter rides and pools for kids and the less adrenaline-addicted. 'Minis' (three- to four-year-olds) are charged €12 admission.

Big Blue Diving DIVING
(☑ 971 68 16 86; www.bigbluediving-mallorca.net; Carrer de Martí Ros García 6, Palmanova; snorkelling per person €39, 1-/2-dive package with equipment €73/93; ⊙ Apr-Oct) The first freediving outfit on Mallorca, this well-run dive centre right on Palmanova beach offers the whole array of PADI courses. Scuba and open water courses for beginners are €269 and €399 respectively.

Cruceros Costa de Calvià BOATING
(☑ 971 13 12 11; www.boattour.es; Avinguda de Magaluf 10, Magaluf; ⊙ 11am, 1pm & 3pm Mon-Fri, 11am & 3pm Sat & Sun May-Oct; ⛲) This operator offers two-hour boat trips in a glass-bottomed boat, with a chance of seeing dolphins (adult/child €21/10). There's also speed boat trips (€26/15), waterborne Palma city tours (€30/16) and day-long sea cruises (€38/20). It departs from the main beach in Magaluf, calling at Palmanova 15 minutes later.

Drinking & Nightlife

While restless young Germans party at the Platja de Palma's beer gardens, their British equivalents cut loose in the nightspots of Magaluf. This is big stag- and hen-night territory and the drinking antics of the Brits in Magaluf have become legendary (for the wrong reasons). In 2020, the regional government addressed the piss-up problem with several laws including banning organised pub crawls and happy hours, as well as a ban on party boats, alcohol vending machines, free bars and adverts for alcoholic drinks in both Magaluf and Playa de Palma. This is the first law of its kind in Europe to restrict the promotion and sale of alcohol in specific tourist areas.

Nikki Beach BAR
(☑ 971 12 39 62; https://mallorca.nikkibeach.com; Avenida Notario Alemany 1, Magaluf; ⊙ 11am-8pm late Apr-Sep; ☎) Sushi, champagne, plush white loungers, bronzed bods, DJ beats and summertime barbecues are what Magaluf-based Nikki Beach has to offer. There's also a yacht pickup service, should you require one.

Information

For hotel information try www.palmanova-magaluf.com, run by the local hoteliers' association.

Magaluf Tourist Office (☑ 971 13 11 26; www.visitcalvia.com; Carrer de Pere Vacquer Ramis 1, Magaluf; ⊙ 9am-6pm) Open year-round.

Palmanova Tourist Office (☑ 971 68 23 65; www.visitcalvia.com; Passeig de la Mar 13, Palmanova; ⊙ 9am-6pm Apr-Oct, to 2pm Nov-Mar)

❶ Getting There & Away

Buses 104, 106 and 107 connect Palma with Palmanova/Magaluf (€3.10, 50 minutes).

Western Mallorca

Best Places to Eat

➡ Trespaís (p99)

➡ Es Verger (p117)

➡ Molón (p115)

➡ Béns d'Avall (p111)

➡ QuitaPenas (p105)

Top Beaches

➡ Cala Blanca (p98)

➡ Cala Portals Vells (p100)

➡ Cala Banyalbufar (p102)

➡ Platja d'en Repic (p113)

Why Go?

'A sky like turquoise, a sea like lapis lazuli, mountains like emerald, air like heaven', enthused Romantic composer Chopin of his new home Valldemossa in 1838. His words ring true almost two centuries later in western Mallorca.

The Serra de Tramuntana range ripples all along the west coast, surveying the Mediterranean from above. Skirted by olive groves and pine forest, its razorback limestone mountains plunge 1000m down to the sea like the ramparts of some epic island fortress. Whether you hike their highland trails, bike their serpentine roads and steep inclines, or breeze along the cliff-flanked coastline by boat, these mountains will sweep you off your feet with their beauty and drama.

When to Go

Spring and autumn are peak season for cyclists in the Tramuntana, but otherwise you'll have its gorgeous coves, trails and flower-flecked heights pretty much to yourself. Most hotels and restaurants open Easter to October. In summer, coastal resorts and villages are full to bursting point, but vast expanses of wilderness mean you can always find a quiet retreat, be it a *finca* (farmhouse), castle or monastery. The festival season gets into full swing as the heat rises: both Deià and Valldemossa host classical musical concerts in summer. True pilgrims walk through the night from Palma to Lluc in August.

Western Mallorca Highlights

1 Deià (p107) Relishing the poetic loveliness of the winner in Mallorca's hill-town beauty pageant.

2 Monestir de Lluc (p118) Driving the length of the coast from seaside Port d'Andratx to this peaceful monastery.

3 Valldemossa (p103) Listening to Chopin on your iPod as you wander through narrow lanes.

4 Biniaraix (p114) Walking through citrus, almond and olive groves to this cute-as-a-button town.

5 Sóller (p108) Finding vintage trains, Miró and Modernista flair in the island's zesty orange capital.

6 Sa Calobra (p117) Feeling your heart do somersaults as you drive the snaking road.

7 Castell d'Alaró (p117) Climbing to the impregnable fortress ruins.

8 Illa de Sa Dragonera (p99) Diving the transparent depths.

9 Sa Foradada (p106) Wandering the coast as the setting sun paints the Mediterranean in aquarelles.

10 Cala Llamp (p98) Savouring this stunning cove round the headland from Port d'Andratx.

BALEARIC SEA

0 — 10 km
0 — 5 miles

Valle
Port
Canc

Cala Banyalbufar
Torre des Verger
Banyalbufar
Ma1

Esp

Cala d'Estellencs
Estellencs
Ma1101

Mirador de Ricardo Roca
S e r r a   d e   T r a m u n t a n a
Puigpun
Ma1041

Cala d'En Basset
Puig Galatzó (1025m)
Galilea

Illa de Sa Dragonera
Illa Es Pantaleu
Sant Elm
S'Arracó
Ma10
Es Capdellà
Calvià

Cala es Conills
Andratx

Port d'Andratx
Es Camp de Mar
Costa d'en Blanes

Cap de Sa Mola
10
Cala Blanca
Cala Fornells
Peguera
Costa de Sa Calma
Ma1
Be

Cala Llamp
Cap des Llamp
Magalu
Sa Porrassa
Cala Vi

Illa dels Conills
Illa Malgrat
Santa Ponça

Cap Negret
El Toro
Sol de Mallorca
Cala de Cap Falc

Cala de Penyes Rofjes
Portals Vells
Cala Portals

Illa del Toro
Cap de Cala Figuera

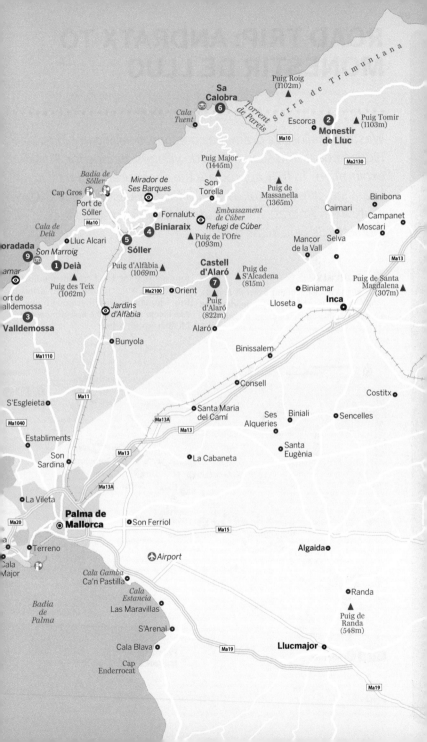

ROAD TRIP: ANDRATX TO MONESTIR DE LLUC

Western Mallorca's dramatic coastline, swelling uplands, hidden coves and scenic seaside villages are ripe for exploration. To fully appreciate the sheer drama of this coastline, hire a car (or bike) and take this astonishing 140km route from Andratx in the south to the pilgrimage site of Monestir de Lluc in the north.

❶ Andratx

Start at the ancient inland town of **Andratx** (p98), 4km north of harbourside **Port d'Andratx** (p98) and a relaxing inland base for exploring the coast and mountains. The road (Ma10, which forms the main artery for this trip) climbs steadily through pine forests before revealing the first glimpses of the Mediterranean below.

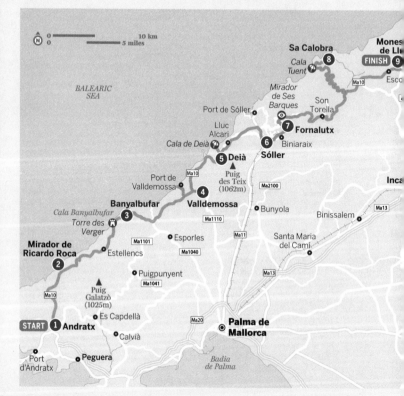

1 Day 140km

Great for... Outdoors, History & Culture

Best Time to Go: June to October

● ●

② Mirador de Ricardo Roca

About 14km from Andratx, pull into the parking lot opposite Restaurant El Grau and climb up to the Mirador de Ricardo Roca for some of the most extraordinary views anywhere along the west coast.

③ Banyalbufar

A further 4km on you pass through **Estellencs** (p101), a pretty village with stunning views of 1025m **Puig Galatzò** (p101). Continue 5km to the iconic **Torre des Verger** (p101), one of the Mediterranean's most dramatically sited watchtowers. The tower lies on the outskirts of **Banyalbufar** (p101), another charming clifftop coastal village, worth a stop for its attractive stone-walled farming terraces and local bodega. From here the road winds inland; at the road junction after 7km, take the narrow road north, which climbs through pine trees and boulders before crossing a high plateau.

④ Valldemossa

The main road heads towards Valldemossa, but before getting there take the turn-off west to **Port de Valldemossa** (p106), an exhilarating 5.5km descent down to the water's edge and a solitary seafood restaurant. Back on the main road it's only a further 1.5km to **Valldemossa** (p103), a worthwhile stopover at the halfway point of the route. The main attractions here are the striking **Real Cartuja de Valldemossa monastery** (p103) and a good supply of restaurants and bars.

⑤ Deià

It's another nine spectacular kilometres beyond the Valldemossa turn-off along the Ma10 to the romantic village of **Deià** (p107), surrounded by hills and shadowed by 1062m Puig des Teix. Don't miss the brief 3km detour down off the main road to **Cala de Deià** (p107), one of Mallorca's prettiest coves, with a lovely shingle surf beach and a popular bar-eatery. From the main road, the views of the tiny hamlet of Lluc Alcari, with its terracotta roofs and Mediterranean backdrop, are also exceptional.

⑥ Sóller

From Deià it's 10km to **Sóller** (p108), a valley town with a fabulous location deep in the Serra de Tramuntana. Stop in for a ride on the vintage **tram** (p112) or visit two of Mallorca's best art galleries, before rolling on to a pair of Mallorca's loveliest villages, Biniaraix and Fornalutx.

⑦ Fornalutx

It's about 7km from Sóller to Fornalutx, but don't miss the detour off the main Ma10 to the charming hamlet of **Biniaraix** (p114) – only 2km from Sóller so you could walk it – where the lovely town square has a single cafe and the village church. Continue on to the larger but still sweet stone-built village of **Fornalutx** (p115), with its postcard mountain views and photogenic town square. From Fornalutx, the Ma10 climbs sharply up to the viewpoint of **Mirador de Ses Barques** (p115), passing high-altitude lakes in the shadow of Mallorca's highest mountains. The vistas down the coast from the lookout are superb. By the time you reach the turn-off to Sa Calobra, the mountains appear bare and otherworldly.

⑧ Sa Calobra

One of the most exhilarating parts of the route is following the hair-raising 12km of hairpin bends down to the popular white-pebble cove of **Sa Calobra** (p118). On the way back, turn off and continue some 2km to the less-crowded but magical inlet of **Cala Tuent** (p118). After enjoying some time on the beach, wind back up to the main road and continue north to Monestir de Lluc.

⑨ Monestir de Lluc

Magnificently nestled in a valley overlooked by the mountains, **Monestir de Lluc** (p118), a huge monastery complex and place of pilgrimage, is the final stop on this road trip. Spend the afternoon exploring the cloistered gardens and museum before continuing on or heading south to Palma.

THE SOUTHWEST

Look beyond the occasional blip of tasteless development and you'll find a sprinkling of little-known treasures in Mallorca's southwest crook. Use Andratx, Port d'Andratx or Sant Elm as your springboard for day trips to the exquisite coves of Portals Vells or a boat trip over to Illa de Sa Dragonera. Activities on this stretch abound, with crystal-clear sea for all manner of water sports.

Andratx

POP 12,150

The largest town in southwest Mallorca, Andratx lies well inland (as a defensive measure against pirate attack), while its harbour, Port d'Andratx, is 4km away. Andratx has a low-key, untouristy vibe and makes a relaxed base for exploring the coast to the west and the mountains that spread to the northeast.

Castell de Son Mas　　　HISTORIC BUILDING
(Avinguda de la Cúria) The 16th-century Castell de Son Mas, on the hill at the northern end of town, is an elegant defensive palace that now houses the *ajuntament* (town hall), as well as the tourist office.

Església de Santa Maria d'Andratx　　CHURCH
(Carrer de General Bernat Riera; ⊙hours vary) This lovely church with its striking bell tower was built in the 18th century on the site of the original 1248 house of worship.

Bar Restaurante Sa Societat　　MALLORCAN €€
(☑971 23 65 66; Avinguda Juan Carlos I 2; mains €11-19, 2-course menú €9-16; ⊙1-4pm & 7.30-11pm Wed-Mon) For fine island fare in a time-warp atmosphere, Bar Restaurante Sa Societat has a courtyard out the back, or you can sit inside beneath exposed beams for *trampó* (tomato, pepper and onion salad), followed by paella, suckling pig with crackling or cod in an aioli crust.

ⓘ Information

Tourist Office (☑971 62 80 19; www.andratx. cat; Avinguda de la Cúria; ⊙10am-2pm Mon-Fri) Housed in the historical town hall at the northern end of town.

ⓘ Getting There & Away

Bus 102 operates a roughly hourly service daily between Palma and Andratx (€4.75, 65 minutes).

Port d'Andratx

POP 3150

Port d'Andratx surrounds a fine, long natural bay that attracts yachting fans from far and wide and moves to an international beat rather than a Mallorcan one. Bristling with art galleries, estate agents and restaurants, the town has an affluent air and a pleasant promenade for a walk and a waterfront meal.

◎ Sights & Activities

★**Cala Llamp**　　　　　　　　　　BEACH
What a difference a bay makes. Located 2km south of Port d'Andratx, beautiful Cala Llamp is where locals gravitate for silence and sparkling, bottle-green water. There's no sand, but you can lie on a shelf of rock that tilts gently into the sea. The scenery is lovely too, with rugged, pine-cloaked cliffs rearing like an amphitheatre around the crescent-shaped cove. It's around a 30-minute walk, or you can drive by taking the Ma1020 from Port d'Andratx and following the signs over the ridge.

Cala Blanca　　　　　　　　　　　BEACH
This very small cove, following a shallow curve down a dirt track from the car park above it, is all small pebbles, boulders and serene views. Pinched between the two jaws of the headland, it's only around 100m wide and sees few visitors, affording peace and quiet. Take the Ma1020 from Port d'Andratx towards Es Camp de Mar and look for the signs.

Llaüts　　　　　　　　　　　　　BOATING
(☑971 67 20 94; www.llauts.com; Carrer de San Carlos 6A; half day €120; ⊙Apr-Oct) A good place for boat rentals, Llaüts offers 4m crafts for those with no boat licence, with prices on request for more experienced boat users. Rates leap by about 10% in August. You'll find it southwest of the main waterfront restaurant strip; opening hours are prone to change, so call ahead.

Diving Dragonera　　　　　　　　DIVING
(☑971 67 43 76; www.aqua-mallorca-diving.com; Avinguda de l'Almirante Riera Alemany 23; 6-/10-dive package €210/340; ⊙8am-7pm mid-Mar–Oct) If you fancy exploring the underwater caves and wrecks around Port d'Andratx and Sa Dragonera, you can take the plunge with this friendly and popular German-run dive shop. It offers the whole shebang of PADI and SSI courses.

Eating

Restaurante El Coche SEAFOOD €€
(☑971 67 19 76; www.restaurantecoche.com; Avinguda de Mateu Bosch 13; mains €14-22; ☺1-3.30pm & 7-10.30pm Wed-Mon; ☎) A slightly classier option than many along the waterfront, refurbished El Coche has been going strong since 1977, outlasting most of the competition in the process. Dishes range from Mallorcan seafood classics like black paella with squid ink to those with a subtle twist, such as the sea bass with prawns and wild asparagus.

★**Trespaís** MODERN MEDITERRANEAN €€€
(☑971 67 28 14; www.trespais-mallorca.com; Carrer Antonio Callafat 24; mains €22-35; ☺6-11pm Tue-Sun; ☎) With its sleek monochrome interior and tree-rimmed patio all aglow with candles, Trespaís is a flicker of new-wave romance. Chef Domenico Curcio, with his Michelin-starred background, has made it the top table in town. Together with his wife, Jenny Terler, he assembles memorable dishes that play up integral flavours.

Drinking & Nightlife

Most of the harbourside restaurants morph into bars as the night wears on. Some reasonable choices can be found at the southwestern end of the strip, with the occasional DJ and live band.

Gran Folies Beach Club BAR
(www.beachclubgranfolies.com; Carrer de Congre 2, Cala Llamp; ☺10am-11.45pm May-Oct; ☎) This bar-restaurant sits right above the rocky cove of lovely Cala Llamp and offers use of a saltwater pool to cavort in between frozen margaritas. It also does breakfast, tapas and full meals and runs events from Mexican nights to G&T tastings. The views are fantastic and there's parking just up the road.

Tim's BAR
(Avinguda de l'Almirante Riera Alemany 7; ☺10am-late; ☎) One of the original bars in the marina, dating from the 70s, Tim's can stay open as late as 4am at the height of summer. It's a fine spot to sink a beer or toast the setting sun with a mojito. Live football is shown on the big screen, and there's music *en vivo* on Friday and Saturday nights.

ⓘ Information

Tourist Office (☑971 67 13 00; www.andratx. cat; Avinguda de Mateu Bosch; ☺9am-4pm Tue-Sat, 9.30am-2.30pm Sun) Well stocked tourist office.

ⓘ Getting There & Away

Most of the 102 buses from Palma continue from Andratx to the port (€1.50, 10 minutes). Bus 100 runs around six times a day between Andratx and Sant Elm (€2.20, 35 minutes), calling in at Port d'Andratx en route.

Sant Elm

POP 410

The narrow country Ma1030 road twists deep into pine forest from S'Arracó to emerge in Sant Elm. While it's by no means a secret, the relative remoteness of this beach resort has kept mass tourism at bay, and there's something magical about spending an evening watching the sun drop behind the silhouetted Illa de Sa Dragonera, knowing that the tip of the Serra de Tramuntana lies just around the bend.

◉ Sights & Activities

★**Illa de Sa Dragonera** ISLAND
The uninhabited 4km-long Illa de Sa Dragonera is a ripple of an island that stretches out like a slumbering dragon to the west of Sant Elm. Constituted as a natural park (Parc Natural de Sa Dragonera), the island is accessible by ferry, which lands at a protected natural harbour on the east side of the island. From there you can follow trails to the capes at either end or ascend the **Na Pòpia** peak (Puig des Far Vell, 352m).

Platja Sant Elm BEACH
(Ⓟ) Sant Elm's main town beach is a pleasant sandy strand that faces the gently lapping Mediterranean to the south. Within swimming distance for the moderately fit is **Illa Es Pantaleu**, a rocky islet that marks one of the boundaries of a marine reserve. To the south of Sant Elm's main beach is **Cala es Conills**, a sandless but pretty inlet (follow Carrer de Cala es Conills).

Keida ADVENTURE SPORTS
(☑971 23 91 24; www.keida.es; Plaça de na Caragola 3; ☺hours vary) Keida offers a huge array of activities, from guided hikes (from €45) to half-day boat excursions to Illa de Sa Dragonera (€45), and two-hour paddle-surfing courses (€45). You can also hire a bike (one day €35) or a kayak (half/full day €35/45) here.

Scuba Activa
DIVING, SNORKELLING

(☑971 23 91 02; www.scuba-activa.com; Plaça de Mossèn Sebastià Grau 7; dive incl equipment from €39; ⊙9am-6pm Apr-Oct) This well run dive centre takes you into the depths of the brilliantly clear waters around Illa de Sa Dragonera, among Mallorca's best for scuba diving, with equipment rental and a full range of courses. It also runs one-hour snorkelling trips (€38).

🍴 Eating

There is a large choice of restaurants, cafes and bars right down by the harbour and along Avinguda Jaume I.

⭐ Es Molí
MEDITERRANEAN €€

(☑971 23 92 02; http://esmoli.cat; Plaça de Mossèn Sebastià Grau 2; mains €14.50-21; ⊙1-4pm & 6.30-10pm Apr-Oct; ☎⛵) Tucked away on a plaza close to the sea, (look for the baby-blue Seat 600 car parked outside) the deco here is stripped-back minimalism, the team young and upbeat, and the food Mediterranean with distinct Italian overtones. Everything from salmon carpaccio with mango to home-made ravioli with wild mushrooms, truffle oil and Iberian ham hits the mark perfectly.

ℹ Information

Tourist Office (☑971 23 92 05; www.andratx. cat; Avinguda de Jaume I 28B; ⊙9am-4pm Mon-Sat & 9.30am-2pm Sun) A short walk from the beach.

ℹ Getting There & Around

The 100 bus runs six times a day from Andratx to Sant Elm (€2.20, 40 minutes) via S'Arracó. You can also take the boat between Sant Elm and Port d'Andratx (€8, 20 minutes, daily February to October). If you are driving, dodge the €3.50 beachfront parking fee by heading a little uphill to park.

Ferries to Illa de Sa Dragonera (return €13, 15 minutes, three to four daily February to November) operate from the small harbour north of Sant Elm's main beach. One of the main operators is **Cruceros Margarita** (☑639 617545; www.crucerosmargarita.com; Harbour; €13; ⊙Feb-Nov).

Portals Vells & Cap de Cala Figuera

Take a short detour 20km south of Andratx to the Cap de Cala Figuera peninsula's eastern flank for one of the last remaining stretches of unspoilt coastline in this much-developed corner of the southwest. It feels light-years away from the crowds and bustle in nearby Magaluf.

Three dreamlike inlets, collectively known as Portals Vells, reside in blissful seclusion, backed by pine-clad sandstone cliffs and dazzlingly clear water.

Cala Portals Vells
BEACH

(🏖) The fairest of the beaches known as Portals Vells is Cala Portals Vells. Turquoise waters lap the *platja*, whose sands stretch back beneath rows of straw umbrellas. To the south, a walking trail leads to **caves** that honeycomb the rock walls, one of them containing the rudiments of a chapel, where the altar has been hewn from the rock. According to local lore, Genoese sailors built it in the 15th century to give thanks for their lives being spared in a shipwreck.

Cala Mago
BEACH

Cala Mago is two narrow inlets: one has a restaurant and is frequented by nudists, while, further west, the longer inlet with the narrow, shady beach is prettier.

ℹ Getting There & Away

You'll need your own wheels to reach Portals Vells as there is no public transport. Take exit 14 off the Ma1 towards Portals Vells, passing the Western Park water park and golf club. About 2km through pine woods you reach a junction: turn left following signs to Cala Mago and park above the bay, or head 1.8km south to reach Cala Portals Vells.

SERRA DE TRAMUNTANA

Dominated by the splendid Serra de Tramuntana range, Mallorca's northwest coast and its hinterland are remarkably wild, ensnared by scarred limestone peaks and cliffs that loom over brilliant blue sea like ramparts. Gold-stone villages and ochre hamlets sit atop hillsides, their rhythms and hues providing tantalising insights into ancient Mallorca. The terraces that march up from the coast date back at least to the Moorish occupation, and walkers love the high, rugged interior for its pine forests, olive groves and wildflowers. The region's unique cultural and geographical features have been inscribed by the Unesco World Heritage List.

Andratx to Valldemossa Coast Road

Welcome to one of the Mediterranean's most exhilarating stretches of coastline, embraced by the Ma10 road, which climbs away from Andratx into the pine-clad hills marking the beginning of the majestic Serra de Tramuntana range. Pasted to clifftops and hillsides, the hamlets and lookouts that dot this mostly lonely stretch of road have arresting views of raw coastal beauty.

Estellencs

POP 402 / ELEVATION 151M

Estellencs is an enticingly laid-back and very pretty village of warm-stone buildings scattered around the rolling hills below the Puig Galatzò; the views of the village are stunning, especially from the main road as you approach from the north.

◎ Sights & Activities

Cala d'Estellencs BEACH
From Estellencs, a 1.5km road winds down through terraces of palm trees, citrus orchards, olives, almonds, cacti, pines and flowers to Cala d'Estellencs, a rocky cove with bottle-green water.

Puig Galatzò WALKING
To ascend Puig Galatzò (1025m), a walking trail starts near the Km 97 milestone on the Ma10 road, about 2.5km west of Estellencs. It's not easy going, so you'll need good maps and plenty of water and food. Prepare for a five- to six-hour round trip. An alternative but easily confused trail leads back down into Estellencs.

✖ Eating

Cafeteria Vall-Hermós CAFE €
(📞 971 61 86 10; www.vallhermos.com; Carrer de Eusebio Pascual 6; pizzas €8, tapas €4-6; ⊗ 10am-11pm Thu-Tue) It's all about the sea view at this simple cafe on the main drag through town, particularly at sunset from one of the rattan chairs on the terrace. Go for a coffee and *bocadillo* (filled roll) by day or linger over a glass of red and some tapas by night. The pizzas are filling and reasonable value too.

Sa Tanca MALLORCAN €
(📞 971 14 91 23; Carrer de la Mar 12; tapas €3; ⊗ 10am-10pm Wed-Mon) Tucked away in the narrow lanes below the main street, this traditional family-run bar prepares fresh tapas like *caracoles* (snails), tortilla and fried anchovies, as well as excellent *vino de la casa* (house wine), at prices geared for locals, rather than tourists.

Montimar MALLORCAN €€
(📞 971 61 85 76; Plaça de la Constitució 7; mains €16-30; ⊗ 1-3.30pm & 7-10.30pm Tue-Sun) Head for the terrace overlooking the rooftops and church. Since 1976, this is where the locals have headed for special occasions. It's a bastion of traditional Mallorcan cooking and dishes range from fish soup to fresh wild sea bass baked in salt, suckling pig or *sobrassada* (Mallorcan cured sausage) with honey, while local cheeses are the pick of the desserts.

❶ Getting There & Away

The No 200 Palma–Estellencs bus (€4, 80 minutes, four to 11 times daily) passes through Banyalbufar (€3.20) and also goes through Esporles.

Banyalbufar

POP 590 / ELEVATION 112M

Pretty Banyalbufar finds itself in a cleft in the Serra de Tramuntana's seaward wall, high above the coast. It's a tight, steep rabbit warren of a town, with quiet pot-plant-lined lanes that wind down towards the sea and beckon strollers.

The village, 8km northeast of Estellencs, was founded by the Arabs in the 10th century; the name Banyalbufar means 'built next to the sea' in Arabic. All around the village are carved-out, centuries-old, stone-walled farming terraces, known as *ses marjades,* which form a series of steps down to the sea. They are kept moist by mountain well water that gurgles down open channels and is stored in cisterns. Just west of town along the coast road is the Torre des Verger, one of the most recognisable symbols of Mallorca.

◎ Sights

Torre des Verger TOWER
(Torre de Ses Animes; Ma10) **FREE** One kilometre out of town on the road to Estellencs, the Torre des Verger is a 1579 *talayot* (watchtower), an image you'll see on postcards all over the island. It's one of the most crazily sited structures on Mallorca – one step further and it would plunge into the Mediterranean far below. Climb to the top, fighting off vertigo as you proceed, and scan the horizon

WORTH A TRIP

AN INLAND DRIVE

Offering a change of perspective and fewer tourist numbers, a worthwhile drive peels away from the coast at Sant Elm or Port d'Andratx to head inland. A few hundred metres beyond the Port des Canonge turn-off as you drive east along the Ma10, hang a left onto the Ma1100 southward towards Esporles. After 1km you reach a road junction and the mansion **La Granja**.

From La Granja, follow the Ma1101 south, which plunges through thick woods and slithers down a series of hairpin bends to reach **Puigpunyent**. This typical inland town offers few sights but the luxury, rose-hued hilltop hotel **Gran Hotel Son Net** is reason enough to detour here if money is no object.

From Puigpunyent, make a dash for **Galilea**, a high-mountain hamlet a serpentine 4km south. Climb to the town's church square for views across the valleys and a drink in the bar next door, or head even higher up this straggling place for a greater sense of altitude.

Back in Puigpunyent, take the Ma1101 to Esporles.

for yachts in the water from the place where sentinels once warned of pirates.

Cala Banyalbufar BEACH

A steep 1km walk downhill past terraced slopes from Banyalbufar brings you to this rugged shingle and pebble, seaweed-scattered cove, where you can swim or sip a cold one at the beach shack on the rocks and look out over the dark turquoise water; there's also a lovely waterfall nearby.

Bodega Son Vives WINERY

(☑609 601904; www.sonvives.com; Ma10; ⊙11am-7pm Thu-Sun May-Oct) High on the hill at the southern entrance to the village, this small winery has cellar-door tastings and sales in summer. It offers a number of fusion wines, but its best drop comes from the locally grown malvasia grape. Son Vives also produces olive oil.

✕ Eating

With some very good restaurants in town, Banyalbufar is a worthy spot for lunch or dinner.

Pegasón y el Pajarito Enmascarado MEDITERRANEAN €

(☑971 14 87 13; Carrer del Pont 2; mains €13-16; ⊙1-7pm Tue-Sun) Stone walls, checked tablecloths and cobbled-together vintage furnishings give this button-cute bistro a distinctly boho feel. It's tucked into the corner of a narrow backstreet just under the main road, with a plant-dotted patio for people watching. The chalked up daily menu is brief but always includes seafood, meat and vegetarian options.

Ca'n Paco MALLORCAN €€

(☑971 61 81 48; Carrer de la Constitució 18; mains €11.50-17.50; ⊙1-5pm & 7.30-11pm Tue-Sun) On the road leading down to Cala de Banyalbufar, this traditional haunt stays true to its Mallorcan roots with generous portions of *arroz negro* (black rice cooked in squid ink) and grilled fish. Its *gató con helado de almendra,* a moist sponge with almond ice cream, takes some beating, as do the terrace views as the sun sinks into the sea.

Son Tomàs MALLORCAN €€

(☑971 61 81 49; Carrer de Baronia 17; mains €14-22; ⊙12.30-4pm & 7-10pm Wed-Mon; 🛜🚻) This classic place at the west end of the village draws cyclists seeking snacks to its streetside tables, while the upstairs restaurant is first class. Family owned since 1983, much of the produce is grown on their own land. Popular dishes include the *lechona* (suckling pig; €17.90) and the classic *frito mallorquín* (fried lamb offal and vegetables).

🛍 Shopping

Malvasia de Banyalbufar WINE

(☑971 14 85 05; www.malvasiadebanyalbufar.com; Carrer de Comte Sallent 5; ⊙11am-2pm & 5-8pm Tue-Sat, to 2pm Sun Jun-Aug, shorter hours Sep-May) This shop run by a cooperative of local wineries was set up to promote the locally grown malvasia grape. It's the perfect place to pick up a bottle of wine for a picnic or to take back home.

❶ Getting There & Away

The No 200 Palma–Estellencs bus (€4, 80 minutes, four to 11 times daily) passes through Banyalbufar (€3.20) and also goes through Esporles.

Esporles

POP 4956

Cradled between the mountain folds in the foothills of the Tramuntana, this pretty village of ochre-stone townhouses is set beside a generally dry stream and has a Saturday market. The pace is very laid-back in the cafe-lined alleys presided over by a neo-Gothic church, dedicated to St Peter. Esporles can be animated at night, as many folk from Palma have opted to live here and commute to the capital.

Walk up the road alongside the church (keeping the church to your right) and up Carrer Costa de Sant Pere for the pleasant 2½-hour **Camí des Correu walk** to Banyalbufar, along the GR221.

Esporles is a delightful stop-off for lunch or dinner and has several recommended restaurants, conveniently located near the leafy main street, shaded by lofty horse chestnut trees.

La Granja HISTORIC BUILDING
(☑971 61 00 32; www.lagranja.net; Carretera de Esporles-Banyalbufar; adult €15.50, child €9; ⊙10am-7pm May-Sep, to 6pm Oct-Apr; ℗) This magnificent *possessió* (rural estate) has been turned into something of a kitsch Mallorca-land exhibit, with folks in traditional dress. The grand mansion is, however, well worth the visit, as are its extensive gardens. Some elements of the property date to the 10th century. You could spend hours exploring the period-furnished rooms, olive and wine presses, grand dining room, stables, workshops and some medieval instruments of torture in the cellars. The admission includes a wine tasting.

El Mesón La Villa MALLORCAN €€
(☑971 61 09 01; Carrer de Nou de Sant Pere 5; mains €15-25; ⊙1-4pm & 8-11pm Thu-Sat, 1-4pm Mon & Tue) Locals wax lyrical about the *asados* (roasts) at El Mesón La Villa, where a chef can usually be found shovelling lamb and suckling pig into a wood-fired clay oven to slow-bake to juicy perfection. The setting matches the rustic, hearty food, with its beams and farming implements, all of which assures it a faithful local following.

Es Brollador SPANISH €€
(☑971 61 05 39; Passeig del Rei 10; mains €11.50-21.50; ⊙10am-10pm) With its tiled floors, high ceilings and rear courtyard, Es Brollador makes a pleasant stop for anything from a morning coffee to lunch or dinner. The pork sirloin with a sauce made with *sobrassada* is good; lighter meals are also served. The outdoor tables under green parasols are perfect for people watching.

❶ Getting There & Away

The No 200 Palma–Estellencs bus (€4, 80 minutes, four to 11 times daily) passes through Esporles (€3.20) and Banyalbufar.

Valldemossa

POP 2027 / ELEVATION 425M

Crowned by the spire of its Carthusian monastery, which slowly lifts the gaze to the Tramuntana's wooded slopes, Valldemossa is one of the island's most eye-catching sights. Set on a gentle rise, the village insists on aimless wandering and chance discoveries along pinched lanes, as breathtaking vistas onto the surrounding valley and hills and pockets of almost indescribable charm await. The allure of Valldemossa's tree-lined, cobbled lanes, stout stone houses and impressive villas means there's no shortage of visitors, and that the bulk of the restaurants and bars serve average fare at inflated prices. But it's not hard to slip away from the crowds to find a part of Valldemossa for yourself and revel in its manifold beauty.

◎ Sights

Valldemossa's rich ecclesiastical heritage, especially in the astonishing monastery that dominates the village and the settlement's celebrated connections with Frédéric Chopin and George Sand, means there is no shortage of specific sights to explore beyond ambling around Valldemossa's beguiling lanes.

Around town you may notice that most houses bear a colourful tile depicting a nun and the words *Santa Catalina Thomàs, pregau per nosaltres* (St Catherine Thomas, pray for us). Yes, Valldemossa has its very own saint.

★**Real Cartuja de Valldemossa** MONASTERY
(www.cartujadevalldemossa.com; Plaça Cartoixa; adult/child €9.50/6; ⊙10am-4.30pm Mon-Sat Feb-Oct) This grand old monastery, which

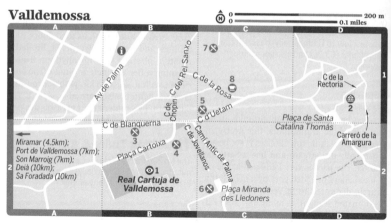

Valldemossa

Valldemossa

◎ Top Sights
1 Real Cartuja de Valldemossa B2

◎ Sights
2 Casa Natal de Santa Catalina
Thomàs D1

✖ Eating
3 Forn Ca'n Molinas B2
4 Gelatimossa B2
5 Hostal Ca'n Marió C1
6 La Posada C2
7 QuitaPenas C1

◎ Drinking & Nightlife
8 Aromas C1

was also a former royal residence has a chequered history. It was once home to kings, monks and a pair of 19th-century celebrities: composer Frédéric Chopin and George Sand. A series of cells now shows how the monks lived, bound by an oath of silence they could only break for half an hour per week in the library. Various items related to the time Sand and Chopin spent here, including Chopin's pianos, are also displayed.

The building's origins date back to 1310 when Jaume II built a palace on the site. After it was abandoned, the Carthusian order took over and converted it into a monastery, which was greatly expanded in 1388. Following the rules of the order, just 13 monks lived in this cavernous space. The monastery was turned into rental accommodation (mostly for holidaymakers from Palma) after its monks were expelled

in 1835. Entry includes piano recitals (eight times daily in summer) and Jaume II's 14th-century **Palau de Rei Sanxo**, a muddle of medieval rooms jammed with furniture and hundreds of years of mementos, gathered around a modest cloister.

Casa Natal de Santa Catalina Thomàs   HISTORIC BUILDING
(Carrer de la Rectoria) The Casa Natal de Santa Catalina Thomàs, the birthplace of St Catherine Thomas, is tucked off to the side of the parish church, the **Església de Sant Bartomeu**, at the eastern end of the town. It houses a simple chapel and has a facsimile of Pope Pius VI's declaration beatifying the saint in 1792 on display; she was canonised in 1930.

Born in 1531 she is said to have had visions of (and was tempted by) the devil from a precocious age. Apparently this was a good thing and she wound up becoming a nun in the Església de Santa Magdalena in Palma, where she died in 1574. Sor Tomasseta, as she is affectionately known, has been venerated by locals ever since. There are no fixed opening hours, but you'll rarely find the doors closed.

🎉 Festivals & Events

Sunday is market day in Valldemossa.

Festa de la Beata   RELIGIOUS
(☉ 28 Jul) Valldemossa celebrates the life of Santa Catalina Thomàs with a donkey-drawn carriage parade and kids dressed in peasant garb throwing sweets to the crowds.

Festival Chopin   MUSIC
(www.festivalchopin.com; ☺Aug) Classical-music performances are held in Valldemossa's Real Cartuja (p103) throughout August; most of the works are by Chopin, although music by other composers is also featured. Tickets go for between €20 and €30.

✖ Eating

A sprinkling of long-established and cheerful eateries festoons the streets; many are clearly signposted. Few are of outstanding culinary significance, yet many are elegantly housed and feature excellent views of the mountain, the valley or the lovely architecture of Valldemossa.

★QuitaPenas   TAPAS €
(☑626 840006; www.quitapenasvalldemossa.com; Carrer Vell 4; tapas €3-15; ☺noon-4pm & 6.30-9.30pm) Spread over three stone-clad rooms in a former simple village house, this unpretentious tapas bar serves highly appertising takes on *pa amb oli* (bread with olive oil and vine-ripened tomatoes) or tangy *sobrassada* with caramelised fig. Couple with chilled Mallorcan wine or one of the local craft brews.

Gelatimossa   ICE CREAM €
(www.gelatimossa.com; Plaça de Cartoixa 18; per scoop €2; ☺11am-10pm Jun-Sep, shorter hours Oct-May) Pistachio, Mallorcan almond, lemon, peach, watermelon, banana, coffee and yoghurt...how ever will you choose? It's all home-made and delicious at this friendly *gelateria*. Grab a cone, or a tub, and head to the garden behind the Real Cartuja (50m away).

Forn Ca'n Molinas   BAKERY €
(☑971 61 22 47; Carrer de Blanquerna 15; coca de patata/ensaïmada €1.20/1.25; ☺9am-7.30pm)

This place along the main pedestrian drag has been baking up the local speciality of *coca de patata* (a bready, sugar-dusted pastry) and the island-favourite *ensaïmades* (light pastry spirals dusted with icing sugar) since 1920. Head for the delightful garden terrace out back. There's a whole cornucopia of other sweet and savoury pastry delights, including *crenadillo chocolate* (chocolate-filled pastry), *hosaldre mermalade, piñon, almendra* (puff pastry square filled with marmalade, pine nuts or almonds) and butter croissants, plus crusty bread rolls with cheese or ham (handy for hikers). There is another branch in town, along Carrer de la Rosa.

Hostal Ca'n Marió   MALLORCAN €
(☑971 61 21 22; http://hostalcanmario.net; Carrer d'Uetam 8; mains €8.50-14; ☺1.30-3.30pm & 8-10pm Wed-Mon) This fourth-generation family-run restaurant dates from 1877 and possibly little has changed, decor-wise, since then. There are no towers of food with elegant drizzles here, but rather good honest Mallorcan dishes, such as *lomo com col* (pork loin with cabbage), *cargols* (snails), stuffed aubergines and *tumbet*, a garlicky aubergine, tomato, potato and courgette bake.

La Posada   MODERN MALLORCAN €€
(☑665 822320; www.laposadamallorca.com; Plaça Miranda des Lledoners 3; ☺noon-10pm; ☎) Grab a table on the small terrace for fabulous valley views. This stylish eatery sets a mellow and relaxing tone with a refreshingly brief menu that covers the gambit of vegetarian, meat and seafood options, all prepared with a soupcon of innovation, like the salad with figs and Mahon cheese

---

CHOPIN'S WINTER OF DISCONTENT

Valldemossa owes much of its fame to the fact that the ailing composer Frédéric Chopin and his domineering lover, writer George Sand, spent their 'winter of discontent' here in 1838–39. Their stay in the town – at the grand Real Cartuja de Valldemossa (p103) no less – wasn't an entirely happy experience and Sand later wrote *Un hiver à Majorque* (A Winter in Mallorca), which, if nothing else, made her perennially unpopular with Mallorquins. Chopin's poor health, the constant rain and damp, and the not-always-warm welcome from the villagers, who found these foreigners rather too eccentric, turned a planned idyllic escape from the pressure cooker of social life in Paris into a nightmare. But time is a great healer and Valldemossa makes great mileage from its discontented former guests, with a music festival in Chopin's name and references to the couple visible all over town.

or red tuna tataki with mango and passion-fruit coulis.

Drinking & Nightlife

Cafe-bars abound in the centre of town; while few are particularly notable and many are over-visited by tourists, finding a chilled beer is not hard.

Aromas CAFE
(☑971 61 23 41; Carrer de la Rosa 25; ☺noon-7pm Tue-Sat; 🐾) With chequerboard floor, warm terracotta walls and jazzy music, this sedate and arty cafe is a relaxed spot to sip speciality teas or thick hot chocolate. It's a tempting alternative to the tourist-stuffed cafes and out back there's a fragrant garden.

ℹ Information

Tourist Office (☑971 61 20 19; www.ajvalldemossa.net; Avinguda de Palma 7; ☺10am-6.30pm Mon-Fri, to 2pm Sat & Sun) On the main road running through town, about two minutes' walk from the main bus stop.

ℹ Getting There & Away

The 210 bus from Palma to Valldemossa (€1.90, 30 minutes) runs four to nine times a day.

Three to four of these continue to Port de Sóller (€2.65, one hour) via Deià.

Port de Valldemossa

About 1.5km west from Valldemossa on the road to Banyalbufar, a spectacular mountain road (the Ma1113) clings to cliffs 5.5km all the way down to Port de Valldemossa. The giddying sea and cliff views are breathtaking and the descent is akin to traversing a precipice, with a village glimpsed through the trees a very long way down below. Drivers should never take their eye off the road and there's only one place to pull over for photos. At journey's end, a shingle and algae 'beach' awaits, backed by low red cliffs and a cluster of a dozen or so houses, one of which is home to the justifiably popular Restaurant Es Port.

Restaurant Es Port SEAFOOD €€
(☑971 61 61 94; www.restaurantesport.es; Carrer Ponent 5; mains €9.50-24.80; ☺10am-10pm Jun-Aug, shorter hours Sep-May; ℗) Seafood is the mainstay here, as you'd expect, and it all somehow tastes better out on the 1st-floor terrace on a midsummer's evening. Rice dishes steal the show, as does the excellent

---

WORTH A TRIP

AN ARCHDUKE'S ROMANTIC ABODES

Head northeast of Valldemossa on the spectacular coastal road that twists to Deià and you will come across two of the most remarkable residences on the island, both of which belonged to Habsburg Archduke Ludwig Salvator (1847–1915), a hopeless romantic who found his idea of heaven right here.

The first is Miramar (www.sonmarroig.com; Carretera de Valldemossa-Deià; adult/child €4/free; ☺10am-5.30pm Mon-Sat May-Oct, shorter hours Nov-Apr). This splendid sea-facing mansion, 5km north of Valldemossa, is built on the site of a 13th-century monastery and has a *tàfona* (olive-oil press), a cloister and landscaped gardens to explore. Ramon Llull, the evangelist and patron saint of Catalan literature, founded the monastery, where he wrote many of his works and trained brethren for the task of proselytising among the Muslims. Walk out the back and enjoy the clifftop views.

About 7km from Valldemossa is another of Habsburg Archduke Ludwig Salvator's residences, Son Marroig (www.sonmarroig.com; Carretera de Valldemossa-Deià; adult/child €4/free; ☺9.30am-6pm Mon-Sat May-Oct, shorter hours Nov-Apr). It's a delightful, rambling mansion jammed with furniture and period items, including many of the archduke's books. But above all, the views are the stuff of dreams.

Ask permission to wander down to Sa Foradada, the strange hole-in-the-wall rock formation by the water, which resembles an elephant from afar. It's a stunning 3km walk (one way) down through olive groves tinkling with sheep bells and along paths flanked by pine trees and caves. A soothing swim in the lee of this odd formation is the reward. Avoid the midday heat as there is little shade. The fiery sunsets here are riveting stuff.

seafood mixed grill, while the *calamares al ajillo con patatas* (cuttlefish cooked with potato cubes and lightly spiced) is perfectly prepared.

ⓘ Getting There & Away

There is no public transport down to the port, but it's a lovely, if mildly hair-raising, drive down.

Deià

POP 768 / ELEVATION 222M

When the late-afternoon sun warms Deià's honey-coloured houses – which clamber steeply up a conical hillside – and the sea deepens to darkest blue on the horizon, it's enough to send even the most prosaic of souls into romantic raptures. This eyrie of a village in the Tramuntana is flanked by steep hillsides terraced with vegetable gardens, citrus orchards, almond and olive trees and even the occasional vineyard – all set against the magnificent mountain backdrop of the Puig des Teix (1062m).

Deià was once a second home to writers, actors and musicians, the best known of whom (to Anglo-Saxons at any rate) was the English poet Robert Graves.

◉ Sights

Climbing up from the main road, the steep cobbled lanes, with their well-kept stone houses, overflowing bougainvillea and extraordinary views across the sea, farm terraces and mountains, make it easy to understand why artists and many other bohemians have loved this place since Catalan artists 'discovered' it in the early 20th century.

★ Casa Robert Graves HISTORIC BUILDING
(Ca N'Alluny; www.lacasaderobertgraves.com; Carretera Deià-Sóller; adult/child €7/3.50; ⊙10am-5pm Mon-Fri, to 3pm Sat; Ⓟ) Casa Robert Graves is a fascinating tribute to the British writer and poet who moved to Deià in 1929 and had his house built here three years later. It's a well-presented and rewarding insight into his life and work; on show you'll find period furnishings, a detailed film on his life, love life and writings, and sundry books, pictures and everyday objects that belonged to Graves himself.

Cala de Deià BEACH
A 3km drive from Deià (take the road towards Sóller), or a slightly shorter walk, is Cala de Deià, one of the most bewitching of the Serra de Tramuntana's coastal inlets. The enclosed arc of the bay is backed by a handful of houses and the small shingle beach is lapped by crystal-clear water crested with white surf. Competition for a parking spot a few hundred metres back up the road can be intense; be sure to get here early.

Es Puig VIEWPOINT
(Ⓟ) From Es Puig, the hill at the heart of Deià, you peer across the rooftops of the higgledy-piggledy village and take in the full sweep of the valley to the glinting Mediterranean beyond. At the top is the modest parish church, the **Església de Sant Joan Baptista** (whose Museu Parroquial, a collection of local religious paraphernalia, rarely opens). Opposite is the small town cemetery. Here lies 'Robert Graves, Poeta, 24-4-1895 – 7-12-1985 E.P.D' (*en paz descanse,* meaning 'may he rest in peace').

✴ Festivals & Events

Festival Internacional de Deià MUSIC
(☑678 989536; www.dimf.com; Son Marroig, Carretera de Valldemossa-Deià; €20; ⊙Thu May-Sep) Outside Deià on the Serra de Tramuntana coast, the Son Marroig mansion hosts the Festival Internacional de Deià, a series of light-classical concerts.

✕ Eating

The Ma10 passes though the town centre, where it becomes the main street and is lined with bars, restaurants and shops, particularly at the village's eastern end. Quality varies, but there are some high-quality mainstays sprinkled among the others, most of which come and go with the years.

Bistro Rullan BISTRO €€
(☑971 18 86 70; Carrer de Arxiduc Luis Salvador 14A; tapas €5-8, mains €12-20; ⊙noon-10pm Wed-Sun) This handsome house dates from the 1930s and now accommodates a popular bistro specialising in Mediterranean- and French-inspired cuisine. There is a romantic candlelit courtyard with heart-stirring valley views and an extensive gin menu (try the

rhubarb and hibiscus). There's also a lighter lunchtime tapas menu with unusual choices like a soft toasted tortilla (burrito) with fillings like chicken and avocado.

Sa Vinya SPANISH €€
(☑971 63 95 00; www.restaurant-savinya.com; Carrer de Sa Vinya Vella 4; mains €12-26; ☺1-11pm Tue-Sun Feb-Nov; 🐾) Cobbled steps climb up to Sa Vinya and its subtly lit terrace, overlooking citrus groves and the Tramuntana's wooded peaks. It's a truly magical spot for dinner, and freshness shines through in typical Spanish seafood dishes like prawns in a garlic and chilli sauce, fried calamari and seafood paella. They also make a good burger and even better chocolate brownie.

Sebastian MEDITERRANEAN €€
(☑971 63 94 17; http://restaurantesebastian.com; Carrer de Felipe Bauzà 2; mains €15-20; ☺7.30-10.30pm; 🐾) A former stable with bare stone walls and crisp cream linen, Sebastian is a refined experience. The short, sweet menu offers three fish and three meat mains, each enhanced with a delicate sauce or purée. What's available depends on the season, but you can expect dishes such as hake with a lobster and pea ravioli and green asparagus.

Ca's Patró March SPANISH €€
(☑971 63 91 37; Cala de Deià; mains €10-25; ☺10am-11pm Jun-Aug, shorter hours Sep-May; 🅿) This is probably the pick of the two places overlooking the water at Cala de Deià (p107) for its slightly elevated views, but it's a close-run thing. It has a wide range of grilled meat and fish dishes – the star of which seems to be the Sóller *gambas*. It's run by the third generation of a local fishing family.

Can Lluc SEAFOOD €€
(☑649 198618; Cala de Deià; mains €10-20; ☺10.30am-7pm May-Oct; 🅿) If you can't bear to drag yourself too far from your towel, this simple bar-eatery fronting Cala de Deià is ace. Cold drinks, grilled sardines and calamari with a squirt of lemon on a lazy summer's afternoon – bliss. It's a useful alternative when the other Cala de Deià restaurant is full, which is often the case. Service can be rather harried.

⭐**Es Racó d'es Teix** MODERN MALLORCAN €€€
(☑971 63 95 01; www.esracodesteix.es; Carrer de Sa Vinya Vella 6; mains €36-38, 3-course lunch menú €38, with wine €52, 4-/6-course tasting

menú €80/120; ☺1-3pm & 7.30-10.30pm Wed-Sun Feb-Oct; 🐾) An island legend, German chef Josef Sauerschell has one Michelin star and it is well deserved. Standouts are the hearty meat dishes – anything from veal carpaccio with artichokes and clams to Mallorcan suckling pig, trotters with foie gras and rack of lamb with an olive crust and figs. Josef runs the restaurant with his wife, Leonor, originally from Deià.

🛍 Shopping

Gres ART
(Carrer de Arxiduc Luís Salvador 4; ☺10am-1pm & 4.30-6.30pm Mon-Fri, 10am-6pm Sat) The ceramics on sale here are world class and the work of native Mallorcan artist Dora Good, now living and working in New York. Her mother Grace is also an accomplished ceramicist and holds workshops here during the winter months.

ℹ Getting There & Away

Deià is 15 minutes up the winding road from Valldemossa on the 210 bus route between Palma (€2.95, 45 to 60 minutes) and Port de Sóller (€1.65, 30 to 40 minutes). As Deià is so visited, parking can be tricky (even though paid parking spaces are provided, they can be full). But you may be able to find a spot to park alongside the Ma10 roadside just east of town.

Sóller

POP 14,150

The picturesque town of Sóller lies in a valley surrounded by the dramatic peaks of the Serra de Tramuntana. The Arabs saw the potential of the valley, known as the Vall d'Or (Golden Valley), and accounts of orange and lemon groves, watered from sources in the hills, date from the 13th century. The citrus-fruit export market laid the foundations for the great wealth of the town, reflected in its railway line to Palma (1912), tram line to the Port de Sóller (1913) and the grand merchant houses that throng the town, such as those strung out along Gran Via and Carrer de Sa Lluna.

Worth visiting in its own right, with its vintage train and tram rides, graceful modernist architecture and galleries showcasing Picasso and Miró, Sóller is also a wonderful base for exploring the west coast and the Tramuntana. It is also the trailhead for some stirring mountain hikes.

Sóller

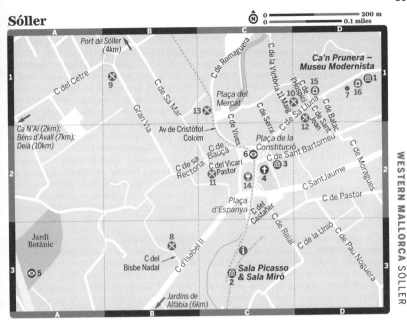

Sóller

◉ Sights & Activities

Simply wandering Sóller's tangle of narrow streets is a pleasure. In any direction, within a few minutes you exchange tight, winding lanes lined with tall and grand wooden doors for country roads bordered by stone walls, behind which flourish orange and lemon groves. Start your exploring at the leafy main plaza in the centre of town.

★ **Sala Picasso & Sala Miró** GALLERY
(Plaça d'Espanya 6, Estación de Tren; ◷10.30am-6.30pm) **FREE** In two rooms at street level in Sóller's station are two fascinating, introspective and contemplative art exhibitions:

the Sala Picasso and Sala Miró. Few train stations boast such a splendid artistic legacy. The Sala Picasso contains more than 50 gently illuminated ceramics from the hands of Picasso from 1948 to 1971, many bearing the artist's trademark subjects: dancers, women, bullfighting. The Sala Miró is beautiful, home to playful, mysterious and beguiling prints from the Catalan master; Miró's maternal grandmother was from Sóller.

★ **Ca'n Prunera – Museu
Modernista** GALLERY
(⌨971 63 89 73; http://canprunera.com; Carrer de Sa Lluna 86-90; adult/child €5/free; ◷10.30am-6.30pm Mar-Oct, closed Mon Nov-Feb)

One of Mallorca's standout galleries, Ca'n Prunera occupies a landmark modernist mansion along Carrer de Sa Lluna. The list of luminaries here is astonishing – works by Joan Miró, along with single drawings by Toulouse-Lautrec, Picasso, Gauguin, Klimt, Kandinsky, Klee, Man Ray and Cézanne. Also part of the permanent collection is a gallery devoted to Juli Ramis (1909–90), a Sóller native and world-renowned painter who had his studio in the neighbouring village of Biniaraix, plus works by Miquel Barceló, Antoni Tapiès and Eduardo Chillida.

Plaça de la Constitució   SQUARE
Thronged with tables and seats from the cafes on its northern, eastern and western perimeters, the lovely main square, Plaça de la Constitució, is 100m from the train station. The tram line bends its way across the square, conveying the loaded and tooting tram to the beaches of Sóller Port. Filled with children playing in the evenings, stuffed with panama-wearing visitors and home to the beautiful Església de Sant Bartomeu, the square is Sóller's vibrant heart and soul.

Església de Sant Bartomeu   CHURCH
(Plaça de la Constitució; ⊙11am-1.15pm & 3-5.15pm Mon-Thu, 11am-1.15pm Fri & Sat, noon-1pm Sun) `FREE` A disciple of architect Antoni Gaudí, Joan Rubió landed some big commissions in Sóller. The town did not want to miss out on the wave of modernity and so Rubió set to work in 1904 on the renovation of the 16th-century Església de Sant Bartomeu. The largely baroque church (built 1688–1723) preserved elements of its earlier Gothic interior, but Rubió gave it a beautiful, if unusual, modernist facade.

The interior is sombre overhead, but several of the bright and gilded side chapels poke from the gloom among rows of devotional candle flames, while the fine altarpiece is a towering and ostentatious focal point. To the left of the altar is a small copy in oil of *The Last Supper*. You'll have a wonderful perspective by walking towards the altar, and then turning for a view of the chandelier, organ and luminous rose window. The church's candelabra-like summit is visible from all over town, set against the looming backdrop of the Serra de Tramuntana.

Jardí Botànic & Museu Balear de Ciències Naturals   GARDENS, MUSEUM
(www.jardibotanicdesoller.org; Carretera Palma-Port de Sóller; adult/child €8/free; ⊙10am-6pm Mon-Sat) A short stroll 600m west from Sóller's town centre onto the busy road to Sóller Port brings you to the peaceful Jardí Botànic, with collections of flowers and other plants native to the Balearic Islands – everything from holm oaks to magnolias and myrtle and the endangered caraway pine – alongside other Mediterranean samples. The same ticket includes entrance to the **Museu Balear de Ciències Naturals** (Natural Science Museum) and its elementary insights into the flora and fauna of the Balearics; the fossil collection is of particular note.

Banco de Sóller   HISTORIC BUILDING
(Plaça de la Constitució) Joan Rubió i Bellver, a Catalonian student of Antoni Gaudí, designed the strikingly modernist frontage of the 1912 Banco de Sóller (nowadays Banco de Santander), which is separated by a narrow road from the Església de Sant Bartomeu (the facade of which he also created). The bank is an imposing and roughly hewn stone building, with two large, circular galleries, windows framed within lacy wrought-iron grilles and a carved lion gazing ferociously out over the square from the edifice's corner.

👉 Tours

Tramuntana Tours   ADVENTURE
(☑971 63 24 23; www.tramuntanatours.com; Carrer de Sa Lluna 72; bicycle rental per day €12-75; ⊙9am-1.30pm & 3-7.30pm Mon-Fri, 9am-1.30pm Sat) This experienced operator organises a range of activities-based guided excursions, including canyoning (from €80), sea kayaking (€50), hiking (from €25) and mountain biking (from €24, without bike rental) in the Serra de Tramuntana, as well as renting out as-new bikes. It also has a gear shop. If it's not open, try the sister shop in Port de Sóller (p113), which has longer opening hours.

⭐ Festivals & Events

Es Firó   FIESTA
(⊙early May) Around the second weekend of May, Sóller is invaded by a motley crew of Muslim pirates. Known as Es Firó, this conflict (involving about 1200 townsfolk)

between *pagesos* (town and country folk) and Moros (Moors) is full of good-humoured drama and copious drinking. It re-enacts an assault on the town that was repulsed on 11 May 1561.

✖ Eating

A large and much-visited town, Sóller has a fine choice of restaurants, cafes and bakeries, serving a tantalising range of Mallorcan and Mediterranean food. For picturesque views, head to Béns d'Avall on the winding road to Deià.

Sa Fàbrica de Gelats ICE CREAM €
(Avinguda de Cristòfol Colom 13; per scoop €1.50; ⊘9am-10pm Jul & Aug, shorter hrs Sep-Jun) Legendary ice cream. Among the 40 or so trays of locally made flavours, those concocted from fresh orange or lemon juice are outstanding. There's a large terrace out back.

Luna 36 MODERN MEDITERRANEAN €€
(☑971 94 21 79; www.luna36.es; Carrer de Sa Lluna 36; mains €19-27; ⊘12.30-3pm & 6.30-10pm Mon-Sat; ☎) This Danish-owned restaurant is a burst of colour on Carrer de Sa Lluna. Aim for a seat in the lovely courtyard garden, framed by scarlet bougainvillea. The bread is homemade daily and the dishes are prepared with the same ethos, strictly depending on what is fresh in season. Expect black-rice risotto, white tuna with dill sauce, and similar.

Casa Alvaro TAPAS €€
(☑871 70 93 15; www.casalvaro.com; Carrer del Vicari Pastor 17; tapas €4.50-10.50; ⊘noon-4pm & 7pm-midnight Wed-Mon, 1.30-4.30pm & 7.30pm-midnight Sun; ☎) Scoot down a cobbled lane off the main plaza to find this delightful place sporting a minimalist-traditional bodega look. Sample innovative art-on-a-plate tapas like artichokes on a bed of chestnut puree, crispy calamari, or pork belly with fava beans and wakame seaweed. Between two and three of these gorgeous combos will result in a full belly and a smile on your face.

Ca'n Llimona ITALIAN €€
(☑971 63 81 75; www.canllimonasoller.com; Calle de la Victòria 12; mains €15-20; ⊘1-4pm & 7.30-10pm) Step inside and the cherry red-cum-lemon motif decor immediately transports you to Sorrento. The journey continues with the enticingly brief menu – no endless

choice of pasta and pizza here. The pasta is made daily and sauces are simple and fresh, like fresh lemon pesto with cherry tomatoes. The owners also make their own herb teas, available for purchase.

Ca'n Boqueta MEDITERRANEAN €€
(☑971 63 83 98; Gran Via 43; 3-course menú €17; ⊘1-3.15pm & 7.45-10.15pm Tue-Sat, 1-3.15pm Sun) A tastefully converted townhouse bistro, with art on the walls, beamed ceilings and a garden patio, Ca'n Boqueta offers creative cooking with a seasonal touch. Starters like cherry gazpacho and scallops with white zucchini cream are a delicious lead to mains such as seafood cannelloni with a white truffle sauce.

★ Béns d'Avall SEAFOOD €€€
(☑971 63 23 81; www.bensdavall.com; Urbanització Costa Deià, off Carretera Sóller-Deià; tasting menus €64-94; ⊘1-3.30pm & 7-9.30pm Wed-Sat, 1-3.30pm Tue & Sun; 🅿☎) From its clifftop perch overlooking the sea, this restaurant's terrace is pop-the-question-at-sunset romantic. Not only that, it's the home turf of Benet Vicens, one of Mallorca's foremost chefs. The nouvelle Balearic-style tasting menu follows the seasons, with dishes like lobster ravioli with rabbit loin and sorrel sauce, fruit-filled suckling pig slow-cooked to crackling perfection, or Tramuntana lamb with eggplant confiture.

Barretes MALLORCAN €€€
(☑971 63 12 28; www.hotelcalbisbe.com; Hotel Ca'l Bisbe, Carrer del Bisbe Nadal 10; menús €29.50-38.50; ⊘8-10.30pm Mar-Oct; 🅿☎) Converted from an old olive mill, Barretes has heavy wood beams in the lantern-lit dining room or al fresco seating on the poolside terrace. The menu is a cut above the norm, with refined dishes like slow-cooked cod with calamari noodles and black-olive crusted lamb with basil risotto, expertly matched with local wines. Watching the sun set over the Tramuntana lends a romantic mood.

🍷 Drinking & Nightlife

Sóller's Plaça de la Constitució, right at the heart of town, is strewn with cafes and bars. A drink here is the ideal way to people-watch and measure the town's comings and goings.

Sa Butigueta BAR
(Avinguda de Jeroni Estades 9; ☎) Free of tourist trimmings and paraphernalia, this down-to-earth Mallorcan bar-cafe-restaurant serves

affordable drinks and tapas. Also acting as a club for locals, this is the place to come to for a clutter-free, authentic vibe, where locals deal cards and chat, quaffing the best-priced booze in town. Take a seat on Avinguda des Born, facing the church, and watch the tram grind by.

🛍 Shopping

Arte Artesanía
JEWELLERY

(☑ 971 63 17 32; www.arteartesania.com; Carrer de Sa Lluna 43; ⊙ 10.30am-8pm Mon-Fri, to 3pm Sat) A dynamic and inspiring artistic space that's simply bursting with ideas, Arte Artesanía is at once classy and avant-garde, with its designer jewellery and small range of paintings, ceramics and sculpture. It's the work of Spanish and international artisan-designers, and exhibitions are often hosted upstairs and also in the small basement room.

Ben Calçat
SHOES

(☑ 971 63 28 74; www.bencalcat.es; Carrer de Sa Lluna 74; ⊙ 9.30am-8.30pm Mon-Fri, to 1.30pm Sat) The place for authentic Mallorcan handcrafted *porqueras*, shoes made from recycled car tyres. The funky bowling-shoe designs in rainbow-bright colours won't appeal to everyone, but this is very Mallorca. Prices start at around €65.

ℹ Information

Tourist Office (☑ 971 63 80 08; www. visitsoller.com; Plaça d'Espanya 15; ⊙ 10am-4.30pm Mon-Fri, 9am-1pm Sat) Sóller's tourist office carries plenty of informative brochures and maps.

ℹ Getting There & Away

BUS

Bus 211 shoots up the Ma11 from Palma to Sóller (€2.45, 30 minutes, up to five daily). Bus 210 takes the long way to/from Palma (€4.05) via Valldemossa (€2.20, 40 to 50 minutes) and Deià (€1.60). A local service connects Sóller with Fornalutx (€1.50, 15 minutes, two to four daily) via Biniaraix.

CAR & MOTORCYCLE

When coming from Palma, you have the option of taking the tunnel (now free of charge) or opting for the mountainous switchbacks up to the pass, with some great views back down towards Palma en route. If you aim to do that, take the last turn-off for Sóller before the tunnel. For other magnificent views down to Sóller and its splendid valley, take the mountain road from Fornalutx to the Sóller–Port de Sóller road. There are handy petrol stations on either side of the road just before the tunnel on the Palma side.

TRAIN

The train journey from Palma to Sóller is a highlight. From April to October, trains (€16; www.trendesoller.com) run from Palma to Sóller six times a day from 10.10am to 7.30pm and five times in the other direction from 9am to 6.30pm. There is a reduced service in November, December, February and March, with four trains per day in each direction.

TRAM

Sóller's antique open-sided **trams** (Tranvías; one way €7; ⊙ every 30 or 60min 8am-8.30pm)

WORTH A TRIP

JARDINS DE ALFÀBIA

The **Jardins de Alfàbia** (☑ 971 61 31 23; www.jardinesdealfabia.com; Carretera de Sóller Km 17; adult/child €7.50/free, adult Nov & Mar €5.50; ⊙ 9.30am-6.30pm Mon-Sat Apr-Oct, to 5.30pm Mon-Fri, to 1pm Sat Mar) reside in the shadow of the rugged Serra d'Alfàbia mountain range stretching east of Sóller. This endearingly faded *finca* with a baroque facade looks like it was stripped from a Florentine basilica. The rambling house is surrounded by gardens, citrus groves, palm trees and a handful of farmyard animals. The murmur of water gurgling along irrigation canals hints at the place's past as the residence of an Arab Wāli (viceroy).

Little remains of the original Arab house, except for the extraordinary polychromatic coffered ceiling, fashioned from pine and ilex, immediately inside the building's entrance. It is bordered by inscriptions in Arabic and is thought to have been made around 1170. To the right of the inner courtyard is the *tafona* (large oil press), a mix of Gothic, Renaissance and baroque styles. The interior is stuffed full with period furniture, plus there is a magnificent 1200-volume library. On display here is the original *Llibre de les Franqueses* (Book of Franchise), written by King Jaume I as the basis for all rights in Mallorca after the Christian conquest.

run to Port de Sóller on the coast and back. They depart from outside the train station but also stop at the northwest corner of Plaça de la Constitució on the way to the Port. Generally, they run from Sóller to Port de Sóller every 30 minutes from 8am to 8.30pm and in the other direction from 8.30am to 9pm (pick up a timetable from the tourist office or visit the station).

Port de Sóller

POP 2909

Sóller's outlet to the sea is a quintessential Mallorcan fishing and yachting harbour, arrayed around an almost perfectly enclosed bay. More than a decade ago, millions of euros were poured into sprucing up the port but, as with all such places, the atmosphere wavers between classy and crass. The architecture reflects French and even Puerto Rican influences, as these were the two main destination countries of many Mallorcan emigrants, some of whom returned with cash and imported tastes.

The sunsets can be stunning, especially in midsummer, when – from the right vantage point – the sun dips into the sea precisely between the jaws of the port's two headlands.

🏃 Activities

The bay is shaped something like a jellyfish and shadowed by a pleasant, pedestrianised and restaurant-lined esplanade. It makes for pleasant strolling, especially around the northern end where the heart of the original town is gathered together.

The beaches are OK, although hardly the island's best. The pick of the crop is **Platja d'en Repic** at the southern end of the bay, not least because it's nicely removed from the streams of passers-by. Keep walking in the same direction around the rocky headland for even more peace and quiet and some fantastic perches for jumping into the sea.

⭐ Mezzo Magic   BOATING
(☏ 664 679875; www.mezzomagic.co.uk; Carrer de L'Església; per person half/whole day from €80/100, yacht half/whole day from €500/700; ☺ 10am-7pm) Mezzo Magic provides stirring chartered yacht voyages all up and down the coastline, to Cala Deià, Sa Calobra, Cala Tuent and Sa Foradada. It also sails the boat further afield (even as far as Ibiza, Formentera and Menorca) for an entirely

different perspective on the island and the Mediterranean, with all the drama of a yachting expedition. Sunset tours are also on the menu and they are open all year-round.

Octopus Dive Centre   DIVING
(☏ 971 63 31 33; www.octopus-mallorca.com; Carrer del Canonge Oliver 13; 1 dive with/without own equipment €45/60, 2 dives €80/99; ☺ 8.30am-7pm mid-May–Oct) Dive with Octopus Dive Centre, a five-star English-run PADI centre with first-rate equipment, courses and dives that range from beginner to expert and depart from shore or off a boat. It operates boat dives at about 30 sites along the Serra de Tramuntana coast.

Nàutic Sóller   BOATING
(☏ 609 354132; www.nauticsoller.com; Platja d'en Repic; 1-person sea kayak per hr/half day/day €10/30/50, 2-person €15/45/75) This place rents out sea kayaks and can also arrange motorboat rental (half/whole day €120/170). Skippers can be provided for excursions.

👉 Tours

Tramuntana Tours   ADVENTURE
(☏ 971 63 27 99; www.tramuntanatours.com; Passeig Es Través 12; bicycle rental per day €12-75, 3hr sea-kayaking €50; ☺ 9am-7.30pm Mar-Oct) This excellent gear shop and activity-tour operator right on the waterfront is the place to come for sea kayaking and bicycle hire. It can also arrange guided hikes into the Serra de Tramuntana, canyoning, mountain biking, boat charters and deep-sea fishing. There's another office in Sóller (p110).

Barcos Azules   BOATING
(☏ 971 63 01 70; www.barcosazules.com; Passeig Es Través 3; adult/child one-way €21/8, return €30/125; ☺ hours vary; 🚌) Tour boats do trips to Sa Calobra (up to four times daily) and Cala Tuent (up to once a day Monday to Friday, minimum seven people) and Sa Foradada (up to once every day, minimum seven people). Get tickets at a booth on the dock, next to the Tourist Office.

🍴 Eating

Port de Sóller waterfront is lined with eateries. Most serve fish and seafood and the quality varies wildly, but there are a few quite outstanding places.

Randemar INTERNATIONAL €€

(📱971 63 45 78; www.randemar.com; Passeig Es Través 16; mains €14-22; ⊗12.30pm-midnight mid-Mar–early Nov; 🛜) You almost feel like you're turning up to a *Great Gatsby*-style party in this pseudo-waterfront mansion, but few make it that far, preferring to linger over cocktails on the candlelit terrace to the back-beat of mellow music. The menu trots the globe from sushi to pasta to yes, even kangaroo. Desserts are a delicious contemporary take on the classics.

Kingfisher SEAFOOD €€€

(📱971 63 88 56; www.kingfishersoller.com; Carrer San Ramon de Penyafort 25; mains €20-28; ⊗noon-late Tue-Sat; 🛜) Sit out beneath one of the vast white parasols and enjoy the breeze as it lifts from the port waters. Kingfisher has it all: friendly and warm service, a fine setting, soothing jazzy music and fine homely fare. The fish and chips is all chunky, juicy cod, a smear of the smoothest of smooth mushy peas, gorgeous potatoes and gherkins, served on a slate plate.

Es Passeig MEDITERRANEAN €€€

(📱971 63 02 17; www.espasseig.com; Passeig de Sa Platja 8; mains €17-27; ⊗1-3.30pm & 6.30-10pm Wed-Sun, 6-10pm Tue Mar-Oct; 🛜🚭) Grab one of the sea-facing terrace tables or aim for one by the window at this artfully understated, yet triumphant restaurant. The bright, creative dishes are richly inflected by the seasons and presented with a razor-sharp eye for detail – no coincidence given chef Marcel Battenberg's Michelin-star credentials. Families are welcome – there's a good kids' menu.

ℹ️ Information

Tourist Office (📱971 63 30 42; Carrer del Canonge Oliver 10; ⊗9am-3.15pm Mon-Fri Apr-Oct) Located within a shiny refurbished train carriage, right in the heart of the town.

ℹ️ Getting There & Away

Most buses to Sóller terminate in Port de Sóller. If driving, you must choose between going to the centre (take the tunnel) or the Platja d'en Repic side (follow the signs). The trams *(tranvías)* to Sóller run along the waterfront. Several car and scooter-rental offices line Passeig Es Través.

If you want to look good on Mallorca's roads, snappy **Bullimoto Vespa** (📱971 63 26 96; www.bullimoto.com; Carrer d'Antoni Montis 6; per day from €38) rents three types of Vespa (two automatic, one manual), all in white and fancy, sparkling condition. Bullimoto also runs Vespa tours of the island.

Biniaraix

From either Fornalutx or Sóller, it's a pleasant 2km drive, pedal or stroll to the sweet hamlet of Biniaraix, with the brooding Tramuntana peering over its shoulder. Sights are few – which is why most people continue on to neighbouring Fornalutx – but there's something special about pausing, however briefly, in a place where most visitors arrive on foot, or along narrow country lanes lined with drystone walls. The village started life as an Arab *alquería* or farmstead and has a pleasant central square.

To go for a sublime ramble, walk up Carrer de Sant Josep from the church to the turning at the top of the road, where the old wash house stands (women of Biniaraix would scrub their clothes here) and turn right where a sign says 'Barranc de Biniaraix Cúber'; this walk will take you into a splendid gorge.

The **walking trail** to Biniaraix is well signposted from the centre of Sóller. You can also walk from Fornalutx, either by following the winding road down from the *plaça* towards Sóller, or by taking the far more attractive path alongside the Fornalutx Cemetery and past the terraced fields on the edge of the village, via the small settlement of **Binibassí**.

Plaça de Sa Concepció SQUARE

The very small, but utterly charming, central square is the focal point of the village, home to an inviting little bodega, a tall solitary plane tree that affords shade to walkers seeking a breather and the Església de la Immaculada Concepció.

Església de la Immaculada Concepció CHURCH

(Plaça de la Concepció) The sweet Church of the Immaculate Conception just up the steps from the *plaça* at the heart of Biniaraix dates from the late 16th century. Topped with a bell tower (added in the 19th century), the church interior has a barrel-vaulted ceiling and a graceful array of round arches.

Bar Bodega Biniaraix CAFE €

(Plaça de Sa Concepció; snacks from €5; ⊗9am-9.30pm Apr-Oct, 10.45am-9.30pm Nov-Mar) This charmer of a bar/cafe sits alone on the square in Biniaraix, with a host of tables set out front. It's a lovely spot for a *cafe con leche* with lashings of peace and quiet, a glass of Mallorcan wine, fresh orange juice and perhaps some *pa amb oli* or a slice or two of the moist homemade almond cake.

❶ Getting There & Away

A local service (€1.50, 15 minutes, two to four daily) connects Sóller with Biniaraix, before continuing to Fornalutx (€1.50). Alternatively, the walk from Sóller is a pleasant way to arrive and you can continue on foot to Fornalutx.

Fornalutx

POP 725

On foot, there are three ways to reach Fornalutx (the name means 'oven light'), one of Mallorca's most enchanting stone-built villages. The first is along a narrow, scenic route from Biniaraix, passing through the minute hamlet of Binibassi and then terraced groves crowded with orange and lemon trees. Another is the road that drops down off the Ma10, with aerial views of the village's stone houses and terracotta roofs. The more prosaic route is along the winding vehicular road from Sóller.

Whichever way you choose, the mountainous backdrop means Fornalutx is postcard pretty, and the effect is heightened as you draw near, with green shuttered windows, flower boxes, well-kept gardens and flourishing citrus groves. Many of the houses are owned by expats (Germans and Brits in the main), but it's a far cry from the comparative bustle of Sóller. Like Biniaraix, Fornalutx is believed to have its origins as an Arab *alquería*.

◉ Sights

Fornalutx rewards those who simply wander. Begin with the lanes around the central Plaça d'Espanya at the top of the road and pop into the ajuntament with its cool courtyard dominated by a palm tree. You can follow the course of the town stream east past fine houses and thick greenery, or climb the stairs heading north out of the town from the Església de la Nativitat de Nostra Senyora. Keep heading up the steps, and if you take a left fork on Carrer de Tramuntana, you will eventually make it to a dead end and the last house in the village; keep going straight up and you can head off up into the hills.

Plaça d'Espanya   SQUARE
The communal heart of the village, this gorgeous square is flanked on one side by the magnificent steps up to the church, the side wall of which occupies another flank; the steps continue on up to the top of the village and beyond, forming a delightful clamber for visitors. On a further side of the square, a cafe occupies pole position on, alongside a small supermarket. Opposite here stands the principal village fountain, supplying fresh, potable water.

Mirador de Ses Barques   VIEWPOINT
(P) The viewpoint of Mirador de Ses Barques, about 6km above Fornalutx, has phenomenal views all the way down to Port de Sóller; the restaurant here is handy for fresh orange juice and cake (rather than the food). Parking is plentiful out front, or across the road at the bend. You can also walk down from here on an engaging hike to Fornalutx below, or indeed clamber up from the village.

**Església de la Nativitat
de Nostra Senyora**   CHURCH
The lovely church of Fornalutx presides over the square, the sound of its sonorous bell marking the hours and quarter hours travels over the terracotta tiles of the village before being swallowed up by the hills. It stops at around 10pm so residents can get some shut-eye.

Ajuntament   HISTORIC BUILDING
(Town Hall; Carrer de Vicari Solivellas 1) A minute's walk from the square, pop into the old town hall with its cool courtyard dominated by a palm tree. Outside, water runs along one of several irrigation channels, leading down to the old wash house, where local women used to scrub clothes. If you keep going down the steps, you will reach the fabulous torrent that runs down from the hills and gushes onward to Sóller during the rains.

✗ Eating

The village is liberally scattered with restaurants and cafes, most of which are located around the central *plaça* or occupy shady roadside terraces (with panoramic views) about 500m out of the centre on the Ma2121 road leading northeast out of town.

★ Molón   FUSION €€
(☑ 871 87 23 23; www.molonrestaurant.com; Carrer Arbona-Colom 3; tapas €7-14; ⊙ 12.30-3.30pm & 7-10.30pm Mon-Sat May-Oct; ☎) The

WESTERN MALLORCA FORNALUTX

DON'T MISS

DRIVING BETWEEN SÓLLER & BUNYOLA
....

A dramatic driving route winds its way south of Sóller. To begin with, climb the valley into the hills (the tunnel isn't as pretty) and enjoy the views to Palma as you bend with the switchbacks on the other side. Before entering Bunyola and the towns that lie beyond, it's worth pausing to visit a grand reminder of Moorish Mallorca: the Jardins de Alfàbia (p112).

menu at Molón revolves around generously sized tapas which are designed to be shared around the table. But these are no ordinary tapas: imaginative combinations like fresh oysters with gin and cucumber jelly and lamb kofta with red pepper hummus and tzatziki reign supreme. Too highfalutin? Opt for a plate of hand-cut chunky chips with some battered hake. The trio of desserts is delicious.

Ca N'Antuna   MALLORCAN €€
(🖉971 63 30 68; Carrer Arbona-Colom 6; mains from €12.50; ⊙12.30-4pm & 7.30-11pm) With tables facing the stupendous view of the mountains from its outdoor terrace, this long-standing restaurant has an appetising focus on wholesome Mallorcan fare, and doesn't skimp on portions. The *lechona* is ample and succulent, while the roast lamb is worth coming back for. Reserve ahead for a table with a view; otherwise you get a seat roadside.

Es Turó   MALLORCAN €€
(🖉971 63 08 08; www.restaurante-esturo-fornalutx.com; Carrer Arbona-Colom 12; mains €107-21.50; ⊙noon-10.30pm Fri-Wed) The views over the village from this restaurant to the Tramuntana peaks at sunset are glorious. The menu is solidly Mallorcan, from *pa amb oli* to *arros brut* ('dirty' rice) and crisp, although dry, *lechona*. Be sure to try the zingy juice, freshly squeezed from local oranges.

ⓘ Getting There & Away
A local service connects Fornalutx with Sóller (€1.50, 15 minutes, two to four daily), via Biniaraix.

Bunyola
POP 6662

This drowsy town, known for olive oil and its *palo* (herbal liquor) distillery, resides at the foot of lush terraced hillsides and the wild grey peaks of the Tramuntana. The rickety wooden train that trundles between Palma and Sóller stops here. It's a fabulous base for rock climbing and – back at ground level – for observing Mallorcan village life in the central square, Sa Plaça, which hosts a small Saturday morning market.

Bunyola does not have an excellent range of restaurants in town, but Orient and Alaró are not far away, and are both stocked with good dining options. Alternatively, Sóller has an excellent selection of restaurants.

Església de Sant Mateu   CHURCH
(Carrer de l'Església 2; ⊙mass) Next to the main square in the heart of town, the Església de Sant Mateu was built in 1230 but was largely redone in 1756. You'll only be allowed to peek inside during mass.

Sa Gubia   CLIMBING
Just west of Bunyola, where the foothills of the Tramuntana thin to the flatlands around Palma, rises this magnificent rock amphitheatre – a holy grail to climbers, who come to play on 125 multi-pitch routes graded 4 to 8, including some excellent, fully bolted long climbs. The **Cara Oeste** (West Face) ranks as one of Europe's most impressive limestone walls.

Ca'n Topa   MALLORCAN €
(🖉971 14 84 67; Careterra Palma a Soller Km 22.1; snacks €5-10; ⊙hours vary) Its high-on-a-hill location on the windy mountain road to Sóller makes Ca'n Topa a much-loved pit stop of cyclists and hikers, who love its languid rhythm, poolside deck, snacks (pizzas, *bocadillos*, cakes and the like) and ice-cold drinks after exploring the Tramuntana.

ⓘ Getting There & Away
Buses and trains running between Palma and Sóller stop at Bunyola (the bus stop is at Sa Plaça, and the train station a short walk west of the centre). Local bus 221 runs twice a day east to Orient (€2, 30 minutes). This is a microbus service and you need to book a seat in advance by calling 617 365365.

Alternatively, hit the hairpin bends up the cross-mountain road and down into the Sóller valley.

Orient

POP 35

With its huddle of ochre houses clustered on a slight rise, pretty Orient is one of the loveliest little hamlets on the island. A few houses on the north side of the road seem set to slide off, as if they're an afterthought.

The 9km road (the Ma2100) that wends northeast from Bunyola to Orient attracts swarms of lithe, lycra-clad cyclists. The first 5km is a promenade along a valley brushed with olive and cypress trees that slowly crests a plain and the Coll d'Honor (550m) before tumbling over the other side of a forested ridge. The next 2km of serried switchbacks flatten out on the run into Orient. All the way, the Serra d'Alfàbia is in sight to the north.

★ **Mandala**   INTERNATIONAL €€
(☑971 61 52 85; Carrer Nou 1; mains €17-25; ☺8.30-10.30pm Tue-Sun Jun–mid-Sep, shorter hours mid-Sep–Nov & Mar-May, closed Dec-Feb; ▣) Spicy smells drift enticingly from this unassuming-looking den of fusion cooking, tucked away on a picturesque cobblestone street. Snag a table on the patio overlooking the verdant valley that surrounds the town and dine on French classics like steak tartar, *bouillabaisse* (Provençal fish stew) and superb rack of lamb, or Asian takes like Thai prawn curry. Bookings are essential.

ⓘ Getting There & Away

The 221 bus runs from Bunyola to Orient (€2) twice a day, but must be reserved the day before (call 617 36 53 65).

Alaró

POP 5438 / ELEVATION 252M

Topped by castle ruins, Alaró is pleasantly sleepy and rewards those who linger. Head for Plaça de la Vila, flanked by the Casa de la Vila (town hall), the parish church and a couple of cafes. The square springs to life at its Saturday morning market. Cafes also congregate around Carrer Petit and Carrer de Jaume Rosselló.

★ **Castell d'Alaró**   CASTLE
(off Carretera Alaró-Bunyola) Perched at an improbable, almost comical angle on a gigantic fist of rock, Castell d'Alaró is one of the most rewarding castle climbs on the island. The ruins are all that remain of the last redoubt of Christian warriors who could only be starved out by Muslim conquerors around 911, eight years after the Moors invaded Mallorca. The astonishing views, from Palma to Badia de Alcúdia, are something special. If the two-hour walk up doesn't appeal, you can cover most of the ascent by car.

★ **Es Verger**   SPANISH €€
(☑971 18 21 26; Camí des Castell; mains €8-16; ☺9am-9pm Tue-Sun) On the zigzagging road up to Castell d'Alaró, this gloriously rustic haunt is well worth the trek, bike ride or gear-crunching ascent. The sheep hanging out in the car park are a menu give-away. In his *Mediterranean Escapes* series of books, UK-based chef Rick Stein praises the lamb *(cordero)* as the moistest he has ever tasted – and right he is.

Traffic   MALLORCAN €€
(☑971 87 91 17; www.canxim.com; Plaça de la Vila 8, Hotel Can Xim; mains €12-22; ☺12.15-5.15pm & 8-11.30pm Mon & Thu-Sun, 8-11pm Wed; ▣ ᐂ) The pick of the places on Plaça de la Vila, this countrified restaurant at the Hotel Can Xim rolls out Mallorcan specialities with a few innovative twists. Meats such as rabbit and suckling pig are definitely the strong point, but the cod with *sobrassada* and honey is terrific, too. Choose between the terrace and the beamed, tiled interior.

ⓘ Getting There & Away

The Palma–Inca train calls at the Consell-Alaró train station (20 to 30 minutes), where it connects with local bus 320 for Alaró (€1.50, 15 minutes).

Cala de Sa Calobra & Cala Tuent

The hairpin-riddled 12km helter-skelter of a road down to Sa Calobra and Cala Tuent is one of Mallorca's top experiences. Whether you're swooning over the giddy ravine views, gulping as a coach squeezes through an impossibly narrow cleft in the rock, or aping Tour de France winner Bradley Wiggins with a thigh-burning pedal to the top (he does it in 26 minutes, for the record), this spectacularly serpentine road, which branches north off the Ma10, is pure drama. Carved through the rock and skirting narrow ridges as it unfurls to the coast, it is the feat of Italian engineer Antonio Paretti, who built it in 1932; its twists and turns were inspired by tying a tie, some say (explaining the section of road that turns round before threading under itself).

◉ Sights

If you come in summer, you won't be alone. Legions of buses and fleets of pleasure boats disgorge battalions of tourists. It's a different world to Sa Calobra on a quiet, bright midwinter morning. From the northern end of the road a short trail leads around the coast to a rocky river gorge, the Torrent de Pareis, and a small white-pebble cove with fabulous (but usually crowded) swimming spots.

To flee for some peace and quiet, nip down a turn-off west to reach restful and gorgeous Cala Tuent.

Cala Tuent BEACH
To skip the Sa Calobra crowds, follow a turn-off west, some 2km before Sa Calobra, to reach Cala Tuent, a tranquil emerald-green inlet in the shadow of Puig Major, with a single tall pine tree right by the beach. The broad pebble-and-shingle beach is backed by a couple of houses and a great, green bowl of vegetation that climbs up the mountain flanks. Cars park alongside the road near the beach, but things can get tight.

Sa Calobra BEACH
Past the turning to Cala Tuent, the road winds down to this small and undeniably attractive white-pebble cove, but it's a coach-fest during the summer crush, when carloads of visitors also descend. There is parking at the end of the road, but you will need to pay. A short trail and walkway leads around the coast to a rocky river gorge, the **Torrent de Pareis**, the dramatic conclusion to the torrent's descent from Escorca.

Puig Major MOUNTAIN
Mallorca's tallest peak (1445m) can be seen from all round these parts. It's topped with a globular radar station, built by the US.

✖ Eating

Before getting behind the wheel to take on the wriggling bends back to the Ma10, have a seat booked for a meal in the old *finca* (farmhouse) of Es Vergeret, which looks out on to awesome views. Alternatively, you can find a few rather average restaurants in Sa Calobra.

Es Vergeret MALLORCAN €€
(📄 971 51 71 05; www.esvergeret.com; Camí de Sa Figuera Vial 21; mains €15-20; ⊘ 12.30am-4.30pm

Mar-Oct) A narrow country lane forking from the road to Cala Tuent on the dramatic drive down passes sheep farms and olive groves before reaching this glorious old *finca,* where astonishing views take in the full sweep of the bay below and the mountains. The terrace is a cracking spot for a lazy lunch of paella, grilled fish or lamb chops.

❶ Getting There & Away

One bus a day (bus 355, Monday to Saturday, May to October) comes from Ca'n Picafort (9.30am) via Alcúdia, Cala Sant Vicenç, Pollença and the Monestir de Lluc. It returns at 3pm. The whole trip takes just under four hours to Sa Calobra (with a one-hour stop at the Monestir de Lluc) and 2½ hours on the return leg. From Ca'n Picafort, you pay €9.05 one way. Boats make excursions to Sa Calobra and Cala Tuent from Port de Sóller.

Monestir de Lluc

The site's sacred nature is heavily embroidered with ancient lore. Back in the 13th century, a local shepherd reputedly saw an image of the Virgin Mary in the sky. Later, a similar image appeared on a rock. Others say it was an Arab shepherd boy who discovered an image of a beautiful woman in 1238 and, returning with a monk from Escorca, saw a holy crown suspended over the spot. Another story relates how a statuette of the Virgin was found here and taken to Escorca. The next day it was back where it had been found. Three times it was taken to Escorca and three times it returned. A chapel was built near the site to commemorate the miracle, possibly around 1268. The religious sanctuary came afterwards. Since then thousands of pilgrims have come every year to pay homage to the 14th-century (and thus not the original) Statue of the Virgin of Lluc.

◉ Sights

★**Monestir de Lluc** MONASTERY
(www.lluc.net; Plaça dels Peregrins; monastery & gardens free, museum adult/child €2/free; ⊘ 10am-5pm; 🅿) Entered via a cloistered garden, the monastery is a huge complex, dating mostly from the 17th and 18th centuries. Off the imposing central courtyard rises up the grand façade of the late-Renaissance **basilica**, behind which is a rather gloomy interior and a fine altarpiece by Jaume Blanquer; the **Virgin Mary and Infant Jesus statuette** is contained in a room behind the altar. The

church received an ornate, baroque-style revamp in the early 20th century, based on plans drawn up by Gaudí.

The dark effigy of the Virgin Mary and the infant Jesus (holding a book open with the letters *alpha* and *omega* inscribed upon the pages) attracts formidable piety from the frequent line of pilgrims who file up the steps to face the statuette in prayer and who often then make a donation in the tray. The statue is known as La Moreneta (the Black Madonna) because of the statuette's age-darkened complexion.

If you're lucky, you might hear the **Els Escolanets** (also known as Els Blauets, the Little Blues, because of the soutane they wear), the monastery's boarding-school boys choir. This institution dates to the early 16th century.

The **museum** is well-worth visiting, showcasing prehistoric finds including Talayotic artefacts, folk art and crafts, religious icons and a stash of vibrant paintings by Catalan Impressionist Josep Coll Bardolet. An English-language card detailing the contents of each gallery is available at the museum front desk. The Lluc ticket gives entry to the museum, the extensive **Jardí Botànic** (botanical garden) and the **swimming pool** (at the conclusion to the botanical garden, no lifeguard) in the monastery's serene grounds.

The monastery also offers fittingly austere accommodation (guests are required to make their own bed).

The **Magnolia Garden**, just before the central courtyard, contains four specimens of *magnolia grandiflora,* which flowers with huge velvety petals in summer.

Camí dels Misteris del Rosari RELIGIOUS SITE

FREE An old stone trail, partly shaded by holm oaks, leads up the **Pujol des Misteris** (Hill of the Mysteries), which rises behind the monastery complex. The path recounts the mysteries of the rosaries, with monuments and three bronze reliefs. A place for peaceful contemplation, it also offers stirring views on the way up, especially into the valley behind. From the austere cross (fenced off with barbed wire) at the top, linger for grandstand views and the boulder-strewn peaks of the Tramuntana.

Centre d'Informació Serra de Tramuntana MUSEUM

(☑ 971 51 70 83; www.serradetramuntana.net; Carretera Lluc a Pollença; adult/child €2/free; ⊙ 9am-4.30pm; ℗) Opposite the monastery complex, this interpretation centre has audiovisual displays and a small museum providing information on the Serra de Tramuntana. Here you can brush up on regional flora and fauna, including bird species such as Eleonora's falcon and Balearic shearwater, and learn about farming in the mountains. The centre has a stock of multilingual leaflets detailing walks in the area, and the friendly staff can arrange camping in the grounds of Lluc for around €5 per night.

WESTERN MALLORCA MONESTIR DE LLUC

THE PATHS OF PILGRIMS

Like so many before him, Antoni Gaudí made the pilgrimage to the Monestir de Lluc in April 1908, leaving a donation of 25 pesetas. In October that same year he returned, this time with his protégé Joan Rubió. He redesigned the church in the same baroque style as the chancel and oversaw the creation of the stone monuments that grace the Pujol des Misteris, which rises behind the monastery complex.

Numerous walking routes leave from the monastery. One is a challenging 11km, five-hour circuit of **Puig de Massanella** (1365m), Mallorca's second highest peak, with sensational vistas from its summit. Another is a 9km, 3½-hour circuit of **Puig Tomir** (1103m), a stiff, rocky ascent into the lonely heights of the Tramuntana, where you may sight vultures and falcons. Another route is a four- to five-hour hike around **Puig Roig** (1102m), to the northwest of the monastery; this route should only be done on Sundays as some of the route traverses private land. Lluc is also a stop on the long-distance GR221 between Sant Elm and Pollença.

For the true spirit of blister-footed pilgrimage, join thousands of Mallorcans on the Marxa des Güell a Lluc a Peu (p120), a 42km all-night march from the Plaça Güell in Palma to the Monestir de Lluc, taking in farmland, hill towns and the Serra de Tramuntana by torchlight.

Festivals & Events

Marxa des Güell a Lluc a Peu   RELIGIOUS
(⊙1st Sat Aug) Annual 42km walk from Palma to Lluc held on the first Saturday of August.

Eating

The most convenient restaurant for travellers is Sa Fonda in the refectory at the monastery itself.

Sa Fonda   SPANISH **€€**
(☑971 51 70 22; Plaça del Lledoner; mains €9-18.50; ⊙8-10.30am & 1-11pm; ℗) Housed in the expanded pilgrims' refectory at the monastery, this rambling restaurant is a historic spot for breakfast, lunch or dinner at a varnished table below marble arches and wood beams. The all-Mallorcan menu stars dishes such as *frito mallorquín*, suckling pig from the oven (€16.50) and grilled sole (€17).

ⓘ Getting There & Away

Up to two buses a day (May to October) run from Ca'n Picafort to the Monestir de Lluc (€6.55, 1¾ hours) on their way to Sóller and Port de Sóller. From Palma, two all-stops buses (€4.80; buses 330 and 354) to Inca continue to Lluc via Caimari from Monday to Saturday (one on Sunday).

Northern Mallorca

Best Places to Eat

➡ Mirador de La Victòria (p137)

➡ Restaurante Jardín (p136)

➡ Bellaverd (p131)

Best Historic Sights

➡ Pol·lèntia (p132)

➡ Calvari (p126)

➡ Església de la Mare de Déu dels Àngels (p126)

➡ Medieval Walls of Alcúdia (p132)

➡ Alcúdia's Historic Mansions (p134)

Why Go?

Bordered by dramatic and sublime coastal scenery, fringed with white-sand bays, dotted with cultured towns (where fiestas inspire a celebratory mood) and blessed with a top portfolio of exciting adventure sports, Northern Mallorca is both an untamed and cultivated region of Mallorca.

The Serra de Tramuntana is at its most fabulous where the range culminates on the Cap de Formentor, flicking out into the Med like a dragon's tail. The road that wraps around its clifftops elicits gasps of wonder from drivers and cyclists. Across the water, the pine-forested peninsula of Cap des Pinar is hiking heaven. Elsewhere, kitesurfers, scuba divers, cavers, cliff jumpers and paragliders harness its unique coastscapes and steady breezes.

Resorts here have a low-key, kid-friendly vibe. Inland, towns have retained an authentic and historic Mallorcan air: from medieval-walled Alcúdia to Pollença, with its charming cafe-rimmed plazas, pilgrim trails and live-to-party summer festivals.

When to Go

Some of the beach resorts barely have a pulse until May or after October (Cala Sant Vicenç, for instance), and the best beach weather runs from June to August. Pollença is one big fiesta in August. Yet our favourite times to visit are spring and autumn – migrating birds flock to the Parc Natural de S'Albufera, the roads are quieter (especially out along the Cap de Formentor), Pollença's Good Friday celebration is captivating, and Alcúdia hosts a terrific market in early October. Cooler weather is better for hitting the walking trails and cycling the gradients, too.

Northern Mallorca Highlights

1 Cap de Formentor (p132)
Getting high on the views on
this coastal thriller.

2 Pollença (p126) Counting
your blessings pilgrim-style on
the 365-step Calvari.

3 Penya Rotja (p124)
Hiking to see the north coast
reduced to postcard format.

**4 Santuari de la Mare de
Déu des Puig** (p126) Lifting
your spirits with sensational
views.

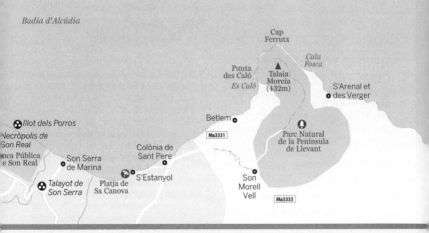

Cala Figuera

Cap de Formentor
1 Moll del Patronet

umat 334m)

Cala Murta *Cala Gossalba*

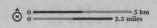

N 0 ———————— 5 km
0 ———————— 2.5 miles

MEDITERRANEAN SEA

Cap des Pinar

3 Penya Rotja

8 Platja des Coll Baix

Museo Sa Bassa Blanca

Badia d'Alcúdia

Cap Ferrutx

Cala Fosca

Punta des Caló
Es Caló

▲ Talaia Moreia (432m)

S'Arenal et
des Verger

Betlem

4 Parc Natural de la Península de Llevant

Illot dels Porros
Necròpolis de Son Real
nca Pública e Son Real

Son Serra de Marina

Colònia de Sant Pere

Ma3331

4 S'Estanyol

Talayot de Son Serra Platja de Sa Canova

Son Morell Vell

Ma3333

5 Talaia d'Alcúdia (p136)
Clambering up to some of the island's finest wraparound views.

6 Parc Natural de S'Albufera (p137) Bird-spotting in the rushes.

7 Alcúdia (p132) Winging back to Roman and medieval times.

8 Platja des Coll Baix (p136) Descending on foot to this gorgeously remote beach with cerulean waters.

HIKING THE COAST OF NORTHERN MALLORCA

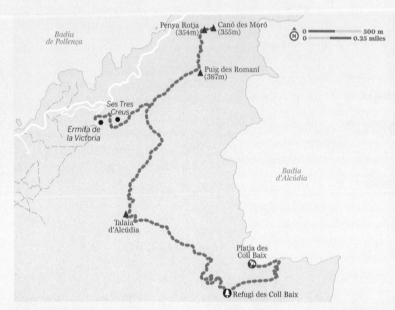

Badia de Pollença

Penya Rotja (354m) — Canó des Moró (355m)

Puig des Romaní (387m)

Ses Tres Creus

Ermita de la Victoria

Badia d'Alcúdia

Talaia d'Alcúdia

Platja des Coll Baix

Refugi des Coll Baix

0 — 500 m
0 — 0.25 miles

HIKING TOUR: THREE COASTAL PEAKS

START ERMITA DE LA VICTÒRIA
END PENYA ROTJA
LENGTH 6KM; 2½–3 HOURS

One of Mallorca's most dramatic and exciting coastal walks, this medium-level hike takes you along precipitous ridges and clifftops to three crags, perched like eyries above the Cap des Pinar peninsula. Look out for the Mallorcan wild goat (*Capra ageagrus hircus*) that inhabits these rocky heights. It's wise to avoid the midday heat; take a map and plenty of water. Make sure you wear sturdy shoes, too.

From the **Ermita de la Victòria** (p136) hermitage, head up the hill along the wide path through the pine forest, passing the signposted **Ses Tres Creus** – three crosses among the trees, overlooking the Badia de Pollença. Turn left after around 15 minutes, following signs to Penya Rotja and Penya des Migdia, onto a narrow footpath that wends up-

hill through woods, then gently downhill (watch out for roots across the way that can trip you up). Don't follow the signs for Talaia d'Alcúdia, which is an alternative hike (described below) – Pause for sensational Badia de Pollença and Formentor views to the west. Sheer walls of rock now rise above you and the sea glints far below. Pass overhanging cliffs and, at a fork in the path, veer right and follow cairns uphill for 1½ hours to crest **Puig des Romaní** (387m), where a superb panorama awaits.

From the summit, return to the main trail, which descends gradually along a ridge as it skirts a bluff, with the cliffs to your left falling away sharply. Squeeze through a vertiginous tunnel that burrows through the rock. Entering old coastal fortifications with gun emplacements, follow the path that skirts the knife-edge cliff face, using the fixed rope to negotiate the steepest parts, to reach the top of **Penya Rotja** (354m) after 1½ hours. Topped by a cannon, the 360-degree lookout takes in the full sweep of Mallorca's north

The rocky, pine-sprouting coastline of the Cap des Pinar, thrusting into the blue Mediterranean, is one of Mallorca's most rewarding and scenic hiking destinations.

coast, reaching across Cap des Pinar to the Badia d'Alcúdia, Pollença and Formentor.

An optional boulder-strewn scramble takes you up to the cannon atop **Canó des Moró** (355m), where you'll most probably be alone with the goats, wild rosemary and striking views across the peninsula to the cobalt waters pummelling **Platja des Coll Baix** (p136) far below. Retrace your steps along the same path back to Ermita de La Victòria.

An alternative, shorter hike from the Ermita de La Victòria is to commence the trek as above, but to instead follow the signs right up to **Talaia d'Alcúdia** (p136), ascending the rocky path for a final scramble up some boulders to panoramic views of the Badia de Pollença and the Badia d'Alcúdia from the summit, where you find the remains of an old watchtower (*talaia*). From here, it's a 40-minute hike down a zigzagging path (follow the blue marks) to the pine trees and the **Refugi des Coll Baix**, where there are picnic tables and a shelter, and a bit further away downhill to the right, a car park. Mallorcan wild goats are often seen around here in abundance. To return to Ermita de La Victòria from here is a 90-minute journey along the way you have come, but you can also follow the signposted path down through the trees to idyllic **Platja des Coll Baix** (p136) below.

WALKING TRAILS ON THE CAP DE FORMENTOR

The peninsula has various trails that lead down to pebbly beaches and inlets. The walk from **Port de Pollença** to crescent-shaped **Cala Bóquer** is signposted off a roundabout on the main road to Cap de Formentor. This valley walk, with the rocky Serra del Cavall Bernat walling off the western flank, is an easy 3km hike.

About 11km along the peninsula from Port de Pollença, trails lead off left and right from the road (there is some rough parking here) to **Cala Figuera** on the north flank and **Cala Murta** on the south. The former walk is down a bare gully to a narrow shingle beach, with mesmerising waters. The latter is through mostly wooded land to a stony beach. Each is around a 40-minute descent.

Near Cala Murta is quiet **Cala Gossalba**, reached via a shady 30-minute walk (try to park at the bay just before Km 15 and descend the trail opposite). From here you can head right to traverse cliffs to the next cove. This is the trailhead for Formentor's most memorable hike. Ascend the boulder-speckled gully behind the cove and then follow the serpentine old military path up to the summit of 334m **Fumat** (around 1½ hours from the cove). The crag has knockout 360-degree views of the cape to the east and the Badia de Pollença to the south, with the peaks of the Tramuntana rising like shark fins to the west. From here, retrace your steps and veer left onto a trail that leads back to the road and the parking bay.

A couple of other small inlets to check out along the coast are **Cala des Caló** and **Cala En Feliu**. Walkers can also hike to or from the cape along the **Camí Vell del Far**, a poorly defined track that criss-crosses and at times follows the main road. At Port de Pollença you can link with the GR221 trail that runs the length of the Serra de Tramuntana.

The Pollença and Port de Pollença tourist offices can give you booklets that contain approximate trail maps, which for these walks should be sufficient.

POLLENÇA & AROUND

Pollença

POP 16,189 / ELEV 41M

Pollença is quite beautiful. On a late summer afternoon, when its stone houses glow in the fading light, cicadas strike up their drone and the burble of chatter floats from cafe terraces lining the Plaça Major, the town is like the Mallorca you always hoped to discover. Its postcard looks and vaguely bohemian airs have drawn artists, writers and luminaries from Winston Churchill to Agatha Christie over the years. Saunter through its gallery- and boutique-lined backstreets or pull up a ringside chair on the square at sundown to watch the world go by, and you too will be smitten. Even better, check into one of Pollença's lovely hotels and overnight here to make the most of its historic charm.

◉ Sights & Activities

★**Calvari**   CHRISTIAN SITE
(Carrer del Calvari) They don't call it Calvari (Calvary) for nothing. Some pilgrims do it on their knees, but even just walking up the 365 cypress-lined steps from the town centre to the lovely 18th-century hilltop chapel, the **Església del Calvari**, with its simple, spartan and serene interior, is penance enough. This may not be a stairway to heaven, but there are soul-stirring views to savour back over the town's mosaic of terracotta rooftops and church spires to the Tramuntana beyond. There's a small cafe at the top next to the church, and you may find a guitarist playing for small change at the top of the steps.

★**Església de la Mare de Déu dels Àngels**   CHURCH
(Plaça Major; ◷ 11am-1pm & 3-5pm Jun-Aug, shorter hours Sep-May) A church was first raised on this site in Gothic style shortly after the conquest in 1229, but was given a complete makeover in the 18th century, so what you see today overlooking the Plaça Major is predominantly baroque. The unusually simple rough-sandstone facade is a superb backdrop to the square. Illuminated by a rose window, the interior has an unusual and barrel-vaulted ceiling with extravagant ceiling frescoes (some restored with a heavy hand) and a magnificent, overblown altarpiece.

★**Santuari de la Mare de Déu des Puig**   MONASTERY
(Puig de Maria; ◷ 9am-6pm Oct-Mar, 8.30am-8.30pm Apr-Sep) **FREE** South of Pollença, off the Ma2200, one of Mallorca's most tortuous roads bucks and weaves up 1.5km of gasp-out-loud hairpin bends to this 14th-century former nunnery, which sits atop the 333m **Puig de Maria**. If you come pilgrim style (the best way), the stiff hike through woods of holm oak, pine and olive will take you around an hour – Pollença shrinks to toy-town scale as you near the summit. Be sure to avoid the midday heat and pack some water.

No taxi driver is foolhardy enough to venture here, which speaks volumes about the road, but if you crank into first gear, take it steady and say your prayers, you might just make it to the final parking bay, around a 20-minute walk from the refuge.

At the top, take a contemplative stroll through the refectory, kitchen, heirloom-filled corridors, and incense-perfumed Gothic chapel of the former nunnery. That's if you can tear yourself away from the view. Though modest in height, this fist of rock commands one of Mallorca's finest outlooks: to the west the hauntingly beautiful peaks of the Tramuntana range, to the east the gently curving bays of Alcúdia and Pollença and the jagged Formentor peninsula.

You can stay the night in a **converted hermit's cell** (☑971 18 41 32; Puig de Maria, Pollença; s/d/tr €20/25/30; ☏) to rise at an ungodly hour for a spectacular sunrise, or simply enjoy the silence over a bite to eat. The paella is one of the best you'll here.

Museu de Pollença   MUSEUM
(Carrer de Guillem Cifre de Colonya; ◷ 10am-1pm & 5.30-8.30pm Tue-Sat Jun-Sep, 11am-1pm Tue-Sat Oct-May) **FREE** This museum's star feature is the 17th-century baroque cloister of the Convent de Sant Domingo – a picture of tranquillity and poise – in which the museum is housed. At the entrance is a small collection of pottery, while upstairs awaits a superb collection of modern and contemporary art, where you can also find a bright Buddhist Kalachakra mandala created from coloured grains of sand, donated by the Dalai Lama to the town in 1990.

Església de la Mare de Déu del Roser   CHURCH
(Carrer de Guillem Cifre de Colonya) Part of the Museu de Pollença, the Església de la Mere

Pollença

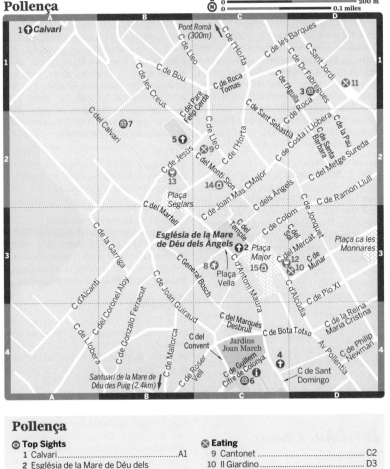

Pollença

de Déu del Roser is a marvellous old and now-empty church whose space is used for art exhibitions and contemporary art installations.

Pont Romà   BRIDGE
(Carrer del Pont Romà) On the northern outskirts of town, this two-arched bridge originally dates to Roman days, although it was much restored in medieval times.

Casa-Museu Dionís Bennàssar
MUSEUM

(☑971 53 09 97; www.museudionisbennassar.com; Carrer de Roca 14; adult/child €3/free; ⊘10.30am-2pm & 5-8pm Tue-Sat, 10.30am-2pm Sun Apr–Oct) This museum, the former home of local artist Dionís Bennàssar (1904–67), hosts a permanent collection of his works. Downstairs are early etchings, watercolours and oils, depicting mostly local scenes. Works on the other floors range from a series on fish that is strangely reminiscent of Miquel Barceló's efforts in Palma's cathedral, to a series of nudes and portraits of dancing girls.

Museu Martí Vicenç
MUSEUM

(☑971 53 28 67; www.martivicens.org; Carrer del Calvari 10; ⊘10am-2pm & 5-8pm Mon & Wed-Sat, 10am-2pm Sun Apr-Oct, 10am-2pm Mon & Wed-Sun Nov & Mar) FREE A short way up the Calvari steps is the Museu Martí Vicenç. The weaver and artist Martí Vicenç Alemany (1926–95) bought this property, once part of a giant Franciscan monastery that also included the nearby former Església de Monti-Sion (Carrer de Jesús), in the 1950s. His works are strewn around several rooms.

Món d'Aventura
ADVENTURE SPORTS

(☑971 53 52 48; http://mondaventura.com; Plaça Vella 8; canyoning €50-55; ⊘10am-2pm & 4.30-8.30pm Mon-Fri, 10am-2pm Sat & Sun) Sports and adventure activities provider Món d'Aventura has canyoning, caving, kayaking, climbing, coasteering and hiking all covered. This is one of the most reputable adventure sports operators on the north coast.

🎉 Festivals & Events

Davallament
RELIGIOUS

(⊘Mar/Apr) At this haunting Good Friday re-enactment of the Passion Play, the body of Christ is solemnly paraded down the 365 steps of Calvari during Davallament ('Lowering') by torchlight. It is one of the island's most moving and evocative Easter celebrations.

Festes de la Patrona
CULTURAL

(⊘late Jul-early Aug) Dress up as a swashbuckling pirate or all in white and throw yourself into the crowd to celebrate the big and boisterous Festes de la Patrona, with mock battles between the Moros i Cristians (Moors and Christians) to mark the siege and attack by Saracen pirates in 1550, led by the infamous Turkish pirate Dragut (1500–65). A famous victory for the townsfolk, the 'battle' is the high point of the festival.

Townsfolk, dressed up as scimitar-waving Moorish pirates and pole-toting villagers, engage in several mock battles, to the thunder of drums and blunderbusses, around town on the afternoon of 2 August. The night before, the town centre is the scene of one almighty drinking spree, with folk thronging the bars and squares, and live concerts blaring through the night from 11pm. No wonder the following day's battles don't get started until 7pm! Spectacular fireworks conclude the festivities.

La Fira
FOOD & DRINK

(⊘2nd Sun in Nov) A massive market held in the Convent de Sant Domingo, the Plaça Major and elsewhere around town.

Festival de Pollença
CULTURAL

(☑971 53 40 11; www.festivalpollenca.com; Convent de Sant Domingo, Carrer de Guillem Cifre de Colonya; ⊘late Jul-Aug) Orchestras, exhibitions and film screenings come to the highly atmospheric Sant Domingo cloister for this summer arts festival, running since 1962.

🍴 Eating

Plaça Major is encircled by good-natured eateries and cafe-bars where tables are scattered about, providing sustenance to legions of diners morning, noon and night; some of the better options are only a short walk away, tucked down the side streets.

Cantonet
ITALIAN €€

(☑971 53 04 29; Carrer del Monti-Sion 20; mains €12-20; ⊘noon-3pm & 7-11pm; 🕿) As day slides into dusk, this restaurant terrace in front of the Església de Monti-Sion is an entrancing choice, with views reaching across the old town rooftops to the Puig de Maria beyond. Settle down to mussels in oregano sauce, gilthead bream in a Sardinian wine sauce or lamb cutlets grilled with honey and thyme.

Il Giardino
ITALIAN €€

(☑971 53 43 02; www.giardinopollensa.com; Plaça Major 11; mains €17-24, set meals €14.50-19.50; ⊘restaurant 12.30am-3pm & 6.30-10.30pm Apr-Oct, patisserie 9am-3pm & 5-7pm Mon-Sat, 9am-3pm Sun; 🎵) For many, this is the pick of the restaurants on Plaça Major, with a fine terrace and friendly service. The menu whispers longingly of *bella Italia,* with mains like lasagne with salmon, fresh goat cheese and zucchini hitting the sweet spot. Its adjacent patisserie and chocolate shop is a delectable post-dinner detour or breakfast choice. Children are well provided for.

La Placeta

SPANISH €€

(971 53 12 18; www.laplacetarestaurant.com; Carrer Sant Jordi 29; mains €13.50-16; ⊙12.30-3pm & 7.30-11pm Tue-Sun; 🚻) Everyone raves about La Placeta at Hotel Sant Jordi, whether for its pretty alfresco setting on the square, child-friendly waiters or no-nonsense home cooking. Dishes as simple as prawns sautéed with artichokes and lamb roasted in its own juices, accompanied with Madeira wine, reveal true depth of flavour.

🍷 Drinking & Nightlife

With several fine cocktail bars and cafe-bars of note dotted about its atmospheric historic centre, Pollença is an excellent place for an evening drink, preferably coupled with a stay in town.

Club Pollença

BAR

(Plaça Major 10; ⊙7am-midnight) Observe Pollença life in all its guises over drinks and tapas on the terrace of this rambling colonial-flavoured cafe with a superb position on Plaça Major, which first opened its doors in 1910. Grab a front-row seat, enjoy the spectacle and soak up the town's manifest charms.

U Gallet

BAR

(971 84 94 29; Carrer de Jesús 40; ⊙11am-2am Apr-Oct, 6pm-1am Fri-Mon Nov-Mar) Known also to locals as the 'Gallito' (cockerel) and full of enticingly cosy nooks and posters of Bowie, the Rolling Stones and Ed Sheeran, this excellent drinking hole is a very welcome choice on Carrer de Jesús, with great cocktails and G&Ts. The vibe is chilled, though sports gets a say on the TV too.

🛍 Shopping

Pollença is filled with engaging and creative little boutiques and its shopping is the best on the island outside Palma.

La Merceria

ARTS & CRAFTS

(🗹 652 023568; Carrer del Monti-Sion 3; ⊙10am-2pm & 5-9.30pm Tue-Fri, 10am-2pm Sat & Sun) This gloriously retro emporium merges vintage style with contemporary design. Among the unique trinkets and gifts are nostalgic sepia postcards of old Pollença, Barcelona fashion, handmade straw boaters for a dash of Gatsby glamour, funky lampshades, gorgeous ceramics, cool glassware, creative candles, ace photos, art, jewellery and uplifting designs. Out back there's a fab collection of kids' books and clothing.

Sunday Market

MARKET

(Plaça Major; ⊙8.30am-1pm Sun) Held year-round, Pollença's Sunday market is one of the largest and liveliest in Mallorca. Fruit, veg, cheese, wine, herbs and spices are concentrated in the Plaça Major, with handicrafts and other stalls taking over an ever-widening arc of surrounding streets.

ℹ Information

Tourist Office (🗹 971 53 50 77; www.pollensa.com; Carrer de Guillem Cifre de Colonya; ⊙8.30am-1.30pm & 2-4pm Mon-Fri, 10am-1pm Sun May-Oct, shorter hours Nov-Apr) Right by the Museu de Pollença, this tourist office is a mine of information on the town and its surrounds, with helpful staff and loads of literature.

ℹ Getting There & Away

From Palma, bus 340 heads nonstop for Pollença (€5.50, 45 minutes, up to 12 daily). It then continues on to Port de Pollença (€1.50, 20 minutes, up to 30 daily). Bus 345 runs from Pollença to Cala Sant Vicenç (€1.50, 20 minutes, frequent).

Cala Sant Vicenç

POP 300

One of the loveliest little corners of the northern Mallorcan coast, Cala Sant Vicenç is arrayed around four jewel-like *cales* (coves) in a breach in the Serra de Tramuntana, with fine views across stunning turquoise waters northwest towards the sheer limestone cliffs of Cap de Formentor. The village is really only open for business from May to October, then largely shuts up shop.

It doesn't take more than 20 minutes to walk the entire distance between Cala Sant Vicenç's four beaches: Cala Barques, Cala Clara, Cala Molins and Cala Carbó.

If you walk for 15 minutes along Carrer Temporal from behind Cala Clara and then down Carrer de Dionís Bennàssar, you'll reach a rise with park benches and the Coves de L'Alzineret, seven funerary caves dug in pre-Talayotic times (c 1600 BCE).

The best restaurants overlook Cala Barques, and serve an appetising – if not particularly outstanding – variety of fresh seafood.

atemrausch

ADVENTURE SPORTS

(🗹 622 12 21 45; www.facebook.com/atemrausch; Carre del Temporal 9; kids/trekking/mountain/road bikes per day from €8/15/25/25; ⊙9.30am-1pm &

CLIFF JUMPING IN CALA SANT VICENÇ

Jumping off a cliff may sound suicidal, but it's a thrilling summer pursuit around the ragged cliffs of Cala Sant Vicenç, where locals diving from giddy heights make it look like a piece of cake. If you plan to take the plunge, however, we highly recommend getting a guide.

Experience Mallorca (p138) guides know the rocks like the backs of their hands. You'll jump off cliffs between 3m and 12m in height, which sounds easy-peasy, but don't be fooled – the moment when you leap and plunge is every bit as nerve-shattering as it is exhilarating.

4-7pm Mon-Sat May-Oct) This German-run one-stop shop specialises in adventure sports, from kayaking and snorkelling to mountain biking and scuba diving. They rent out all kinds of bicycles, including kid-sized ones; rates fall the longer you rent the bike. Bike insurance is €2 per day.

Bar-Restaurant Cala Barques MALLORCAN €€
(☑971 53 43 36; Cala Barques; mains €13-26; ⊗12.30-3.30pm & 7.30-10.30pm Tue-Sun May-Oct) The location, on a perch overlooking Cala Barques, is excellent. Pair the scenery with grilled fish, squid and other seafood, or appetising steaks and roasts, and you've an excellent combo.

ℹ Information

Tourist Office (☑971 53 32 64; Plaça de Cala Sant Vicenç; ⊗9am-4pm Mon-Fri, 10am-1pm Sat May-Oct) A short walk away from Cala Barques.

ℹ Getting There & Away

Cala Sant Vicenç is 6.5km northeast of Pollença, off the road towards Port de Pollença. The 345 bus runs to Cala Sant Vicenç (€1.50, 20 minutes, up to six times daily) from Pollença and from Port de Pollença.

Port de Pollença

POP 6596

This low-key resort at the northern cusp of the Badia de Pollença looks out onto entrancing views over to the jagged formations of the Formentor peninsula. Yes, tourism is quite full-on, but the marina, cafe-lined promenade and long arc of sand still makes an appealing base for families and water-sports enthusiasts.

🏖 Beaches

The beaches immediately south of the main port area are broad, sandy and gentle. Tufts of beach are sprinkled all the way along the shady promenade stretching north of town – these rank among Port de Pollença's prettiest corners. South along the bay towards Alcúdia, the beaches become a grey gravel mix, frequently awash with poseidon grass. At the tail end of this less-than-winsome stretch, the stiff breezes on **Ca'n Cap de Bou** and **Sa Marina** (just before entering Alcúdia) are among the best on the island for wind- and kite-surfing.

🏃 Activities

Some of the island's finest diving is in the Badia de Pollença. There's plenty of wall and cave action, and reasonable marine life (rays, octopuses, barracudas and more) along the southern flank of the Formentor peninsula and the southern end of the bay leading to Cap des Pinar.

Rich Strutt HIKING
(☑668 542274; www.mallorcanwalkingtours.com) An English-speaking guide with almost 30 years' experience. Rich is based in Port de Pollença and offers a huge number of day hikes (or longer treks) for groups of four or more.

Rent March CYCLING
(☑971 86 47 84; www.rentmarch.com; Carrer de Joan XXIII 89; bike rental per day €8-45, e-bikes from €16.90; ⊗9am-1pm & 3.30-8pm) In business for decades, Rent March hires out all sorts of bikes, from basic bicycles to mountain bikes, e-bikes, tandems, lightweight racer bikes and children's bikes. It also rents out scooters and motorbikes, and provides villa accommodation.

Sail & Surf Pollença SAILING, WINDSURFING
(☑971 86 53 46; www.sailsurf.eu; Passeig de Saralegui 134; beginner windsurfing/sailing courses €132/145; ⊗9am-6pm Mon-Sat Apr-Oct, shorter hours Nov-Mar) Come here for two- to three-day courses in sailing and windsurfing. Those with experience can also rent equipment. Discounts available for children under 14.

Scuba Mallorca
DIVING

(☎971 86 80 87; www.scubamallorca.com; Carrer d'Elcano 23; dive package from €80, equipment extra €20; ☺8am-6.30pm Apr-Oct, shorter hours Nov-Mar; 🅿) Scuba Mallorca is a PADI five-star rated outfit offering some 20 different diving courses for both certified and non-certified divers (minimum age 10). There's single Try Dive trips (€80, maximum depth 9m), double Try Dive outings (€140, maximum depth 12m) and Bubble-maker for kids.

Kayak Mallorca
KAYAKING

(☎971 91 91 52; www.piraguasgm.com/kayak mallorca; Playa de la Gola; 3hr trip incl transport per person from €40, rental per hr/half-day/full-day from €15/30/40; ☺10am-1pm Mon-Wed & Sat, 10am-1pm & 5-8pm Thu & Fri) On the beach south of the marina, experienced outfit Kayak Mallorca organises trips for all skill levels, whether you fancy paddling around the coast to Cap des Pinar or via caves to Formentor. It also rents out and sells kayaks and runs kayaking courses, as well as selling stand-up paddle-boards.

 Eating

A market kicks off every Wednesday on Plaça Miguel Capllonch, two blocks inland, northwest of the marina. The port is also well supplied with a tempting range of restaurants.

★Bellaverd
VEGETARIAN €

(☎971 86 46 00; www.pensionbellavista.com; Carrer les Monges 14; breakfast from €4.50, mains €9.50-23.50; ☺8.30am-midnight Tue-Sun; 🖉🅿) Sit in a gorgeous setting under the canopy of an ancient fig tree in the courtyard garden of this arty enclave, which also hosts the occasional sculpture workshop. The kitchen cooks up a healthy spread of vegetarian and vegan dishes, from creative salads to pumpkin, leek and walnut filo parcels, goat's cheese lasagne or simple spaghetti with pesto. Kids are catered for, as well.

Celler La Parra
MALLORCAN €

(☎971 86 50 41; Carrer de Joan XXIII 84; mains €10-16.50; ☺1-3pm & 7-11pm; 🅿) In business since the 1960s, this atmospheric, rustic and old-style Mallorcan restaurant is something of a rarity in these parts. It serves up genuine island fare, from fresh fish to *frito mallorquín* (sautéed lamb offal), *lechona* (roast pork) and *tumbet* (Mallorcan ratatouille). Throw in a wood-fired oven, wine-cellar decor and nary a pizza in sight, and you'll soon see why it's well worth a visit.

❶ Information

Tourist Office (☎971 86 54 67; www.puerto pollensa.com; 1 Passeig Saralegui; ☺9am-8pm Mon-Fri, to 4pm Sat May-Sep, shorter hours Oct-Apr) On the waterfront in front of the marina.

❶ Getting There & Away

The 340 bus from Palma to Pollença continues to Port de Pollença (€1.50, 20 minutes direct or 30 minutes via Cala Sant Vicenç). Bus 352

PORT DE POLLENÇA TO CAP DE FORMENTOR BY ROAD

The stirring journey from Port de Pollença to the Cap de Formentor is a highlight of the region and a memorable expedition either by car or on two wheels.

The road quickly climbs away from Port de Pollença, affording splendid views of the bay, and whips its way towards the blustery cape. The traffic moves at a snail's pace here in summer, owing to a succession of **lookouts** with ranging views, such as the **Mirador de Sa Creueta**, 3km northeast of Port de Pollença. Look out to the east and spot the small islet of **Illot del Colomer**. From the same spot you can climb a couple of kilometres up a side road to the **Talaia d'Albercuix**, an 18th-century watchtower-constructed to warn of pirates. The location was selected for its far-ranging 360-degree views. Time your journey to climb up for sunset, if you can.

From here, the Ma2210 sinks down through the woods some 4km to **Platja de Formentor** (Platja del Pi), a slender beach with soft sand and inviting waters. The road then slithers another 11km from Hotel Formentor out to the cape and its 19th-century **Cap de Formentor Lighthouse**, where the views look south to Cap Ferrutx at the far side of the Badia d'Alcúdia. The short walking track (the **Camí del Moll del Patronet**) leads south to another supreme **viewpoint**.

makes the run between Port de Pollença and Ca'n Picafort (€2.70, one hour), stopping at Alcúdia (€1.60, 15 minutes) and Port d'Alcúdia (€1.60, 25 minutes) along the way. The 353 runs to Formentor (€1.55, 20 minutes). Bus 445 runs to Cala Millor (€9.50, 95 minutes, once daily) on the south coast. Bus 446 runs south to Cala Ratjada (€8.50, twice daily, 75 minutes), via Artà (€6.85, one hour), as does bus 448.

Cap de Formentor

The most dramatic stretch of Mallorca's coast, Cap de Formentor is an other-worldly domain of razor-edge cliffs and wind-buckled limestone peaks jutting far out to sea; from a distance, it looks like an epic line of waves about to break. This is a fantastic choice for a cycle or drive (p131), or a hike (p125).

ℹ Getting There & Away

The 18km stretch from Port de Pollença (via the Ma2210) is naturally best done with your own vehicle, bicycle or feet, although the 353 bus runs from Port de Pollença to Platja de Formentor (€1.55, 20 minutes, four daily Monday to Saturday; summer months only).

BADIA D'ALCÚDIA

Alcúdia

POP 19,793

Just a few kilometres inland from the coast, ancient Alcúdia is a beautiful town of quiet charm and character, ringed by mighty medieval walls that enclose a maze of narrow lanes, historic mansions, cafe-rimmed plazas and warm-stone houses. On the fringes of town survive the entrancing remains of Pol·lèntia, once the island's prime Roman settlement.

◉ Sights

★ **Pol·lèntia**   ARCHAEOLOGICAL SITE
(www.pollentia.net; Avinguda dels Prínceps d'Espanya; adult/child incl Museu Monogràfic €4/2.50; ⊙ 9.30am-9pm Mon-Sat, 9am-1pm Sun May-Oct, shorter hours Nov-Apr) Ranging over a sizeable (but walkable) area, the fascinating ruins of the Roman town of Pol·lèntia lie just outside Alcúdia's walls. Founded around 70 BCE, it was Rome's principal city in Mallorca and is the most important archaeological site on the island. Pol·lèntia

reached its apogee in the 1st and 2nd centuries CE and covered up to 20 hectares. To the north, the one-room Museu Monogràfic has a fascinating but limited collection on Pol·lèntia.

The sheer geographical spread of Pol·lèntia (most of it not excavated) suggests it was a city of some scale and substance.

In the northwest corner of the site is the Sa Portella residential area – with the foundations, broken pillars and remains of the walls of *domus* (houses) separated by two streets. The best-preserved of the houses is the Casa dels Dos Tresors (House of the Two Treasures), a typical Roman house, centred on an atrium, which stood from the 1st to the 5th centuries CE. The 14.4cm bronze head of a young girl was found in the Casa del Cap de Bronze (House of the Bronze Head) nearby.

A short stroll away are the remnants of the Forum, which boasted three temples and rows of *tabernae* (shops). Finally, you can walk another few hundred metres to reach the fascinating 1st-century-CE Teatre Romà (Roman Theatre), which seems to be returning into the rock from which it was hewn. The semi-circular *orchestra* at the front and the *cavea* (where spectators were seated) still survive. It wasn't until the late 19th century that the remains were identified as being a theatre. The theatre alone, with a diameter of 75m and a former capacity of around 1000 spectators, is worth the entrance fee.

Visitors are free to wander among the ruins.

★ **Museu Monogràfic**
de Pol·lèntia   MUSEUM
(www.pollentia.net; Carrer de Sant Jaume 30; adult/child incl Pol·lèntia €4/2.50; ⊙ 9.30am-8.30pm Tue-Sat, 10am-2pm Sun May-Sep, shorter hours Oct-Apr) This one-room museum has a fascinating although limited collection of statue fragments, coins, jewellery, household figurines of divinities, scale models of the Casa dels Dos Tresors and Theatre and other remains excavated from the ruins of the Roman town of Pol·lèntia. It's well presented but labels are only in Catalan; but you can ask for the 'English guidebook' pamphlet from the helpful receptionist.

★ **Medieval Walls**   LANDMARK
Although largely rebuilt, Alcúdia's fine city walls are impressive. Those on the north side are largely the medieval originals while

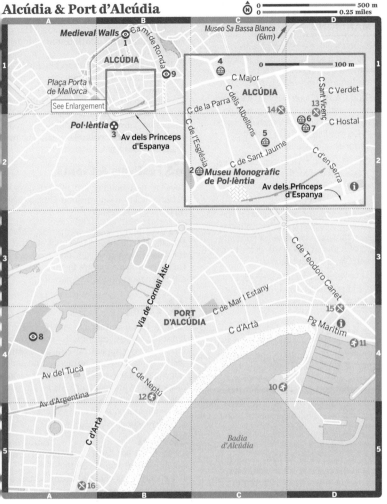

NORTHERN MALLORCA ALCÚDIA

ALCÚDIA'S HISTORIC MANSIONS

Alcúdia's old town is dotted with grand, handsome and impressive mansions, within a short walk of each other. Here are some of the finest examples:

Ca'n Canta (Carrer Major 18) A fine old home with stunning carvings around its 1st-floor windows, just west of Plaça de sa Constitució, opposite the entrance to Carrer dels Albellons.

Ca'n Domènech (Carrer dels Albellons 7) One of Alcúdia's finest, this large, grand and noble building has a largely unadorned facade.

Ca'n Fondo (Carrer d'en Serra 13) This stolid and imposing building with classical carvings around its 1st-floor windows is a short walk north of the turning with Carrer de Sant Jaume.

Ca'n Torró (Carrer d'En Serra 15) This grand old building is next door to Ca'n Fondo.

near the **Porta Roja** (Red Gate) are remnants of an 18th-century bridge. From the bridge, you can climb up and walk around 250m atop the walls, as far as Carrer del Progres, with fine views over town and towards the distant hills. Beyond the bridge to the northeast, the Plaça de Toros (bullring) has been built into a Renaissance-era bastion.

Porta del Moll   GATE
(Porta de Xara; Carrer del Moll) A magnificent sight at the east end of the old town sporting two towers, this solitary 14th-century gate is one of the two surviving gates of Alcúdia.

Museo Sa Bassa Blanca   GALLERY
(Fundación Yannick y Ben Jakober; ☑tours 971 54 98 80; www.fundacionjakober.org; Camí de Coll Baix; adult/child €10/7, 2-6pm Tue free, house tours €25, guided art tours €10, sculpture park & rose garden alone €5; ⊙10am-1pm & 2-6pm Mon-Sat) Around 6km east of Alcúdia, in a Hispano-Moorish-style house, this eclectic cultural institution concentrates on children's portraits from the 16th to 19th centuries. It also has exhibition space devoted to contemporary artists, a sculpture garden featuring works by the British artist couple Ben Jakober and Yannick Vu, and the Espacio SoKraTES, showcasing art from the likes of Mallorcan painter Miquel Barceló and a 10,000-crystal curtain by Swarovski. A highlight of tours of the principal Hassan Fathy building is the 15th century Mudejar coffered ceiling.

There's also an observatory, an aquarium and a camera obscura. Spring, when the rose garden is in full bloom, is a fine time to visit. To reach the gallery, follow the signs to Fundació and Bonaire. At Bodega del Sol restaurant, turn right and follow the road, which turns into a potholed track. The museum is on the right.

★☆ Festivals & Events

Tuesday and Sunday are market days in Alcúdia, held on and around Passeig Mare de Déu de la Victoria.

Fira d'Alcúdia   CULTURAL
(⊙early Oct) The big annual market event is the Fira d'Alcúdia on the first weekend in October; produce market together with traditional dances, music and parades.

✕ Eating

Alcúdia has a rewarding selection of restaurants, largely catering to the sizeable influx of day trippers. Several are notable for their locations on attractive and quiet side-streets, their traditional settings complemented with excellent Mallorcan and international menus – but there's no shortage of choices with alfresco seating for avid people-watchers.

Ca'n Costa   MALLORCAN €€
(☑971 54 53 94; Carrer Sant Vicenç 14; mains €12-19; ⊙12.30-3pm & 6.30-11pm Tue-Sun; ⊛) It feels little has changed at this grand old house since it was built in 1594, with its beams and oil paintings still intact. There's alfresco seating for balmy days and a menu packed with Catalan and Mallorcan classics like *suquet,* a rich fish casserole, cod with *sobrassada* (tangy cured pork sausage) and roast suckling pig.

Ca'n Pere   MEDITERRANEAN €€
(☑971 54 52 43; www.hotelcanpere.com; Carrer d'en Serra 12; mains €9-22; ⊙noon-4pm & 6-10.30pm) This attractive stone-walled courtyard restaurant in the hotel of the same name serves up fresh Mediterranean cuisine such as black ravioli filled with prawns and salmon. Service can be slow when things are busy.

ℹ Information

Tourist Office (☑ 971 54 90 22; Passeig de Pere Ventayol; ⊙ 8.30am-5pm Mon-Sat May-Oct, to 2.30pm Nov-Apr) This helpful tourist office has maps, leaflets and stacks of info on Alcúdia and its surrounds.

ℹ Getting There & Away

The 351 bus from Palma to Platja de Muro calls at Alcúdia (€5.45, 45 minutes, up to 16 daily). Bus 352 connects Ca'n Picafort (€1.85, 45 minutes) with Alcúdia as often as every 15 minutes from May to October. Local service 356A connects Alcúdia with Port d'Alcúdia and Platja d'Alcúdia (€1.55, 15 minutes, every 15 minutes from May to October).

Port d'Alcúdia

POP 4850

Draped along the northeastern corner of the Badia d'Alcúdia, Port d'Alcúdia is a very busy beach-holiday centre with an appealing waterfront, marina and fishing harbour. Dotted with palms, its gently sloping, fine-sand beach has shallow water and plenty of activities geared towards families.

⊙ Sights

Cova de Sant Martí CAVE
An otherworldly religious shrine and grotto in a 20m-deep hollow, Cova de Sant Martí dates back to the 13th century. Find it at the foot of Puig de Sant Martí crag (behind the BelleVue Club Hotel); the tourist office (p136) can point you in the right direction. A pilgrimage leads to the cave on the Sunday after Easter.

Hidropark AMUSEMENT PARK
(☑ 971 89 16 72; www.hidroparkalcudia.com; Avinguda del Tucá; adult/child 3-10yr/under 3yr €24.90/17.90/free; ⊙ 10am-6pm July-Aug, to 5pm May, June, Sept & Oct) Amuse the kids at this water park with slides, a wave pool and infant splash area. It's about 600m inland from the beach. It's ever so slightly cheaper to book online.

🏃 Activities

Pro Cycle Hire MOUNTAIN BIKING
(☑ 971 86 68 57; www.procyclehire.com; Carrer del Corb Mari 6; bike hire per day from €17) This top-choice outfit both rents out high-grade bikes and takes tours around the island, including three-day tours over the flats and into the steep gradients of the mountains, as well as

a punishing one-day 327km, 12-hour lap of Mallorca.

Alcudiamar Sports & Nature WATER SPORTS
(☑ 871 577017; www.sportsandnaturealcudiamar. com; Port Turistic i Esportiu; ♿) This water-sports specialist offers a full range of PADI courses, from day baptism courses to advanced open-water diver certificates. It also arranges kayak rental and tours, sailing and windsurfing courses and boat trips to sea caves.

Wind & Friends WATER SPORTS
(☑ 971 54 98 35, 661 745414; www.windfriends.com; Carrer de Neptú; ⊙ Apr-Oct) On the waterfront, next to the Hotel Sunwing, this outfit organises sailing, windsurfing and kitesurfing. A five-day beginners' course in windsurfing costs €260 (children €210); a three day course is also available at €170. Boat, kayak and stand-up paddle-board rental (from €10) is also available. A basic five-day sailing course is €280 (children €210).

Transportes Marítimos Brisa BOATING
(☑ 971 54 58 11; www.tmbrisa.com; Passeig Marítim; ⊙ May-Oct) Transportes Marítimos Brisa offers catamaran trips (adult/child €58/29, five hours), excursions to Platja de Formentor (€26/13, four hours) and coasts, coves and caves of east Mallorca (€36/18, three hours) plus trips to see dolphins and the sunrise (€49/38, two hours).

Alcanada Golf Club GOLF
(Club de Golf Alcanada; ☑ 971 54 95 60; www. golf-alcanada.com; Carretera del Faro; 9/18 holes from €62/105) Named after a small lighthouse-crowned islet to the south, this 18-hole (par 72) course enjoys an enviably splendid and scenic location, with gorgeous views of the sea (which may take your eyes off the ball).

🎉 Festivals & Events

Festival de Sant Pere FIESTA
(⊙ 29 Jun) This festival celebrates the port's patron saint. The week leading up to this day is a time of concerts, kids shows and activities and on the big day a statue of Sant Pere is paraded on land and sea.

🍴 Eating

The emphasis in Port d'Alcúdia swerves more towards quantity rather than quality, but there are a few places of genuine culinary worth and certainly no shortage of restaurant options, reaching all the way down to the Platja de Muro.

Willy's Hamburger
FAST FOOD €

(☑ 971 89 04 82; www.willymallorca.com; Avenida S'Albufera 21; snacks & light meals €3-12; ⊙ 8am-2.30pm Thu-Tue; ⛷) This *snackeria* in Platja de Muro is a hit with locals for its ultra-fresh, homemade fast food. Despite being as busy as a beehive in summer, there's always a friendly welcome. Burgers are good, as is the *pepito de lomo* (pork loin in a bap with garlicky aioli, €4.20).

Como en Casa
SPANISH €€

(☑ 971 54 90 33; www.restaurantcomoencasa.com; Carrer dels Pins 4; mains €7-16; ⊙ 6pm-midnight Tue-Sun; ⛷⛷) Tucked down a side street near the marina, Como en Casa always has a good buzz and warm welcome. Snag a table on the terrace for dishes rich in local ingredients and home-grown veg. Try the zingy flavours in seared tuna on kiwi-mango salad or creamy vegetarian curry. Tasty kids' menu and several meat-free choices too.

★ Restaurante Jardín
MEDITERRANEAN €€€

(☑ 971 89 23 91; www.bistrodeljardin.com; Carrer dels Tritons; mains €18-25; ⊙ 1-3.30pm & 7-11pm Fri & Sat, 1-4pm Sun; ⛷) The smart interior of this Michelin-starred restaurant may be out of step with the nondescript villa facade, but uniform excellence inspires the menu. A swirl of flavours permeates each dish, from suckling lamb shank with glazed vegetables to grilled octopus with potatoes and black olive mayonnaise. Meals conclude sweetly with desserts like chocolate and hazelnut cake, all exquisitely presented. Book ahead.

❶ Information

Tourist Office (☑ 971 54 72 57; www.alcudia-mallorca.com; Passeig Marítim; ⊙ 8am-8.30pm Mon-Fri, 8.30am-3.30pm Sat & Sun Mar-Oct) Located in a booth behind the marina; can supply local maps.

❶ Getting There & Around

Boats (€25 to €52, 1½ to two hours, two daily) leave for Ciutadella on the island of Menorca from the ferry port.

Regular buses run from here to Alcúdia (€1.60, 15 minutes) and Port de Pollença (€1.60, 25 minutes).

Easy Rider (☑ 606 543099, 971 54 50 57; www.easyridermobilityhire.com; Playa de Muro) Mobility hire provider.

Cap des Pinar

From Alcúdia and Port d'Alcúdia, the phenomenally beautiful Cap des Pinar thrusts eastward into the deep blue and, together with Cap de Formentor away to the north, encloses the Badia de Pollença within its embrace. The cape bristles with Aleppo pine woods at its eastern end as it rises to precipitous cliffs. Its walking trails are hands down some of the most spectacular on the island. The headland is military land and off-limits, but the rest is well worth it.

From Alcúdia, head northeast through residential Mal Pas and Bonaire to a scenic route that stretches to Cap des Pinar. After 1.5km of winding coastal road east of Bonaire you reach the beach. With such beautiful panoramas out to sea, it's hardly surprising there's a particularly fine option for a meal on Cap des Pinar.

★ Platja des Coll Baix
BEACH

It's a fantastic ramble to Platja des Coll Baix – and what a bay! Snug below sheer, wooded cliffs, this shimmering crescent of pale pebbles and translucent water is soul-stirring stuff. The catch: it's only accessible on foot or by boat. Come in the early morning or evening to see it at its peaceful best. From Alcúdia, it's about 8km to an open spot in the woods where you can park. Follow the purple road signs for the Museo Sa Bassa Blanca (p134), aka Fundación Yannick y Ben Jakober, and keep on for another 2km.

From this spot, you could climb the south trail to Talaia d'Alcúdia, then follow the signs to Coll Baix, a fairly easy half-hour descent. The main trail will lead you to the rocks south of the beach, from where you have to scramble back around to reach Platja des Coll Baix.

★ Talaia d'Alcúdia
MOUNTAIN

Accessed by a lovely, relatively undemanding 30- to 40-minute hike through the pine trees, this astonishing viewpoint has 360-degree wide-angle views over the surrounding sea. From the Ermita de La Victòria (☑ 971 54 99 12; www.lavictoriahotel.com; Carretera Cap des Pinar; s/d €50/60, breakfast €8), take the road up into the pines behind the Mirador de la Victòria and follow the signs. The Talai d'Alcúdia – a 16th-century lookout tower – is a final scramble up some boulders at the top, where the views are simply awesome.

You can also get here by following the signs up from the picnic ground beyond the final car park for Platja des Coll Baix, if you want to tie in a trip to the beach and climb up to the viewpoint.

Platja s'Illot   BEACH

A curtain of pines rises behind Platja s'Illot, a pretty cove beloved of locals where crystal-clear water and an islet make it great for a spot of snorkelling. You'll need to bring a towel to lay on as there are no sunbeds, but there is a cafe for beachside snacking and the views ranging across to Cap de Formentor are something else. Just don't expect to have them all to yourself on a summer's day.

Mirador de La Victòria   MALLORCAN €€

(☑971 54 71 73; www.miradordelavictoria.com; Carretera Cap des Pinar; mains €7.50-26; ⊗1-3.30pm & 7pm-midnight Tue-Sun May-Oct, shorter hours Nov-Apr; P 🖍) Climb the steps through pine forest past the Ermita de La Victòria to reach this gorgeous rustic restaurant, with no-nonsense home cooking and amazing views out over the treetops towards Cap de Formentor. Besides local dishes like *caracoles* (snails) and *lomo con col* (pork loin wrapped in cabbage), the grilled fish and rice dishes are also fine.

❶ Getting There & Away

The 356B bus (€1.60) runs from Alcúdia to Bonaire three times a day, but no further than that. By far the best way to reach the Ermita de La Victòria and the start of the walk is to drive up the winding road to the top.

SOUTH OF ALCÚDIA

Ca'n Picafort

Ca'n Picafort, and its southern extension, Son Baulo, is a somewhat raw and raggedy package-tour frontier town. But the beaches are pretty decent and some interesting archaeological sites dot the surrounding terrain. The main resort backs on to Platja de Santa Margalida, a crowded shallow beach with turquoise water.

For a wilder feel, swing southwest of town to Platja de Son Real. This almost 5km stretch of coast, with snippets of sandy strands in among the rock points, is backed only by low dunes, scrub and bushland dense with Aleppo pines.

★Parc Natural de S'Albufera   PARK

(☑971 892 250; www.mallorcaweb.net/salbufera; ⊙visitor centre 9am-6pm Apr-Sep, to 5pm Oct-Mar) [FREE] The 688-hectare Parc Natural de S'Albufera, west of the Ma12 between Port d'Alcúdia and Ca'n Picafort, is prime birdwatching territory, with 303 recorded species (more than 80% of recorded Balearic species), 64 of which breed within the park's boundaries. More than 10,000 birds overwinter here, among them both residents and migrants. Entrance to the park is free, but permits must be obtained from the visitor centre, which is a 1km walk from the entrance gates on the main road.

The so-called Gran Canal at the heart of the park was designed to channel the water out to sea. The five-arched Pont de Sa Roca bridge was built over it in the late 19th century to ease travel between Santa Margalida and Alcúdia. The park is considered a Ramsar Wetland of National Importance and, in addition to the bird species, around 400 plant species have been catalogued here. In spring, wildflowers bloom, bringing vibrant splashes of colour.

The visitor centre can provide information on the park and its birdlife, and is the trailhead for several walks through the protected wetlands. From here, 14km of signposted trails fan out across the park. There are four marked itineraries, from short 725m (30 minutes) routes to 11.5km (3½ hours) trails, two of which can be covered by bike. Of the six timber birdwatching observatories, or *aguaits* – come inside and watch in silence – some are better than others. You'll see lots of wading birds in action from the Bishop I and II *aguaits* on the north side of the Gran Canal.

★Platja de Muro   BEACH

Around 5km south of Port d'Alcúdia (on the bus line to Ca'n Picafort), Platja de Muro is a long, alluring stretch of sand, with extensive blue views of the Badia d'Alcúdia. The setting, with pale, soft sand backed by pines and the dunes of the Parc Natural de S'Albufera, is a winner. The water is shallow and azure, but crowds can get intense in summer.

Finca Pública de Son Real   FARM

(☑971 18 53 63; ⊙10am-5pm) Much of the area between the coast and the Ma12 has been converted into the Finca Pública de Son Real. Its main entrance is just south of the Km 18 milestone on the Ma12, and the former farm buildings host an information office for those who wish to walk the property's several coastal trails. There's also a museum zooming in on traditional Mallorcan rural life.

Necròpolis de Son Real — ARCHAEOLOGICAL SITE

(Punta des Fenicis) By the sea about 10 minutes' walk southeast of Platja de Son Bauló, this necropolis appears to have been a Talayotic cemetery with 110 tombs (in which the remains of more than 300 people were found). The tombs assume the shape of mini-*talayots* (ancient watchtowers) and date as far back as the 7th century BCE. Some believe this was a graveyard for commoners.

Illot dels Porros — ARCHAEOLOGICAL SITE

Not far from Necròpolis de Son Real, the island called Illot dels Porros also contains remains of an ancient necropolis. It's a fairly easy swim for the moderately fit.

Experience Mallorca — ADVENTURE SPORTS

(☑ 687 358922; www.experience-mallorca.com; Avenida son Noguera 7, Llucmajor; activities €45-75; ☺ 9am-9pm) If you want to crank up the thrill factor a notch or two, head for this adventure specialist, who will raise your pulse with activities such as canyoning, cliff jumping, coasteering, caving, abseiling, trekking and rock climbing.

ℹ Information

Tourist Office (☑ 678 378319, 971 85 07 58; Plaça Jaume I; ☺ 9am-2pm & 3-5pm Mon-Fri, 9am-2pm Sat & Sun) This helpful tourist office is located close to the marina.

ℹ Getting There & Away

Bus 390 runs from Palma to Ca'n Picafort (€6.70, 1¾ hours, up to eight daily). Bus 352 is the main service between Ca'n Picafort and Port de Pollença (€2.70, 1¼ hours), via Port d'Alcúdia (€1.65, 45 minutes).

Colònia de Sant Pere

Named after the patron saint of fishers (St Peter), this peaceful former fishing village is an antidote to the tourist resorts to the west, but historic attractions are limited. The huddle of houses has expanded beyond the central square and church to accommodate a small populace that seems to be on permanent vacation.

In the centre of town you'll find the **Platja de la Colònia de Sant Pere** and southwest beyond that is the small marina and fishing port. About 2.5km west of Colònia de Sant Pere, you'll reach **Platja de Sa Canova**, a fine and tranquil sweep of sand that reaches all the way to Son Serra de Marina. From the village of S'Estanyol the only way to Sa Canova is on foot, but it's not a long walk as S'Estanyol is almost on the beach's edge.

Sa Xarxa — SEAFOOD €€

(☑ 971 58 92 51; www.sa-xarxa.com; Passeig; mains €12-20; ☺ 1-11pm Tue-Sun Mar-Oct) The tables arrayed under tamarind trees along the waterfront here have incredible sea and sunset views. Seafood is good, especially the catch of the day, done simply in a salty crust. Everything, such as the carpaccio of angler fish with lime yoghurt, gets the delicate touch. Inside, it's largely wood, with model ships, walls crammed with pictures and panama hats hanging from pegs.

ℹ Getting There & Away

Bus 481 runs from Colònia de Sant Pere to Artà (€2.10, 25 minutes) three or four times a day from Monday to Friday.

The Interior

Best Places to Eat

➡ Celler Es Grop (p146)

➡ Ca Na Toneta (p144)

➡ Joan Marc Restaurant (p144)

➡ Terra di Vino (p143)

➡ Celler Ca'n Amer (p144)

Best Viewpoints

➡ Ermita de Santa Magdalena (p143)

➡ Santuari de Nostra Senyora de Cura (p147)

➡ Castell de Santueri (p151)

➡ Santuari de Sant Salvador (p150)

Why Go?

Mallorca's occasionally overlooked but entirely serene interior is the island's alter ego to its coastal buzz. This is where the island's rural heart beats strongly in church-topped villages, where locals fiercely guard their traditions – and throw some of Mallorca's most spirited *fiestas*.

Although the sapphire sea is rarely more than an hour's drive away, the terrestrial interior is a quite different realm, with ranging plains and meadows stippled with vineyards, and olive, almond, citrus and carob trees. The dramatic Serra de Tramuntana looms to the northwest and the sublime Serra de Llevant elevates the land off to the east.

Cyclists welcome the relaxing flats, though there's no shortage of gradients to get the legs pumping afresh, with roads winding to the sacred mountain-top sights of Santuari de Nostra Senyora de Cura on Puig de Randa, Ermita de Santa Magdalena or the Santuari de Sant Salvador. Join them for astonishing views.

When to Go

Unlike the coast, inland Mallorca tends to remain open for business year-round: Palma folk like nothing better than escaping from city life in the depths of winter (shallow as they are) and finding a rural retreat for a heartwarming meal or a quiet night's sleep. The last third of the year is the rainiest (although there hasn't been much of that in recent years) and average lows only drop to 8°C or 9°C in January. High summer, on the other hand, is reliably sweltering.

The Interior Highlights

1 Bodegas Macià Batle
(p142) Touring the vineyards
and finishing with a glass or
two at this lauded winery.

2 Festes de la Verema
(p143) Throwing grapes

and cavorting with devils at
Binissalem's annual harvest
festival.

**3 Santuari de Sant
Salvador** (p150) Taking

divine inspiration from the
views at this hilltop hermitage.

4 Els Calderers (p148)
Seeing how the rural *señors*
lorded over the land at this
mansion-museum.

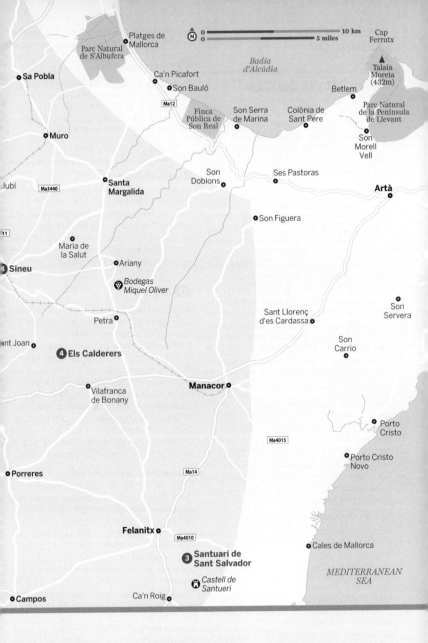

5 Caimari (p144)
Tramping the olive groves, then eating like a king in this sweet hillside town.

6 Coves de Campanet (p145) Creeping into the belly of the island through these elaborate caverns.

7 Santuari de Nostra Senyora de Cura (p147) Driving or cycling up to some of the most astonishing views on Mallorca.

8 Sineu (p145) Wandering the markets and stone streets of this comely hill town.

THE CENTRAL CORRIDOR

Santa Maria del Camí

POP 7167

Santa Maria del Camí is an attractive little town, with a couple of pretty squares, but it's not exactly exciting. If you're coming from Palma, as you roll into town the Ma13A widens to become the bar-lined Plaça dels Hostals, often populated by flocks of refuelling cyclists.

★ **Bodegas Macià Batle**   WINERY
(☑ 971 14 00 14; www.maciabatle.com; Camí de Coanegra; ⊙ 9am-6.30pm Mon-Sat; P) Based just outside of central Santa Maria, one of Mallorca's biggest names in wine, Bodegas Macià Batle has been using has been using the area's 300 annual days of sun to produce great grapes since 1858, Bodegas Macià Batle is based just outside of central Santa Maria. Tastings are free, or you can arrange a one-hour tour of the vineyard and production facilities, finishing with four wines and nibbles (adult/child €15/6, five per day March to October; three per day in quiet months). You can also admire their labels, designed by contemporary artists.

Convent de Nostra Senyora de la Soledat   CONVENT
(Plaça dels Hostals 30) The centrepiece of Plaça dels Hostals is the 17th-century Convent de Nostra Senyora de la Soledat, aka Can Conrado. If the main doors happen to be swung open, you can peer into the magnificent front courtyard, while a peek into the rear gardens can be had around the corner from Carrer Llarg.

Festes de Santa Margalida   FIESTA
(⊙ Jul) Held over almost three weeks in July, with the key day of 20 July, this festival involves concerts, traditional dances and communal meals.

Moli des Torrent   MALLORCAN €€€
(☑ 971 14 05 03; www.molidestorrent.de; Carretera de Bunyola 75; mains €20-26; ⊙ 1-3pm & 7-10pm Fri-Tue; P) The area's most atmospheric restaurant, set in a stone windmill on the country road leading north of Santa Maria to Bunyola. Sit in the vaulted interior or on the pretty patio for delightful home cooking that makes the most of the seasons, from Mallorcan *gambas* with *tumbet* (essentially prawns with ratatouille) to veal and sweetbreads with chanterelle risotto. Book ahead.

❶ Getting There & Away

Santa Maria is around halfway along the Palma–Inca train line, a stop on all three island lines. Fares in either direction cost €1.85, journey times range between 18 and 23 minutes, and there are frequent services every day.

Binissalem

POP 8316

The Romans brought their winemaking nous to Binissalem some 2000 years ago and this handsome little town at the foot of the Tramuntana, its long streets lined with stone buildings and orange trees, has been wedded to the grape ever since.

◉ Sights

Celler Tianna Negre   WINERY
(☑ 971 88 68 26; www.tiannanegre.com; Camí des Mitjans; ⊙ cellar door 9am-6pm Mon-Fri Mar-Oct, to 4pm Nov-Feb, tours by prior arrangement; P) ✐ With 20 hectares of biological plantings, architect-designed buildings and sincere commitment to sustainability, Tianna Negre is at the bleeding edge of winemaking. Happily, the results – made from manto negro, prensal blanc and other varieties – are excellent. Tours and tastings start at €20 for a sample of three wines and cheese, and run to €50 for three hours, tapas and premium wines.

Casa-Museu Llorenç Villalonga   MUSEUM
(☑ 971 88 60 14; www.fundaciocasamuseu.cat; Carrer de Bonaire 25; ⊙ 10am-2pm Mon-Fri, plus 4-8pm Tue & Sat) FREE Binissalem's prosperity as a wine-making town was reflected in the construction of several notable 18th- and 19th-century mansions. One that has been well preserved is Can Sabater, a country residence of the Catalan writer Llorenç Villalonga and now the Casa-Museu Llorenç Villalonga. Inside, note the 18th-century wine vats and room set aside for the crushing of grapes underfoot, and the many artefacts of the author's life, including his Civil War diary. Summer concerts are held in the garden.

Ca'n Novell   WINERY
(☑ 971 51 13 10; Carrer de Bonaire 17; ⊙ 8am-1pm & 2-3pm Mon, 8am-1pm & 2-10pm Tue, 3-8pm Wed-Fri, 8.30am-2pm Sat) Locals fill their own bottles

(€1.5 to €3 per litre) from the vast, 18th-century vats at this delightfully old-school winery. Fashioned from olive wood and bound by sturdy rings of oak, these grand old barrels were a standard feature of cellars and mansions across much of this part of the island. They also bottle extra-virgin olive oil and hold 'micro-theatre' and other cultural events in the evocative space, heady with vinous fumes.

José Luis Ferrer WINERY
(📋 971 10 01 00; www.vinosferrer.com; Carrer del Conquistador 103; guided tours from €10; ⊙ 10am-7pm Mon-Fri, to 6pm Sat year-round, 10am-2pm Sun Apr-Oct) One of Mallorca's largest and most celebrated wineries, José Luis Ferrer, was launched in 1931. To get a better insight into the wine-making process, hook onto one of the 45-minute guided tours, which start at 11am and 4.30pm most days, and include a three-wine tasting. More extensive (and expensive) tours are offered; call ahead to book. There's also the option of taking a train around the vineyards.

✵ Festivals & Events

Festes de la Verema FIESTA
(⊙ Sep; 🎪) This vintage festival, renowned for its climactic grape fight, is actually a week-long bash of wine tastings, concerts, readings, exhibitions and a wild night-time *correfoc* (fire run), with fire-breathing devils dashing through the streets to the crashing of firework displays. But of course it's the grape fight that gets most people's juices flowing.

✗ Eating

The restaurants and bars dotted around the Plaça Església and surrounding streets are fine places to sample the local wine over a few tapas and get into the slow-moving swing of things.

★ Terra di Vino ITALIAN €
(📋 871 91 02 26; Carrer de sa Creu 3; mains from €13; ⊙ 1-4pm & 7-11pm Wed-Mon; 🔊) There's a brief menu, but this superb, small restaurant immerses diners deeply and alluringly in the warm aromas of Italia, each dish infused with flavour and permeated with expertise. Service is amiable and the pasta is a delight. Space can be at a premium inside, but you can take to the tables outside, just off the main square.

❶ Getting There & Away

Binissalem is on all three train lines between Palma (€1.85, 20 to 30 minutes) and Inca (€1.85, eight minutes) with frequent services in both directions every day. Be aware that morning T1 express services from Palma don't stop here.

Inca

POP 32,137

There are two main reasons for coming to Inca, Mallorca's third city – it has some of the finest traditional *cellers* (basement restaurants) on the island, and it's at the heart of the Mallorcan leather industry: globally coveted Spanish shoe brands Camper and Farrutx took their first baby steps here. Otherwise, the journey to the nearby Ermita de Santa Magdalena provides an inspiring and enjoyable car or bike journey, rewarded by terrific views.

◉ Sights

★ Ermita de Santa Magdalena VIEWPOINT
(📋 971 50 40 08; Puig Santa Magdalena; ⊙ church 11.30am-7pm May-Oct, to 4pm Nov-Apr) **FREE** For extraordinary views, make the pilgrimage to this hermitage with 13th-century origins, which sits astride the **Puig de Santa Magdalena** (307m). From the little chapel, your gaze will take in the full sweep of the plains to the Serra de Tramuntana and the Alcúdia and Pollença bays. It's a terrific starting point for hikes, providing you've brought sturdy footwear. Pilgrims ascend to the chapel in numbers on Diumenge de l'Àngel (Angel Sunday, a week after Easter Sunday).

Claustre de Sant Domingo CONVENT
(📋 871 91 45 00; Plaça de Sant Domingo; ⊙ 8am-3pm & 4-8pm Mon-Fri, 10am-1.30pm Sat) **FREE** The last Dominican convent to be founded in Mallorca, Claustre de Sant Domingo is notable for its baroque architecture. Attached to the 17th-century convent-church of the same name, it was built in 1730, used as a prison in the Spanish Civil War, and is now a cultural and arts centre, hosting musical and dramatic performances, art exhibitions and the like.

Església de Santa Maria Major CHURCH
(Plaça de Santa Maria Major; ⊙ 10.30am-1pm Thu May-Oct) Inca's baroque church stands proud on Plaça de Santa Maria Major. Its greatest

THE INTERIOR INCA

treasure is a Gothic retable of Santa Maria d'Inca, painted in 1373 by the early Mallorcan artist Joan Daurer.

✨ Festivals & Events

Dijous Bo CULTURAL
(Holy Thursday; ⊘Nov) The town's biggest shindig is on the third Thursday in November, with processions, livestock competitions, sporting events, a fun fair and concerts.

🍴 Eating

A peculiarity of Inca is its *cellers*, basement restaurants in some of the oldest buildings in the town centre.

★Celler Ca'n Amer MALLORCAN €
(☑971 50 12 61; www.celler-canamer.es; Carrer de la Pau 139; mains €16-18, lunch menú €24; ⊘1-4pm & 7.30-11pm Mon-Sat, 1-4pm Sun; P) Refinements to Mallorcan classics are the hallmark of Tomeu Torrens, who slings the pans at this lively *celler,* rustically charming with its wooden beams and huge wine barrels. The house speciality is lamb shoulder stuffed with eggplant and *sobrassada* (paprika-spiced cured pork sausage), but the suckling pig with spot-on crackling and seafood options such as stuffed courgette are equally delicious. Reserve.

★Joan Marc Restaurant MEDITERRANEAN €€
(☑971 50 08 04; www.joanmarcrestaurant.com; Plaça del Blanquer 10; mains/menús €12-16/34-68; ⊘1-3.30pm & 8-10.30pm Tue-Sat, 1-3.30pm Sun, closed Jan; 🖉) A total contrast to Inca's dark and traditional *cellers* is this light, imaginative restaurant. The minimalist decor is softened by nature-themed design touches like tree-trunk coat hangers and almond shells. Sunny, herby flavours shine in Joan Marc's deft cooking: perhaps wild *corvina* (fish) with garlic soup, ham and olives, or roasted aubergine with house-made *sobrassada* and Mahon cheese.

Celler Ca'n Ripoll MALLORCAN €€
(☑971 50 00 24; www.restaurantcanripoll.com; Carrer de Jaume Armengol 4; mains €10-22; ⊘1-3.45pm & 7.30-11.30pm Mon-Sat, 1-3.45pm Sun) Delve down to this enormous, cathedral-like 18th-century *celler,* with a high-beamed ceiling resting on a series of stone arches. On the menu are hearty island specialities like the superb roast suckling pig (€19.95) and

cod with *sobrassada* (€14.95). It's not quite valet parking, but they can arrange a place to park your bike.

🛍 Shopping

ReCamper SHOES
(☑971 88 82 33; www.camper.com; Carrer Cuartel 91, Polígon Industrial; ⊘10am-8pm Mon-Sat) Snag a bargain at Camper's factory outlet, which does a brisk trade in seconds and end-of-lines.

Mercat d'Inca MARKET
(⊘8am-1.30pm Thu) Sprawling over most of the town centre, Inca's Thursday market is one of the biggest on the island, with hundreds of stalls doing a brisk trade in everything from honey and herbs to ceramics, flowers, fabrics and fruit and veg. Local leather is wheeled out in massive fashion in the shape of jackets, bags and shoes.

ℹ Getting There & Away

If you're not driving down the Ma13 motorway from Palma, get the train along the same route (€3.15, 30 minutes, frequent services).

Caimari

POP 773

Where fields of almonds, olives and carob yield to the foothills of the Serra de Tramuntana, and sheep-bells ring to the munching of wind-fallen figs, this gorgeous little town quietly goes about its business. Travellers are increasingly switching on to Caimari's manifest charms, but the locals seem to take it in their stride, and the rhythm of their lives doesn't seem to have changed much at all.

Caimari's bars are still very much local affair, but entirely friendly and welcoming of outsiders.

★Ca Na Toneta MALLORCAN €€€
(☑971 51 52 26; www.canatoneta.com; Carrer des Horitzó 21; menú €45; ⊘8-11pm daily Apr-Oct, 8.30-11pm Fri, 1.30-11pm Sat & Sun Nov-Feb) Making loving use of the fruits of local producers, and what they grow themselves, Ca Na Toneta is an exceptional country restaurant that invites diners to linger over six courses – whatever the chef has created for the day's degustation.

Sa Ruta Verda
CAFE

(☑ 636 681091; Carrer Nuestra Senyora Virgen del Lluc 62; ☺ 9am-6pm Feb-Nov; 🛜) Beloved of the many cyclists that pedal through this part of the island, gearing themselves up for the climb through the Tramuntana, Sa Ruta Verda pumps out coffee, juices, *pa amb oli* (bread with oil) and homemade energy bars with genuine enthusiasm. It also stocks tools, accessories and clothing for cyclists who find themselves in a bind.

Bar Ca'n Tomeu
BAR

(☑ 971 50 00 08; www.facebook.com/barcantomeucaimari; Carrer de Ses Tavernes 9; ☺ 6am-10pm) A typical Mallorcan bar through and through, this traditional local is a welcome spot just off the main square and a good bolthole for a *cafe con leche* (white coffee) or a *cerveza* (beer), with bites for snackers and tables flung outside on the street.

ⓘ Getting There & Away

It's nice to travel under your own steam if you want to fully explore these quieter parts of the island. If you're reliant on buses, the 330 connects Caimari with Palma (€3.75, one hour, six daily) while the 332 goes to Inca (€1.50, 15 minutes, up to five daily).

Campanet
POP 2612

Set above a beautiful and somnolent stretch of little-visited countryside quilted with orchards and sheep-grazed meadows, Campanet is an elegant and alluring village, worth a brief detour. Encrusted onto a sharp ridge, the town's central square, Plaça Major, is dominated by a looming Gothic church (although the surrounding cafes always seem busier than the less popular Mass).

A handful of welcoming, good-value cafes and restaurants clusters around Plaça Major and along Carrer Llorenç Riber, leading southeast down the hill out of town.

★ Coves de Campanet
CAVE

(☑ 971 51 61 30; www.covesdecampanet.com; Camí de ses Coves; adult/child 5-10 yr/under 5yr €15/8/free; ☺ 10am-6.30pm summer, to 5.30pm winter) An eerie forest of wax-like stalactites and stalagmites, the Coves de Campanet aren't as flashy as some of Mallorca's other cave systems, and are perhaps more authentic for it. There are guided tours every 45 minutes and visits last just under an hour. Scientists find these caves especially interesting

as they're home to a local species of blind, flesh-eating beetles. Find them 3km north of town, and if driving on the Palma–Sa Pobla motorway, take exit 377.

Bar es Club
MEDITERRANEAN €

(☑ 971 51 60 48; www.baresclub.com; Plaza Major 25; mains from €7; ☺ 7am-1am) Much-loved by cyclists seeking a breather or just to fuel up on breakfast, this restaurant/bar/cafe serves excellent pizza, pastas and paella (you often need to book a day ahead for the latter), enjoying a lovely position on the square. The outside tables are popular, so consider reserving, especially for an al fresco dinner. An affordable kids menu is also at hand.

ⓘ Getting There & Away

Ideally you need your own transport to reach the best of what Campanet and surrounds have to offer. Otherwise, the 333 bus links Campanet with Inca (€1.50, 20 minutes, up to nine per day).

Sineu
POP 3764

Once a centre of kingly power, now a quietly grand stone settlement mounting a prominence in the central Mallorcan plain, Sineu is one of the most engaging of the island's inland towns. It's also one of the oldest – a local legend traces the town's origins back to Roman Sinium, while the link to the Islamic settlement of Sixneu is less tenuous. Not as ambiguous is the antiquity of its two traditional rural fairs, one weekly, one annual, both dating to the early 14th century.

◉ Sights

Església de Santa Maria
CHURCH

(Plaça Sant Marc) Rebuilt after a calamitous fire in 1505, this sombre Gothic church, with its detached campanile, is Sineu's most significant, and the heart of the town. It houses a museum of medieval pottery that opens when the weekly market (p146) takes over Sa Plaça, every Wednesday morning.

Convent de la Concepció
CONVENT

(Carrer del Palau 17) Between 1309 and 1349, this was the site of the Mallorcan kings' second palace (after Palma), making Sineu the de facto capital of rural Mallorca. In 1583 it was given to the Order of the Immaculate Conception, who rebuilt extensively in the 17th century, and still live here today. A two-minute stroll southwest of Sa Plaça, the convent has a *torno,* a small revolving door through which you can receive pastries made by the nuns, in return for a few euros.

⚜ Festivals & Events

Sineu's Easter processions are some of the largest and most impressive on the island.

Sa Fira   FAIR
(Plaça des Fossar; ⊘ early May) Sineu's annual Sa Fira is a major agricultural spring fair held on the first Sunday of every May, and dates to 1318.

Festa del Siurell   FIESTA
(Llubí; ⊘ Feb) The little town of Llubí, 10km due north of Sineu, is worth visiting on the Saturday before the Tuesday of Carnaval. The Festa del Siurell involves townsfolk dressing up as *siurells,* traditional Mallorcan ceramic whistles. That night, a big *siurell* is burned in effigy in Plaça de l'Església, dominated by the outsized Església de Sant Feliu.

✕ Eating

Beyond the more generic tapas bars in the main squares, Sineu has some excellent Mallorcan restaurants, worth seeking out.

★ Celler Es Grop   MALLORCAN €€
(☑ 971 52 01 87; Carrer Major 18; mains €14-18; ⊘ 9.30am-4pm & 7-11pm Tue-Sun) Watch your step as you descend into this cheerful, white-washed 18th-century cellar, lined with huge old wine vats and other historical ephemera. Galician cuisine vies with Mallorcan favourites on the meat-heavy menu – the roast spring lamb and rice dishes aree fervently recommended.

Sa Fàbrica   MALLORCAN €€
(☑ 971 52 06 21; Carrer del Estació 1; mains €11-18; ⊘ noon-4pm & 7pm-midnight Wed-Mon; 🖭) Most come for the seafood, steaks and brochettes of Mallorcan pork, served sizzling hot from the grill at this convivial restaurant, housed in a former carpet factory. The lamb shoulder and rice dishes are also top-notch. Pep the owner keeps everything ticking over nicely.

🔒 Shopping

Sineu Market   MARKET
(Mercat de Sineu; ⊘ 8am-2pm Wed) One of rural Mallorca's most venerable traditions, Sineu's weekly market has taken over the town centre every Wednesday morning since 1306. Spreading out from Sa Plaça and down to the Plaça des Fossar, it sells livestock, leathergoods, ceramics, food and much more from all over the island, while the surrounding bars and cafes do a merry trade.

ⓘ Getting There & Away

T3-line trains call at Sineu from Palma (€3.05, 45 minutes, regular) and Manacor (€2.35, 20 minutes, regular). The station is about 100m east of Plaça des Fossar.

Sa Pobla & Muro

Sa Pobla, a grid-street rural centre and the end of the (railway) line from Palma, is in Mallorca's agricultural heartland. It has only a few attractions, but gets a shot of cultural adrenaline during several lively festivals and the weekly Sunday market. Five kilometres south across the potato flats, Muro is a dignified hilltop town with a handsome church at its apex.

⊙ Sights

Can Planes   MUSEUM
(Carrer d'Antoni Maura 6, Sa Pobla; adult/child €2/ free; ⊘ 4-8.30pm Tue-Fri, 10am-1pm Sat & Sun) The handsome manor house Can Planes contains the **Museu d'Art Contemporani**, a changing display of works by Mallorcan and foreign artists residing on the island. Upstairs, the **Museu de Sa Jugueta Antiga** is a touching collection of old toys.

Església de Sant Joan Baptista   CHURCH
(☑ 971 53 70 22; Carrer Bisbe Ramon de Torrella 1, Muro) Muro boasts an outsized parish church, a brooding, early-17th-century Gothic sandstone creation reminiscent of Sineu's main church. Its detached campanile is the town's most prominent landmark, and can be seen for miles across the plain.

⚜ Festivals & Events

Festes de Sant Antoni Abat   CULTURAL
(⊘ 16-17 Jan) This festival in both Sa Pobla and Muro has a little bit of everything with processions, fireworks, folk music, dancing, costumed devils and blessings for beasts of burden. Pre-festival activities run for a week, but the night of the 16th is the liveliest.

Sa Pobla International Jazz Festival

MUSIC

(www.facebook.com/mallorcajazzsapobla; Plaça Major, Sa Pobla; ☺ Jul/Aug) Jazz comes to Sa Pobla every August for this festival. Shows kick off in the Sala Es Cavallets, on Plaça Major Sa Pobla, at 10.30pm, and cost €5.

❶ Getting There & Away

From Palma take the T2 (Tren Sa Pobla) to both Sa Pobla and Muro (€3.75, around one hour, up to 17 services per day); the same service connects with Inca (€2.05, 15 to 20 minutes).

THE SOUTHEAST

Algaida

POP 5500 / ELEV 201M

A typically sober and dignified central Mallorcan town, Algaida has few sights beyond the gothic **Església de Sant Pere i Sant Pau** and nearby **Església de la Mare de Déu de la Pau de Castellitx**. Its greatest attractions are the **Festes de Sant Honorat** (16 January) and the **Festa de Sant Jaume** (25 July). On both occasions, *cossiers* dance for an appreciative local audience. The origins of the *cossiers* and their dances are disputed, but always a group of dancers, six men and one woman, plus the devil, perform various pieces that end in defeat for the fiend. If you're hunting for wholesome Mallorcan traditional fare, not modish sophistication, you can eat happily here.

★ Santuari de Nostra Senyora de Cura

MONASTERY

(Sanctuary of Our Lady of Cura; ☎ 971 12 02 60; www.santuaridecura.com; Puig de Randa; ☺ 8am-7pm daily Apr-Oct, 10am-4.45pm Mon-Fri Nov-Mar) This gracious monastery stands atop the 548m hill of Puig de Randa. Like most monasteries, it was built partly for defensive purposes, though the views are simply divine. Ramon Llull lived here as a hermit in the 13th century, praying in a cave (open 10am to 2pm, ask for a key from the cafe reception), and in the 16th century the Estudi General (university) in Palma created the Collegi de Gramàtica here. You can stay the night (doubles €53–65, suites €80).

The views across the plains to the Serra de Tramuntana are quite extraordinary. There's also a **museum** and an attractive and well-tended garden and you can eat or simply have a coffee at the monastery's cafe, with outside seating. Driving up here is no problem and there's ample parking. The Santuari, which is variously signposted as 'Santuari de Cura' or simply 'Cura', is 5km beyond the small village of Randa, southwest of Algaida.

Museu de Gordiola

MUSEUM

(☎ 971 66 50 46; www.gordiola.com; Carretera Palma-Manacor Km 19; ☺ museum & shop 9am-6.30pm Mon-Sat, 9.30am-1.30pm Sun, glassworks 9.30am-1.30pm & 3pm-6pm Mon-Fri, 9.30am-noon Sat; ⓟ) FREE The Museu de Gordiola glassworks and museum, set in a mock-Gothic palace and named for a family that's made glass since 1719, has a glassworks on the ground floor where you can observe the glassmakers and furnaces in action. Upstairs, the stained-glass illuminated museum has a riveting collection of glass items from around the world, some of great beauty and colour. The on-site shop contains some lovely pieces too. The museum lies 2.5km west of town on the Ma15.

Ca'l Dimoni

MALLORCAN €

(☎ 971 66 50 35; Carretera Vella de Manacor Km 21; mains €12-15; ☺ noon-midnight Thu-Tue) On Algaida's northern fringes, Ca'l Dimoni is rustic Mallorca through and through, with wood beams, chunky tables, cured sausages hanging from the rafters and an open fire where chefs sizzle up meaty mains. There's always a good local buzz here, as well as heart-warming dishes like *frit Mallorquín* (fried lamb innards), *cargols* (snails) and *arros brut* ('dirty' rice).

❶ Getting There & Away

The 490 bus stops in Algaida on its way from Palma to Portocolom (€2.45, 30 minutes, up to 10 daily), and the 454 runs from Algaida to Cala Millor (€7.10, 80 minutes, once daily, Monday to Saturday). In summer, seasonal buses also connect Algaida with the east-coast resorts.

Montuïri

POP 2867

Riding a hill above ranging farmland, Montuïri is one of Mallorca's oldest towns, dating back to the Moorish dominion of the island. Known for its apricots, it's appropriate that its handsome stone buildings glow an apricot hue in the morning sun. The sandstone **Església de Sant Bartomeu** dominates

WORTH A TRIP

SA FONT

Sa Font (Carrer de Sa Font) FREE is one of the few reminders of the Arab presence on the island. This complex *qanawat* (well and water distribution structure) is difficult to date but was taken over by the Muslims' Christian successors after 1229. It lies in Pina, 5.5km northwest of Montuïri, just 50m south of the Església de Sants Cosme i Damià, on the road to Lloret de Vistalegre. Head down Carrer de Sa Font from the church and it's on the far side of the road.

central Plaça Major, through which runs Carrer Major, graced by the occasional mansion and bar. Montuïri has a few very pleasant bars spilling out onto the Carrer de Palma, running through its heart.

★ **Museu Arqueològic**
de Son Fornés   MUSEUM
(☑971 64 41 69; www.sonfornes.mallorca. museum; Carrer d'Emili Pou, Molí d'en Fraret; adult/ child €3.50/free; ☺10am-5pm Mar-Oct, to 2pm Mon-Fri Nov-Feb) Housed in an 18th-century mill on the northwest edge of town, this enthusiastic, well-curated little museum explores the prehistoric Talayotic civilisation of Mallorca. Many exhibits are from the nearby Son Fornés talaiot (watchtower), inhabited from around 900 BCE to the 4th century CE. One of Mallorca's most important archaeological sites, the *talaiot* is easy enough to visit: head 2.5km northwest out of Montuïri on the Ma3200 towards Pina and you'll see it to the right (east) of the road.

Festa de Sant Bartomeu   CULTURAL
(☺Aug) The main event of this celebration in honour of Montuïri's patron saint is the dance of the *cossiers* (a group of dancers, six men and one woman, plus the devil), both on the 24th and the eve before.

S'Encuentro   RELIGIOUS
(☺Mar/Apr) On Easter Sunday, a figure of Christ resurrected is met in a parade by a figure of the Virgin Mary, who does some excited hops to show her joy at the resurrection of her son.

S'Hostal   BAR
(☑971 64 60 49; Carrer Constitució 58; ☺7am-midnight Tue-Sun) Renowned for taking the ubiquitous Mallorcan bar snack *pa amb oli* (bread with oil) to the limits of its potential, this greenery-draped roadside bar downhill from central Montuïri is one of those 'local secrets' travellers delight in uncovering.

❶ Getting There & Away

The 411 connects Palma and Montuïri (€4.05, 30 minutes, up to six daily). It stops outside the bar S'Hostal, down the hill to the south of the centre of town.

Petra

POP 2816

The birthplace of Catholic saint and missionary Juníper Serra, Petra is a quiet, comely midland town, its former prominence demonstrated by long streets of solid stone houses, and two impressive churches, dating to the 16th and 17th centuries. With an in-town winery, a couple of very nice places to eat and an intriguing museum, it's an undemonstrative and relaxing place that rewards an extra few hours' exploration.

◉ Sights

Unhurried Petra's principal claim to historical fame is its favourite son, Juníper Serra, born here in 1713. A Franciscan missionary and one of the founders of what is now the US state of California, he could have had no inkling of his destiny as he grew up in this rural centre. Colourful majolica tiles depicting his missionary exploits enliven an already-handsome town – the street housing the museum dedicated to him is one of the prettiest in Mallorca.

★ **Els Calderers**   HISTORIC BUILDING
(☑971 52 60 69; www.elscalderers.com; Camino Els Calderers; adult/child €9/4; ☺10am-6pm Apr-Oct, to 5pm Nov-Mar; ℗) On a pretty country back road between Montuïri and Petra, this stout rural mansion has been converted into a period museum. Els Calderers was built around 1750, on the site of an estate granted to the eponymous Calderers family in 1285. Sold to the Verí family in the 18th century, its grand dimensions, extensive grounds and well-preserved collection of antique

Mallorcan furnishings strongly evoke a vanished world of aristocratic privilege.

Museu Fra Juníper Serra MUSEUM

(www.spiritualmallorca.com; Carrer des Barracar 6-10; €5; ⊙10am-1.30pm Mon-Fri) The Museu Fra Juníper Serra contains mementos of Juníper Serra's missionary life. Next door is the house in which he was born, while all over the streets in this part of town are ceramic depictions of his eventful life. Entry is via the Spiritual Mallorca ticket (€5).

Bodegas Miquel Oliver WINERY

(☑971 56 11 17; www.miqueloliver.com; Carretera Petra-Santa Margalida Km 1.8; ⊙10am-6pm Mon-Fri & 11am-1.30pm Sat; ℙ) Going strong since 1912, Bodegas Miquel Oliver is one of the island's most respected winemakers. You can pick up a decent bottle of red at the cellar door, a little over 1km north of town, for under €10. There is also a variety of private tours, focusing on wine, wine-making, viticulture, vineyards and tapas.

✖ Eating.

Es Celler MALLORCAN €€

(☑971 56 10 56; www.restaurantesceller.com; Carrer de l'Hospital 46; mains €12-15; ⊙noon-11.45pm) Step down off the street and into this wonderfully cavernous cellar restaurant with soaring ceilings and old wine barrels. Its specialities are barbecued meats, roast lamb and roast suckling pig, but it also rustles up Mallorcan classics like *berenjenas rellenas de carne* (meat-stuffed aubergines), *arros brut* (dirty rice) and *tumbet*.

❶ Getting There & Away

Petra is one stop short of Manacor (€1.45, nine minutes) on the Palma–Manacor (T3) train line and gets at least one service an hour in both directions. From Palma, the trip takes just under an hour and costs €3.75.

Manacor

POP 42,600

Manacor, Mallorca's second-largest city, is perhaps best known as the birthplace of tennis great Rafael Nadal – fans can head direct to the Rafa Nadal Museum Xperience (p150) – and as a centre of furniture manufacturing. There are definitely more compelling attractions to be found elsewhere, but don't discount this place entirely.

❍ Sights

Església de Nostra Senyora

Verge dels Dolors CHURCH

(Plaça del General Weyler; ⊙8.30am-12.45pm & 5.30-8pm) The massive Església de Nostra Senyora Verge dels Dolors lords it impressively over the Manacor skyline. Raised on the site of the town's former mosque with a hybrid Gothic/neo-Gothic style, reflecting the fact that construction began in the 14th century and wasn't completed until the 19th century. It's well worth popping in to admire the splendid arches and stonework, dappled with sunlight through stained glass, and the magnificent altarpiece. The church is stuffed with small chapels, including 10 in the nave.

THE INTERIOR MANACOR

Manacor

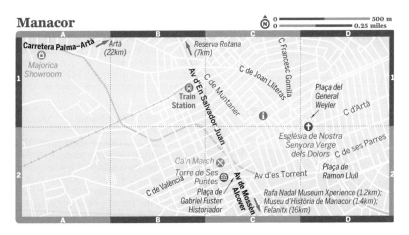

Museu d'Història de Manacor — MUSEUM

(☎971 84 30 65; www.museudemanacor.com/ca; Carretera Cales de Mallorca; ☉9am-2pm Wed-Mon, plus 5-7.30pm Thu-Sat mid-Sept–May, to 8.30pm June–mid-Sept, closed Sun mid-Sept–May) FREE This intriguing museum contains fascinating exhibits relating to the Roman, Byzantine, Vandal, Muslim and later eras of the region, including Roman mosaics that form the most important collection of mosaics in the Balearic Islands. There are also important pieces of ancient sculpture, metalwork and ceramics.

Rafa Nadal Museum Xperience — MUSEUM

(☎971 17 16 83; https://sportxperience.rns portscentre.com; Carretera Cales de Mallorca; adult/child €15/10; ☉10am-2.30pm) Admire the top moments of the Mallorcan tennis star's career on the court in the Exhibition Room, then get your pulse moving on a variety of simulators (including tennis, through Formula 1 to mountain cycling and other sports) in the Experience Room. Tickets sales stop at 2pm.

Torre de Ses Puntes — HISTORIC BUILDING

(Plaça de Gabriel Fuster Historiador; ☉6.30-8.30pm) Once part of the city's defences, this 14th-century tower has received some (mostly sensitive) modern, plate-glass additions, and is now used for the odd exhibition. It's around 500m west of the tourist office.

✗ Eating

Above and beyond the expected pool of perfectly good Mallorcan restaurants and tapas bars, there are a few excellent places to eat in Manacor.

Ca'n March — MALLORCAN €€

(☎971 55 00 02; www.canmarch.com; Carrer de València 7; mains €13.50-24, menús €14.50-25; ☉1-3.30pm Tue-Sun, plus 8.30-11pm Fri & Sat) Fish prepared with a minimum of fuss using salt from Es Trenc and Mallorcan olive oil is a strong point at this warm, traditional haunt, which has been knocking out the plates since 1925. Or you can opt for rice dishes like lobster and rice, vegetable paella or black rice (cuttlefish with ink, plus rice).

Reserva Rotana — MEDITERRANEAN €€€

(☎971 84 56 85; www.reservarotana.com; Camí de Bendris Km 3; mains €24-32; ☉7-11pm Mar-Oct) A slice of rural luxury, this tucked-away *finca* (estate) offers genteel ambience and polished service in its beamed dining room and flower-draped garden. Top-notch ingredients and careful cooking shine in dishes like lamb loin with Joselito bacon, porcinis, walnut and rosehip, or turbot with potatoes and lovage. The *finca* is situated 7km north of Manacor, off the Ma3321.

🛍 Shopping

Most visitors come to Manacor for the manufactured pearls, but you'll also find some fine woodwork on sale.

Majorica Showroom — JEWELLERY

(www.majorica.com; Carretera Palma-Artà Km 47; ☉9.30am-8pm Jun-Sep, to 5pm Nov-Feb, to 6pm Mar-May & Oct) This company, the best-known Manacor pearl manufacturer, was founded by German Eduard Heusch in 1890 and now has its two-storey showroom on the edge of town on the road to Palma. Upstairs you can see a handful of people working on the creation of pearls.

ℹ Information

Tourist Office (☎662 350891; www.visitmanacor. com; Plaça del Convent 3; ☉9am-2pm Mon-Fri)

ℹ Getting There & Away

The T3 train connects Manacor and Palma (€3.45, 65 minutes, hourly between 6.17am and 10.20pm). Plenty of buses on cross-island routes also call in, terminating in front of the train station, a 10-minute walk from Plaça del General Weyler.

Felanitx

POP 17,500

Felanitx is an important regional centre with a reputation for ceramics, white wine and capers (the culinary type). A handsome if unspectacular town, it's perhaps most visited as the gateway to two stunning hilltop sites nearby.

★ Santuari de Sant Salvador — MONASTERY

(www.santsalvadorhotel.com; ☉church 8am-11pm) One of inland Mallorca's most spectacular viewpoints, the hermitage Santuari de Sant Salvador crowns a hilltop 5km southeast of Felanitx and 509m above sea level. Built in 1348, the year of the Black Death, it's plausible that the hermits were safe here. The church, added to over the years, is a strange mix, with gaudy columns and an elaborate cave nativity scene offset by an unadorned barrel-vaulted ceiling and a delicately carved stone altarpiece.

Apart from the monastery, there's a prominent cross (built in 1957) on a neighbouring peak, while the car park is dominated by an enormous, 35m-high statue of Christ the King, atop a column. At every turn, the views are heavenly. For the full experience, you can stay the night in one of the tastefully converted cells at the **Petit Hotel Hostatgería Sant Salvador** (☑971 51 52 60; www.cancalcohotels.com; Puig San Salvador, Santuari de Sant Salvador; d/apt Feb-Oct from €45/90; Ⓟ 🛜).

Castell de Santueri   CASTLE
(☑691 223679; http://santueri.org; €4; ⊙10am-6.30pm Mar-Oct) This clifftop castle, whose proud walls rise seamlessly from a craggy natural peak, offers spectacular views, extending southeast far out to sea. The castle was built by the Moors, and not taken until 1231, two years after the rest of the island had fallen. To get here from Felanitx, take the Ma14 for 2km, then follow the signs to the left (east). The road winds 5km to the base of the castle.

You can also reach the Santuari de Sant Salvador on a 4km-long path through the hills from the castle.

ℹ Getting There & Away

From Palma the 490 (and 491 express) connect with Felanitx (€5.40, one hour, up to 12 daily).

Eastern Mallorca

Best Places to Eat

➜ Forn Nou (p157)

➜ Cases de Son Barbassa (p160)

➜ VORO (p163)

➜ Andreu Genestra (p160)

➜ Es Coll d'Os (p162)

➜ Restaurant Sa Llotja (p165)

Best Historic Architecture

➜ Sa Torre Cega (p160)

➜ Castell de Capdepera (p159)

➜ Santuari de Sant Salvador (p156)

➜ Torre de Canyamel (p163)

➜ Ermita de Betlem (p158)

➜ Transfiguració del Senyor (p156)

Why Go?

There's a reason tourists arrive in Eastern Mallorca in their hundreds of thousands on their annual solar pilgrimage: this is one of the prettiest coasts on the island. Ignore the less sightly resorts and you will discover a rocky eastern coastal landscape that also conceals perfectly formed caves, coves and inlets, some of which are accessible only on foot and are largely immune to development.

This region is also home to the quite spectacular scenery of the Parc Natural de la Península de Llevant which elevates you to fine views of the Mediterranean and, if you keep going, to the beautifully situated Ermita de Betlem.

Stunning medieval towns such as Artà and Capdepera – the Santuari de Sant Salvador rising over the former and a formidable castle looming over the latter – supply all the history you may need, while the coastline between Porto Cristo and Portocolom reveals a seductive string of secluded coves and bays.

When to Go

You could be forgiven for thinking that Eastern Mallorca hibernates throughout winter, rumbling into life only from April to October. There's an element of truth in this: many restaurants, hotels and other businesses only open in these months (although an increasing number are extending from February to November). Winters are relatively mild and the beauty of Eastern Mallorca's coast and hill towns have a special allure without the crowds. Most towns and villages celebrate Sant Antoni with great gusto in mid-January.

HIKING THE EASTERN COAST

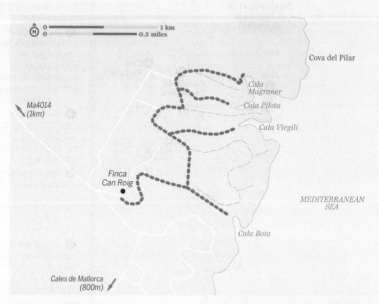

Cova del Pilar

Cala Magraner

Cala Pilota

Cala Virgili

MEDITERRANEAN
SEA

Cala Bota

Finca
Can Roig

Ma4014
(1km)

Cales de Mallorca
(800m)

FOUR COVES HIKE

START FINCA CAN ROIG
END FINCA CAN ROIG
LENGTH 13KM; 3-3½ HOURS

Just north of Cales de Mallorca the chaos of the resorts falls away and nature resumes. Over the 6km between Cales de Mallorca and Cala Romántica, there's only pine-specked rocky coves, pitted cliff faces and the alluring aquamarine of the Mediterranean.

The walk begins at **Finca Can Roig**, a rural estate. To get here, take the Carretera Porto Cristo–Portocolom (Ma4014) and at Km 6 turn east towards Cales de Mallorca. Continue 2.2km and veer left; after 200m you'll reach the entrance to Can Roig. Leave your car here and walk up the path; you will shortly reach a gate, which you can access on the right-hand side (with signs to the beach).

Continue along the wide, rocky track; after about 15 minutes, a slightly narrower path turns off to the right. Follow it alongside a small gully and through patches of

trees to reach **Cala Bota**, a sheltered (and often deserted) cove with a small sandy beach. A steep trail meanders around and above the cove, giving a bird's-eye view of its beauty.

From Cala Bota, retrace your steps and take the second right towards the next cove, **Cala Virgili**. The track brings you to a smaller trail that heads off right down to this narrow, cliff-flanked cove, with limpid water for a refreshing dip. (The walk down takes about 10 minutes.)

Return to the main trail and follow it. You'll pass a small trail on your right, but keep straight until you come upon a second path. Take it towards the **Cala Pilota**, a lovely cove backed by cave-pocked cliffs, with brilliantly turquoise water.

Head back to the main trail and continue. Ignore the first right and instead take the second, which rolls down to the final cove, **Cala Magraner**, the grandest of the bunch both in size and beauty. The trail is wide at first but stops in a clearing; another,

The dented coastline and pure azure waters of the eastern Mallorcan coast – approaching their most beautiful and least developed condition between Cales de Mallorca and Cala Romántica – are superb for hiking.

narrower trail leads you for the last few minutes. After splashing in the crystalline waters and exploring the small caves that dot the rock, walk the main trail back to Finca Can Roig.

HIKING IN THE PARC NATURAL DE LA PENÍNSULA DE LLEVANT

Hikers are in their element in the Parc Natural de la Península de Llevant. The **information office** (p159) at **S'Alquera Vella de Baix** – where you can park – supplies a map highlighting 13 trails totalling 25km through the region.

A classic walk leads from here to the coast and down to the little beach at **S'Arenalet des Verger**, where you can overnight at a **campsite** (✉reservations 9am-4pm Mon-Fri 971 17 76 52; www.caib.es; S'Arenalet des Verger; per person €5) or **refuge** (✉reservations 9am-4pm Mon-Fri 971 17 76 52; www.caib.es; S'Arenalet des Verger; r €40-60) if you've booked ahead. Reckon on around two hours' walking time. Alternatively, to reach the same point from the east along the coast, you could start at **Cala Estreta** (where you can leave your car, as it's outside the park proper). This walk follows the coast to **Cala Matzoc** (p162), on past the 18th-century watchtower **Torre d'Albarca** and west. It takes another hour to reach S'Arenalet des Verger, inside the park and on the cusp of the nature reserve.

Hikes departing from S'Alquera Vella de Baix that head towards S'Arenalet des Verger include the 6.5km-long **Cami dels Presos** (route number 3) – the Prisoners' Path – which follows an ancient path built by Republican prisoners in the early 1940s to construct an artillery battery (never completed) on the **Puig de Sa Tudossa**, which concludes the hike. The trek passes by the ruins of the **Campament des Soldats** (Soldiers' Camp) – at the foot of the **Puig des Porrassar** – a camp where the prisoners were kept, where you can still see the barracks, stables and various storage rooms surrounding a courtyard. There is the option of linking up with the hike up **Talaia Freda** (564m; route number 13) from near here too. Alternatively, continue along winding route number 3 to the Puig de Sa Tudossa above, where you have the option of linking up with either route number 5 or 6, two different paths which take you down to the beach at S'Arenalet des Verger Another alternative is to trek 1km to the top of Puig des Porrassar (481m; 30 minutes) from the camp (route number 12), or hike south for 30 minutes along route number 4 from the camp to **Es Verger**, 1.5k away, from where route number 1 returns to S'Alquera Vella de Baix or route number 2 (one hour) leads to **Albarca**.

To reach S'Alquera Vella de Baix take the Ma3333 north of Artà in the direction of the Ermita de Betlem and follow the signposted turn-off right at Km 4.7, from where it's a further 600m to the car park.

COASTAL HIKES IN CALA RATJADA

Give the crowds in Cala Ratjada the slip by taking the **walking trail** that leaves from the far northern end of Cala Agulla and heads through the pines of a protected natural area towards the pristine **Cala Mesquida**, a beach backed with dunes. The round trip is 10km. Along the way, a smaller trail veers off to the right at the signpost for the *'torre'*, the Talaia de Son Jaume II watchtower. The trail (7km round trip from Cala Agulla) is marked with red dots, and the reward at the end is a spectacular panoramic view.

THE NORTHEAST

There's great hiking, swimming, horse riding and birdwatching in the northeast, yet its attractions aren't solely natural. The medieval hill towns of Artà and Capdepera retain countless antique treasures, while the raucous resort town of Cala Ratjada is a reminder of what much of Mallorca's eastern coast has become.

Artà

POP 7671

The antithesis of Cala Ratjada's buzzing resort culture just a few kilometres away, the quiet inland town of Artà beckons with its maze of narrow streets, appealing cafes, an attractive main square (Plaça del Conqueridor) and medieval architecture, all dominated by the magnificent form of an imposing 14th-century hilltop fortress.

◉ Sights & Activities

★**Santuari de Sant Salvador**　CASTLE
(Carrer del Castellet; ⊙8am-8pm Apr-Oct, shorter hours Nov-Mar) FREE Rising high and mighty above Artà, this walled fortress was built atop an earlier Moorish enclave and encloses a small church. The 4000-sq-metre complex, extensively restored in the 1960s, reveals all the hallmarks of a medieval bastion, down to the stone turrets ringing the top and the metre-thick walls. The views from here sweep over the rooftops of the medina-like old town and beyond to the bald, bumpy peaks of the Serra de Llevant.

★**Ses Païsses**　ARCHAEOLOGICAL SITE
(off Carretera Artà-Capdepera; adult/child €2/free; ⊙10am-5pm Mon-Fri, to 2pm Sat) Just beyond Artà proper lie the remains of a 3000-year-old Bronze Age settlement, the largest and most important Talayotic site on the island's eastern flank. The site's looming stone gateway, composed of rough, 8-tonne slabs, is an impressive transition into the mystery-shrouded world of prehistoric Mallorca. You can traverse the tree-shaded site in under 30 minutes, but may appreciate a longer visit. From the large roundabout east of Artà's tourist office, follow the signs towards Ses Païsses.

Museu Regional d'Artà　MUSEUM
(⊡971 82 97 78; Carrer de l'Estel 4; adult/child €2/free; ⊙10am-3pm Tue-Sat) This little museum opens a window on Artà's fascinating past. There's a natural history section, and another tracing the development of the city through time, with Bronze Age, Talayotic, Punic, Roman and Moorish artefacts, including ceramics, jewellery, bronzes and funerary gifts. There's also space for rotating exhibitions, often featuring local art, traditions and culture.

Transfiguració del Senyor　CHURCH
(Carrer del Mal Lloc; adult/child €2/free; ⊙10am-5pm Mon-Sat) This church, built atop the foundations of a Moorish mosque, was begun soon after the Christian reconquest, although the restored facade dates to the 16th century. Inside, note the large rose window, the ornately carved mahogany pulpit and the 14 chapels in the nave. There's also a small museum exhibiting artefacts such as precious altarpieces and a silver cross bearing a sliver of Palma Cathedral's relic of the True Cross (brought here in 1512).

Manacor–Artà Greenway　CYCLING
(www.viasverdes.com) This easy cycle route between the two eponymous cities follows a disused railway over 29km of packed-earth and gravel pathway. Occasional sea glimpses and a quieter perspective on the rural northeast are your rewards. You can rent bikes in the tourist office (p158) at the disused train station in Artà.

★☆ Festivals & Events

Festes de Sant Antoni Abat　CULTURAL
(⊙16-17 Jan) During this intriguing Catalan festival, everyone dresses in traditional costume and heads to the Santuari de Sant Salvador for dancing, music and a downright odd display of backward-facing equestrians swinging long sticks.

Eating

Artà has some brilliantly atmospheric restaurants and cafes, many with a boho vibe

---

ⓘ ARTÀ CARD

If you're planning on doing a fair bit of sightseeing, buy the Artà Card (€3) at the tourist office (p158). It gets you entry to the major sights, including the Museu Regional d'Artà (p156), the church and museum of Transfiguració del Senyor (p156), Ses Païsses (p156) and reduced entry to the Coves d'Artà (p163), near Canyamel.

Artà

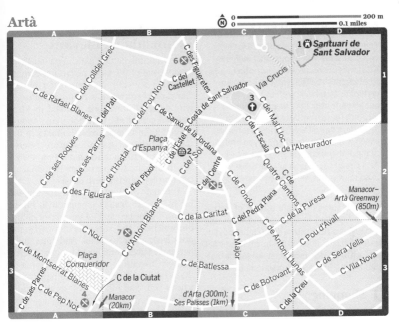

and sidewalk seating. Carrer de la Ciutat, the prettiest street in town, is lined with shops, restaurants and cafe-dotted squares. Prices tend to be higher than in most other places in Mallorca, partly due to the tourist influx, but quality is also high.

★ **Forn Nou** MEDITERRANEAN €€
(☑971 82 92 46; www.fornnou-arta.com; Carrer del Centre 7; 3-course dinner €30, mains from €21; ☺6.30-11pm; 🛜) Forn Nou's terrace perches high above Artà's medieval maze and peers across the rooftops to the church and fortress. The season-driven menu changes twice monthly, but you can expect clean, bright Mediterranean flavours, along the lines of Atlantic anchovies with roasted peppers and paprika, or lobster risotto.

Gaudí el Restaurante MEDITERRANEAN €€
(☑971 82 95 55; www.santsalvador.com; Carrer del Pou Nou 26; mains €21-25; ☺1-3pm & 7-10pm Tue-Sun; 🛜) Gathered around an inner courtyard lit by tealights and purportedly designed by Antoni Gaudí, this is a fabulously intimate setting for lunch or dinner. Dishes such as sole *meunière* with Sòller oranges, ham and artichokes, or salmon *tataki* with green seaweed risotto and *wakame*, indicate ambition in the kitchen. Live music accompanies the tapas on Tuesday night.

Artà

◉ **Top Sights**
1 Santuari de Sant Salvador D1

◉ **Sights**
2 Museu Regional d'Artà B2
3 Transfiguració del Senyor C1

✕ **Eating**
4 Cafe Parisien A3
5 Forn Nou C2
6 Gaudí el Restaurante B1
7 Mar de Vins B3

Mar de Vins INTERNATIONAL €€
(☑971 59 64 10; Carrer d'Antoni Blanes 34; mains €12-16; ☺11am-10.30pm Mon-Sat; 🛜🖉🍴) Our favourite hangout to linger over coffee and a good book, this cafe conceals one of Artà's loveliest garden patios. The interior is cosy, with its cobbled floor, paintings and marble-topped tables, and there are plenty of vegetarian options to complement carnivorous Spanish favourites, such as chicken *croquetas* and meltingly tender *albóndigas* (meatballs).

Cafe Parisien MEDITERRANEAN €€
(☑971 83 54 40; Carrer de la Ciutat 18; mains €15-18; ☺10am-11pm Mon-Sat, 5-11pm Sun; 🛜) White wrought-iron chairs, modern art and swing

CYCLING AROUND ARTÀ

The tourist office hands out an excellent brochure called Bike Tours that includes a dozen route maps and descriptions through the area that you can complete on foot or by bike. The office also rents out bikes. Particularly recommended is the 7km route from Artà to the Ermita de Betlem hermitage (the last section of which is relentlessly steep). If you prefer things flat and car-free, the Manacor–Artà Greenway (p156) follows a disused railway between the two cities.

music give this boho cafe a dash of Parisian class. Swathed in jasmine and vines, the courtyard is a beautiful spot on a balmy day. The food has a market-fresh, international slant, with lighter fare such as salads balanced by curries and European dishes.

🛍 Shopping

d'Artà
ARTS & CRAFTS

(☑ 971 83 69 81; http://darta.es; Avinguda de Costa i Llobera 7; ⊘ 9am-8pm, reduced hours winter) Housed in Artà's handsome, disused train station and incorporating the tourist office, this collective venture displays the wares of local, traditional artisans for sale. Beautiful leatherwork, handsome ceramics and handmade clothes are sold alongside herbal liquors, organic smallgoods made from Mallorcan black pigs, single-flower honeys, dried fruit and other lip-smacking bounty. Upstairs you'll find exhibitions of local art.

ℹ Information

Tourist Office (☑ 971 83 69 81; http://darta. es; Avinguda de Costa i Llobera 7; ⊘ 10am-5pm Mon-Fri, to 2pm Sat) Artà's local craft and cultural centre incorporates a helpful tourist office with plenty of info and maps of the area. It also sells the Artà Card (p156) and rents out bikes.

The office is located at the former, and long disused, train station.

ℹ Getting There & Away

Bus services to/from Artà's Avinguda de Costa i Llobera include bus 411 to Palma (€9.90, 90 minutes, four to five daily) via Manacor (€2.95, 25 minutes), and bus 446 to Port d'Alcúdia (€5.45, one hour, three daily Monday to Saturday) and Port de Pollença (€6.85, 70 minutes).

Parc Natural de la Península de Llevant

This beautiful nature park, 5km north of Artà, is one of the most rewarding corners of Mallorca's east. It's dominated by the **Serra de Llevant**, a low mountain range of wind-sculpted limestone, cloaked in Mauritanian grass broken by holm oak, Aleppo pine and fan palms, and culminates in the **Cap Ferrutx**, a dramatic nature reserve (off-limits to the public) that drops vertiginously into the Mediterranean from Mallorca's northern and eastern coasts.

Although parts of the park are accessible by car, it's hugely popular with hikers (p155), cyclists and binocular-wielding birdwatchers; the latter are drawn by the prevalence of cormorants, Audouin's gulls, peregrine falcons and booted eagles. There's a lovely hike up to the secluded church of the Ermita de Betlem via the mirador, from where you can hike down to the Badia d'Alcúdia.

Ermita de Betlem
CHRISTIAN SITE

FREE Founded in 1805, Ermita de Betlem is still home to hermits who live a life of seclusion and self-sufficiency. The alluring views over country and wind-whipped coast make the steep up-and-down road to this hermitage a joy. The lovely stone-built exterior of the church stands in contrast to its modern whitewashed interior, ceiling frescoes and cave nativity scene, complete with stalactites and stalagmites. Stroll up the neighbouring hilltops to see all the way to Menorca.

There's a small shop selling rosaries and Catholic keepsakes to the right of the door. To reach the hermitage, take the narrow paved road (the Ma3333) beginning in Artà, which meanders for around 5km through pine woodland and fields before climbing steeply to reach the top of the ridge, then winding down a further 2.5km. You can also climb up from (or walk down to) Betlem below. On the drive up, you'll see the Badia d'Alcúdia appear at a bend in the road: it's an astonishing sight.

Mirador de la Ermita de Betlem
VIEWPOINT

Breathtaking viewpoint (not just for exhausted cyclists) high up on the way to the Ermita de Betlem, with glorious views of the Badia d'Alcúdia and Cap Ferrutx.

ℹ️ Information

Parc Natural de la Península de Llevant Information Office (📞 900 15 16 17; http:// ibanat.caib.es; S'Alqueria Vella de Baix; ⏱ 9am-4pm) The park office can help with itinerary maps and organises guided walks, generally in Catalan and Spanish.

ℹ️ Getting There & Away

You'll need your own wheels: buses can only get you as close as Artà or Betlem.

Capdepera

POP 11,600

More of a fortified town than a town with a castle, Capdepera's stirring medieval fortress is visible from across the plains of northeastern Mallorca, its magnitude a reminder of the centuries in which it was the only protection from the degradations of pirates. The remainder of the village that clusters below its walls is pleasant, in parts beautiful, but the castle is the still main attraction.

◎ Sights & Activities

★ **Castell de Capdepera** CASTLE
(📞 971 81 87 46; www.capdeperacastell.com; Carrer del Castell; €3; ⏱ 10am-8pm Jun-Sep, to 7pm Apr, May & Oct, to 5pm Nov-early Jan & early Feb-Mar) Lording it over Capdepera is this early-14th-century fortress. A walled complex built on the ruins of a Moorish fortress, the castle is one of the best preserved on the island. Constructed as a self-contained fortified town by Jaume II (son of the conquering Jaume I), it was a bastion of safety (from pirate attacks) and royal power in this part of the island. Within the walls, a simple stone church contains a valuable wooden crucifix dating to the 14th century.

Capdepera Golf GOLF
(📞 971 81 85 00; www.golfcapdepera.com; Carretera Artá-Capdepera, Km 3.5; 9 holes €39-49, 18 holes €59-97; ⏱ 8am-7pm summer, 9am-3pm winter) Designed to make the most of the topography by US golf architect Dan Maples, this 18-hole course is highly regarded.

🎊 Festivals & Events

Mercat Medieval CULTURAL
(⏱ May) Commemorating the foundation of the town by Jaume II in 1300, this fair sees Capdepera given over to medieval costumes, and events on the third weekend in May.

Festa de Sant Antoni RELIGIOUS
(St Anthony's Feast Day; ⏱ 16-17 Jan) Adapted from a pre-existing pagan festival, this archaic Balearic celebration of a 3rd-century Egyptian saint is ushered in by bonfires and masked dances.

EASTERN MALLORCA CAPDEPERA

BIRDWATCHING IN MALLORCA

Just about anywhere in Mallorca is good for birdwatching, but the northern, eastern and southern coasts are prime territory for twitchers.

Parc Natural de S'Albufera (p137) A marshy birdwatchers' paradise where some 230 species, including moustached warblers and shoveler ducks, vie for your attention. The park is home to no less than two-thirds of the species that live here permanently or winter on Mallorca and is a Ramsar Wetland of International Importance.

Parc Nacional Marítim-Terrestre de l'Arxipèlag de Cabrera (p173) These protected offshore islands draw marine birds, migrants and birds of prey, including fisher eagles, endangered Balearic shearwaters, Audouin's gulls, Cory's shearwaters, shags, ospreys, Eleonora's falcons and peregrine falcons.

Parc Natural de la Península de Llevant (p158) Watch for cormorants and Audouin's gulls in this rugged promontory north of Artà.

Parc Natural de Mondragó (p176) Falcons, turtle doves and coastal species.

Embassament de Cúber In the shadow of the Puig Major de Son Torrella, watch for raptors and other mountain species.

Vall de Bóquer Near Port Pollença, this rocky valley is home to warblers, Eurasian Scops owls, red-legged partridges, peregrine falcons, and other mountain and migratory species.

Cap de Formentor (p132) Species on this dramatic peninsula include all manner of warblers, blue rock thrushes, crag martins, Eleonora's falcons, pallid swifts, migrating raptors and, if you're lucky, the Balearic shearwaters.

Eating

Capdepera's best eating is to be found near, but not in, the town. Several upscale hotels in the surrounding countryside also lay claim to some top-notch, enticing restaurants.

★ Cases de Son Barbassa MEDITERRANEAN €€
(☎971 56 57 76; www.sonbarbassa.com; Camí de Son Barbassa; mains from €24, 3-course menu €34.50; ⏲12.30-3pm & 7-10pm) Follow a narrow lane to this blissfully secluded *finca* (rural estate) which notches up the romance with its terrace and sweeping country views. Set among olive, almond and carob trees, it makes plenty of garden and market produce in dishes likes turbot in champagne with clam and oysters, and suckling pig cooked to crackling perfection – prepared with home-grown olive oil.

★ Andreu Genestra MODERN EUROPEAN €€€
(☎971 56 59 10; http://andreugenestra.com; Carretera Cala Mesquida, Km 1; 5/8/10 courses €58/74/105; ⏲1.30-3pm & 7-10.30pm Sat & Sun, 7-10.30pm Mon-Fri Apr-Nov; P ❄ 📶) Michelin-starred Mallorcan chef Genestra runs this wonderful rural restaurant, attached to (but independent from) the Predi Son Jaumell hotel, nestled among his own olive groves and vineyards. Shades of his experience at Mugaritz and El Bulli shine through his fixed-price menus, yet Mallorcan ingredients such as *cocarroi* (pastry) and local *butifarra* sausage are given due respect.

Information

Tourist Office (☎971 55 64 79; Carrer des Centre 9; ⏲8am-3pm Mon-Fri) In the town centre.

Getting There & Away

Bus 411 links Capdepera to Palma (€11, 1½ hours, up to five daily), via Artà (€1.50, 15 minutes) and Manacor (€4.05, 40 minutes). Bus 441 also runs along the east coast, stopping at all the major resorts, including Porto Cristo (€3.35, 55 minutes, up to eight daily) and Cala d'Or (€9.20, 1¾ hours); a change may be necessary to complete the trip.

Cala Ratjada

POP 6500

Cala Ratjada is the Jekyll and Hyde of Mallorca's eastern resorts. Wander along the promenade that skirts the contours of the coast and plump for one of the quieter bays and it can be pretty and sometimes even peaceful. It's also a terrific base for water-borne activities. But come high season, the resort adopts a second persona as the Costa de Bavaria, with rollicking beer gardens attracting a tanked-up 18-to-30 crowd, doing a brisk trade in currywurst and other German grub. You'll need to push beyond its centre to find Mallorca again (which is never too far away).

Sights

★ Sa Torre Cega HISTORIC BUILDING
(☎971 81 94 67; www.fundacionbmarch.es; off Carrer d'Elionor Servera; adult/child €4.50/free; ⏲tours 10.30am-noon Wed-Fri, 11am-6pm Sat & Sun May-Nov, 10.30am-noon Wed, Fri & Sat Feb-Apr) Named for the 15th-century 'blind tower' (unsighted by similar watchtowers) at its centre, this coastal estate was built in the early 20th century by the noted architect Guillem Reynés Font. The beautiful Mediterranean garden is home to a collection of over 40 works by noted Spanish, Catalan and Latin American sculptors, such as Eusebio Sempere, Juan de Ávalos, Xavier Corberó and Agustín Cárdenas. All guided visits must be booked in advance through the tourist office (p162).

Far de Capdepera LIGHTHOUSE
This lighthouse on Mallorca's easternmost tip is the endpoint of a lovely drive, walk or cycle through pine forests, around 1.5km east of Sa Torre Cega. Sitting 76m above the sea, the lighthouse – long crucial for sailors fighting the fierce winds that assail the east coast – began operating in 1861 (and was only electrified in 1969), and the views from here (all the way to Menorca on a clear day) are wonderful.

Activities

Skualo Adventure Sports DIVING
(☎971 56 43 03; www.mallorcadiving.com; Carrer Lepanto 1; 2-day scuba course €290, 2hr snorkelling €45; 👪) This reputable dive centre has an array of PADI courses and snorkelling excursions, many to the pristine waters around the Parc Natural de la Península de Llevant (p158). It also arranges other activities, including speedboating (€45, 50 minutes) and cave tours (with swimming in saltwater and freshwater caves, €65, three hours).

Rancho Bonanza HORSE RIDING
(☎619 680688; www.ranchobonanza.com; Carrer de Ca'n Patilla; 1/2hr ride €20/40, full-day excursion per person €70; 👪) The best of a few options on the pine-shaded outskirts of town,

Cala Ratjada

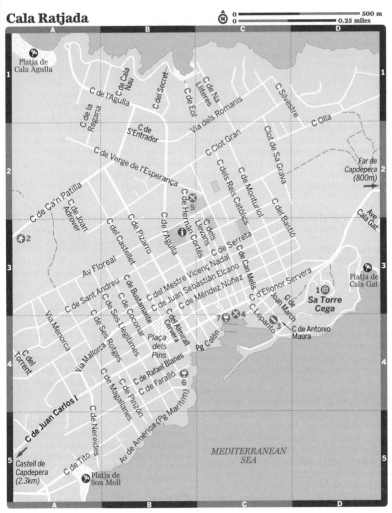

Bonanza runs excursions daily to quiet bays and along rural lanes. One-hour pony rides (€10) are available for kids six years and under, as are riding lessons (€20) and bareback riding (€20 per hour).

Illes Balears Ballooning BALLOONING
(☎607 647647; www.ibballooning.net) Balloons for awe-inspiring trips (dawn/sunset flight per person €170/180) or private hire (€300).

✖ Eating

Dining pickings in Cala Ratjada are more international than in many Mallorcan towns,

TRANQUIL COVES AROUND CALA RATJADA

Heading north from Cala Ratjada, you'll find a wonderfully undeveloped stretch of coast-line flecked with beaches. Long-time favourites of nudists, these out-of-the-way coves are no secret, but their lack of development has kept them calm and pristine.

Broad, family-friendly **Cala Mesquida**, surrounded by sand dunes and a small housing development, is the most accessible, with free parking, a few beach bars in season and a regular bus service (bus 471) from Cala Ratjada (€1.90, 25 minutes, up to eight daily).

It requires more determination to access the undeveloped coves due west. Of-ten-windy **Cala Torta**, tiny, sheltered **Cala Mitjana** and the beachless **Cala Estreta** are all found at the end of a narrow road that ventures through the hills from Artà, yet a more interesting way to arrive is via the one-hour walking path from Cala Mesquida.

Further west, and following a 20-minute trek along the coast from Cala Estreta, **Cala Matzoc** comes into view. Often empty, the spacious sandy beach backs onto a hill where you'll find the ruins of a prehistoric *talayot* (watchtower).

but there's good Mallorcan seafood too, nat-urally, and you're never short of choice.

★ Es Coll d'Os   MEDITERRANEAN €€

(☑971 56 48 55; www.escolldos.com; Carrer de Verge de l'Esperança 5; 3-course menu €35; ☺6.30-10.30pm Mon-Sat) This family-run *finca* res-taurant feels light years away from some of the tacky tourist places in Cala Ratjada. Sit on the vine-draped terrace for a meal that tastes profoundly of the seasons, creatively prepared with organic, home-grown herbs and vegetables, lamb reared on the nearby estate and fish drawn from local waters.

Ca'n Maya   SEAFOOD €€

(☑971 56 40 35; www.canmaya.com; Carrer d'El-ionor Servera 80; mains €15-30; ☺noon-4pm & 7pm-midnight Tue-Sun Apr-Nov; ☏) This cen-trally located restaurant dates to 1938 and is perhaps the most authentic and low-key of Cala Ratjada's seafood places. Its glassed-in, harbourside terrace is ideal for lingering over fried squid, razor clams, grilled monk-fish, spider-crab rice, Norwegian lobster, *paella* and many other delicacies from the Mediterranean's briny depths.

🍷 Drinking & Nightlife

Cala Ratjada is one place in northeastern Mallorca where you can really go hog-wild, especially around Carrer des Coconar and Carrer d'Elionor Servera.

Royal   BAR

(☑971 81 82 22; Carrer d'Elionor Servera 74; ☺9am-1am; ☏) A much-loved sunset spot, the Royal has a classy terrace overlooking the narrow end of the harbour. There's mu-sic from 8pm on Thursday (DJs), Friday (fla-menco) and Saturday (jazz), and the kitchen

pumps out a high standard of seafood, sal-ads and food from the grill, including a very good-value lunch menu (€10; noon to 3pm).

Café Noah's   BAR

(☑971 81 81 25; www.cafenoahs.com; Avinguda de América 2; ☺9am-2am) The sea views are entrancing from the terrace of this slick lounge bar: straddling the waterfront prom-enade, it's a prime spot for people watching and cocktail sipping. Inside there are comfy leather sofas and DJs to get the crowd on their feet on Friday to Sunday nights in sum-mer. A decent and internationally inventive menu rounds off an appealing choice.

ℹ Information

Tourist Office (☑971 81 94 67; www.ajcap depera.net; Centre Cap Vermell, Carrer de l'Agulla 50; ☺9am-1pm & 4-8pm Mon-Fri; ☏) Located in the white town hall building; there is free wi-fi in the plaza out the front. Visit in the morning for English-speaking service.

ℹ Getting There & Away

Bus 411 links Palma de Mallorca and Cala Rat-jada, via Artá, with up to five runs daily in each direction (€11.45, two hours). From May to Oc-tober, a daily bus trundles frequently to nearby beaches and sights like Cala Mesquida, Cala Agulla and Coves d'Artà (all €1.85).

Canyamel

POP 315

Little Canyamel is naturally more sedate compared to the bigger resorts along the eastern seaboard, although it does have its share of medium-rise development, and the attractive **Platja de Canyamel** can get very crowded in summer (the well-heeled inhabitants whose expensive houses cling to the southern slopes above the town keep well clear of all that). Inland, a fine medieval tower turned cultural centre rises next to the road and there's a majestic cave complex that sees far fewer visitors than similar sites along this pitted coast.

◉ Sights & Activities

Coves d'Artà CAVE
(☑971 84 12 93; www.cuevasdearta.com; Carrer de Coves de s'Ermita; adult/child 7-12yr/child under 7yr €15/7/free; ⊙10am-6pm Apr-Jun & Oct, to 7pm Jul-Sep, to 5pm Nov-Mar) Head 1km north of Canyamel and pass through an unassuming fissure in the rock wall that buffers the coast and you'll find yourself in a stunning warren of limestone caves – the possible inspiration for Jules Verne's *Journey to the Centre of the Earth*. First up is a soaring vestibule, home to the 22m-tall stalagmite known as the 'Queen of Columns', while subsequent rooms include the 'Chamber of Purgatory' and 'Chamber of Hell'. Guided tours leave every 30 minutes.

Torre de Canyamel CASTLE
(☑971 84 11 34; Carretera Artà-Canyamel, Km5; adult/child €3/free; ⊙10am-3pm & 5-8pm Tue-Sat, 10am-3pm Sun) Just 3km inland from Canyamel and signposted off the main coast road, the striking Torre de Canyamel – a 23m-high, restored 13th-century defensive tower of golden stone, named for the sugar cane once grown in the district – is a rewarding detour. There's a restaurant, event space and a permanent exhibition tracing 700 years of development in the area, through artefacts from the Morell Ethnographic Collection.

Canyamel Golf GOLF
(☑971 84 13 13; www.canyamelgolf.com; Avinguda d'es Cap Vermell; 9/18 holes from €49/83; ⊙7.30am-9pm Jun-Aug, shorter hours Sep-May) Making sensitive (and challenging) use of some lovely terrain, this 18-hole course is one the island's most attractive. One of its idiosyncratic features is a stone hut, adding a scenic complication to the game. It's also home to turtles, so be careful near the water hazards.

Pula Golf GOLF
(☑971 81 70 34; www.pulagolf.com; Carretera Son Servera-Capdepera, Km 3; 9 holes €39-49, 18 holes €65-97; ⊙8am-7pm) Designed by José María Olazabal, this PGA Tour 18-hole course is

Mallorca's longest and most demanding (par 72). There's also a hotel and country club, housed in a 16th-century rural villa.

✕ Eating

If you're looking for an alternative to unexceptional hotel restaurants and standard seaside bars, head inland to Porxada de Sa Torre, at the foot of the Torre de Canyamel.

★ Porxada de Sa Torre MALLORCAN €€
(☑971 84 11 34; www.torredecanyamel.com/es; Carretera Artà-Canyamel, Km5; mains €17-20; ⊙1-3.30pm & 7-11pm Tue-Sun, 7-11pm Mon) Opening onto a garden terrace, Porxada de Sa Torre is a beacon of Mallorcan cooking, serving *tumbet,* perfectly roasted rabbit with onions, and widely famed *lechona* (suckling pig, roasted over holm oak). You're welcome in the kitchen to see how the dishes are prepared, while stone-and-wood architecture, an ancient olive press and friendly service complete the charming package.

★ VORO MEDITERRANEAN €€€
(☑871 811 234; www.vorobyparkhyattmallorca. com; Park Hyatt Mallorca, Urbanización Atalaya de Canyamel; 11-/16-course tasting menu €110/140; ⊙7-9.30pm Tue-Sat; 🅟) With superchef Álvaro Salazar at the helm and its name deriving from the Latin root-word for 'devour', Michelin-starred VORO seeks to push boundaries with top-class service and an exquisitely creative menu, which also keeps its eye on Mediterranean cuisine. There are two tasting menus, backed up by a superlative wine list.

❶ Getting There & Away

Bus 472 connects Canyamel with Cala Ratjada (€1.90, 25 minutes, nine per day, Monday to Saturday, two on Sunday). Bus 473 heads to Artà (€1.90, 20 minutes, three daily Monday to Saturday).

CALA MILLOR TO PORTOCOLOM

For the millions of tourists who gush every year onto its sandy beaches, splash in its gentle waves and hang their sunhats in swish, all-inclusive resorts, the coast from Cala Millor to Portocolom is a Mediterranean paradise. But for those who mourn the loss of Mallorca's once-pristine coastline, the overdevelopment is nothing short of a catastrophe. From humble beginnings in the 1930s, Cala Millor has grown to be a beast of a resort – the largest on Mallorca's eastern coast. But the crowd-weary shouldn't be put off entirely. Head inland to cosy rural hotels and drive, cycle or hike to off-the-beaten-path beaches, such as **Cala Romántica** or **Cala Varques**.

Porto Cristo

POP 7300

Mallorca's grandest caves, the otherworldly Coves del Drac, ensure Porto Cristo is a perennially popular day-trip destination, attracting civilian spelunkers by the busload. It's true that as a resort it lacks some of the bang of glitzier destinations elsewhere on the coast, but what Porto Cristo lacks in glamour it makes up for in quiet charm.

◉ Sights & Activities

★ Coves del Drac CAVE

(Dragon's Caves; ☑ 971 82 07 53; www.cuevasdeldrach.com; Carretera Cuevas; adult/child €16/9; ◉ 10am-5pm Mar-Oct, 10.30am-3.30pm Nov-early Mar) Over-visited and probably overpriced, the Coves del Drac are by no means over-rated. Of all of Mallorca's accessible cave complexes, this is the least forgettable. A 1.2km shuffle with the inevitable crowd, accompanied by a multilingual commentary, leads through chamber after chamber of impossible shapes, colours and dimensions. The one-hour tour finishes at a vast amphitheatre and lake, where you'll enjoy a brief boat-borne classical music recital.

Skualo Adventure Sports & Dive Centre DIVING

(☑ 971 81 50 94; www.mallorcadiving.com; Passeig del Cap d'Es Toll 11; 2 dives without/with equipment €80/105; ◉ 9am-6pm Mon-Sat Easter-Oct) This first-rate dive centre offers scuba 'baptisms' (€95) for novices, plus a wide array of PADI courses. It also offers snorkelling (€45) and two-hour sea-kayaking excursions (€49), as well as a three-hour sea-cave excursion (€69), with the chance to swim. There are eight notable dive sites within reach, offering varied topography and lots of sea life..

✦ Festivals & Events

Festa de Sant Antoni RELIGIOUS

(◉ 16 & 17 Jan) Porto Cristo goes all out with a bonfire and 'dance of the devils' for the eve of Sant Antoni, the traditional blessing of animals.

✕ Eating

Several fish restaurants line the waterfront where you'll be paying for the view of the harbour and sandy cliffs, but some have good menus.

La Magrana CAFE €€

(☑ 971 82 15 33; Plaça de Déu del Carme 15; mains €15-16; ◉ 9am-4pm Tue-Sat, 10am-2pm Sun Nov-Feb; ☜ ⚑) Uphill from town, on a quiet church square, this cute green-shuttered cafe cultivates a boho vibe, with its appealing jumble of vintage knick-knacks, pot plants, wicker chairs, art and bold colours. Take a seat in the garden terrace for fresh juices, ice creams and light bites like *pa amb oli* (bread with oil) with Serrano ham and cannelloni with fresh salad.

Quince SEAFOOD €€

(☑ 971 82 18 30; www.restaurantequince.com; Carrer Verí 1; mains €12-28; ◉ 11.30am-10pm Thu-Tue; ☜) With a tastily located slot overlooking the Porto Cristo harbour, good-looking Quince is a charmer, with a varied, cosmopolitan and world-ranging menu spanning flavours from chicken *gyoza* to fillet of 'Cuban style' black pork with fried bananas, *ceviche* made from the catch of the day, fish stew, fresh Mallorcan prawns, fried baby squids with *tzatziki aioli,* and spare ribs.

Sa Pedra SEAFOOD €€

(☑ 971 82 09 32; Carrer Verí 4; mains €15-25; ◉ noon-4pm & 7-11pm Wed-Mon; ☜ ⚑) Sa Pedra is a smart Porto Cristo choice with a good-looking perch and terrace overlooking the boats in the marina, serving crowd-pleasing seafood paella (€16.90), home-made fish croquettes (€16.25), fried baby squid (€16.25), meaty mains and a tot-satisfying kids menu. Vegetarians can aim for the vegetable paella.

ℹ Information

Tourist Office (☑ 971 84 91 26, 662 350882; www.visitmanacor.com; Plaça de l'Aljub; ◉ 9am-3pm Mon-Fri) At the end of the wharf.

ℹ Getting There & Away

Eight bus lines serve Porto Cristo, among them bus 412 to Palma (€8.80, 1½ hours, up to 10 daily) via Manacor (€1.95, 30 minutes); buses 441, 445 and 448 connect to other east-coast resorts, including Cala Ratjada.

EASTERN MALLORCA PORTO CRISTO

SECLUDED COVES SOUTH OF PORTO CRISTO

The creviced and fissured coast running south of Porto Cristo is textured with a series of beautiful, unspoilt coves, many of them signposted from the Ma4014 highway linking Porto Cristo and Portocolom. The largest and most developed of the bunch is **Cala Romántica** (S'Estany d'en Mas; P), a 160m-long wedge of pale golden sand flanked by cliffs and calm turquoise shallows; you should find it very quiet in the low season. A few hotels form one of the island's more serene resorts, and a rough promenade has been hewn out of the rock face by the sea.

Further south of Cala Romántica lies a string of beautiful spots, such as **Cala Varques** (Cala Barques), known for the cave on the cliff above the cove, **Cala Sequer**, **Cova del Pilar**, best explored by kayak, or **Cala Magraner**, a wild and secluded cove at the foot of a gorge and weather-pitted cliffs, popular with climbers and hikers (p154). None has direct car access (in fact, some would be more easily reached by boat).

Portocolom

POP 4294

A rather sleepy place as far as east-coast holiday resorts go, Portocolom has resisted the tourist onslaught with dignity and a measure of grace. Claimed rather dubiously as the birthplace of Christopher Columbus by those who dispute his Genoese origins, it's a thoroughly maritime town based on a large, handsome natural harbour (one of the few on the island). Fishing boats, sailing boats and the odd luxury yacht bob in the calm waters of its large horseshoe-shaped bay, while divers are drawn to its proximity to some of the island's best sites.

Within reach of Portocolom are some fine beaches, such as the immaculate little cove of **Cala Marçal** and, at the northern end of town, scenic and gentle **Cala s'Arenal**, the locals' preferred beach. On the eastern headland at the mouth of the bay, there's the mid-19th-century lighthouse, **Far de sa Punta de ses Crestes**.

🏃 Activities

Starfish   BOATING
(http://starfishboat.com; Moll Comercial; ☉May-Oct; 🚣) A glass-bottomed tour is a great way to explore the coastline south of Portocolom. Boarding at Portocolom Marina, or Cala Marçal just to the south, Starfish runs several daily trips to Cala d'Or (adult/child €25/14) and Cala Figuera (€32/14), calling at stunning coves and beaches on the way.

Skualo Adventure Sports Centre   DIVING
(☏971 83 41 97; www.mallorcadiving.com; Ronda del Creuer Balear 53; introductory dive €95;

☉8.30am-8pm Mon-Sat Apr-Oct) A well respected dive centre, with snorkelling (€49), sea-kayaking (two- to three-hour excursion €49) and three-hour sea excursions to coastal caves (€69). It's also branched out into stand-up paddleboarding, speedboating and, of course, dive-certification courses.

🍴 Eating

Portocolom's reputation as a relaxed holiday spot attracts a slightly older, wealthier crowd than some other east-coast resorts. Accordingly, the dining options are good!

★ Restaurant Sa Llotja   SPANISH €€
(☏971 82 51 65; www.restaurantsallotjaportoco lom.com; Carrer dels Pescadors; mains €21.50-24.50; ☉1-3pm & 7-11pm Tue-Sun; 🐾) A slick, glass-fronted restaurant with a wonderful terrace overlooking the harbour, Sa Llotja does delicious renditions of established dishes with slightly conservative restraint. Starters might be grilled scallops or tagliatelle with lemon sauce and red shrimps, while mains include monk-fish wrapped in egg with lemon mayonnaise or steak tartar.

ℹ Information

Tourist Office (☏971 82 60 84; www.visitfelanitx.es; Avinguda de Cala Marçal 15; ☉9am-4pm & 6-9pm Tue-Fri, 9am-1pm Sat & Sun, 9am-4pm Mon) At the southern end of town, on the road to Cala Marçal.

ℹ Getting There & Away

Eight bus lines service Portocolom, including the coastal routes 441, 448 and 449 (varied prices, dozens daily). Buses 490 and 491 (express) go to/from Palma (€7.20, 1¾ hours).

Southern Mallorca

Best Places to Eat

➜ Restaurante Petite Iglesia (p175)

➜ Sal de Coco (p172)

➜ Casa Manolo (p173)

➜ Port Petit (p176)

Best Beaches

➜ Cala Pi (p170)

➜ Cala Llombards (p174)

➜ Cala Mondragó (p176)

➜ Cap de Ses Salines to Colònia de Sant Jordi (p168)

➜ Cala Santanyí (p174)

➜ Platja de Ses Covetes (p171)

Why Go?

The forbidding and rugged geography of the coast between the Badia de Palma (Bay of Palma) and Colònia de Sant Jordi has preserved this area as one of Mallorca's least developed seaboard regions. Much of the shoreline is ringed by high, impenetrable cliffs lashed endlessly by the churning Mediterranean waters and swept by winds. It may not always be highly accessible, but the untamed, raw beauty of the coastline is hypnotising.

Devoted to agriculture and conservation, this part of the island has been spared the worst excesses of overdevelopment that have scarred parts of Mallorca, providing glimpses of how all of the island's coast must once have looked. Amid the cliffs lie intimate coves, long swathes of fine sand and some sublime geology. Whether tightly pinched between rock, or fading into rough scrub of pine and juniper, some of Mallorca's best beaches are sheltered here, awaiting discovery.

When to Go

Mallorca's southern beaches live for the summer, to the extent that you won't find much going on if you arrive before Easter or after October. November to March, when the island is at its quietest and coolest, can still be a superb time to visit; you're likely to have the place to yourself, including some eerily quiet resort towns with just a handful of restaurants, hotels and shops open. Summer is undoubtedly the peak season; if crowds turn you off, just seek out one of many resort-free stretches of coastline or hike at will.

Southern Mallorca Highlights

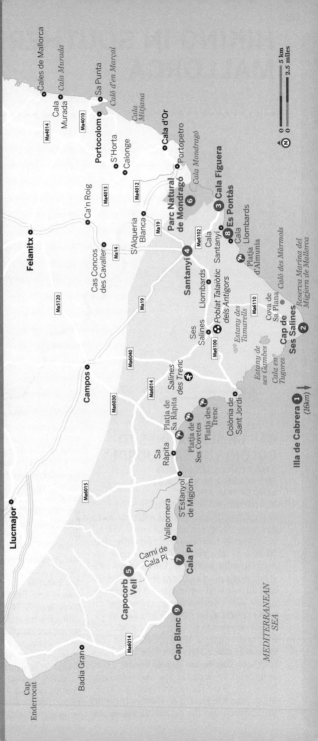

1 Illa de Cabrera (p173) Boating to Mallorca's sole national park, a precious ark of unspoilt habitat.

2 Cap de Ses Salines (p168) Hiking to the tiny coves dotting the island's southeastern extremity.

3 Cala Figuera (p175) Following the photographic tour of this delightful fishing village's harbour.

4 Santanyí (p174) Pottering through handsome stone streets.

5 Capocorb Vell (p170) Wandering the prehistoric relics of the Talayotic people.

6 Parc Natural de Mondragó (p176) Swimming and birdwatching among beaches and wetlands.

7 Cala Pi (p170) Trekking down to the sands of this cove.

8 Es Pontàs (p174) Gazing onto this sublime natural sea arch.

9 Cap Blanc (p170) Tracing the coast's contours from the lighthouse.

HIKING IN SOUTHERN MALLORCA

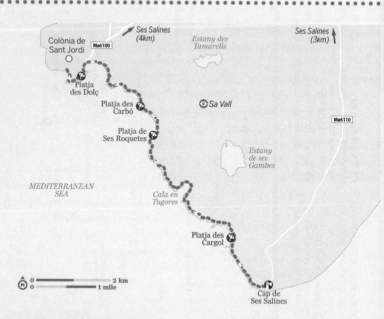

CAP DE SES SALINES TO COLÒNIA DE SANT JORDI

START CAP DE SES SALINES
END COLÒNIA DE SANT JORDI
LENGTH 9KM; 3 HOURS

The coastal trail between Cap de Ses Salines and Colònia de Sant Jordi is a flat but rocky trek across battered rock outcrops and secluded sandy beaches, perfect for swimming. Be sure to take plenty of water – there are no freshwater sources and there's very little shade along the way. Plants you'll see on the trail include wild asparagus and leafy *azucena de mar* (sea purslane), whose fragrant white flowers appear in July and August.

As returning to pick up your car after the hike will require a taxi trip, it's most convenient to take a taxi (€15) from Ses Salines (p170) to **Cap de Ses Salines** (p172). From here, head towards the sea and turn right (west). You'll see the Mediterranean glistening to your left, the Illa de Cabrera (p173) in the distance and the private **Sa Vall estate**, owned by the March family, bordering the walk on your right.

After 30 minutes of a fairly flat walk over the ruddy-coloured rocks that dominate the coast here (the same that give Palma's Catedral its striking colour), you'll come upon the first 'virgin' beach of the walk, **Platja des Cargol**, which is protected by a natural rock pier. In summer it can get quite crowded.

Continue along the coast for further coves and beaches, like **Cala en Tugores** (which you should reach in an hour's walk), **Platja de Ses Roquetes** and **Platja des Carbó** (after 2¼ hours) and finally **Platja des Dolç** (the full three hours). The beaches, with their fine-as-flour sand and gentle gradient (and thus waves) are simply gorgeous. Even with summer crowds, an idyllic backdrop of juniper trees and squawking seagulls ensures that it always feels like an escape.

At the western end of Platja des Dolç is Colònia de Sant Jordi (p171), the end of the walk. If you want to return to Ses Salines, jump on bus 502 (€1.50).

Pristine coastline can be hard to come by in Mallorca, but the walk from Cap de Ses Salines to Colònia de Sant Jordi has it in abundance.

HIKING THE ILLA DE CABRERA

The best-known walking route on the Illa de Cabrera (p171) in Parc Nacional Marítim-Terrestre de l'Arxipèlag de Cabrera heads up to a restored 14th-century **castle** (p171) – the Castillo de Cabrera – a fortress once used to keep from the island. The 30-minute walk from the **park information office** (p171) at the port to the castle meanders along the western flank of the island before bringing you to the 80m-high bluff where the castle looms and from where magnificent views range to Mallorca.

Another route runs south for the 15-minute walk along the west side of the island past a **church** and the **Cabrera National Park Refuge** (p173) to the beach of **Sa Plageta** (p173). Surrounded by low pine-clad hills, this peaceful beach is a delightful place for a picnic and/or a watery romp. You can hike south of the beach along a trail to a **memorial** to French Prisoners on the island who died on Cabrera during the Napoleonic Wars; there is also a **museum** (☎630 982363; adult/child €2/free; ⊙11.30am-1pm & 4-6pm) not far from here, housed in a *celler* (wine cellar) with displays relating to the history and culture of the island. The farmhouse-turned-museum was once home to the Feliu family, which owned the entire island in the early 20th century. Trekking west along the shore from Sa Plageta will bring you to **S'Espalmador** (p173), a peaceful little cove south of, and sheltered by, the point of the same name (Punta de S'Espalmador).

Other possible routes – some of which require a guide – lead to the **N'Ensiola lighthouse** (four hours, permission required), the southern sierra of **Serra de Ses Figueres** (2½ hours, permission required), or the highest point of the island, the 172m **Picamosques** (three hours, permission required).

RAFAEL MARTIN-GAITERO/SHUTTERSTOCK ©

Illa de Cabrera (p173)

Cala Pi

POP 412

An intimate, geographically blessed and very likeable resort, Cala Pi overlooks a gorgeous white-sand, pine-flanked slither of a beach. On the coast, a circular 17th-century (and recently restored) defence tower stands testament to the Mallorca of centuries past, when the threat from North African pirates was constant. Today the tower gazes out onto quite sublime views of the sapphire seas beyond. Typical Mallorcan restaurants, with local as well as foreign tourists in their sights, make up the perfectly pleasant suite of options around Cala Pi. Summer terraces, paella, suckling lamb shoulder – it's a pleasant refrain of classic dishes and settings.

★ **Cala Pi** BEACH

Reached via a steep staircase (follow the signs along Camí de la Cala Pi), this beach is only 50m wide but it is a beauty, stretching more than 100m inland and flanked on either side by craggy cliffs that ensure the startlingly turquoise water in the inlet stays as still as bath water. There are no facilities at beach level – just rows of boathouses – so bring any provisions you're likely to need.

★ **Capocorb Vell** ARCHAEOLOGICAL SITE

(971 18 01 55; Carretera Arenal-Cap Blanc, Km 23; €3; 10am-5pm Fri-Wed;) At this sprawling prehistoric village, you can wander along rocky pathways and beside rough stone structures that date to 1000 BCE. The site, which includes 28 dwellings and five *talayots* (square and round stone towers made with – in the case of Capocorb Vell – no mortar). First excavated in the early 1900s, it gives a great sense of the scope and layout of the mysterious settlement. There's a small bar at the entrance where you buy the tickets and, beyond that, a place to park.

Restaurante Miguel SPANISH €€

(971 12 30 00; Carrer de la Torre 13; mains €17-27.50, set meal €24; 11am-11pm Tue-Sun Mar-Oct) Set back from the ruddy headland that sustains Cala Pi's highly photogenic 16th-century 'fire tower', Restaurante Miguel is a Mallorcan-style 'farmhouse' with a huge, inviting patio. Miguel cooks up excellent seafood dishes like paella, lobster and seafood casserole and seabass with clams, as well as heartier Mallorcan specialities like rabbit with onions. There's a kids' menu for young ones (€8.55).

❶ Getting There & Away

Bus 525 links Cala Pi and Palma once in the morning and once in the evening (€5.75, 70 minutes).

Sa Ràpita

POP 10,000

The main settlement along this stretch of coast, Sa Ràpita is a sleepy seaside village whose rocky shoreline, lashed and haranged by waves, provides a scenic diversion from a largely nondescript town, as does the alluring profile of nearby Illa de Cabrera. Neighbouring Vallgornera has the longest cave on the island.

Most of the places to eat along waterfront Avinguda de Miramar – in other words, most of the places in Sa Ràpita – hedge their bets between Mallorcan favourites and pizza and pasta. You can eat perfectly well, but the choice is unspectacular.

WORTH A TRIP

CAP BLANC

If you're travelling the coast road from Palma to Capocorb Vell and Cala Pi, take the short detour to this wind-shredded, atmospheric headland. If you're on the Ma6014 highway south from S'Arenal, turn right at the sign pointing to 'Cap Blanc'. You'll soon come across the **Far de Cap Blanc** (Cap Blanc Lighthouse).

You can't get right up to the lighthouse, which dates to 1863 and whose lightbeam was originally fuelled by olive oil. But you can wander through gaps in the fence by the road leading to the lighthouse to explore the surrounding rugged coastline. From here, the views along the ruddy cliffface are nothing short of breathtaking, with Palma and the western mountains in one direction, the Illa de Cabrera in the other, and seabirds circling the Mediterranean sky overhead. If the wind isn't too fierce, this makes a fabulous picnic spot. But be careful with kids or dogs – there's no fence and the drop is abrupt, and almost certainly fatal.

Platja de Ses Covetes
BEACH

This 200m sweep of pale, silky sand and gin-clear water forms part of the **Reserva Marina del Migjorn de Mallorca** (a protected marine reserve), so no buildings mar its backdrop of dunes and pines. It's unspoilt but not uncrowded. Walking east along the shore, you'll come upon **Platja des Trenc**. Platja de Ses Covetes is past Sa Ràpita and off the Ma6030 highway.

Xaloc
MALLORCAN €€

(☑ 971 64 06 35; Carrer del Xaloc 36; mains €8.50-17; ☺ 12.30-3.30pm & 7.30-11pm Tue-Sat, 12.30-3.30pm Sun) This little backstreet Mallorcan joint comes highly recommended by locals for its paellas, grilled fish, grilled squid, lamb shoulder and other Balearic favourites.

❶ Getting There & Away

From Palma, bus 515 heads to Sa Ràpita (€5.50, one hour, up to seven daily).

Colònia de Sant Jordi

POP 2734

A once-sleepy fishing village that was 'discovered' by tourism in the 1950s, Colònia de Sant Jordi's popularity with *palmero* vacationers has made it the biggest beach resort of the southern coast. Prim and with well-laid-out streets that form a chequerboard across a gently rolling landscape, the town is family friendly and surrounded by some of the best and least-developed beaches on Mallorca. Perhaps most enticingly, it's also the embarkation point for the marine wilderness of the Illa de Cabrera archipelago.

◉ Sights & Activities

Colònia de Sant Jordi's main attractions are its wonderful beaches and seafront promenade. Best known is the Platja des Trenc, a 20-minute walk from the northwestern end of town.

Centro de Visitantes Parque Nacional de Cabrera
AQUARIUM

(☑ 971 65 62 82; www.cvcabrera.es; cnr Carrer Gabriel Roca & Plaça del Dolç; €8; ☺ 10am-2am & 3-6pm Feb-Nov) FREE At the northeastern end of town, watched over by a whale-skeleton sentry, this stone-and-glass swirl of a building is part aquarium and part interpretation centre for the offshore marine environs of the Parc Nacional Marítim-Terrestre de l'Arxipèlag de Cabrera. Free and fascinating, your visit to 18 aquariums and over 70 species ends with a climb up a spiral ramp that wraps around an extraordinary mural by Miguel Mansanet, based on 16th-century Mallorcan maps of the Mediterranean.

Platja des Trenc
BEACH

Platja des Trenc, the largest undeveloped beach on Mallorca, runs 2km northwest from the southern edge of Colònia de Sant Jordi. With long stretches of frost-white sand, azure water and a restful setting among pine trees and rolling dunes, des Trenc proves just how pretty the Mallorcan coast was before development got out of hand. Officially a nudist beach, des Trenc draws a mixed clothed and unclothed crowd, many of whom take advantage of the sun loungers for hire.

Piraguas Mix
KAYAKING

(☑ 660 470723; www.piraguasmixkayaks.com; Camí de Alcaria Rotja, Campos; sea kayaks per day from €30, double kayaks €50, guided excursions per person €30; ☺ 8.30am-8.30pm) One of the most respected sea-kayaking outfits on the island. Call to meet in central Sant Jordi if you'd like to hit the water.

Team Double J
CYCLING

(☑ 971 65 57 65; www.teamdoublej.com; Avinguda de la Primavera 7A; aluminium road bike per day/week €15/70, carbon road bike €30/135; ☺ 9.30am-1.30pm & 3-7pm Mon-Fri, from 5pm Sat & Sun Feb-Oct) This outfit rents good-quality bikes, if you're tackling rough terrain or serious road distance, and can also provide maps and information on area routes. Call or email to arrange rental outside standard opening months. They also rent e-bikes (per day/week €25/140).

Mar Cabrera
BOATING

(☑ 971 65 64 03; www.marcabrera.com; Carrer Gabriel Roca 20; adult/child from €45/26; ☺ 8am-10pm Feb-Nov) Mar Cabrera operates a speedboat service and tours of the Illa de Cabrera (p171) and coves of the southern coast.

Excursions a Cabrera
BOATING

(☑ 971 64 90 34; www.excursionsacabrera.es; Carrer Dofí 1l; adult/child boat €45/26, speedboat €49/30; ☺ 8am-10pm high season, to 4pm low season, closed Nov-Feb; ❸) Round-trip tours by speedboat or slower boats from Colònia de Sant Jordi to the marine- and birdlife-rich Parc Nacional Marítim-Terrestre de l'Arxipèlag de Cabrera (p173). There are several departures daily.

✖ Eating & Drinking

Colònia's bars – most densely gathered on and behind the waterfront promenade Carrer Gabriel Roca – can get quite lively on a high-season Friday night.

Sal de Coco   MEDITERRANEAN €€

(☑971 65 52 25; www.restaurantsaldecoco.com; Moll de Pescadors; mains €15-20, menús €28; ⊗8am-11pm Wed-Mon Mar-Nov; 🛜) This slick, art-strewn bistro takes its name from the sea salt gathered on the rocks around Colònia de Sant Jordi. Marta Rosselló puts an original take on Mediterranean flavours in dishes like homemade fish and spinach ravioli with shrimp sauce, cuttlefish and mushroom risotto and just-right steak tartare – all beautifully presented and revealing true depth of flavour.

Marisol   SEAFOOD €€

(☑971 65 50 70; Carrer Gabriel Roca 63; mains €16-20; ⊗10am-11pm; 🛜) This seaside restaurant is a reliable choice: try the saltcrust hake, or the dory or scorpion fish (when it's super-fresh), which is sold by the kilo. Or you could opt for pasta, pizza, fish and shellfish, rice dishes or stews at a table on the spacious covered terrace by the water.

ℹ Information

Tourist Office (☑971 65 60 73; Carrer Gabriel Roca; ⊗10am-2pm & 5-9pm May-Sep, 10am-2pm & 4-6pm Oct, 10am-2pm Tue-Sun Feb & Mar)

ℹ Getting There & Away

Bus 502 connects Palma to Sant Jordi (€6.65, 1¼ hours, up to six daily), which continues to Ses Salines (€1.50, 10 minutes).

Ses Salines

POP 4900

Used as a source of salt since the days of the Romans, Ses Salines (Salt Pans) is a beautifully preserved agricultural centre that has quickly gained recognition as one of inland Mallorca's most attractive towns. With quality bars, restaurants and hotels, plus grocers selling local wines, salt and other produce that some travellers crave, it's transformed itself from a rural waystation to a destination in its own right.

Plus, it's surrounded by some lovely rural scenery, crisscrossed by walking and cycling trails within whiffing distance of the salty sea.

◉ Sights

★ Cap de Ses Salines   LIGHTHOUSE

(Carretera de Cap de Ses Salines) Follow the Ma6110 highway 12km south of Ses Salines to reach the Cap de Ses Salines, a beautiful bluff on Mallorca's southernmost tip with a **lighthouse** (Far des Cap de ses Salines; closed to the public) dating back to 1863. There's not much here, but stretching out along either side are wonderfully unspoilt beaches protected by the Reserva Marina del Migjorn de Mallorca.

The eastern beaches are hewn out of the coastal cliffs that run up towards exquisitely beautiful coves like **Caló des Màrmols**, beaches like the **Platja d'Almunia** and caves like **Cova de Sa Plana**. A rugged coastal path links them all in a 9km trail (p168).

Poblat Talaiòtic
dels Antigors   ARCHAEOLOGICAL SITE

FREE About 1km south of Ses Salines (follow the signposts off the road to Colònia de Sant Jordi) is this neglected archaeological site. There's no visitor centre, the gate is always open and only sun-bleached plaques remain, so use your imagination to see how these low stone walls and mounds would have once constituted a prehistoric settlement. There's not much room to park so you'll need to leave your car by the side of the road, but the site receives few visitors.

☞ Tours

Salines des Trenc   TOURS

(☑673 43 34 56, 971 65 53 06; www.salinasdestrenc.com; Carretera Colònia de Sant Jordi-Campos, Km 8.5; ⊗10-11.30am & 1-3pm Tue-Sat) If you fancy getting the inside scoop on Salines des Trenc's famous *flor de sal* (hand-harvested sea salt), you can join a 45-minute tour of the salt pans. Tours are available in Spanish, English and German, staggered across the opening hours listed above and explore the salt production process and its history, as well as the 170-plus bird species living in the surrounding wetlands.

✖ Eating & Drinking

★ Casa Manolo
MALLORCAN €€

(☎ 971 64 91 30; www.bodegabarahona.com; Plaça Sant Bartomeu 2; mains €17-23; ☺ 11am-4pm & 7.30-11pm Tue-Sun) With its photo-plastered walls and ceilings strung with Serrano hams, this corner bar looks much as it did when it opened in 1945. While the aged, Josper-grilled meat is fantastic, the real secret to its staying power lies in the rice, seafood and fish dishes. Try lobster stew or *arròs notari*, a rice dish overflowing with seafood and a rich squid-ink sauce.

★ Mon de Vins
WINE BAR

(☎ 971 64 97 73; www.llumdesal.es; Carrer del Batle Andreu Burguera Mut 14; ☺ 10.30am-10.30pm) A wonderful place to sample the wines of Mallorca (and further afield), this outpost of Robert Chaves' burgeoning Llum de Sal (local organic gourmet salt) empire is strewn with tempting bottles and opens onto an inviting courtyard. Take a bottle away, stay and wash down quality tapas with a few sympathetic glasses, or do both: the choice is yours.

ⓘ Getting There & Away

The easiest way to arrive here is with your own wheels, not least because they are essential for freedom to explore the surrounding attractions. If you're reliant on public transport, bus 502 runs to Palma (€7.50, 80 minutes, up to seven daily), Santanyí (€1.50, 10 minutes), Campos (€2.45, 25 minutes) and Colònia de Sant Jordi (€1.50, 10 minutes).

Illa de Cabrera

Nineteen uninhabited islands and islets make up the only national park in the Balearic Islands, the **Parc Nacional Marítim-Terrestre de l'Arxipèlag de Cabrera** (☎ 971 72 50 10; ☺ Easter-Oct), an archipelago whose dry, hilly islands are known for their birdlife, rich marine environment and abundant lizard populations. The Illa de Cabrera, the largest of the archipelago and the only one you can visit, sits 16km off the coast of Colònia de Sant Jordi. Other islands are used for wildlife research. Only 200 people per day (300 in August) are allowed to visit this highly protected natural area, so reserve your place at least a day ahead. The main park authority (p84) is in Palma. The only accommodation on the island is the **Cabrera National Park Refuge** (☎ 971 65 62 82; Illa de Cabrera; r Jun-Sep €65, May & Oct €55; ☺ May-Oct).

Many enjoy the wonderfully calm beaches, **Sa Plageta** and **S'Espalmador**. The park has an extremely fragile ecosystem and there are few hiking trails open to the public – for most of them you'll either need to tag along with a guide or request permission from the park information office on Cabrera.

Castillo de Cabrera
CASTLE

(☎ 630 982363; www.balearsnatura.com; Illa de Cabrera) Attacked, damaged and rebuilt repeatedly since its 14th-century origin, this squat hexagonal tower guards Cabrera's eastern harbour. At one point it was converted into a prison for French soldiers, more than 5000 of whom died after being abandoned in 1809 towards the end of the Peninsular War. It now enjoys a slightly more peaceful retirement, watching tourists rather than pirates disembarking below.

ⓘ Information

Park Information Office (☎ 630 982363; http://en.balearsnatura.com; Port of Cabrera; ☺ 8am-2pm & 4-8pm May-Oct) Advice and permits for hikes and other things to do on the island.

ⓘ Getting There & Away

Although private boats can come to Cabrera if they've requested navigation and anchoring permits in advance from the park authority, nearly all visitors arrive on the organised tours. Excursions a Cabrera (p171) runs both slow

> ### SNORKELLING OFF THE ILLA DE CABRERA
>
> The Illa de Cabrera is a wonderful place for snorkelling. While you need special permission to dive here, you can snorkel off the beach without it. Or, in July and August, sign up at the park information office for the guided snorkelling excursions offered by park rangers.

WILDLIFE WATCHING ON THE ILLA DE CABRERA

Illa de Cabrera is prime territory for birdwatching: marine birds, birds of prey and migrating birds all call the islands home for at least part of the year. Common species include fisher eagles, endangered Balearic shearwaters, Audouin's gulls, Cory's shearwaters, shags, ospreys, Eleonora's falcons and peregrine falcons.

Terrestrial wildlife is also abundant. The small Balearic lizard is the best-known species here: it has few enemies on the archipelago and 80% of the species population lives on Cabrera.

boats and speedboats from Colònia de Sant Jordi; Mar Cabrera (p171) operates a speedboat service.

On the cruise back to Colònia de Sant Jordi, the boat stops in **Sa Cova Blava** (Blue Cave), a gorgeous cave with crystalline waters where passengers can take a dip. Speedboats also stop here.

Santanyí

POP 12,112

Wedged between the Parc Natural de Mondragó and Ses Salines, Santanyí has been well and truly discovered by holiday-makers. Travellers flock to this handsome inland town, where honey-coloured churches shelter a fine array of bars, boutiques, ceramic shops and restaurants. Such is its popularity with well-heeled German tourists in particular that every second shop now seems to be an estate agent or art gallery.

Most of the action spirals around the church-dominated Plaça Major, especially on market days (Wednesdays and Saturdays) when stalls selling local produce, leather goods and trinkets fill every available central street. Once they pack up, the square is returned anew to laid-back cafes and bars that subtly entice you to linger over tapas and drinks, long into the evening.

Diners are spoilt in Santanyí – every second door hides a tapas bar or restaurant, although prices are inflated by the tourist trade and its appetite.

★ **Es Pontàs**　　　　　NATURAL FEATURE

One of the top photo-ops on the south coast, this natural arch in between Cala Santanyí and Cala Llombards is a simply stunning sight. If you're fortunate to get here for sunrise, it's a standout image and one guaranteed to garner Instagram likes-a-plenty. You can park your car nearby and walk the short distance to the *mirador* overlooking the sublime and wave-thrashed rock form.

★ **Cala Llombards**　　　　　BEACH

(🏄) A petite cove defined by rough rock walls topped with pines, Cala Llombards is a truly beautiful place. A beach-hut bar and sun loungers shaded by palm-leaf umbrellas constitute the extent of human intervention. The view is soul-satisfying – turquoise waters, a sandy beach and the reddish rocks of the cliffs that lead like a promenade towards the sea. To reach Cala Llombards, follow the sign off the Ma6102 down a stone-walled road bordered by meadows of grazing sheep.

Cala Santanyí　　　　　BEACH

Cala Santanyí's popular but not overcrowded beach is the star in a scenic show that also includes a gorgeous, cliff-lined cove and impossibly cobalt-coloured waters. The beach sits at the bottom of a ravine of sorts where there is a car park (it's a stiff walk or cycle ride back to the resort centre). A small path leads along the coast, where the natural rock arch El Pontàs rises out of the surf. This is a popular spot to snorkel.

Alchemy　　　　　EUROPEAN €€

(📞 971 65 39 57; www.alchemysantanyi.com; Plaça Major 9; mains €18-22; ⊙9am-11pm) Despite the name, Alchemy has little to do with molecular gastronomy or culinary experimentation. With its pretty courtyard, slick bistro interior and warm welcome, it keeps its look, feel and food refreshingly simple. You can select from a morning *ensaïmada* (spiral pastry), tapas, duck confit with pear chutney, salt cod with roasted peppers, or simply grilled meat, seafood, pasta or pizza.

Es Molí de Santanyí　　　　　TAPAS €€

(📞 971 65 36 29; Carrer de Consolació 19; tapas €7-14; ⊙1-11pm mid-Feb–mid-Nov) Located in an old windmill on the road leading east from Santanyí, this sprawling stone-built restaurant has a lovely garden terrace shaded by palms and rubber trees. With a tasty line in tapas, the menu is all imaginative, well-executed morsels for assembling your own little feast.

ℹ️ Getting There & Away

Bus connections with Palma are plentiful: take bus 501 (€6.75, 1¼ hours, up to seven daily) or bus 502 (€6.57, 1¾ hours with transfer, up to seven daily).

Cala Figuera

POP 627

A twisting fissure in the coastal slab of southern Mallorca forms the impossibly picturesque and extremely photogenic harbour town of Cala Figuera. Steep scrubby escarpments rise up on all sides from the glassy water, leaving little space for the few houses, bars and restaurants to cling to. Despite its great charm, and proximity to some of Mallorca's busiest resorts, it remains the fishing village it has always been. While some yachts line up beside the smaller working boats, local fishermen still make their way down the winding inlet before dawn, returning in the evening to mend their nets. Many of their houses have no street access, only private slipways for their launches. An easy-to-follow and signposted **photographic trail** *(ruta fotogràfica)* leads around the harbour.

Cala Figuera is a quiet, relaxing place. But there's nothing to stop you taking that relaxation even further, with a few drinks in one of the bar-restaurants overlooking the picturesque harbour.

Red Star Tours BOATING

(☑664 243464; www.redstartours.com; Carrer de Virgen del Carmen 52; ☉10am-1pm & 3-5pm) Hop aboard for a 90-minute tour of the surrounding bays including Cala Santanyí (adult/child €30/22), or a two-hour tour (€42/28) taking in a string of little-known coves and secluded beaches. Red Star also rents kayaks (from €15 for one hour), stand-up paddleboards (from €15 for one hour) and rigid inflatable boats (€85 for two hours).

⭐ **La Petite Iglesia** FRENCH €€

(☑971 64 50 09; Carrer de la Marina 11; mains €17-19, menú €20; ☉9am-1pm & 6-11pm Mon-Sat, 6-11pm Sun; 🖽) Inhabiting the shell of a little sandstone church, with outdoor tables under the trees, this atmospheric place serves up terrific French home cooking. Everything is spanking fresh, from the house-baked bread to whatever fish was hauled up to the harbour that day, with special mention going to the lip-smacking terrines and slow-cooked dishes, such as *boeuf bourguignon*.

L'Arcada MALLORCAN €€

(☑971 645 032; Carrer de Virgen del Carmen 80; mains €15-20; ☉noon-10.30pm Apr-Oct) Watch the boats blink in the port at this laid-back hillside restaurant. The seafood – from grilled calamari to Mallorcan prawns and stuffed courgettes – is good, naturally, but don't overlook island-wide faves such as paella, pork loin with *tumbet* (Mallorcan ratatouille) and rabbit with onions.

Bon Bar BAR

(☑673 79 59 69; Carrer Virgen de Carmen 27; ☉10am-midnight Tue-Sun, to 10pm winter; 🛜) Views – that's what this place is all about. High above the main body of the inlet and with uninterrupted vistas, this is the place to nurse a cocktail, or a *pa amb oli* (bread with oil and other toppings: €11 to €14) or ice cream if it's too early for a drink.

ℹ️ Getting There & Away

Bus 503 connects Cala Figuera with Palma (€7.30, 1½ hours, four daily Monday to Saturday, with transfer at Santanyí) and Santanyí (€1.50, 20 minutes).

Portopetro

POP 634

This intimate fishing port's quiet appeal is immediately apparent as you stroll its steep, shady streets and look out over the protected natural inlet that originally made this town such a hit with fishers. There's no beach in the town centre, but that helps explain why it's escaped the development rampant in Cala d'Or, just to the north.

A string of good Mallorcan restaurants – nothing fancy, but all worth their salt and all with waterside terraces for good weather – lines the marina.

Petro Divers DIVING

(☑971 65 98 46; www.petro-divers.eu; Es Calo d'es Moix 8; ☉8.30am-6.30pm Mar-Nov; 🖽) This diving outlet offers the full array of PADI and SSI courses, from intro and children's dives to open-water diving certifications. A single dive will set an already-certified diver back €40; the more you book, the cheaper it gets. Petro rents gear and runs up to four trips per day when things are busy.

ℹ️ Getting There & Away

Bus 501 connects Portopetro with Palma (€8.70, 1¾ hours, up to 10 daily) and Cala d'Or (€1.70, 10 minutes).

Parc Natural de Mondragó

A natural park encompassing beaches, protected dunes, wetlands, coastal cliffs and inland agricultural land, the 766-hectare Parc Natural de Mondragó is a beautiful area for swimming or hiking, but is best known as a birdwatching destination. Only 95 hectares of the park are publicly owned: much of the remainder is still divided into small dry-stone-walled fields known as *rotes,* bearing almonds, figs, carob and olives.

Most people who head this way come to take a dip in the lovely Cala Mondragó (🏊), one of the most attractive coves on the southeast coast. Sheltered by large rocky outcrops and fringed by pine trees, it's formed by a string of three protected sandy beaches connected by rocky footpaths. To explore the region, there are five short trails through the park.

ℹ Information

The small **park office** (☎ 971 18 10 22; http://en.balearsnatura.com; Carretera de Cala Mondragó; ☺ 9am-4pm) by the Ses Fonts de n'Alis car park (cars/motorbikes/caravans €5/2/9) has maps of walking trails. Information boards detail the local birdlife and plant species.

ℹ Getting There & Away

Cala Mondragó is 2km south of Portopetro. High-season bus 507 links Cala Mondragó with Cala d'Or (€1.85, 45 minutes, up to five daily Monday to Saturday, summer only) and a few other seaside resorts.

Cala d'Or

POP 3622

Although the pretty cove beaches and calm, azure waters are still here, they can be hard to find amid the endless bustle of this flashy, overgrown resort. Cala d'Or's five small calas each have their own centre, where pubs, restaurants and souvenir shops flourish, making it difficult to get a handle on the place.

Sea Riders   BOATING
(☎ 615 998732; www.searidersweb.com; Avinguda de Cala Llonga; 90min trip adult/child €35/25; ☺ May-Oct) Sea Riders, in Cala Llonga, offers

> ### WILDLIFE WATCHING IN THE PARC NATURAL DE MONDRAGÓ
> ....
> Birdwatchers have a ball with the varied species found in the area. Among the species that nest here are peregrine falcons, Audouin's gulls, Balearic shearwaters, European shags and rock pigeons. Take one of the walking trails that crisscross the park for plenty of birdwatching opportunities. Also keep an eye out for Algerian hedgehogs, Hermann's tortoises and Balearic toads.

speedboat rides between a string of beaches and bays, including Cala Mitjana, Cala Ferrera, Cala Egos, Cala Mondragó, Portopetro and Cala Figuera, with up to three departures between 11am and 5pm daily in July and August (and twice daily at 11am and 3.30pm in May, June, September and October).

Port Petit   MEDITERRANEAN €€€
(☎ 971 64 30 39; www.portpetit.com; Avinguda de Cala Llonga; mains €23.50-34.50, lunch menu €21.50, 3-/5-course gourmet menu €37.50/49.50, 6-course degustation €69.50; ☺ 1-3.30pm & 7-11pm Wed-Mon Apr-Oct; 🅿) One of Cala d'Or's top tables, Port Petit adds an innovative spin to local seafood and produce, served on a covered terrace whose dazzling whiteness matches the yachts below. Dishes like fresh lobster sautéed in lime butter, squid with sepia rice or rack of lamb slow-roasted in its own juices are cooked with aplomb.

ℹ Information

There are two tourist offices in town: **one** (☎ 971 65 74 63; Carrer d'en Perico Pomar 10; ☺ 9am-2pm Mon-Fri) just north of the central grid, and the **other** (☎ 971 65 97 60; Avinguda de la Cala d'Or 4; ☺ 10am-4pm Mon-Fri) inland from Cala Ferrera.

ℹ Getting There & Away

Bus 501 heads to Portopetro (€1.70, 10 minutes, up to eight times daily), then on to Palma (€8.70, 1¾ hours, up to 10 daily). Bus 441 runs along the eastern coast, stopping at all the major resorts.

Jardins de Alfàbia (p112)

Understand Mallorca

History

Mallorca's position in the heart of Europe's most fought-over sea has placed it in the path of the great sweeps of Mediterranean history, and events in that wider theatre have transformed the island time and again. But for all its experience of invasion, war, prosperity and hunger, Mallorca has rarely been at the heart of great European affairs. It's the perfect blend of historical riches and contemporary getaway.

The Talayotic Period

The Balearic Islands were separated from the Spanish continent a mere eight million years ago. They were inhabited by a variety of animal life that carried on in splendid isolation until around 9000 to 10,000 years ago, when the first groups of Epipaleolithic people set out from the Spanish coast in rudimentary vessels and bumped into Mallorca.

The earliest signs of human presence on the island date to around 7200 BCE. In the following 6000 years, the population, made up of disparate groups or tribes, largely lived as hunter-gatherers in caves or other natural shelters. Around 2000 BCE they started building megalithic funerary monuments, but at the time the pyramids were being constructed in Egypt, Mallorca was home to only a basic civilisation.

Things were shaken up in Mallorca and Menorca around 1200 BCE with the arrival of warrior tribes, probably from Asia Minor, who overwhelmed the local populace. They are known today as the Talayotic people, after the dry-stone *talayots* (towers) that are their chief material legacy, still scattered across many Mallorcan sites. The circular (and sometimes square- or hull-shaped) stone edifices are testimony to an organised and hierarchical society. The most common circular *talayots* could reach a height of 6m and had two floors. Their purpose is a matter of conjecture: were they symbolic of the power of local chieftains, or their burial places? Were they used for storage or defence? Or were they perhaps religious sites? There were at least 200 Talayotic villages across the island: simple ceramics, along with artefacts in bronze (swords, axes, necklaces), have been found on these sites.

TIMELINE	7200 BCE	c 1200 BCE	c 700 BCE
	Archaeologists date the first human settlements in Mallorca to this time, based on carbon-dated findings in the southwest of the island in Cova de Canet, a cave near Esplores.	Warrior tribes invade Mallorca, Menorca, Corsica and Sardinia. Those in Mallorca and Menorca are known today as the Talayotic people because of the *talayots* (stone towers) they built.	Phoenician traders install themselves around the coast, extending their influence across Mallorca. Balearic slingers serve as mercenaries in Carthaginian armies.

The ancients knew Mallorca and Menorca as the Gymnesias Islands, from a word meaning 'naked' (it appears that at least some of the islanders got about with a minimum of covering). Talayotic society seems to have been divided into a ruling elite, a broad subsistence-farming underclass and slaves. It is not known if they had a written language.

Contact with the outside world came through Greek and Phoenician traders, although the Carthaginian Phoenicians attempted to establish a foothold in Mallorca and failed. They did, however, enrol Mallorcans as mercenaries: Balearic men were noted for their skill as slingers, having learned to use these simple weapons with deadly accuracy as children. These sling-wielding Mallorcan and Menorcan *foners* (Catalan for 'warriors') gave themselves the name 'Balears', possibly derived from an ancient Greek word meaning 'to throw'. And so their island homes also came to be known as the Balearics. These men weren't averse to payment, developing a reputation as slings for hire: in Carthaginian armies they would shower a deadly hail of stones on the enemy before the infantry advanced. Also carrying daggers or short swords for hand-to-hand combat, they wore virtually no protection. Balears played their part in the Carthaginian victory over the Greeks in Sicily in the 5th century BCE, and again in the Punic Wars against Rome.

Romans, Vandals & Byzantines

When the Roman Consul Quintus Cecilius Metelus approached the shores of Mallorca in 123 BCE, possibly around Platja des Trenc in the south, he did not come unprepared. Knowing that the island warriors were capable of slinging heavy stones at his ships' waterline and sinking them, he had come up with a novel idea. Using heavy skins and leather, he effectively invented the first armoured vessels. Stunned by their incapacity to inflict serious damage, the Mallorcan warriors fled inland before the advance of Metelus's legions. Within two years the island had been pacified.

Metelus had 3000 settlers brought over from mainland Iberia, and founded two military camps in the usual Roman style (with the intersecting main streets of the *decumanus* and *cardus maximus*). Known as Palmeria (or Palma) and Pol·lèntia, they soon developed into Mallorca's main towns. Pol·lèntia, neatly situated between the two northeast bays of Pollença and Alcúdia, was the senior of the two.

As Pol·lèntia was embellished with fine buildings, temples, a theatre and more, some Roman citizens opted for the rural life, building grand country villas. None remain today, but it is tempting to see them as the precursor to the Arab *alqueries* (farmsteads) and Mallorcan *possessions* (country estates).

HISTORY ROMANS, VANDALS & BYZANTINES

Talayotic Sites

Ses Païsses, Artà

Capocorb Vell, Cala Pi

Necròpolis de Son Real, Ca'n Picafort

Museu Arqueològic de Son Fornés, Montuïri

Es Figueral de Son Real, Ca'n Picafort

Illot dels Porros, Ca'n Picafort

123 BCE	426 CE	534	707
On the pretext of ending Balearic piracy, the Roman general Quintus Cecilius Metelus, later dubbed Balearicus, storms ashore and takes control of Mallorca and Menorca.	Raids on Mallorca by the Vandals, central European Germanic tribes that had pillaged their way across Europe to North Africa, lead to the destruction of the Roman city of Pol·lèntia.	Belisarius takes control of the Balearic Islands in the name of the Byzantine Emperor Justinian, who, until his death in 565, attempted to re-establish the Roman Empire across the Mediterranean.	Muslim Arabs from North Africa raid Mallorca for the first time. Four years later they begin the conquest of the Spanish mainland.

The indigenous population slowly adopted the Roman language and customs, but continued to live in its own villages. Plinius the Elder reported that Mallorcan wine was as good as that in Italy, and the island's wheat and snails were also appreciated.

Archaeological evidence of early Christianity – such as the 5th-century CE remains of a basilica at Son Peretó near Manacor – suggests that the new Roman faith had arrived on the island as early as the 4th century. By then storm clouds were gathering, breaking in the form of barbarian assaults on the Roman Empire from the 5th century. The Balearic Islands felt the scourge of the Vandals (an East Germanic tribe that plundered their way into Roman territory) in 426. Forty years later, having crashed across Spain to establish their base in North Africa, they returned to take the islands.

The Vandals got their comeuppance when Byzantine Emperor Justinian decided to try to rebuild the Roman Empire. His tireless general, Belisarius, vanquished the Vandals in North Africa in 533 and took the Balearic Islands the following year. After Justinian's death in 565, Byzantine control over territories in the western Mediterranean quickly waned. By the time the Muslims swept across North Africa in the first years of the 8th century, the Balearic Islands were an independent Christian enclave.

The Islamic Centuries

Some historians claim the funny white, green and red clay figurine-whistles known as *siurells* were introduced to Mallorca by the Phoenicians and may have represented ancient deities. Classic figures include bulls, horse riders and dog-headed men.

In 902 an Arab noble from Al-Andalus (Muslim Spain), Isam al-Jaulani, was forced by bad weather to take shelter in the port of Palma. During his stay he became convinced that the town could and should be taken, along with Mallorca and the rest of the Balearic Islands, and incorporated into the Caliphate of Córdoba. On his return to Córdoba, the Caliph Abdallah entrusted him with the task, and Al-Jaulani returned with a landing party in 902 or 903.

The port town fell easily but Al-Jaulani, now the Wāli (governor) of the territory dubbed 'the Eastern Islands of Al-Andalus' by the Arabs, was compelled to wage another eight years of war against pockets of Christian guerilla resistance throughout the islands. But by the time Al-Jaulani died in 913, the islands had been pacified and he had begun work to expand and improve its only city, now called Medina Mayurka (City of Mallorca).

The Muslims divided the island into 12 districts, and in the ensuing century Mallorca thrived. They brought advanced irrigation methods, allowing the *alqueries* – the farms they established – to flourish. Medina Mayurka became one of Europe's most cosmopolitan cities, and by the end of the 12th century it had a population of 35,000, on par with Barcelona and London. The *al-qasr,* or castle-palace (Palau de l'Almudaina),

869	903	1075	1114–15
Norman raiders sack Mallorca's population centres, just 21 years after an Arab raid from Muslim Spain, which Mallorca's leaders had agreed to in return for being left in peace.	Muslim forces take control of Mallorca in the name of the Caliph of Córdoba in Spain. Local Christian warriors resist for another eight years in redoubts across the island.	Mallorca becomes an independent *taifa* (small kingdom) in the wake of the civil conflicts that shattered the Caliphate of Córdoba into a series of *taifas* across Spain.	A Catalan–Pisan crusading force arrives to end the piracy that is damaging Mediterranean trade. They take Medina Mayurka (Palma) in 1115 and free 30,000 Christian slaves before leaving the island.

was built over a Roman fort, and the grand mosque stood where Palma Catedral does now. With the raising of walls around the new Rabad al-Jadid quarter (roughly Es Puig de Sant Pere), the city reached the extents it would maintain until the late 19th century. It was a typical medieval Muslim city, a medina like Marrakech or Fez. Few of the narrow streets that made up its labyrinth, now called *estrets* (narrows), remain. Medina Mayurka enjoyed close relations with the rest of the Muslim world in the western Mediterranean, although by 1075 the emirs (princes) of the Eastern Islands were independent of mainland jurisdiction.

Al-Jaulani's successors dedicated considerable energy to piracy, which by the opening of the 12th century was the islands' principal source of revenue, arousing the wrath of Christian Europe's trading powers. In 1114, 500 vessels carrying a reported 65,000 Pisan and Catalan troops landed on Mallorca and launched a bloody campaign, entering Medina Mayurka in April the following year. After 10 months' fighting, news of a Muslim relief fleet en route from North Africa persuaded the exhausted invaders to depart, laden with booty, prisoners and freed Christian slaves.

In 1116, a new era dawned in Mallorca, as the Almoravids (a Berber tribe from Morocco) from mainland Spain took control. The Balearics reached new heights in prosperity, particularly under the Wāli Ishaq, who ruled from 1152 to 1185. Then, in 1203, Mallorca fell under the sway of the Almohads, who had taken control of Al-Andalus.

The internecine strife between Muslim factions had not gone unnoticed in Christian Spain, where the Reconquista (the reconquest of Muslim-held territory by the Christian kingdoms) had taken on new impetus after the rout of Almohad armies in the Battle of Las Navas de Tolosa in 1212. By 1250 the Christians would take Valencia, Extremadura, Córdoba and Seville, and the last Muslims would be expelled from Portugal. In such a context, it is hardly surprising that a plan should be hatched to take the Balearic Islands – especially as Mallorca continued to be a major source of piracy, seriously hindering Christian sea trade.

El Conqueridor

On 5 September 1229, 155 vessels bearing 1500 mounted knights and 15,000 infantry weighed anchor in the Catalan ports of Barcelona, Tarragona and Salou, setting sail for Mallorca. Jaume I (1208–76), the energetic 21-year-old king of Aragón and Catalonia, vowed to take the Balearic Islands and end Muslim piracy in the process. Later dubbed El Conqueridor (The Conqueror), Jaume landed at Santa Ponça and, after two swift skirmishes, marched on Medina Mayurka, to which he laid siege. Finally, on 31 December, Christian troops breached the defences and poured into

History Tour

....

Bronze Age/Talayotic Ses Païsses

....

Roman Pol·lèntia

....

Moorish Banys Àrabs, Palma

....

Medieval Alcúdia's walled old town

....

Gothic Catedral, Palma

....

Renaissance/baroque Palma's mansions and patios

1148	1185	1203	1229
Mallorca signs a trade agreement with the Italian cities of Genoa and Pisa, opening Mallorcan markets to the Italians and reducing the threat of further Christian assaults on the island.	The Muslim governor of the island, Wāli Ishaq, dies, ending a period of unprecedented prosperity. His rule represents the high point of Almoravid control over Mallorca.	The Almohads in peninsular Spain defeat the Almoravid regime in Medina Mayurka and take control of the island, although life continues largely unchanged for most of Mallorca's inhabitants.	Under Jaume I, King of Aragón, Catalan troops land at Santa Ponça in Mallorca, defeat the Muslims and camp before the walls of Medina Mayurka.

the city, pillaging mercilessly. In the following months, Jaume I pursued enemy troops across the island, meeting only feeble resistance.

With the conquest of Mallorca complete, Jaume proceeded to divide it up among his lieutenants and allies. The Arab *alqueries, rafals* (hamlets) and villages were handed over to their new *senyors* (masters). Many changed name, but a good number retained their Arab nomenclature (places beginning with *bini*, meaning 'sons of', are notable examples). Many took on the names of their new lord, preceded by the possessive particle *son* or *sa* (loosely translated as 'that which is of...'). Jaume codified this division of the spoils in his *Llibre del Repartiment*.

Among Jaume's early priorities was a rapid program of church-building, Christianisation of the local populace and the introduction of settlers from Catalonia (mostly from around the city of Girona). For the first century after the conquest, Ciutat (the city) held the bulk of the island's population. The Part Forana ('Part Outside' Ciutat) was divided into 14 districts, but all power in Mallorca was concentrated in Ciutat. Beneath the king, day-to-day governance was carried out by six *jurats*, or 'magistrates'.

The Christian Catalan settlers imposed their religion, tongue and customs on the island, while the bulk of the Muslim population was reduced to slavery. Those that did not flee or accept this destiny had only one real choice: to renounce Islam. The Jewish population would also have a troubling time of it.

In the Part Forana the farmsteads came to be known as *possessions* and were the focal point of the agricultural economy upon which the island would largely come to depend. The *possessions* were run by local managers who were faithful to their (frequently absentee) noble overlords, and were often well-off farmers themselves. They employed *missatges* (permanent farm labour) and *jornalers* (day wage labourers), both of whom generally lived on the edge of misery. Small-farm holders frequently failed to make ends meet, ceded their holdings to the more important *possessions* and themselves became *jornalers*.

Mallorca's connection to the seafaring trade routes of the Mediterranean ensured that it was particularly vulnerable to the ravages of the plague, which hit the island repeatedly, decimating the population in the process.

Crown of Aragón

On Jaume I's death in 1276, his territories were divided between his two sons, Jaume II and Pere II. In the succeeding years Mallorca was torn in the contest between the two, a dynamic that persisted under their heirs. By 1349, the previously independent Kingdom of Mallorca was tied into the Crown of Aragón, although it retained a high degree of autonomy.

The fortunes of Mallorca, particularly Palma, closely followed those of Barcelona, the Catalan headquarters of the Crown of Aragón and its trading hub. In the middle of the 15th century, both cities (despite setbacks such as outbreaks of the plague) were among the most prosperous in the

1229	1267	1276	1343
Jaume I enters the city, which his troops sack, leaving it in such a state that a plague the following Easter kills many of the inhabitants and invading soldiers.	Mallorcan icon Ramon Llull has a series of visions that will ultimately transform him into one of the most important Catalan cultural figures in history.	Jaume I dies, almost 50 years after bringing Christian rule to Mallorca. The territories under his rule are divided between his two sons, prompting decades of internecine conflict.	Pere III of the Crown of Aragón invades Mallorca and seizes the crown from Jaume III, who dies six years later in the Battle of Llucmajor, trying to reclaim it.

THE EVANGELISING CATALAN SHAKESPEARE

Born in Ciutat (Palma) de Mallorca, mystic, theologian and all-round Renaissance man before his time Ramon Llull (1232–1316) started off on a worldly trajectory. After entering Jaume I's court as a page, Ramon was elevated to major-domo of Jaume II, the future king of Mallorca. In this enviable position he proceeded to live it up, writing love ditties and reputedly enjoying a wild sex life.

Then, in 1267, he saw five visions of Christ crucified and everything changed. His next years were consumed with profound theological, moral and linguistic training (in Arabic and Hebrew). He founded a monastery (with Jaume II's backing) at Miramar for the teaching of theology and Eastern languages to future evangelists. His burning desire was to convert Jews and Muslims, and he began to travel throughout Europe, the Near East and North Africa to preach. At the same time he wrote countless tracts in Catalan and Arabic, and is considered the father of Catalan as a literary language. In 1295 he joined the Franciscans and in 1307 risked the ire of Muslims by preaching outside North African mosques. Some say he was lynched in Tunisia by an angry mob, while others affirm he died while en route to his native Mallorca in 1316. Certainly, he is buried in the Basílica de Sant Francesc (p58) in Palma. His beatification was confirmed by Pope John Paul II and the long, uncertain process of canonisation began in 2007.

Mediterranean. Palma had some 35 consulates and trade representatives sprinkled around the Med. The city's trade community had a merchant fleet of 400 vessels and the medieval Bourse, Sa Llotja, was an animated focal point of business.

But not all was rosy. In the Part Forana farm labourers lived on the edge of starvation, and crops occasionally failed to such an extent that people dropped dead in the streets, as in 1374. Frequent localised revolts, such as that of 1391 (the same year that furious workers sacked the Call, or Jewish ghetto, in Ciutat), were stamped out mercilessly by the army. A much greater shock to the ruling classes was the 1521 Germania revolt, an urban working-class uprising largely provoked by crushing taxes imposed on the lower classes. The unrest forced the viceroy (by now Mallorca was part of a united Spain under Emperor Carlos V) to flee. In October 1522 Carlos sent in the army, but control was not re-established until the following March.

By then Mallorca's commercial fortunes had declined and by the 16th century its coast had become constant prey to the attacks of North African pirates. Around the island the building of 'fire-towers' (watchtowers communicating by bonfire) and fortifications, many of which stand today, testified to the urgency of the problem. Some of Mallorca's most colourful traditional festivals, such as Moros i Cristians in Pollença and Es Firó in Sóller, date to these times. From the 17th century Spain's

1382	1391	1488	1521
Sac i Sort (Bag and Luck) is introduced, whereby the names of six candidates to be named *jurats* (magistrates) for the following 12 months are pulled out of four bags.	Hundreds of Jews die in a pogrom as farmers and labourers sack the Jewish quarter of Palma. Months later, those involved are released without sentence, for fear of causing greater unrest.	The Inquisition, which had operated from the mainland, is formally established in Mallorca. In the following decades hundreds would die, burned at the stake as heretics.	Armed workers and farm labourers rise up in the beginning of the Germania revolt against the nobles. In October 1522, Carlos V sends troops to Alcúdia to quell the revolt.

THE JEWS IN MALLORCA

The first Jews appear to have arrived in Mallorca in 70 CE, after the destruction of the Temple in Jerusalem. Under Muslim rule, a small Jewish minority thrived in Medina Mayurka; Christian Mallorca, following the 1229 conquest, was not so kind.

Although barred from most professions and public office, Mallorca's Jews were esteemed for their learning and business sense. Jewish doctors, astronomers, bankers and traders – generally fluent in Catalan and/or Spanish, Latin, Hebrew and Arabic – often played key public roles.

By the end of the 13th century, there were perhaps 2000 to 3000 Jews in Ciutat (Palma). They were evicted from the environment of Palau de l'Almudaina and moved to the Call (Catalan equivalent of a ghetto) in the streets around Carrer de Monti-Sion, in eastern Sa Calatrava. Here they were locked in at night and obliged to wear a red and yellow circular patch during the day. In 1315 their synagogue was converted into the Església de Monti-Sion, and they would not have another until 1373. In 1391, rioting farmers killed some 300 Jews in an anti-Semitic pogrom.

In 1435 the bulk of the island's Jews were forced to convert to Christianity and their synagogues were converted into churches. At the beginning of the 16th century they were forced to move from the Call Major to the Call Menor, centred on Carrer de Colom. Now officially Christian, they were nonetheless suspected of secretly practising Jewish rites. They were a particular target for the Inquisition, and the last *auto-da-fé* (trial by fire) of such so-called *judaizantes* took place in 1691, when three citizens were burned at the stake.

Known as *xuetes* (from *xua*, a derogatory term referring to pork meat), they continued to be shunned by many Christians, and couldn't breathe more easily until the 19th century. A veritable flurry of 19th-century Mallorcan writers and poets came from *xueta* families. During WWII, when the Nazis asked Mallorca to surrender its Jewish population, the religious authorities purportedly refused. Today the descendants of these families (who even in the mid-20th century were shunned) are estimated to number between 15,000 and 20,000.

fortunes declined and Mallorca slid into provincial obscurity. Backing the Habsburgs in the War of the Spanish Succession (1703–15) didn't endear Mallorca to the finally victorious Bourbon monarch, Felipe V. In 1716 he abolished all of the island's privileges and autonomy.

Pirate attacks forced Mallorca to be on its guard throughout much of the 18th century, until the island received permission to retaliate without punishment in 1785. At the same time, Mallorcan Franciscan friar Fray Junípero Serra was in California, founding missions that seeded major cities, such as San Francisco and San Diego.

1706	1773	1809	1837
The Austrian pretender to the Spanish throne in the War of the Spanish Succession (1702–15) takes control of Mallorca. Nine years later, Mallorca is conquered by Felipe V.	King Carlos III orders that the Jews of Palma be allowed to live wherever they wish and that all forms of discrimination and mistreatment of the Jewish population be punished.	Thousands of French troops captured in battle in mainland Spain are sent to Illa de Cabrera, where they live in appalling conditions. The survivors would not be released until 1814.	A passenger steamer between Barcelona and Palma begins service, creating a regular link to the mainland. Among its first passengers, in 1838, were George Sand and Frédéric Chopin.

The Napoleonic Wars of the early 19th century had repercussions for Mallorca – waves of Catalan refugees flooded the island, provoking economic and social unrest. The second half of the century saw the rise of the bourgeoisie, an increase in agricultural activity and, in 1875, the opening of the first railway, between Palma and Inca.

Mallorca in the Civil War

The 1931 nationwide elections brought unprecedented results: the Republicans and Socialists together won an absolute majority in Palma, in line with the results in Madrid. The Confederación Española de Derechas Autónomas (Spanish Confederation of the Autonomous Right) won the national elections in 1933 and all the left-wing mayors in Mallorca were sacked by early 1934. The same mayors were back again in a euphoric mood after the dramatic elections of 1936 gave a countervailing landslide victory to the left.

For many generals this was the last straw. Their ringleader, General Francisco Franco, launched an uprising against the central Republican government in July 1936. In Mallorca the insurrection found little resistance. On 19 July rebel soldiers and right-wing Falange militants burst into Cort (the town hall) and arrested the left-wing mayor, Emili Darder (he and other politicians would be executed in February 1937). They quickly occupied strategic points across Palma with barely a shot fired. More resistance came from towns in the Part Forana, but that was soon bloodily squashed.

By mid-August battalions of Italian troops and war planes sent by Franco's fascist ally, Benito Mussolini, were pouring into Mallorca. The island became the main base for Italian air operations and it was from here that raids were carried out against Barcelona, with increasing intensity as the Civil War wore on.

On 9 August 1936, a Catalan-Valencian force (apparently without approval from central command) retook Ibiza from Franco and then, on the 16th, landed at Porto Cristo. So taken aback were they by the lack of resistance that they failed to press home the advantage of surprise. A Nationalist counter-attack begun on 3 September, backed by Italian planes, pushed the hapless (and ill-equipped) invaders back into the sea. Soon thereafter, the Republicans also abandoned Ibiza and Formentera. Of the Balearic Islands, only Menorca remained loyal to the Republic throughout the war.

With Franco's victory in 1939, life in Mallorca mirrored that of the mainland: use of Catalan in public announcements, signs, education and so on was banned. In 1940, rationing was introduced and stayed in place until 1952. Of the nine mayors the city had from 1936 to 1976, four were military men and the others staunchly conservative.

One of the most beautiful descriptions written of the island is the Catalan painter Santiago Rusiñol's *Mallorca, l'Illa de la Calma* (*Mallorca, the Island of Calm;* 1922), in which he takes a critical look at the rough rural life of many Mallorcans.

HISTORY MALLORCA IN THE CIVIL WAR

1912	1922	19 July 1936	1 April 1939
The train line linking Palma with Sóller opens; until then, poor mountain roads had made it easier for the people of Sóller to travel north by sea to France than south by land to Palma.	The first postal service flight takes place between Barcelona and Palma. The service would use flying boats parked in hangars at Es Jonquet in Palma.	The army and right-wing militias take control of Mallorca for General Franco as he launches his military uprising against the Republican government in Madrid.	Franco claims victory in a nationally televised radio speech, three days after Madrid had fallen to Nationalist troops, bringing to an end almost three years of conflict.

Boom Times

In 1950 the first charter flight landed on a small airstrip on Mallorca: no one could have predicted the implications. By 1955 central Palma had a dozen hotels, while others stretched along the waterfront towards Cala Major.

The 1960s and 1970s brought an extraordinary urban revolution, as mass tourism took off vertiginously. The rampant high-rise expansion around both sides of the Badia de Palma – and later along countless other beaches around Mallorca's coast – was the result of a deliberate policy by Franco's central government to encourage tourism in Spain's coastal areas. Many of the hotels built during this period have since been closed, or recycled as apartment or office blocks.

The islanders now enjoyed – by some estimates – the highest standard of living in Spain, but 80% of their economy was (and still is) based on tourism. For decades this led to thoughtless construction and frequent anxiety attacks whenever a season didn't meet expectations. The term *balearización* was coined to illustrate this short-term mentality and the avid overdevelopment of one of the island's most precious resources – its beautiful coastline.

Between 16 and 18 March 1938, Italian air-force bombers based in Mallorca launched 17 raids on Barcelona, killing about 1300 people. Apparently Mussolini ordered the raids without the knowledge of the Spanish Nationalist high command.

A Change of Image

In recent years Mallorca's tourism weathervane has been slowly tilting, with an increasing focus on sustainability, eco-awareness and year-round activities. The island is waking up to the fact that thoughtless construction and anonymous package-holiday hotels are the past, not the future, with resorts, such as the infamous Magaluf, attempting to change from the stag-and-hen knees-up choice to a more family-friendly destination. Along these lines, among other measures, al fresco boozing in certain areas has been banned, as well as happy-hour deals, two-for-one promotions and similar. Undeniably, such intents have not been helped by the fact that the popular UK show, *Love Island*, has been famously filmed in Mallorca over recent years, which led to a 23% increase in Brits travelling to the island in 2018. Overtourism is also being addressed with restrictions on Airbnb rentals, a tourist tax and a concerted move (albeit with resistance) to reduce the number of cruise liners to the capital to just one daily. Thus, while areas of Mallorca still offer the boozy resorts and cheap-as-chips English breakfasts that, for some, define the island, the true light of Mallorcan culture, cuisine, history and hospitality is, we hope, increasingly emerging.

Agritourism has proven to be more than just a passing fad, and more and more *fincas* (working farms) are opening their doors to visitors, offering faultless accommodation in peaceful rural locations and meals that feature Mallorca's fantastic produce. Meanwhile, the urban counter-

1952	1960	1983	2007
After almost 12 years, post–Civil War rationing finally ends on the island. Although many Mallorcans continue to live subsistence lives, the tourism boom will soon transform the island forever.	An estimated 500,000 tourists visit the island, marking the beginning of Mallorcan mass tourism. These figures would increase 50 times over during the decades that followed.	The autonomy statute for the Balearic Islands region (together with those of other Spanish regions) is approved, eight years after Franco's death.	Mallorcan Socialist Francesc Antich ends right-wing Partido Popular rule by forming a coalition government with promises to put a brake on construction projects.

parts to those handsome *fincas,* the venerable aristocratic manor houses of the towns and cities, are being sensitively restored as boutique hotels. If Mallorcan tourism has anything of an image problem, fixing it is simply a matter of accentuating these positives – the heritage, style and native pleasures the island has always boasted.

Though many resorts still go into winter hibernation, hotels in busier towns and villages are now staying open during the low season, mostly to cater for a growing number of travellers who come for the island's outdoor activities. Many of Europe's pro cycling teams rely on Mallorca for their winter training and increasing numbers of people are waking up to the richness and variety of outdoor pursuits the island offers. Adventure sports companies, offering everything from guided hikes and mountain biking to canyoning, caving and coasteering, are rising in number. Their message? Look beyond the beach – Mallorca has year-round substance, variety and appeal.

For an island that is banging the drum about its sustainable tourism, unique landscapes and outdoor activities, the Serra de Tramuntana's inscription on the Unesco World Heritage list of cultural landscapes in 2011 was the icing on the cake. The wild mountains rising in Mallorca's northwestern hinterland are now getting the measure of attention their beauty warrants.

A RIGHT ROYAL DILETTANTE

As the first battles of the Italian campaign raged in 1915, Archduke Ludwig Salvator sat frustrated in Brandeis Castle in Bohemia, writing furiously, but impeded by the fighting from returning to his beloved Balearic Islands. He died in October that year of blood poisoning after an operation on his leg.

Ludwig had been born in 1847 in Florence, the fourth son of Grand Duke Leopold II. He was soon travelling, studying and visiting cities all over Europe. From the outset he wrote of what he saw. His first books were published one year after his first visit to the Balearic Islands in 1867. He returned to Mallorca in 1871 and the following year bought Miramar. He decided to make Mallorca his main base – a lifestyle choice that many northern Europeans would seek to imitate over a century later.

Salvator was an insatiable traveller. In his private steam-driven yacht *Nixe* (and its successors) and other forms of transport, he visited places as far apart as Cyprus and Tasmania. Hardly a year passed in which he didn't publish a book on his travels and studies, possibly the best known of which are his weighty tomes on *Die Balearen* (*The Balearics*). His love remained Mallorca (where royals and other VIPs visited him regularly) and, in 1877, local deputies awarded him the title of Adopted Son of the Balearic Islands. Four years later he was made an honorary member of the Royal Geographic Society in London.

2009	2011	2019	2020
The Basque separatist group, ETA, detonates a series of bombs, killing two policemen and causing havoc at the height of Mallorca's July and August summer tourist seasons.	The conservative Partido Popular (PP) storms back into power, winning an absolute majority in regional elections. The Unió Mallorquina, kingmaker in 2007, loses all of its seats.	Left-leaning party Partido Socialista Obrero Español (PSOE) make history by becoming the largest party in the regional assembly after regional elections.	Balearic Islands pass several laws aimed at cracking down on alcohol-fuelled holidays.

Corruption & the Political Climate

Over the past decade or so, the Mallorcan political scene has been rife with corruption. Linked inextricably to the cash-cow tourist economy that feeds around 80% of Mallorca's GDP, this corruption has a cease-lessly corrosive effect on good business practice and public confidence. Illegal property construction and infrastructure contracts for roads and flyovers to nowhere have long sapped public faith in political leadership. In 2014, the former Balearic Islands' president and Popular Party (PP) minister, Jaume Matas, was sentenced to a six-year jail term for fraud. Then, in 2017, PP member Álvaro Gijón and the former vice president, Gabriel Barceló, were forced to resign over accusations of corruption.

More recently, the Spanish national election held in November 2019 resulted in a narrow win for Partido Socialista Obrero Español (PSOE; Spanish Socialist Workers' Party) in Mallorca. However there was also a rise of the extreme right in the Balearic Islands, more specifically, for the Vox party which had already caused controversy by supporting the stag-ing of a bullfight in August 2019 in Palma, after a brief two-year period of prohibition.

The COVID-19 Pandemic

With around 25% of the island's economy dependent on tourism, Mallor-ca was particularly exposed to the tourism downturn prompted by the global COVID-19 pandemic.

The first COVID-19 case on the island was a British tourist in Palma in early February 2020. Despite upbeat and premature predictions that Spain would only suffer a handful of cases, at the time of writing Spain had recorded almost 2.5 million confirmed cases and over 67,000 deaths from COVID-19, with almost 1000 of the fatalities on Mallorca.

Heavily geared to the tourist dollar, the Mallorcan economy went into freefall. The first half of 2020 saw a vast 92% drop in hotel bookings compared to the same period in 2019. With a 40% drop in GDP for the second quarter of 2020, many businesses pulled down their shutters and long queues formed at foodbanks.

Optimism briefly returned when the island reopened to tourists in spring 2021, but the influx of visitors from Spain and Germany saw infections soar-ing again, prompting further despair. The uncertainty was exemplified by a precipitous 50% drop in tourist inflows to the island in July 2021 compared to the same month in 2019 and one third of hotels were not even operating in August. However, the island's high vaccination rate – almost 82% of the target population having received their full course of vaccinations at the time of writing – was restoring hope for the future, though considerable uncertainty remained.

2020	2020	2021	2021
In February, a British man becomes the first COVID-19 case in Mallorca.	The COVID-19 pandemic causes a 20-year setback in the economy of the Balearic Islands.	In May, Spain lifts COVID-19 travel restrictions for citizens of 10 low-risk countries, including the UK and Japan.	By October, 81.6% of the target population of the Balearic Islands is fully vaccinated against COVID-19.

Landscape & Wildlife

All of the Balearics are beautiful, but Mother Nature really pulled out the stops for Mallorca. Whether you're slow-touring the wild west, where limestone cliffs drop suddenly to curvaceous bays and water 50 shades of blue; rambling through the hinterland, where hills rise steep and wooded above meadows cloaked in wildflowers, olive groves and citrus orchards; or lounging on flour-white beaches on the south coast, you can't help but feel that Mallorca's loveliness is often underrated. Trust us – it's stunning.

Mallorca's Landscape

Mallorca, shaped like a rough trapezoid, is the largest island of the Balearic archipelago. Technically, the island chain is an extension of mainland Spain's Sistema Penibético (Beltic mountain range), which dips close to 1.5km below the Mediterranean and peeks up again to form the islands of Mallorca, Menorca, Ibiza and Formentera. The stretch of water between the archipelago and the mainland is called the Balearic Sea.

The Coast

Mallorca's coastline is punctuated for the most part by small coves, save for three major bays. The Badia de Palma in the south is the most densely populated corner of the island. The two large, shell-shaped bays of the north, the Badia de Pollença and Badia d'Alcúdia, are enclosed by a series of dramatic headlands, Cap de Formentor, Cap des Pinar and Cap Ferrutx.

A series of plunging cliffs interspersed with calm bays marks the south, which is where you'll also find Mallorca's two main island networks: the Illa de Sa Dragonera (offshore from Sant Elm) and the 19-island Parc Nacional Marítim-Terrestre de l'Arxipèlag de Cabrera (from Colònia de Sant Jordi).

Mountains

The island's defining geographic feature is the 90km-long Serra de Tramuntana, a Unesco World Heritage Cultural Landscape since 2011. Spectacularly buckled and contorted, this range of peaks, gullies and cliffs begins close to Andratx in the southwest and reaches its dramatic finale in the northern Cap de Formentor. The highest summits are in the centre of the range, northeast of Sóller, but the steep-sided western flanks that rise abruptly from the Mediterranean shore and shelter numerous villages give the appearance of being higher than they really are. The range is for the most part characterised by forested hillsides (terraced with agriculture in some areas) and bald limestone peaks. A number of tributary ranges, such as the Serra d'Alfabia and Els Cornadors, both close to Sóller, are sometimes named separately.

On the other side of the island, the less-dramatic Serra de Llevant extends from Cap Ferrutx in the north to Cap de Ses Salines in the south; the offshore Illa de Cabrera is considered an extension of the range. Its highest point is the easily accessible Santuari de Sant Salvador (509m).

Between the two, in the centre of the island, extends the vast fertile plain known as Es Pla.

Caves

Mallorca, particularly along its eastern and southern coasts, is drilled with caves created by erosion, waves or water drainage. The caves range from tiny well-like dugouts to vast kilometres-long tunnels replete with lakes, rivers and astounding shapes sculpted by the elements. Although underground, most of the caves actually sit above sea level. The best-known are the Coves del Drac (p<?>) outside Porto Cristo; Coves d'Artà (p<?>) in Canyamel; Coves de Campanet (p<?>) in Campanet; and Coves de Gènova (p<?>), which are close to Palma.

Wildlife

Mallorca's animal population is fairly modest in both numbers and variety, but this is more than compensated for by the abundant birdlife, which makes the island a major Mediterranean destination for twitchers.

Land Animals

The most charismatic (and easily visible) of Mallorca's land species is the Mallorcan wild goat *(Capra ageagrus hircus),* which survives in reasonable numbers only in the Serra de Tramuntana, Cap des Pinar and Parc Natural de la Península de Llevant.

Other mammals include feral cats (a serious threat to bird populations), ferrets, rabbits and hedgehogs. Lizards, turtles, frogs and bats make up the bulk of the native populations. Lizards thrive on Mallorca's islands due to the lack of human population and introduced species, particularly on the Illa de Sa Dragonera, where they have the run of the island, and the Illa de Cabrera; the latter provides a refuge for 80% of the last surviving Balearic lizards *(Podarcis lilfordi).*

You'll also find spiders, more than 300 moth species and 30 kinds of butterflies.

....

MALLORCA'S PARKS

A full 40% of the island falls under some form of official environmental protection.

PARK	FEATURES	ACTIVITIES	WHEN TO VISIT
Parc Nacional Marítim-Terrestre de l'Arxipèlag de Cabrera (p<?>)	Archipelago of 19 islands and islets; home to 130 bird species and diverse marine life	Birdwatching, hiking, scuba diving, snorkelling, swimming	Easter-Oct
Parc Natural de S'Albufera (p<?>)	Vital wetland sheltering 400 plants and 230 species of birds, many of them on migration paths between Europe and Africa	Birdwatching (including 80% of the birds recorded on the Balearic Islands), cycling	Spring & autumn
Parc Natural de Mondragó (p<?>)	Rolling dunes, juniper groves, vibrant wetlands and unspoilt beaches close to east-coast resorts	Hiking, picnicking, swimming	May-Sep
Parc Natural de la Península de Llevant (p<?>)	Flora and fauna	Walking, birdwatching	May-Sep
Parc Natural de Sa Dragonera (p<?>)	Two small islets and the 4km-long Dragonera Island; endangered gull population	Snorkelling, scuba diving	May-Sep

Marine Life

Sperm whales, pilot whales and finback whales feed not far offshore. Also swimming here are bottlenose dolphins, white-sided dolphins and other species. Scuba divers often spot barracuda, octopus, moray eels, grouper, cardinal fish, damsel fish, starfish, sea urchins, sponges and corals.

Birds

As a natural resting point between Europe and Africa, and as one of the few Mediterranean islands with considerable wetlands, Mallorca is a wonderful birdwatching destination (p<?>). Coastal regions in particular draw hundreds of resident and migratory species, especially during the migration periods in spring and autumn.

With more than 200 species it's all but impossible to predict what you'll see. The birds can be divided into three categories: sedentary (those that live on the island year-round), seasonal (those that migrate south after hatching chicks or to escape the cold winters in northern Europe) and migratory (those that rest briefly in Mallorca before continuing their journey).

Endangered Species

The populations of Mallorca's threatened species of Mediterranean birds, tortoises and toads are recovering thanks to the conservation and controlled breeding efforts of Mallorca's parks and natural areas.

Endangered species here include the spur-thighed tortoise and Hermann's tortoise, the only two tortoises found in Spain, as well as the Loggerhead turtle and bird species, such as the red kite.

In 2006 the endemic Mallorcan midwife toad's status was changed to 'vulnerable' from 'critically endangered' on the IUCN Red List of Threatened Species. But there's not such good news about the Balearic shearwater, a water bird that has suffered greatly because of feral cats; IUCN listed it as the most endangered species in Europe in 2016.

The *Plants of the Balearic Islands,* by Anthony Bonner, is the definitive guide to Mallorca's flora and the ideal companion for budding botanists who plan to spend lots of time hiking.

Plants

The Balearic Islands claim more than 120 endemic species and provide a fertile home to countless more.

Mountains & Plains

On the peaks of the Serra de Tramuntana, Mallorca's hardy mountain flora survives harsh sun and wind. Thriving species tend to be ground-huggers or cliff species such as *Scabiosa cretica* (with exotic-looking lilac blooms), which burrow into rock fissures to keep their roots well drained.

On Mallorca's rocky hillsides and flat plains, where oak forests once grew before being burned or destroyed to create farmland, drought-resistant scrubland flora now thrives. Expect to see evergreen shrubs like wild olives and dwarf fan palms, as well as herbs such as rosemary, thyme and lavender. Other plants include heather, broom, prickly pear (which can be made into jam) and 60 species of orchid.

Endemic plants include the lovely *Paeonia cambessedesii,* a pink peony that lives in the shade of some Serra de Tramuntana gullies, and *Naufraga balearica,* a clover-like plant found on shady Tramuntana slopes.

Forests & Ferns

Where evergreen oak forests have managed to survive you'll find holly oaks, kermes oaks and holm oaks growing alongside smaller, less noticeable species such as violets, heather and butcher's broom. Most interesting to botanists are endangered endemic species like the shiny-leaved box *(Buxux balearica)* and the needled yew *(Taxus baccata),* a perennial tree that can grow for hundreds of years. A specimen in Esporles is thought to be more than 2000 years old.

POSEIDON'S GRASS

Beach-lovers in northern Mallorca are occasionally put off by beaches with great rafts of what many mistake for algae. This is sea grass (Poseidon grass or poseidonia), vital for the hindering of erosion on the seabed. The oxygen it gives off helps clean the water, attracts abundant sealife and slows global warming by absorbing carbon dioxide. Thick layers on some beaches actually help keep them intact. It can give off an unpleasant odour, but its presence is nonetheless good for the maritime environment.

Humidity-seeking ferns (more than 40 species) have found marvellous habitats near Mallorca's caves, gorges and streams. In other areas, clusters of poplars, elms and ash trees, introduced species, form small forests.

Coastal Species

Along the shore, plants have had to adapt to constant sea spray, salt deposits and strong winds. One of Mallorca's most beloved coastal species is samphire *(fonoll marí),* a leafy coastal herb that was given to sailors as a source of scurvy-preventing vitamin C. These days it's marinated and used in salads. Other common species are the spiny cushion-like *Launaea cervicornis,* and *Senecio rodriguezii,* whose purpleflowers earned it the nickname of *margalideta de la mar* (little daisy of the sea).

In the wetlands, marshes and dunes of Mallorca, a variety of coastal freshwater flora prosper. Duckweed is one of the most common plants here, though it is often kept company by bulrush, yellow flag iris, sedge and mint. These sand-dwelling species often have white or pale-green leaves and an extensive root system that helps keep them anchored in the shifting sands.

Environmental Threats

The uninhibited construction that began in the 1960s and 1970s has influenced everything from birds' nesting habits to plant habitats, rainwater run-off and water shortages. Although the government is more environmentally aware now than in decades past, the relationship between development and environmental protection remains uneasy.

One of the most pressing concerns for environmentalists is the prevalence of invasive plant species. Many destructive species were first introduced in local gardens but have found such a good home in Mallorca that they're crowding out endemic species. A good example is *Carpobrotus edulis,* called 'sour fig' in England and locally dubbed *patata frita* (French fry) or *dent de león* (lion's tooth) because of its long, slender leaves. A robust low-lying plant, it chokes native species wherever it goes.

A Green Future?

You need only take one look at Mallorca to see the island's potential for producing renewable energy. The island has an average of 300 days of sunshine a year, and steady winds prevail on the coast. Yet until fairly recently the island was dragging its heels when it came to clean energy, despite its natural resources.

Things are slowly changing; in 2011 Siemens set a precedent by introducing a high-voltage direct current (HVDC) in the form of a 244km submarine cable between Palma and Valencia. The HVDC provides renewable energy from the Spanish mainland totalling some 25% of the energy consumed by both residents and tourists. Though it is early days, it is hoped that in the near future the island will derive the vast majority of its power from renewable sources, including wind, solar and hydro-electric power.

Mallorcan Architecture

For an overview of Mallorca's architectural spectrum, a visit to Palma should be high on your list. You'll glimpse Arab baths and Renaissance residences where Mallorcan aristo-crats once swanned around, baroque *patis* (patios) and Modernista mansions. And, of course, Palma's Gothic cathedral, as unique as it is vast. The next chapter is still to be written: the wave of innovation sweeping contemporary Spanish architectural circles is barely beginning to wash over Mallorca.

First Beginnings

Remains of the *talayots* (stone towers) of the first Balearic peoples are found at various sites around the island. Most settlements of these so-called Talayotic peoples were encircled by high stone walls, within which were numerous dwellings and the towers, which were built of stone, usu-ally without the use of mortar. It is thought that some of the *talayots* may have served as watchtowers, others tombs, but little is known about these structures or the lives of those who built them. Although Talayotic cultures survived roughly until the Roman arrival of 123 BCE, many of the structures seen today date back to 1000 BCE. The best preserved sites are at Ses Països (p156) and Capocorb Vell (p170).

Despite ruling over Mallorca for more than two centuries and despite their reputation as mighty builders, the Romans left behind surprisingly few signposts to their presence. This dearth of Roman ruins on Mallorca is most likely attributable to the fact that the Romans, unlike their pre-decessors, occupied the prime patches of coastal real estate, which was then built over by subsequent civilisations. The only meaningful extant Roman site in Mallorca – Pol·lèntia (p132), in Alcúdia in the island's north – is also believed to have been its largest city.

Muslim Mallorca

Mallorca has remarkably little to show for its three centuries of Muslim rule, not least because the mosques they built were invariably occupied by conquering Christian armies in the 13th century, and were subse-quently converted into churches. Palma's Catedral (p53) and Església de Sant Miquel (p65) are two such examples – nothing of their origi-nal form survives. And mosques were not the only buildings to be appro-priated by the new Christian rulers and transformed beyond recognition – the Palau de l'Almudaina (p54) was first built by the Romans, then adapted by a succession of Muslim governors, before becoming the seat of royal (Christian) power on the island.

Defensive fortresses on strategically sited hilltops were another fea-ture of the Islamic occupation but, again, most were taken over and much modified by Christian forces in the centuries that followed. Castell de Capdepera (p159) is perhaps the most impressive example.

Buildings of Muslim Mallorca
....
Banys Àrabs, Palma
....
Jardins d'Alfàbia, Serra de Tramun-tana
....
Porta de l'Almud-aina, Palma
....
Remnants of 12th-century Arab wall, Palma
....
Castell de Santueri, Felanitx

Mallorcan Gothic

The Catalan slant on the Gothic style, with its broad, low-slung, vaulting church entrances and sober adornment, inevitably predominated in Catalan-conquered Mallorca. Guillem Sagrera (c 1380–1456), a Catalan architect and sculptor who had previously worked in Perpignan (today in France), moved to Mallorca in 1420 to take over the direction of work on the Catedral (p53), the island's foremost Gothic structure. Sagrera is considered to be the greatest architect and sculptor of the period in Mallorca. He designed one of the Catedral's chapels and the Gothic chapter house, and, more importantly, he raised Sa Llotja (p68), Mallorca's other standout Gothic monument.

As in other parts of Spain, Islamic influences were evident in some aspects of building throughout the Gothic period. In Mallorca this Mudéjar style is not immediately evident in external facades, but a handful of beautiful *artesonados* (coffered wood ceilings) remain. Those in Palma's Palau de l'Almudaina (p54) are outstanding. The beautiful *artesonado* in the manor house at the Jardins de Alfàbia (p112) appears to be an Islamic relic.

> The return to Christian rule in 1229 came too late for Romanesque architecture to truly make its mark on Mallorca. Perhaps only the Palau de l'Almudaina in Palma shows some traces of the style.

Renaissance & Baroque

Renaissance building had a rational impulse founded on the architecture of classical antiquity, but it seems to have largely passed Mallorca by. Some exceptions confirm the rule, such as the (later remodelled) main entrance to Palma's Catedral (p53), the Consolat de Mar (p68) building and the mostly Renaissance-era sea walls. Although decorated in baroque fashion, the Monestir de Lluc (p118) is basically late Renaissance, and was designed by sculptor and architect Jaume Blanquer (c 1578–1636).

The more curvaceous and, many would say, less attractive successor to the Renaissance was a moderate, island-wide baroque that rarely reached the florid extremes that one encounters elsewhere in Europe. It is most often manifest in the large churches that dominate inland towns. In many of the churches, existing Gothic structures received a serious

ARCHITECTURAL INSIGHT

Pol·lèntia (p132) Roman ruins in Alcúdia, with remnants of houses, temples and a theatre.

Patis (p67) Flit back to Renaissance and baroque times in the *patis* in Palma's historic centre.

Museu Regional d'Artà (p156) Take a brief trot through island history. Brush up on your knowledge of *talayots* here.

Palma Catedral (p53) The giant of Gothic, with its flying buttresses, soaring pinnacles and one of the world's largest rose windows.

Ses Païsses (p156) Close to Artà, this is one of Mallorca's largest and most impressive Talayotic sites.

Banys Àrabs (p59) Palma's Arab baths are the most important remaining monument to Muslim domination of the island.

Castell d'Alaró (p117) The enigmatic ruins of a medieval fortress.

Ca'n Prunera (p109) A classic example of a Modernista mansion in Sóller.

Es Baluard (p66) This contemporary gallery seamlessly merges with Palma's Renaissance seaward walls.

Old Alcúdia (p132) The medieval walls here are among the island's best preserved.

reworking, evident in such elements as barrel vaulting, circular windows, and bloated and curvaceous pillars and columns. Church exteriors are in the main sober (with the occasional gaudy facade). An exception can be found in the *retablos* (*retaules* in Catalan), the grand sculptural altarpieces in most churches. Often gilt and swirling with ornament, this was where baroque sculptors could let their imaginations run wild.

Yet perhaps the most pleasing examples of Mallorca's interpretation of the baroque style comes in the *patis* that grace old Palma's mansions. Drawing on Islamic/Andalusian and Roman influences, dictated by a warm Mediterranean climate, these courtyards represent one of Spain's most subtle baroque forms.

Although baroque is the predominant form, a handful of noble Palma houses betray Renaissance influences, such as the facade of the Cal Marquès del Palmer: standing in front of this building, you might for the briefest of moment think yourself transported to Medici Florence.

Mallorcan Modernisme

Palma

Like most island-wide phenomena, Palma is the centrepiece of Mallorca's Modernista period. A contemporary of Gaudí, Lluís Domènech i Montaner (1850–1923) was another great Catalan Modernista architect who left his mark on the magnificent former Grand Hotel, now the CaixaForum (p65).

The undulating facade of Can Casasayas, built for the wealthy Casasayas family, once known for the sadly lamented confectioner's Confitería Frasquet, is a typical feature of Modernisme. The site is now given over to one of Palma celebrity Marc Fosh's restaurants.

Another eminent and influential figure in the history of Mallorcan Modernisme was Gaspar Bennàssar (1869–1933). Unlike many other Catalan architects who worked on the island, Bennàssar was born in Palma and he played with various styles during his long career, including Modernisme. An outstanding example of this is the Almacenes El Águila (p65), built in 1908 at the height of Modernisme's glory. Each of the three floors is different and the generous use of wrought iron in the main facade exemplifies the style. Next door the use of *trencadís* (ceramic shards) in the Can Forteza Rey facade is classic Gaudí-esque. Can Corbella, on the other hand, dates from roughly the same period, but is dominated by a neo-Mudéjar look.

The seat of the Balearic Islands' Parliament is located in the Círculo Mallorquin, a high-society club on Carrer del Conquistador that local Modernista architect Miquel Madorell i Rius (1869–1936) renovated in 1913.

Sóller

Provincial Sóller can't rival Palma for the breadth of its Modernista buildings, but it does have some outstanding examples of the genre. Most of it is attributable to Joan Rubió, an acolyte of Antoni Gaudí, and the most eye-catching example is the unusual early-20th-century Modernist facade he grafted onto the 18th-century Església de Sant Bartomeu (p110). The adjacent and extravagant Banco de Sóller (p110) is a typically bold example of his approach. Nearby, the Ca'n Prunera Museu Modernista (p109) sports a typically delicate stone facade with muted wrought ironwork; it's also unusual on Mallorca in that it allows you to step beyond the Modernist facade and see the genre's influence upon early-20th-century interiors.

While you can peer into many of Palma's *patis* from the street, architecture buffs would do well to time their visit to Palma with Corpus Christi, when many of these otherwise private spaces are opened to the public.

MALLORCAN ARCHITECTURE MALLORCAN MODERNISME

Arts & Crafts

Mallorca has been a source of inspiration to artists for centuries – Joan Miró felt such an affinity for his maternal homeland that he moved to Palma from his birth city, Barcelona, while local legend Miquel Barceló has added a vibrant splash of colour to galleries across the island. Today you can still encounter deep-rooted arts and crafts traditions, be they in the upbeat ballads sung at *festes* (festivals) or the leather-making factories in Inca, where funky footwear label Camper took its first steps.

Literature

Mallorca's many accomplished writers have not only created works of enduring significance, but have been instrumental in establishing Catalan and Mallorquin as literary languages. The works of many of Mallorca's leading writers, such as Llorenç Villalonga and Baltasar Porcel, have now been translated, inviting outsiders into a rich literary scene little known beyond the Catalan-speaking world.

Those curious to find out more about authors writing in Catalan – in Mallorca and elsewhere in the Catalan-speaking world – should check out www.escriptors.cat, the website of the Association of Catalan Language Writers.

The Early Centuries

Anaïs Nin set an erotic short story, *Mallorca*, in Deià. It appeared in the volume *Delta of Venus* and deals with a local girl who gets into an erotic tangle with a pair of foreigners and pays a high price. Nin stayed in Deià for a year in 1941.

In one sense Mallorcan literature began with the island's medieval conqueror, Jaume I (1208–76), who recorded his daring deeds in *El Llibre dels Fets* (*The Book of Deeds*). He wrote in Catalan, a language that the Palma-born poet and visionary evangeliser Ramon Llull (1232–1316) would elevate to a powerful literary tool. A controversial figure, who many feel should be declared a saint (he has only made it to beatification), Llull has long been canonised as the father of the literary Catalan tongue.

Few Mallorcans grapple with Llull's medieval texts, but most know at least one poem by Miquel Costa i Llobera (1854–1922), a theologian and poet. His *El Pi de Formentor* (*The Formentor Pinetree,* 1907), which eulogises Mallorcan landscapes through a pine on the Formentor peninsula, is *the* Mallorcan poem.

The 20th Century

One of the island's greatest poets was the reclusive Miquel Bauçà (1940–2005). His *Una Bella Història* (1962–85) is a major achievement. Llorenç Villalonga (1897–1980), born into an elite Palman family and trained in medicine, was one of Mallorca's top 20th-century novelists. Baltasar Porcel (1937–2009) was the doyen of contemporary Mallorcan literature. *L'Emperador o l'Ull del Vent* (*The Emperor or the Eye of the Wind,* 2001) is a dramatic tale about the imprisonment of thousands of Napoleon's soldiers on Illa de Cabrera. Carme Riera (b 1948, Palma) has churned out an impressive series of novels, short stories, scripts and more. Guillem Frontera (b 1945, Ariany) has produced some engaging crime novels, particularly the 1980 *La Ruta dels Cangurs* (*The Kangaroo Route*).

In 1936, inspired by a stay in the then little-known town of Pollença, Agatha Christie wrote the short crime thriller *Problem at Pollensa Bay,* which would later be the title for a volume of eight short crime mysteries.

Music

Folk

Mallorca, like any other part of Spain, has a rich heritage in folk songs and ballads sung in Mallorquin. At many traditional *festes* in Mallorcan towns you'll hear the sounds of the *xeremiers,* a duo of ambling musicians, one of whom plays the *xeremia* (similar to the bagpipes) and the other a *flabiol* (a high-pitched pipe).

Contemporary

For those who thought Ibiza was the exclusive Mediterranean home of club sounds, Daniel Vulic (DJ and German radio director in Mallorca) brought out *Cool Vibes Vol 1,* a compilation of strictly Mallorcan chill-out and club music in 2007.

The island's best-known singer-songwriter is Palma's Maria del Mar Bonet i Verdaguer (b 1947). She moved to Barcelona at the age of 20 to join the Nova Cançó Catalana movement, which promoted singers and bands working in Catalan. Bonet became an international success and is known for her interpretations of Mediterranean folk music, French *chanson* (Jacques Brel and company) and experiments with jazz and Brazilian music.

An altogether different performer is Concha Buika. Of Equatorial Guinean origins, she was born in Palma in 1972 and rose through the Palma club circuit with her very personal brand of music, ranging from hip-hop to flamenco to soul. Her second CD, *Mi Niña Lola,* came out in 2007, followed by *Niña de Fuego* a year later, and in 2009 *El Ultimo Trago,* a collaboration with Chucho Valdés, the renowned Cuban jazz pianist. She continues to release albums, most recently in 2019 with *Flamenca: La inspiración de un nuevo.*

Argentine-born, Mallorca-based starlet Chenoa got her break when she stunned all in the TV talent show *Operación Triunfo*. Since 2002 she

---

WRITINGS ABOUT MALLORCA

Mallorca has long inspired foreign writers, both in providing a place in which to write and yielding up rich subject matter for the stories themselves.

➡ *A Lizard in my Luggage* (2006), *Goats from a Small Island* (2009), *Donkeys on my Doorstep* (2010), *A Bull on the Beach* (2012), *A Chorus of Cockerels* (2016) by Anna Nicholas

➡ *Snowball Oranges* (2000), *Mañana Mañana* (2001), *Viva Mallorca* (2004) and *A Basketful of Snowflakes* (2007) by Peter Kerr

➡ *Rafael's Wings: A Novel of Mallorca* (2006), *Von Ripper's Odyssey* (2016) by Sian Mackay

➡ *Tuning Up at Dawn* (2004) and *Bread and Oil: Majorcan Culture's Last Stand* (2006) by Tomás Graves, son of Robert Graves

➡ *Wild Olives: Life in Majorca with Robert Graves* (2001) by William Graves

➡ *Jogging Around Mallorca* (1929) by Gordon West

➡ *British Travellers in Mallorca in the Nineteenth Century* (2006) edited by Brian J Dendle and Shelby Thacker

➡ *Die Insel des Zweiten Gesichts* (*The Island of the Second Vision*, 1953) by German writer Albert Vigoleis Thelen

has churned out seven albums and has become one of the most popular voices in Spanish-Latin pop.

Painting & Sculpture

The Early Centuries

Important artists around the mid-15th century include Rafel Mòger (c 1424–70) and Frenchman Pere Niçard, productive in Mallorca from 1468 to 1470. They created one of the era's most important works, *Sant Jordi*, now housed in Palma's Museu Diocesà (p59). The outstanding sculptor of this time was Guillem Sagrera, who did much of the detail work on Sa Llotja (p68).

Pere Terrencs (active c 1479–1528) returned from a study stint in Valencia with the technique of oil painting – the death knell for egg-based pigments. His was a transitional style between late Gothic and the Renaissance. In a similar category was Córdoba-born Mateu López (d 1581), who landed in Mallorca in 1544 where he and his son became senior painters.

Gaspar Oms (c 1540–1614) was Mallorca's most outstanding late-Renaissance painter. The Oms clan, from Valencia, dominated the Mallorcan art scene throughout the 17th and 18th centuries.

Miquel Bestard (1592–1633) created major baroque canvases for churches, such as the Convento de Santa Clara and the Església de Monte-Sion, in Palma. Guillem Mesquida i Munar (1675–1747) concentrated on religious motifs and scenes from classical mythology.

19th & 20th Centuries

The 19th century brought a wave of landscape artists to Mallorca. Many came from mainland Spain, particularly Catalonia, but the island produced its own painters, too. More than half a dozen notables were born and raised in Palma. Joan O'Neille Rosiñol (1828–1907) is considered the founder of the island's landscape movement. He and his younger contemporaries, Ricard Anckermann Riera (1842–1907) and Antoni Ribas Oliver (1845–1911), both from Palma, were among the first to cast their artistic eyes over the island and infuse it with romantic lyricism.

From 1890 a flood of Modernista artists from Catalonia 'discovered' Mallorca and brought new influences to the island. Some of them, such as Santiago Rusiñol (1861–1931), had spent time in Paris, which was then the hotbed of the art world. Locals enthusiastically joined in the Modernista movement. Palma-born Antoni Gelabert Massot (1877–1932) became a key figure, depicting his home city in paintings such as *Murada i Catedral a Entrada de Fosc* (1902–04). Other artists caught up in this

Best Niche Galleries

....

Es Baluard, Palma

....

Casa-Museu Dionís Bennàssar, Pollença

....

Ca'n Prunera – Museu Modernista, Sóller

....

MIRÓ & MALLORCA

Joan Miró grew up and spent most of his life in Barcelona, but Mallorca was his spiritual home and it became his permanent abode when he moved here in the mid-1950s. The island was an endless source of inspiration to the artist – the horizons, the 'eloquent silence', the pure brilliance of the light, and the vivid blues of the sea that were reflected in works such as *Bleu I, II, III* (1961), a three-part series of intensely hued paintings.

The bustle of Santa Catalina market, the crescent-shaped patterns of Moorish and Mallorcan folk art (baskets, pottery and the ceramic peasant whistles called *siurells*) inspired his increasingly expressive and abstract work.

Here Miró could walk through the streets and listen to the organist in the cathedral unnoticed, and he relished this anonymity. His studio on the outskirts of the city gave him ample breathing space to fully immerse himself in his art. He lived there until his death in 1983, aged 90. You can visit his house and studio, and see many of his paintings, sketches and sculptures, at Fundació Pilar i Joan Miró (p90).

Es Baluard (p66), Palma de Mallorca

wave were Joan Fuster Bonnín (1870–1943) and Llorenç Cerdà i Bisbal (1862–1955), born in Pollença.

Meanwhile Llorenç Rosselló (1867–1902) was shaping up to be the island's most prominent sculptor until his early death. A handful of Rosselló's bronzes, as well as a selection of works by many of the painters mentioned here, can be seen in Es Baluard (p66).

By the 1910s and 1920s symbolism began to creep into local artists' vocabulary. Two important names in Mallorcan painting from this period are Joan Antoni Fuster Valiente (1892–1964) and Ramón Nadal (1913–99), both from Palma.

Contemporary

Towering above everyone else in modern Mallorcan art is local hero and art icon, Miquel Barceló (b 1957, Felanitx). His profile has been especially sharp in his island home since the unveiling in 2007 of one of his more controversial masterpieces, a ceramic depiction of the miracle of the loaves and fishes housed in Palma's Catedral (p53). Barceló, who divides his time between Paris and Mali's Dogon Country, has a studio in Naples and was a rising star by the age of 25. Although he is best known as a painter, Barceló has worked with ceramics since the late 1990s. However, the commission for the Catedral was on a hitherto unimagined scale for the artist.

Less well known but nonetheless prolific is Palma-born Ferran García Sevilla (b 1949), whose canvases are frequently full of primal colour and strong shapes and images. Since the early 1980s he has exhibited in galleries throughout Europe. Joan Costa (b 1961, Palma) is one of the island's key contemporary sculptors, who also indulges in occasional brushwork.

One cannot leave out 20th-century Catalan icon Joan Miró (1893–1983). His mother came from Sóller and he lived the last 27 years of his life in Cala Major, just outside Palma, where his former home is now a museum, the Fundació Pilar i Joan Miró (p90). Working there in a huge studio, he

Glass blowing

maintained a prolific turn-out of canvases, ceramics, statuary, textiles and more, exploring his particular motifs of women, birds and the cosmos.

Crafts

Tourism may have led to the overdevelopment of the Mallorcan coast, but it has enabled the revival of many traditional crafts and artisan workshops, among them those working with metal, ceramics, paper, glass, leather and jewellery.

The Consell de Mallorca tourist office (p206), its airport branch and some municipal tourist offices around the island have information on local handicrafts, notable craftspeople and where their wares can be found.

Glasswork & Leatherwork

Glasswork was first produced on the island way back in the 2nd century BCE and its artisans were part of a network of production and trade centred on Murano in Venice. Mallorcan glass manufacturing reached its high point in the 18th century, after which the industry fell into decline. But one family, the Gordiolas, who first entered the industry in its 18th-century heyday, have been almost single-handedly responsible for Mallorcan glass-making's revival in the mid- to late 20th century. Although you'll find smaller artisans working with glass, the Museu de Gordiola (p147), outside Algaida, is the island's largest producer, and here you can watch traditional glass-blowing techniques.

Thanks to famous shoe manufacturers such as Camper, Mallorca's leather-making industry has become renowned worldwide for the quality of its products. Although smaller traditional manufacturers tend to get drowned out by the larger companies, there's no denying that this industry is a stunning Mallorcan success story. Inca is the capital of Mallorcan shoemaking, with a host of factories and outlets open to the public.

Tram to Port de Sóller (p113)

Survival Guide

Directory A–Z

Accessible Travel

Mallorca is a long way from being barrier-free, but things are slowly improving. Wheelchair access to some museums, official buildings and hotels represents something of a sea change in local thinking.

➡ Be circumspect about hotels advertising themselves as accessible, as this can mean as little as wide doors to rooms and bathrooms, a ramp into reception or other token efforts.

➡ Cobbled streets and flights of steps in hill towns can make getting around difficult.

➡ Palma city buses are equipped for wheelchair access, as are some of those that travel around the island. Some taxi companies run adapted taxis – they must be booked in advance.

➡ Download Lonely Planet's free Accessible Travel guide from http://lptravel.to/AccessibleTravel.

Customs Regulations

➡ There are no duty-free allowances for travel between EU countries and no restrictions on the import of duty-paid items into Spain

Climate

Palma de Mallorca

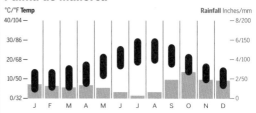

from other EU countries for personal use.

➡ VAT-free articles can be bought at airport shops when travelling between EU countries.

➡ Duty-free allowances for travellers entering Spain from outside the EU include 2L of wine (or 1L of wine and 1L of spirits) and 200 cigarettes, 50 cigars or 250g of tobacco.

Discount Cards

Students, seniors (over 65s), families and young people get discounts of 20% to 50% at many sights. Museum entry is often free for under 12s. From October to April, some four-star hotels and car-hire companies offer discounts for over-55s.

City Cards Some Mallorcan centres offer discount cards entitling holders to entry to multiple

attractions, and other perks. The most useful is the Palma Pass.

Senior's Cards Reduced prices at museums and attractions (sometimes restricted to EU citizens only) and occasionally reduced costs on transport.

Student Cards An ISIC (International Student Identity Card; www.isic.org) can save you up to 50% off stays, attractions and more.

Youth Card Travel, sights and youth hostel discounts with the European Youth Card (Carnet Joven in Spain; www.euro26.org).

EATING PRICE RANGES

The following price ranges refer to a main course.

€ less than €12

€€ €12–20

€€€ more than €20

Electricity

Type C
220V/50Hz

Health

Mallorca doesn't present any health dangers – your main gripes are likely to be sunburn, insect bites, mild stomach problems and hangovers.

Before You Go
HEALTH INSURANCE

➤ If you're an EU citizen, a European Health Insurance Card (EHIC), available from health centres, covers you for most medical care. It will not cover you for non-emergencies, emergency repatriation or procedures you've travelled here specifically for.

➤ Citizens from other countries should find out if there is a reciprocal arrangement for free medical care between their country and Spain.

VACCINATIONS

No jabs are necessary for Mallorca but the WHO recommends that all travellers be covered for diphtheria, tetanus, measles, mumps, rubella and polio, regardless of their destination.

In Mallorca
AVAILABILITY & COST OF HEALTH CARE

➤ If you need an ambulance, call ☑061.

➤ Clinical standards and waiting times are among the best in Europe, and costs are equivalent to other Western European countries.

➤ For emergency treatment go straight to the *urgencias* (emergency) section of the nearest hospital. The island's main hospital is Palma's **Hospital Universitari Son Espases** (☑871 20 50 00; www.hospitalsonespases.es; Carretera de Valldemossa 79), but other important ones are based in Inca and Manacor.

➤ At the main coastal tourist resorts you will generally find clinics with English- and German-speaking staff.

➤ *Farmacias* (pharmacies) offer advice and sell over-the-counter medication. When a pharmacy is closed it posts the name of the nearest *farmacia de guardia* (duty pharmacies) on the door.

HEALTH RISKS

➤ Heat exhaustion occurs following excessive fluid loss. Symptoms include headache, dizziness and tiredness. Treat by drinking plenty of water and/or fruit juice.

➤ Heat stroke is much more serious, resulting in irrational and hyperactive behaviour and eventually loss of consciousness and death. Rapid cooling by spraying the body with water and fanning is ideal.

➤ If you have a severe allergy to bee or wasp stings, carry an EpiPen or similar adrenaline injection.

➤ In forested areas, watch out for the hairy reddish-brown caterpillars of the pine processionary moth. Touching the caterpillars' hairs sets off a severely irritating allergic skin reaction.

➤ Some Spanish centipedes have a very nasty, but nonfatal, sting. The ones to watch out for are those with clearly defined segmentssuch as black and yellow stripes.

➤ In summer, waves of stingers (jellyfish) can wash up on the island's beaches. Vinegar, ice and Epsom salts can soothe the pain of a sting. If unavailable, rub in salt water; fresh water can stimulate the sting. Head to a Red Cross stand (usually present on the main beaches) if you are stung.

➤ Sandflies are found on many Mallorcan beaches. They usually only give a nasty itchy bite but can occasionally cause a rare skin disorder called cutaneous leishmaniasis, a raised lesion at the site of the bite which can leave atrophic scarring.

TAP WATER

Tap water is safe to drink across Mallorca.

Insurance

➤ Comprehensive travel-insurance to cover theft, loss, medical problems and cancellations is highly recommended. Read the fine print, as some policies exclude 'high risk' activities such as scuba diving and canyoning.

➤ EU citizens are entitled to health care in public hospitals (present your European Health Insurance Card).

➤ Check that your policy covers ambulances or an emergency flight home.

➤ Keep all documents and bills if you have to make a claim.

➤ Worldwide travel insurance is available at www.lonelyplanet.com/travel-insurance. You can buy,

PRACTICALITIES

Newspapers English- and German-language dailies are widely available in resorts. Major Spanish newspapers include centre-left *El País* (http://elpais.com) and centre-right *El Mundo* (www.elmundo.es). For Mallorca news, try *Diario de Mallorca* (www.diariodemallorca.es), *Ultima Hora* (http://ultimahora.es) or English-language *Majorca Daily Bulletin* (http://majorcadailybulletin.com).

Radio Regional stations include Radio Balear (www.radiobalear.net) and English-speaking Radio One Mallorca (www.radioonemallorca.com).

Smoking Many Mallorcans smoke, although the ban on smoking in all enclosed public places, once often flouted, is now enforced more rigorously.

Weights & Measures The metric system is used.

extend and claim online any time – even if you're already on the road.

Internet Access

➡ Numerous cafes and bars have free wi-fi. You may need to ask for the password when ordering.

➡ Most hotels have wi-fi, but in some cases the signal is weak beyond the lobby

Legal Matters

➡ By law you are expected to carry some form of photographic identification at all times, such as a passport, national ID card or driving licence.

➡ The blood alcohol limit for driving in Spain is 0.05%. There are stiff fines (up to €1000) for anyone caught exceeding this limit. Levels of 0.12% and above carry a risk of imprisonment.

➡ Cannabis is legal but only for personal use and in very small quantities. Public consumption of any drug is illegal.

➡ If arrested, you will be allotted the free services of a duty solicitor (*abogado de oficio*), who may speak only Spanish (and Mallorquin).

You are entitled to have the nature of the accusation against you explained in a language you understand, and to make a phone call.

➡ If you end up in court, the authorities are obliged to provide a translator.

LGBTIQ+ Travellers

Homosexuality is legal in Spain. In 2005 the socialist president of Spain, José Luis Rodríguez Zapatero, gave the conservative Catholic foundations of the country a shake with the legalisation of same-sex marriage. In Mallorca, Palma is the natural epicentre of a proud and prominent gay culture.

Resources

Ben Amics (☑871 96 54 66; www.benamics.com; Carrer del General Riera 3; ⊙9am-3pm) The island's umbrella association for members of the LGBTIQ+ community.

Gay Mallorca (www.gay-mallorca.blogspot.com) Weekly events listings.

Guía Gay de España (http://guia.universogay.com/palmademallorca) More useful listings of cafes, saunas, nightclubs and restaurants.

Mallorca Gay Map (www.mallorcagaymap.com) A handy guide to gay-friendly attractions (restaurants, hotels, clubs etc); a printed version is available from some municipal tourist offices in Palma.

Maps
Maps of Mallorca
Among the better and clearer island maps:

➡ Freytag and Berndt's *Mallorca* (1:50,000)

➡ Michelin's *No.579 Balears/Balearics* (1:140,000)

➡ Marco Polo's *Mallorca* (1:125,000)

➡ Bike Mallorca's *Mallorca Bicycle Map* (1:100,000)

Walking Maps
Walking maps must be at least 1:25,000 in scale; anything bigger is practically useless. Purchase your maps at hiking shops, or check out map specialists in other countries, for example Stanfords (www.stanfords.co.uk) in the UK.

➡ Alpina Editorial produces three maps to the Serra de Tramuntana range (*Mallorca Tramuntana Sud, Mallorca Tramuntana Central* and *Mallorca Tramuntana Nord*). These come with detailed walk descriptions in a solid booklet. The third map is in Catalan and German only.

➡ Discovery Walking Guides publishes detailed guides to different regions of the island. Their *Walk! Mallorca (North & Mountains),* for example, is packed with walks, basic maps and GPS coordinates. You'll also need to buy additional maps though.

➡ The *Kompass Wanderführer 5910 Mallorca* (in German), by Wolfgang Heizmann, comes with detailed walking maps.

➡ Spain's Centro Nacional de Información Geográfica (www.cnig.es) covers a good part of the island in 1:25,000 scale sheets.

Money

ATMs are widely available in towns and resorts. Credit cards are accepted in most hotels, restaurants and shops.

ATMs

➡ Most debit and credit cards, such as Visa, MasterCard and Cirrus, can be used to withdraw cash from *cajeros automáticos* (ATMs).

➡ ATMs are ubiquitous in towns and major resorts, and accessible 24/7.

➡ There is usually a charge (around 1.5% to 2%) on ATM cash withdrawals abroad which will be clearly shown on the screen before the transaction is completed.

Cash

➡ Cash is king for small purchases in Mallorca, and spare change is handy for coffee pit stops and spontaneous market buys.

➡ Avoid taking more money to the beach than you need for ice cream, drinks, and sunbed and parasol hire (€10 to €15 per day).

➡ Not all banks exchange foreign currencies; those that do will have a clear cambio/change/exchange/ wechsel sign displayed on the exterior of the building.

➡ Exchange bureaux are another option, but commission rates may be high. Western Union is a good bet.

Credit & Debit Cards

➡ Credit and debit cards are generally accepted in hotels, with the exception of some rural B&Bs.

➡ Small, family-run restaurants and cafes might insist on cash – check before ordering to be on the safe side.

➡ Cards can be used to pay for most other purchases. You'll sometimes be asked to show your passport or some other form of photo ID.

➡ Among the most widely accepted cards are Visa, MasterCard, American Express (Amex), Cirrus, Maestro, Plus, Diners Club and JCB.

Taxes & Refunds

Spain's IVA (VAT) goods-and-services tax of up to 21% is included in stated prices. Refunds are available on goods of any purchase amount, if taken out of the EU within three months. Collect a refund form when purchasing and present it (together with the purchases) to the customs IVA refunds booth when leaving the EU. For more information, see www.globalblue.com.

Tipping

Hotels Discretionary: porters around €1 per bag and cleaners €2 per day.

Cafes and bars Not expected, but you can reward good service by rounding the bill to the nearest euro or two.

Restaurants Service charge is included, unless '*servicio no incluido*' is specified, but many still leave an extra 5% or so.

Taxis Not necessary, but feel free to round up or leave a modest tip, especially for longer journeys.

Opening Hours

High-season hours are provided; hours generally decrease in the shoulder and low seasons. Many resort restaurants and hotels close from November to March.

Banks 8.30am–2pm Monday to Friday; some also open 4–7pm Thursday and 9am–1pm Saturday

Bars 7pm–3am

Clubs midnight–6am

Post offices 8.30am–9.30pm Monday to Friday, 8.30am–2pm Saturday

Restaurants 1–3.30pm and 7.30–11pm

Shops 10am–2pm and 4.30–7.30pm or 5–8pm Monday to Saturday; large supermarkets and department stores generally 10am–9pm Monday to Saturday

Post

The Spanish postal system, Correos (www.correos.es), is generally reliable, if a little slow at times. Delivery times are erratic but ordinary mail to other Western European countries can take up to a week; to North America up to 10 days; and to Australia or New Zealand between 10 days and three weeks.

Sellos (stamps) are sold at most *estancos* (tobacconists' shops with 'Tabacos' in yellow letters on a maroon background), as well as post offices. A postcard or letter weighing up to 20g costs €1.70 from Spain to other European countries; rates are higher to other countries. For a full list of prices for certified (*certificado*) and express post (*urgente*) mail, check the 'Fee Calculator' on the Correos website.

Public Holidays

The two main periods when Spaniards (and Mallorcans are no real exception) go on holiday are Semana Santa (the week leading up to Easter Sunday) and August, which also happens to be when half of Europe descends on Mallorca. Accommodation can be hard to find and transport is put under strain.

There are 14 official holidays each year, to which most towns add at least one to mark their patron saint's day. Some places have several traditional feast days; not all of them are official holidays but they're often a reason for partying.

The main island-wide public holidays:

Cap d'Any (New Year's Day) 1 January

Epifania del Senyor (Epiphany) 6 January

Dia de les Illes Balears (Balearic Islands Day) 1 March

Dijous Santa (Holy Thursday) March/April

Divendres Sant (Good Friday) March/April

Diumenge de Pasqua (Easter Sunday) March/April

Festa del Treball (Labour Day) 1 May

L'Assumpció (Feast of the Assumption) 15 August

Festa Nacional d'Espanya (Spanish National Day) 12 October

Tots Sants (All Saints) 1 November

Dia de la Constitució (Constitution Day) 6 December

L'Immacula da Concepció (Feast of the Immaculate Conception) 8 December

Nadal (Christmas) 25 December

Segona Festa de Nadal (Boxing Day) 26 December

Safe Travel

Mallorca is safe, but the usual precautions are advised. The main thing to be wary of is petty theft: keep an eye on your valuables and you should be OK.

Report thefts to the **national police** (☏902 10 21 12; www.policia.es). It is unlikely that you will recover your goods, but you need to make a formal *denuncia* for insurance purposes. To save time, you can make the report by phone (in various languages), or online (search for '*denuncias*').

Telephone

Mallorca's former distinctive blue payphones are being phased out on the grounds that they have become obsolete in the era of mobile telephones.

Mobile Phones

Local SIM cards are widely available and can be used in European and Australian mobile phones. Other phones may need to be set to roaming.

Note that, from June 2017, there are no roaming charges when travelling from and within the EU. Outside of these countries, operators can set their tariffs freely.

Phonecards

Cut-rate phonecards from private companies can be good value for international calls, particularly if you don't have access to Skype or WhatsApp. They can be bought from *estancos* (tobacconists), news-stands and *locutorios* (call centres), especially in Palma and coastal resorts – compare rates if possible.

Telephone Numbers

➡ All telephone numbers in Mallorca (including mobile numbers) have nine digits.

➡ Almost all fixed-line telephone numbers begin with ☏971, although a small number begin with ☏871.

➡ Numbers starting with a '6' are for mobile phones.

➡ Numbers starting with ☏900 are national toll-free numbers, while those starting ☏901 to ☏905 come with varying costs. A common one is ☏902, which is a national standard rate number, but can only be dialled from within Spain. In a similar category are numbers starting with ☏800, ☏803, ☏806 and ☏807.

➡ It is possible to dial an operator in your country of residence at no cost to make a reverse-charge call (*una llamada a cobro revertido*) – pick up the number before you leave home. You can usually get an English-speaking Spanish international operator on 1008 (for calls within Europe) or 1005 (rest of the world).

Time

Mallorca runs on central European time (GMT/UTC plus one hour). Daylight saving time begins on the last Sunday in March and ends on the last Sunday in October.

UK, Ireland, Portugal & Canary Islands One hour behind Mallorca.

USA Spanish time is USA Eastern Time plus six hours, or USA Pacific Time plus nine hours.

Australia During the Australian winter (Spanish summer), subtract eight hours from Australian Eastern Standard Time to get Spanish time; during the Australian summer, subtract 10 hours.

Toilets

Public toilets are rare to non-existent across the island. If you find yourself in need of the facilities, remember that most (but not all) bars and restaurants will expect you to purchase something before or after you use the toilet.

Tourist Information

➡ Almost every town and resort in Mallorca has a walk-up tourist office (*oficina de turismo* or *oficina de información turística*) for local maps and information.

➡ Tourist offices in coastal areas usually open from Easter or May until October and keep surprisingly short hours. If you do find them open, they're usually helpful and overflowing with useful brochures.

➡ In Palma you'll find municipal tourist offices focussing on Palma and its immediate surrounds. There's also the **Consell de**

Mallorca Tourist Office (Map p60; ☎971 17 39 90; www.infomallorca.net; Plaça de la Reina 2, Palma de Mallorca; ☺8.30am-8pm Mon-Fri, to 3pm Sat; ☎), which covers the whole island.

➡ For general information about the Balearic Islands, visit www.illesbalears.es.

Visas

Spain is one of the 26 member countries of the Schengen Convention, under which 22 EU countries (all but Bulgaria, Cyprus, Ireland and Romania) plus Iceland, Norway and Switzerland have abolished checks at common borders.

To work or study in Spain a special visa may be required – contact a Spanish embassy or consulate before you travel.

Citizens or Residents of	Visa Required?
EU & Schengen countries	No
Australia, Canada, Israel, Japan, NZ, UK and the USA	Not required for tourist visits of up to 90 days
Other countries	Check the Foreign Office website (www.exteriores.gob.es).

Extensions & Residence

You can apply for no more than two visas in any 12-month period and they are not renewable once in Spain.

Nationals of EU countries, Iceland, Norway and Switzerland can enter and leave Spain at will and don't need to apply for a *tarjeta de residencia* (residence card), although they are supposed to apply for residence papers and must meet certain criteria.

People of other nationalities who want to stay in Spain longer than 90 days require one of two types of residence card – for less than or more than six months. Getting one can be a drawn-out process, starting with an appropriate visa issued by a Spanish consulate in their country of residence. Start the process well in advance.

Volunteering

Most volunteering opportunities in Spain are on the mainland, but it is worth checking Go Abroad (www.goabroad.com) for projects in Mallorca. *Fincas* (farms) and families offering work and board on a voluntary basis advertise on Work Away (www.workaway.info).

Note that Lonely Planet does not endorse any organisation that we do not work with directly. Travellers should investigate any volunteering option thoroughly before committing to a project.

Women Travellers

Travelling in Mallorca is largely as easy as travelling anywhere else in the Western world. However, you may still occasionally find yourself the object of staring, catcalls and unnecessary comments. Simply ignoring them is usually sufficient.

While topless bathing and skimpy clothes are in fashion on the island's coastal resorts, people tend to dress more conservatively in the towns and inland.

Work

➡ Nationals of EU countries, Switzerland, Norway and Iceland may work freely in Spain, and hence, Mallorca. Virtually everyone else needs to obtain, from a Spanish consulate in their country of residence, a work permit and (for stays of more than 90 days) a residence visa.

➡ Many bars (especially of the UK and Irish persuasion), restaurants and other businesses are run by foreigners and look for temporary staff in summer. Check any local press in foreign languages, which carry ads for waiters, nannies, chefs, babysitters, cleaners and the like.

➡ Translating and interpreting could be an option if you are fluent both in Spanish and a language in demand. You can start a job search on the web, for instance at Think Spain (www.thinkspain.com).

Transport

GETTING THERE & AWAY

Most visitors to Mallorca fly into Palma's international airport, though it's possible to arrive by ferry from points along the Spanish coast (Alicante, Barcelona, Denia and Valencia). The neighbouring islands of Ibiza and Menorca are also linked to Mallorca by both air and ferry.

Flights and tours can be booked online at lonelyplanet.com/bookings.

Entering the Country

Entry and exit procedures in Mallorca are generally smooth and not overly officious.

Passports

Citizens of most of the 27 European Union member states and Switzerland can travel to Spain with their national identity card. All other nationalities, including the UK, must have a full valid passport, and a few even require visas (p207). Full details can be found at the website of the Spanish Foreign Office (www.exteriores.gob.es)

If applying for a visa, check that your passport's expiry date is at least six months away. Non-EU citizens must fill out a landing card.

By law you are technically supposed to carry your passport or ID card with you at all times.

Air

Air is the most convenient and popular way of arriving in Mallorca, so much so that Palma airport is the third-busiest airport in Spain, with connections across Spain and Europe.

Airports & Airlines

Palma de Mallorca Airport (PMI;☎902 404704; www.aena-aeropuertos.es) is 8km east of Palma de Mallorca. Flying to 105 countries, it's Spain's third-largest airport, and one of the busiest in Europe. In summer especially, masses of charter and regular flights form an air bridge to Palma from around Europe, among them many low-cost airlines.

The Arrivals hall is on the ground floor of the main terminal building, where you'll find a **tourist office** (☎971 78 95 56; www.visitpalma.com; Aeroport de Palma; ☺8am-8pm Mon-Sat, to 2pm Sun), money-exchange offices, car hire, tour operators and hotel-booking stands. Departures are on the 2nd floor.

Nearly every European airline serves Mallorca, along with the majority of budget carriers. Airlines flying to the island include the following:

Air Berlin (www.airberlin.com) From London (Stansted), dozens

---

CLIMATE CHANGE & TRAVEL

Every form of transport that relies on carbon-based fuel generates CO_2, the main cause of human-induced climate change. Modern travel is dependent on aeroplanes, which might use less fuel per kilometre per person than most cars but travel much greater distances. The altitude at which aircraft emit gases (including CO_2) and particles also contributes to their climate change impact. Many websites offer 'carbon calculators' that allow people to estimate the carbon emissions generated by their journey and, for those who wish to do so, to offset the impact of the greenhouse gases emitted with contributions to portfolios of climate-friendly initiatives throughout the world. Lonely Planet offsets the carbon footprint of all staff and author travel.

of cities all over Germany and elsewhere in mainland Europe.

British Airways (www.britishairways.com) From London.

easyJet (www.easyjet.com) From 13 UK airports and nine in mainland Europe.

Germanwings (www.germanwings.com) From dozens of UK and mainland Europe airports.

Iberia (www.iberia.es) Flies from many mainland Spanish cities with its subsidiary Air Nostrum.

Jet2 (www.jet2.com) From Belfast, Leeds, Edinburgh and Newcastle.

Lufthansa (www.lufthansa.com) From numerous central European cities.

Ryanair (www.ryanair.com) From numerous UK and mainland European airports.

Vueling (www.vueling.com) From major Spanish cities, as well as other European cities, including Dublin and Florence.

Departure Tax

Departure tax is included in the price of a ticket.

Sea

Ferry services connect Mallorca to the Spanish mainland and to Menorca, Ibiza and Formentera. Most services operate only from Easter to late October, and those that continue into the winter reduce their departure times. Most ferry companies allow you to transport vehicles on longer routes and have car holds (this incurs an additional fee and advance bookings are essential). If you are travelling with your own vehicle, be sure to arrive at the port in good time for boarding.

Prices vary widely according to season; check routes and compare prices at Direct Ferries (www.directferries.com).

Ferry companies that operate to and from Mallorca include the following:

Trasmediterránea (☑902 454 645; www.trasmediterranea.es)

Baleària (☑902 160180; www.balearia.com)

Tours

Joining an organised tour to Mallorca is certainly not necessary – it's an easy destination for independent travel. But some companies offer specialist tours that make it so much easier to indulge your passions.

Mallorca Muntanya (☑639 713212; www.mallorcamuntanya.com; per person from €200) Trekking tours, mostly in the Serra de Tramuntana.

Tramuntana Tours (Map p109; ☑971 63 24 23; www.tramuntanatours.com; Carrer de Sa Lluna 72; bicycle rental per day €12-75; ☺9am-1.30pm & 3-7.30pm Mon-Fri, 9am-1.30pm Sat) Guided hikes in the Serra de Tramuntana.

Mar y Roc (☑680 322171; www.mallorca-wandern.de) Group hiking tours in Mallorca.

Naturetrek (☑in UK 01962 733051; www.naturetrek.co.uk) Eight-day birdwatching tour.

Unicorn Trails (☑in UK 01767 600 606; www.unicorntrails.com) Two-week-long horse-riding tours to choose from.

Cycle Mallorca (www.cyclemallorca.co.uk) Well-organised road-cycling holidays.

Inntravel (www.inntravel.co.uk) A slow-tour specialist offering walking and cycling holidays.

FERRY SERVICES

TO	FROM	COMPANY	PRICE (SEAT)	FREQUENCY	DURATION (HR)	SLEEPER BERTH
Palma	Barcelona	Trasmediterránea, Baleària	from €49	1-2 daily	7½	yes
Palma	Denia	Baleària	from €66	2 daily	8	yes
Palma	Ibiza (Ibiza City)	Baleària	from €46	2 daily	4	yes
Palma	Mahon (Menorca)	Trasmediterránea	from €34	Sun	3½	no
Palma	Valencia	Trasmediterránea, Baleària	from €47	1 daily	8	yes
Port d'Alcúdia	Barcelona	Baleària	from €48	2 daily	6	yes
Port d'Alcúdia	Ciutatdella (Menorca)	Trasmediterránea, Baleària	from €48	2 daily	1-2	no

GETTING AROUND

Transport in Mallorca is reasonably priced, though buses and trains do not cover every corner of the island, and some services dwindle during the low season. For timetables throughout the island, head to **Transport de les Illes Balears** (TIB; ☎971 17 77 77; www.tib.org).

Bicycle

Pro cycling teams' fondness for Mallorca as a winter training ground have really put the island on the cycling map in recent years. It's now one of Europe's most popular destinations for road cycling. Although the uphill slog can be tough in mountainous areas, particularly along the island's western and north-western coasts, much of the island is reasonably flat and can be easily explored by bike.

Wide shoulders, a decent number of bike paths and familiarity with, and accept-ance of, cyclists by other road users make it all the more appealing. Signposts have been put up across much of rural Mallorca indi-cating cycling routes (usually secondary roads between towns and villages).

For an overview of cycling on the island, visit www.illesbalears.es and click on 'Sports & Active Tourism'. It has several routes across the island. Another recommend-ed website with routes grad-ed according to difficulty is http://mallorcacycling.co.uk.

Hire

Bike-hire places are scat-tered around the main re-sorts of the island, including Palma, and are usually highly professional. Prices vary widely, but on average you'll pay between €10 and €15 per day for a city bike, and €20 to €30 per day for an aluminium or carbon road bike. The longer you hire the bike, the cheaper daily rates get, and many hire outfits will deliver the bike to where you are staying.

Bus

The island is roughly divided into five bus zones radiating from Palma.

Bus line numbers in the 100s cover the southwest, the 200s the west (as far as Sóller), the 300s the north and much of the centre, the 400s a wedge of the centre and east coast and the 500s the south. These services are run by a phalanx of small bus companies, but you can get route and timetable infor-mation for all by contacting **Transport de les Illes Balears** (TIB; ☎971 17 77 77; www.tib.org).

Most of the island is ac-cessible by bus from Palma. All buses depart from (or near) Palma's **Estació In-termodal** (Map p56; ☎971 17 77 77; www.tib.org; Plaça d'Espanya) on Plaça d'Espan-ya. Not all lines are especially frequent, and some services slow to a trickle on week-ends. Frequency to many coastal areas also drops from November to April and some lines are cut altogether (such as those between Ca'n Picafort and Sa Calobra or Sóller).

Although services in most parts of the island are ade-quate, out-of-the-way places can be tedious to reach and getting around the Serra de Tramuntana by bus, while possible, isn't always easy. Bus 200 from Palma runs to Estellencs via Banyalbufar for example, while bus 210 runs to Valldemossa and then, less frequently, on to Deià and Sóller. Nothing makes the connection between Estel-lencs and Valldemossa and all but the Palma–Valldemos-sa run are infrequent.

Distances are usually short, with very few services taking longer than two hours to reach their destinations.

Car & Motorcycle

Mallorca's roads are gener-ally excellent, though there are a few coastal hair-raisers in the north and west of the island that are not for faint-hearted drivers (Sa Calobra and Formentor to name two). The narrow roads on these cliff-flanked coasts and the country roads that thread through the interior are ideal for motorbike touring.

The island's main artery is the Ma13 motorway, which slices through the island diagonally, linking Palma in the west with Alcúdia in the north. The Ma1 loops south-west of Palma to Andratx.

While you can get about much of the island by bus and train, especially in high season, having a car will give you far greater freedom. With your own wheels you can seek out the nature parks, secluded coves and moun-tain retreats away from the crowds.

If your car is not equipped with sat nav, it's worth invest-ing in a decent road map to negotiate the island's more offbeat corners. Marco Polo produces a decent one at a 1:125,000 scale.

Automobile Associations

The Real Automóvil Club de España (www.race.es) is the national automobile club. They may well come to assist you in case of break-down, but in any event you should obtain an emergency telephone number for Spain from your own insurer.

Bring Your Own Vehicle

Always carry proof of owner-ship of a private vehicle.

Every vehicle should display a nationality plate of its country of registration. It is compulsory in Spain to carry a warning triangle (to be used in case of break-down) and a reflective jacket. Recommended accessories include a first-aid kit, spare-bulb kit and fire extinguisher.

Driving Licences

EU driving licences are recognised throughout Europe. Those with a non-EU licence are supposed to obtain a 12-month International Driver's Permit (IDP) from their home automobile association to accompany their national licence. In practice, national licences from countries such as Australia, Canada, New Zealand and the USA are usually accepted.

Fuel

You'll find petrol stations (*gasolineras*) in major towns and cities and most large resorts. Make sure you have a full tank if you're exploring rural areas off the beaten track. Choose between lead-free (*sin plomo*; 95 octane) and diesel (*gasóleo*). Petrol prices are on a par with the rest of Europe. You can pay with major credit cards.

Hire

Car-hire rates vary, but you should be able to get an economy vehicle for between €40 and €70 per day; bear in mind that compact cars can be a tight fit for families. Additional drivers and one-way hire can bump up the cost. Extras like child seats (around €10 per day) should be reserved at the time of booking.

To rent a car you have to have a licence, be aged 21 or older and, for the major companies at least, have a credit card. A word of advice: some agencies try to make even more money by charging a hefty fee for fuel, instead of asking you to bring it back with a full tank. Always read the fine print carefully.

All the major car-hire companies are represented on the island. It can pay to shop around, and you might want to check a cost comparison site like www.travelsupermarket.com before going down the tried-and-trusted route. Branches at the airport include the following:

➧ **Avis** (☑902 110261; www.avis.com)

➧ **Europcar** (☑902 105055; www.europcar.com)

➧ **Gold Car** (☑902 119726; www.goldcar.es)

➧ **Hertz** (☑971 78 96 70; www.hertz.com)

➧ **Sixt** (☑902 491616; www.sixt.com)

Insurance

➧ Third-party liability insurance is a minimum requirement in Spain and throughout Europe.

➧ Ask your insurer for a European Accident Statement form, which can simplify matters in the event of an accident.

➧ A European breakdown-assistance policy, such as the AA Five Star Service or RAC European Breakdown Cover, is a good investment.

➧ Car-hire companies provide third-party liability insurance, but make sure you understand what your liabilities and excess are, and what waivers you're entitled to in case of an accident or damage to the hire vehicle.

➧ Insurance that covers damage to the vehicle – Collision Damage Waiver (CDW) – usually costs extra, but driving without it is not recommended.

➧ Car-hire multiday excess insurance can be cheaper online; try www.icarhireinsurance.com or http://insurance4carhire.com.

Road Rules

Blood-alcohol limit 0.05%. If found to be over the limit you can be judged, fined and deprived of your licence within 24 hours. Fines range up to around €1000 for serious offences, and you can even be jailed for a reading of 0.12% and above. Non-resident foreigners will be required to pay up on the spot (at 30% off the full fine).

Legal driving age For cars, 18; for motorcycles and scooters, 16 (80cc and over) or 14 (50cc and under). A licence is required in all cases.

Motorcyclists Must use headlights at all times and wear a helmet if riding a bike of 125cc or more.

Overtaking Spanish truck drivers often have the courtesy to turn on their right indicator to show that the way ahead of them is clear for overtaking (and the left one if it is not and you are attempting this manoeuvre).

Roundabouts (traffic circles) Vehicles already in the circle have the right of way.

Side of the road Drive on the right.

Speed limits In built-up areas, 50km/h; increases to 100km/h on major roads and up to 110km/h on the four-lane highways leading out of Palma.

Train

Four train lines run from Plaça d'Espanya in Palma de Mallorca; **Transport de les Illes Balears** (TIB; ☑971 17 77 77; www.tib.org) has details.

One heads north to Sóller and is a panoramic excursion in an antique wooden train; it's one of Palma's most popular day trips.

The other three lines head inland to Inca, where one terminates and the others shear off to serve Sa Pobla and Manacor. Prices are generally cheaper than buses and departures are frequent throughout the day. Mooted plans to extend the line from Manacor to Artà seem unlikely to come to fruition.

Language

Mallorca is a bilingual island, at least on paper. Since the Balearic Islands received their autonomy statute in the 1980s, the islanders' native Catalan (català) has recovered its official status alongside Spanish. This said, it would be pushing a point to say that Catalan, or its local dialect, mallorquí, had again become the primary language of Mallorca or the rest of the Balearic Islands. Today Spanish remains the *lingua franca*, especially between Mallorquins and other Spaniards or foreigners.

Spanish pronunciation is straightforward as most Spanish sounds are pronounced the same as their English counterparts. Note that the kh in our pronunciation guides is a guttural sound (like the 'ch' in the Scottish loch), ly is pronounced as the 'lli' in 'million', ny as the 'ni' in 'onion', th is pronounced with a lisp, and r is strongly rolled. In our pronunciation guides, the stressed syllables are in italics. If you follow our pronunciation guides given with each phrase in this chapter, you'll be understood just fine.

Spanish nouns (and the adjectives that go with them) are marked for gender – feminine nouns generally end with -a and masculine ones with -o. Where necessary, both forms are given for the words and phrases in this chapter, separated by a slash and with the masculine form first, eg perdido/a (m/f).

Also note that Spanish has two words for the English 'you': when talking to people familiar to you or younger than you, use the informal form, tú, rather than the polite form Usted. The polite form is used in the phrases provided in this chapter; where both options are given, they are indicated by the abbreviations 'pol' and 'inf'.

> **Want More?**
> For in-depth language information, check out Lonely Planet's *Spanish Phrasebook*. You'll find it at shop.lonely planet.com.

BASICS

Hello./Goodbye.	*Hola./Adiós.*	o·la/a·dyos
How are you?	*¿Qué tal?*	ke tal
Fine, thanks.	*Bien, gracias.*	byen gra·thyas
Excuse me.	*Perdón.*	per·don
Sorry.	*Lo siento.*	lo syen·to
Yes./No.	*Sí./No.*	see/no
Please.	*Por favor.*	por fa·vor
Thank you.	*Gracias.*	gra·thyas
You're welcome.	*De nada.*	de na·da

My name is ... *Me llamo ...*   me lya·mo ...
What's your name?
¿Cómo se llama Usted?   ko·mo se lya·ma oo·ste
Do you speak (English)?
¿Habla (inglés)?   a·bla (een·gles)
I (don't) understand.
Yo (no) entiendo.   yo (no) en·tyen·do

ACCOMMODATION

I'd like to book a room.
Quisiera reservar una habitación.   kee·sye·ra re·ser·var oo·na a·bee·ta·thyon
How much is it per night/person?
¿Cuánto cuesta por noche/persona?   kwan·to kwes·ta por no·che/per·so·na

air-con	*aire acondicionado*	ai·re a·kon·dee·thyo·na·do
bathroom	*baño*	ba·nyo
bed	*cama*	ka·ma
campsite	*terreno de cámping*	te·re·no de kam·peeng
double room	*habitación doble*	a·bee·ta·thyon do·ble

guesthouse	pensión	pen·syon
hotel	hotel	o·tel
single room	habitación	a·bee·ta·thyon
	individual	een·dee·vee·dwal
window	ventana	ven·ta·na
youth hostel	albergue	al·ber·ge
	juvenil	khoo·ve·nee

DIRECTIONS

Where's ...?
¿Dónde está ...?   don·de es·ta ...

What's the address?
¿Cuál es la dirección?   kwal es la dee·rek·thyon

Could you please write it down?
¿Puede escribirlo,   pwe·de es·kree·beer·lo
por favor?   por fa·vor

Can you show me (on the map)?
¿Me lo puede indicar   me lo pwe·de een·dee·kar
(en el mapa)?   (en el ma·pa)

behind ...	detrás de ...	de·tras de ...
far away	lejos	le·khos
in front of ...	enfrente de ...	en·fren·te de ...
left	izquierda	eeth·kyer·da
near	cerca	ther·ka
next to ...	al lado de ...	al la·do de ...
opposite ...	frente a ...	fren·te a ...
right	derecha	de·re·cha

EATING & DRINKING

I'd like to book a table.
Quisiera reservar   kee·sye·ra re·ser·var
una mesa.   oo·na me·sa

What would you recommend?
¿Qué recomienda?   ke re·ko·myen·da

What's in that dish?
¿Que lleva ese plato?   ke lye·va e·se pla·to

I don't eat ...
No como ...   no ko·mo ...

That was delicious!
¡Estaba buenísimo!   es·ta·ba bwe·nee·see·mo

Please bring the bill.
Por favor nos trae   por fa·vor nos tra·e
la cuenta.   la kwen·ta

Cheers!
¡Salud!   sa·loo

Key Words

appetisers	aperitivos	a·pe·ree·tee·vos
bar	bar	bar
bottle	botella	bo·te·lya

Signs

Abierto	Open
Cerrado	Closed
Entrada	Entrance
Hombres	Men
Mujeres	Women
Prohibido	Prohibited
Salida	Exit
Servicios/Aseos	Toilets

breakfast	desayuno	de·sa·yoo·no
cafe	café	ka·fe
children's menu	menú infantil	me·noo een·fan·teel
cold	frío	free·o
dinner	cena	the·na
food	comida	ko·mee·da
fork	tenedor	te·ne·dor
glass	vaso	va·so
highchair	trona	tro·na
hot (warm)	caliente	ka·lyen·te
knife	cuchillo	koo·chee·lyo
lunch	comida	ko·mee·da
main course	segundo plato	se·goon·do pla·to
market	mercado	mer·ka·do
menu (in English)	menú (en inglés)	me·noo (en een·gles)
plate	plato	pla·to
restaurant	restaurante	res·tow·ran·te
spoon	cuchara	koo·cha·ra
supermarket	supermercado	soo·per·mer·kado
with/without	con/sin	kon/seen
vegetarian food	comida vegetariana	ko·mee·da ve·khe·ta·rya·na

Meat & Fish

beef	carne de vaca	kar·ne de va·ka
chicken	pollo	po·lyo
duck	pato	pa·to
fish	pescado	pes·ka·do
lamb	cordero	kor·de·ro
pork	cerdo	ther·do
turkey	pavo	pa·vo
veal	ternera	ter·ne·ra
fish	pescado	pes·ka·do
lamb	cordero	kor·de·ro
pork	cerdo	ther·do
turkey	pavo	pa·vo
veal	ternera	ter·ne·ra

Fruit & Vegetables

English	Spanish	Pronunciation
apple	manzana	man·tha·na
apricot	albaricoque	al·ba·ree·ko·ke
artichoke	alcachofa	al·ka·cho·fa
asparagus	espárragos	es·pa·ra·gos
banana	plátano	pla·ta·no
beans	judías	khoo·dee·as
beetroot	remolacha	re·mo·la·cha
cabbage	col	kol
carrot	zanahoria	tha·na·o·rya
cherry	cereza	the·re·tha
corn	maíz	ma·eeth
cucumber	pepino	pe·pee·no
fruit	fruta	froo·ta
grape	uvas	oo·vas
lemon	limón	lee·mon
lentils	lentejas	len·te·khas
lettuce	lechuga	le·choo·ga
mushroom	champiñón	cham·pee·nyon
nuts	nueces	nwe·thes
onion	cebolla	the·bo·lya
orange	naranja	na·ran·kha
peach	melocotón	me·lo·ko·ton
peas	guisantes	gee·san·tes
(red/green) pepper	pimiento (rojo/verde)	pee·myen·to (ro·kho/ver·de)
pineapple	piña	pee·nya
potato	patata	pa·ta·ta
pumpkin	calabaza	ka·la·ba·tha
spinach	espinacas	es·pee·na·kas
strawberry	fresa	fre·sa
tomato	tomate	to·ma·te
vegetable	verdura	ver·doo·ra
watermelon	sandía	san·dee·a

Other

English	Spanish	Pronunciation
bread	pan	pan
butter	mantequilla	man·te·kee·lya
cheese	queso	ke·so
egg	huevo	we·vo
honey	miel	myel
jam	mermelada	mer·me·la·da
oil	aceite	a·they·te
pepper	pimienta	pee·myen·ta
rice	arroz	a·roth
salt	sal	sal
sugar	azúcar	a·thoo·kar
vinegar	vinagre	vee·na·gr

KEY PATTERNS

To get by in Spanish, mix and match these simple patterns:

When's (the next flight)?
¿Cuándo sale (el próximo vuelo)? — kwan·do sa·le (el prok·see·mo vwe·lo)

Where's (the station)?
¿Dónde está (la estación)? — don·de es·ta (la es·ta·thyon)

Where can I (buy a ticket)?
¿Dónde puedo (comprar un billete)? — don·de pwe·do (kom·prar oon bee·lye·te)

Do you have (a map)?
¿Tiene (un mapa)? — tye·ne (oon ma·pa)

Is there (a toilet)?
¿Hay (servicios)? — ai (ser·vee·thyos)

I'd like (a coffee).
Quisiera (un café). — kee·sye·ra (oon ka·fe)

Could you please (help me)?
¿Puede (ayudarme), por favor? — pwe·de (a·yoo·dar·me) por fa·vor

Drinks

English	Spanish	Pronunciation
beer	cerveza	ther·ve·tha
coffee	café	ka·fe
(orange) juice	zumo (de naranja)	thoo·mo (de na·ran·kha)
milk	leche	le·che
tea	té	te
(mineral) water	agua (mineral)	a·gwa (mee·ne·ral)
(red) wine	vino (tinto)	vee·no (teen·to)
(white) wine	vino (blanco)	vee·no (blan·ko)

EMERGENCIES

Help!
¡Socorro! — so·ko·ro

Go away!
¡Vete! — ve·te

Call a doctor!
¡Llame a un médico! — lya·me a oon me·dee·ko

Call the police!
¡Llame a la policía! — lya·me a la po·lee·thee·a

I'm lost.
Estoy perdido/a. — es·toy per·dee·do/a (m/f)

I'm ill.
Estoy enfermo/a. — es·toy en·fer·mo/a (m/f)

Where are the toilets?
¿Dónde están los baños? — don·de es·tan los ba·nyost

SHOPPING & SERVICES

I'd like to buy ...
Quisiera comprar ... kee·*sye*·ra kom·*prar* ...
May I look at it?
¿Puedo verlo? *pwe*·do *ver*·lo
How much is it?
¿Cuánto cuesta? *kwan*·to *kwes*·ta
That's too/very expensive.
Es muy caro. es mooy *ka*·ro
Can you lower the price?
¿Podría bajar un po·*dree*·a ba·*khar* oon
poco el precio? *po*·ko el *pre*·thyo
There's a mistake in the bill.
Hay un error en la cuenta. ai oon e·*ror* en la *kwen*·ta

ATM	cajero automático	ka·*khe*·ro ow·to·ma·*tee*·ko
credit card	tarjeta de crédito	tar·*khe*·ta de *kre*·dee·to
post office	correos	ko·*re*·os
tourist office	oficina de turismo	o·fee·*thee*·na de too·*rees*·m

TIME & DATES

¿Qué hora es? ke o·ra es
It's (10) o'clock.
Son (las diez). son (las dyeth)
Half past (one).
Es (la una) y media. es (la *oo*·na) ee *me*·dya

morning	mañana	ma·*nya*·na
afternoon	tarde	*tar*·de
evening	noche	*no*·che
yesterday	ayer	a·*yer*
today	hoy	oy
tomorrow	mañana	ma·*nya*·na

Monday	lunes	*loo*·nes
Tuesday	martes	*mar*·tes
Wednesday	miércoles	*myer*·ko·les
Thursday	jueves	*khwe*·bes
Friday	viernes	*vyer*·nes
Saturday	sábado	*sa*·ba·do
Sunday	domingo	do·*meen*·g

NUMBERS

1	uno	*oo*·no
2	dos	dos
3	tres	tres
4	cuatro	*kwa*·tro
5	cinco	*theen*·ko
6	seis	seys
7	siete	*sye*·te
8	ocho	*o*·cho
9	nueve	*nwe*·ve
10	diez	dyeth
20	veinte	*veyn*·te
30	treinta	*treyn*·ta
40	cuarenta	kwa·*ren*·ta
50	cincuenta	theen·*kwen*·ta
60	sesenta	se·*sen*·ta
70	setenta	se·*ten*·ta
80	ochenta	o·*chen*·ta
90	noventa	no·*ven*·ta
100	cien	thyen
1000	mil	meel

TRANSPORT

I want to go to ...
Quisiera ir a ... kee·*sye*·ra eer a ...
What time does it arrive/leave?
¿A qué hora llega/sale? a ke o·ra *lye*·ga/*sa*·le
I want to get off here.
Quiero bajarme aquí. *kye*·ro ba·*khar*·me a·*kee*

1st-class	primera clase	pree·*me*·ra *kla*·se
2nd-class	segunda clase	se·*goon*·da *kla*·se
bicycle	bicicleta	bee·thee·*kle*·ta
boat	barco	*bar*·ko
bus	autobús	ow·to·*boos*
car	coche	*ko*·che
cancelled	cancelado	kan·the·*la*·do
delayed	retrasado	re·tra·*sa*·do
motorcycle	moto	*mo*·to
one-way	ida	*ee*·da
plane	avión	a·*vyon*
return	ida y vuelta	*ee*·da ee *vwel*·ta
ticket	billete	bee·*lye*·te
ticket office	taquilla	ta·*kee*·lya
timetable	horario	o·*ra*·ryo
train	tren	tren

CATALAN – BASICS

Good morning.	Bon dia.	bon *dee*·a
Good afternoon.	Bona tarda.	bo·na *tar*·da
Good evening.	Bon vespre.	bon *bes*·pra
Goodbye.	Adéu.	a·*the*·oo
Please.	Sisplau.	sees·*pla*·oo
Thank you.	Gràcies.	gra·*see*·a
You're welcome.	De res.	de res
Excuse me.	Perdoni.	par·*tho*·nee
I'm sorry.	Ho sento.	oo *sen*·to
How are you?	Com estàs?	kom as·*tas*
(Very) Well.	(Molt) Bé.	(mol) be

GLOSSARY

Most of the following terms are in Castilian Spanish which is fully understood around the island. A handful of specialised terms in Catalan (C) also appear. No distinction has been made for any Mallorcan dialect variations.

agroturisme (C) – rural tourism

ajuntament (C) – city or town hall

alquería – Muslim-era farmstead

avenida – avenue

avinguda (C) – see *avenida*

baño completo – full bathroom with toilet, shower and/or bath

bodega – cellar (especially wine cellar)

bomberos – fire brigade

cala – cove

call (C) – Jewish quarter in Palma, Inca and some other Mallorcan towns

cambio – change; also currency exchange

caña – small glass of beer

canguro – babysitter

capilla – chapel

carrer (C) – street

carretera – highway

carta – menu

castell (C) – castle

castellano – Castilian; used in preference to '*Español*' to describe the national language

català – Catalan language; a native of Catalonia. The Mallorcan dialect is Mallorquin

celler – (C) wine cellars turned into restaurants

cervecería – beer bar

comisaría – police station

conquistador – conqueror

converso – Jew who converted to Christianity in medieval Spain

correos – post office

cortado – short black coffee with a little milk

costa – coast

cuenta – bill, cheque

ensaïmada (C) – Mallorcan pastry

entrada – entrance, ticket

ermita – small hermitage or country chapel

església (C) – see *iglesia*

estació (C) – see *estación*

estación – station

estanco – tobacconist shop

farmacia – pharmacy

faro – lighthouse

fiesta – festival, public holiday or party

finca – farmhouse

gasolina – petrol

guardía civil – military police

habitaciones libres – literally 'rooms available'

hostal – see *pensión*

iglesia – church

IVA – *impuesto sobre el valor añadido,* or value-added tax

lavabo – washbasin

librería – bookshop

lista de correos – poste restante

locutorio – telephone centre

marisquería – seafood eatery

menú del día – menu of the day

mercat (C) – market

mirador – lookout point

Modernisme – the Catalan version of the art nouveau architectural and artistic style

monestir (C) – monastery

museo – museum

museu (C) – see *museo*

objetos perdidos – lost-and-found

oficina de turismo – tourist office; also *oficina de información turística*

palacio – palace, grand mansion or noble house

palau (C) – see *palacio*

pensión – small family-run hotel

plaça (C) – see *plaza*

platja (C) – see *playa*

playa – beach

plaza – square

port (C) – see *puerto*

possessió (C) – typical Mallorcan farmhouse

PP – Partido Popular (People's Party)

puente – bridge

puerto – port

puig (C) – mountain peak

rambla – avenue or riverbed

refugis (C) – hikers' huts

retablo – altarpiece

retaule (C) – see *retablo*

robes de llengües (C) – traditional striped Mallorcan fabrics

santuari (C) – shrine or sanctuary, hermitage

según precio del mercado – on menus, 'according to market price' (often written 'spm')

Semana Santa – Holy Week

serra (C) – mountain range

servicios – toilets

tafona (C) – traditional oil press found on most Mallorcan farms

talayot (C) – ancient watchtower

tarjeta de crédito – credit card

tarjeta de residencia – residence card

tarjeta telefónica – phonecard

terraza – terrace; pavement cafe

torre – tower

turismo – tourism or saloon car

urgencia – emergency

Behind the Scenes

SEND US YOUR FEEDBACK

We love to hear from travellers – your comments keep us on our toes and help make our books better. Our well-travelled team reads every word on what you loved or loathed about this book. Although we cannot reply individually to your submissions, we always guarantee that your feedback goes straight to the appropriate authors, in time for the next edition. Each person who sends us information is thanked in the next edition – the most useful submissions are rewarded with a selection of digital PDF chapters.

Visit **lonelyplanet.com/contact** to submit your updates and suggestions or to ask for help. Our award-winning website also features inspirational travel stories, news and discussions.

Note: We may edit, reproduce and incorporate your comments in Lonely Planet products such as guidebooks, websites and digital products, so let us know if you don't want your comments reproduced or your name acknowledged. For a copy of our privacy policy visit lonelyplanet.com/privacy.

OUR READERS

Many thanks to the travellers who used the last edition and wrote to us with helpful hints, useful advice and interesting anecdotes:

Paul Bullivant, Joan Cunningham, Paul Laye, Antje Schönherr, Ross Simpson Brown.

WRITER THANKS

Josephine Quintero

Many thanks to my many friends in Mallorca, including Isabel Carmona, Felipe Diaz and my wonderful Airbnb hostess, Nicole in Palma, as well as other countless people who shared their enthusiasm and love of all things Mallorcan. Thanks too to my ever-supportive family and, not forgetting, the ever-conscientious editorial team at LP.

Damian Harper

Many thanks to everyone who helped with tips along the way in this forever-charming island, especially Robert Landreth, Daniel Hands, Emmanuelle Arbona, Biel and Yunli, Dave in Pollença, Norma Gray, Isabel, Francesco Bellini, Cristina, Steffi, Luisa Martínez, Francoise, Jaime, Miguel, Tomeu, Timothy, Emma and Daisy.

ACKNOWLEDGEMENTS

Climate map data adapted from Peel MC, Finlayson BL & McMahon TA (2007) 'Updated World Map of the Köppen-Geiger Climate Classification', *Hydrology and Earth System Sciences*, 11, 1633–44.

Cover photograph: Cala Fornells, west of Palma de Mallorca, Massimo Ripani/4Corners Images ©

THIS BOOK

This 5th edition of Lonely Planet's *Mallorca* guidebook was researched and written by Damian Harper and Josephine Quintero. The previous edition was written by Damian and Hugh McNaughtan. This guidebook was produced by the following:

Senior Product Editors Sandie Kestell, Angela Tinson

Regional Senior Cartographer Anthony Phelan

Assisting Cartographer Julie Sheridan

Product Editors Will Allen, Paul Harding

Book Designers Catalina Aragón, Brooke Giacomin, Katherine Marsh, Virginia Moreno

Assisting Editors Joel Cotterell, Sasha Drew, Monique Perrin, Maja Vatrić

Cover Researcher Naomi Parker

Thanks to Jessica Boland, Clare Healy, Karen Henderson, Kate James, Sonia Kapoor, Darren O'Connell, Monique Perrin

Index

Map Legend

Sights
- Beach
- Bird Sanctuary
- Buddhist
- Castle/Palace
- Christian
- Confucian
- Hindu
- Islamic
- Jain
- Jewish
- Monument
- Museum/Gallery/Historic Building
- Ruin
- Shinto
- Sikh
- Taoist
- Winery/Vineyard
- Zoo/Wildlife Sanctuary
- Other Sight

Activities, Courses & Tours
- Bodysurfing
- Diving
- Canoeing/Kayaking
- Course/Tour
- Sento Hot Baths/Onsen
- Skiing
- Snorkelling
- Surfing
- Swimming/Pool
- Walking
- Windsurfing
- Other Activity

Sleeping
- Sleeping
- Camping
- Hut/Shelter

Eating
- Eating

Drinking & Nightlife
- Drinking & Nightlife
- Cafe

Entertainment
- Entertainment

Shopping
- Shopping

Information
- Bank
- Embassy/Consulate
- Hospital/Medical
- Internet
- Police
- Post Office
- Telephone
- Toilet
- Tourist Information
- Other Information

Geographic
- Beach
- Gate
- Hut/Shelter
- Lighthouse
- Lookout
- Mountain/Volcano
- Oasis
- Park
- Pass
- Picnic Area
- Waterfall

Population
- Capital (National)
- Capital (State/Province)
- City/Large Town
- Town/Village

Transport
- Airport
- Border crossing
- Bus
- Cable car/Funicular
- Cycling
- Ferry
- Metro station
- Monorail
- Parking
- Petrol station
- S-Bahn/Subway station
- Taxi
- T-bane/Tunnelbana station
- Train station/Railway
- Tram
- U-Bahn/Underground station
- Other Transport

Routes
- Tollway
- Freeway
- Primary
- Secondary
- Tertiary
- Lane
- Unsealed road
- Road under construction
- Plaza/Mall
- Steps
- Tunnel
- Pedestrian overpass
- Walking Tour
- Walking Tour detour
- Path/Walking Trail

Boundaries
- International
- State/Province
- Disputed
- Regional/Suburb
- Marine Park
- Cliff
- Wall

Hydrography
- River, Creek
- Intermittent River
- Canal
- Water
- Dry/Salt/Intermittent Lake
- Reef

Areas
- Airport/Runway
- Beach/Desert
- Cemetery (Christian)
- Cemetery (Other)
- Glacier
- Mudflat
- Park/Forest
- Sight (Building)
- Sportsground
- Swamp/Mangrove

Note: Not all symbols displayed above appear on the maps in this book

OUR STORY

A beat-up old car, a few dollars in the pocket and a sense of adventure. In 1972 that's all Tony and Maureen Wheeler needed for the trip of a lifetime – across Europe and Asia overland to Australia. It took several months, and at the end – broke but inspired – they sat at their kitchen table writing and stapling together their first travel guide, *Across Asia on the Cheap*. Within a week they'd sold 1500 copies. Lonely Planet was born.

Today, Lonely Planet has offices in the US, Ireland and China, with a network of over 2000 contributors in every corner of the globe. We share Tony's belief that 'a great guidebook should do three things: inform, educate and amuse'.

OUR WRITERS

Josephine Quintero

British by birth, Josephine's home is in Andalucía, from where she has travelled extensively, covering some 45 destinations for Lonely Planet in such far flung places as Victoria (Australia) and Mexico City. Other LP titles she has authored and co-authored include *Sweden*, the *Canary Islands*, *Cyprus*, *Ireland*, *Baja California* and several regions in Spain and Italy. Josephine graduated from UC Berkeley in English and lived in the Middle East for several years before moving to the more relaxed shores of southern Spain.

Damian Harper

With two degrees (one in modern and classical Chinese from SOAS), Damian has been writing for Lonely Planet for over two decades, contributing to titles as diverse as *China*, *Beijing*, *Shanghai*, *Vietnam*, *Thailand*, *Ireland*, *London*, *Mallorca* and *Malaysia*.

Published by Lonely Planet Global Limited
CRN 554153
5th edition – May 2022
ISBN 978 17870 17122
© Lonely Planet 2022   Photographs © as indicated 2022
10 9 8 7 6 5 4 3 2 1
Printed in Singapore